ARE 5 Practice Problems

for the Architect Registration Exam

David Kent Ballast, FAIA, NCARB, CSI
Holly Williams Leppo, AIA
Rima Taher, PhD, PE

The Power to Pass®
www.ppi2pass.com

Professional Publications, Inc. • Belmont, California

LEED® is a registered trademark of the U.S. Green Building Council.

National Electrical Code®, NEC®, and NFPA® are registered trademarks of the National Fire Protection Association.

MasterFormat® and SectionFormat® are registered trademarks of the Construction Specifications Institute.

ARE 5 PRACTICE PROBLEMS FOR THE ARCHITECT REGISTRATION EXAM
First Edition

Current release of this edition: 1

Release History

date	edition number	revision number	description
Nov 2016	1	1	New book.

Printed in the United States of America.

PPI
1250 Fifth Avenue, Belmont, CA 94002
(650) 593-9119
ppi2pass.com

ISBN: 978-1-59126-516-0

Library of Congress Control Number: 2016957820

FEDCBA

DIVISIONS

Practice Management

Project Management

Programming & Analysis

Project Planning

Project Development

Construction & Evaluation

TABLE OF CONTENTS

DIVISION 5: PROJECT DEVELOPMENT & DOCUMENTATION

DIVISION 6: CONSTRUCTION & EVALUATION

PREFACE AND ACKNOWLEDGMENTS

ARE 5 Practice Problems for the Architect Registration Exam is written to give you comprehensive practice to help you prepare for the Architect Registration Exam 5 (ARE 5). This book is a companion to the *ARE 5 Review Manual for the Architect Registration Exam*, which gives a comprehensive review for those preparing for the ARE 5.

The ARE 5 contains a variety of problem types, including multiple-choice problems, check-all-that-apply problems, and fill-in-the-blank problems. The ARE 5 has introduced three more types: hot spot problems, drag-and-place problems, and case study problems. We wrote this book to mimic the exam's problem types so that you will become familiar with them as you use *ARE 5 Practice Problems*.

Many people have helped in the production of this book. We would like to thank Gary E. Demele, FAIA, NCARB, and Bradley E. Saeger, AIA, who reviewed the book for technical accuracy and offered many good suggestions for additions and improvements. We would also like to thank all the fine people at PPI, including Steve Buehler, associate director of acquisitions; Nicole Evans, Leata Holloway, and Vanessa Stefani, acquisitions editors; Rebecca Morgan, editorial project manager, Thomas Bliss and Tracy Katz, associate project managers; Scott Marley, senior copy editor; Robert Genevro, Tyler Hayes, Richard Iriye, Ellen Nordman, Ceridwen Quattrin, and Ian A. Walker, copy editors and typesetters; Tom Bergstrom, cover designer and technical illustrator; Sam Webster, publishing systems manager; Cathy Schrott, production services manager; and Grace Wong, director of publishing services.

Although we had much help in preparing this new book, the responsibility for any errors is our own. A list of known errata for this book is maintained at **ppi2pass.com/errata**, and you can let us know of any errors you find at the same place. We greatly appreciate the time you take to help us keep this book accurate and up to date.

David Kent Ballast, FAIA, NCARB, CSI
Holly Williams Leppo, AIA
Rima Taher, PhD, PE

CODES AND STANDARDS USED IN THIS BOOK

ACI 318: *Building Code Requirements for Structural Concrete*, 2014. American Concrete Institute, Farmington Hills, MI.

ADA Standards: *2010 Americans with Disabilities Act (ADA) Standards for Accessible Design*, U.S. Department of Justice, Washington, DC.

AIA: Contract Documents, 2007. American Institute of Architects, Washington, DC.

AISC: *Steel Construction Manual*, 14th ed, 2011. American Institute of Steel Construction, Chicago, IL.

ANSI/ASHRAE 62.1: *Ventilation for Acceptable Indoor Air Quality*, 2016. American Society of Heating, Refrigerating and Air-Conditioning Engineers, Atlanta, GA.

ANSI/ASHRAE 62.2: *Ventilation and Acceptable Indoor Air Quality in Low-Rise Residential Buildings*, 2016. American Society of Heating, Refrigerating and Air-Conditioning Engineers, Atlanta, GA.

ANSI/ASHRAE/IESNA 90.1: *Energy Standard for Buildings Except Low-Rise Residential Buildings*, 2013. American Society of Heating, Refrigerating and Air-Conditioning Engineers, Atlanta, GA.

ANSI/BOMA Z65.1: *Office Buildings: Standard Methods of Measurement*, 2010. Building Owners and Managers Association, Washington, DC.

ASCE/SEI7: *Minimum Design Loads for Buildings and Other Structures*, 2010. American Society of Civil Engineers, Reston, VA.

CSI: MasterFormat, 2016. Construction Specifications Institute, Alexandria, VA.

CSI: SectionFormat, 2009. Construction Specifications Institute, Alexandria, VA.

IBC: *International Building Code*, 2015. International Code Council, Washington, DC.

ICC/ANSI A117.1: *Accessible and Usable Buildings and Facilities*, 2009. International Code Council. Washington, DC.

IECC: *International Energy Conservation Code*, 2015. International Code Council, Washington, DC.

IgCC: *International Green Construction Code*, 2015. International Code Council, Washington, DC.

IMC: *International Mechanical Code*, 2015. International Code Council, Washington, DC.

IPC: *International Plumbing Code*, 2015. International Code Council, Washington, DC.

IRC: *International Residential Code*, 2015. International Code Council, Washington, DC.

LEED: Leadership in Energy and Environmental Design (LEED) 2013 Green Building Rating System for New Construction. U.S. Green Building Council, Washington, DC.

NDS: *National Design Specification (NDS) for Wood Construction*, 15th ed., 2015. American Wood Council, Leesburg, VA.

NEC (NFPA 70): *National Electrical Code*, 2014. National Fire Protection Association, Quincy, MA.

NFPA 101: *Life Safety Code*, 2015. National Fire Protection Association, Quincy, MA.

The Secretary of the Interior's *Standards for Rehabilitation*, 2010. *Code of Federal Regulations*, Title 36, Part 67.

INTRODUCTION

ABOUT THIS BOOK

ARE 5 Practice Problems for the Architect Registration Exam contains over 550 problems organized into six divisions that follow the structure of version 5 of the Architect Registration Exam (ARE 5).

- Division 1: Practice Management
- Division 2: Project Management
- Division 3: Programming & Analysis
- Division 4: Project Planning & Design
- Division 5: Project Development & Documentation
- Division 6: Construction & Evaluation

The problems presented in *ARE 5 Practice Problems* encompass a range of architectural topics focusing on the topics that appear on the ARE 5. Recent developments in architecture and construction in a number of areas are covered on the exam and in this book, including

- building commissioning
- business development and operations
- concrete reinforcement
- conformance with sustainability requirements

- construction manager as adviser or constructor
- contract documents for sustainable projects
- contractor selection
- cost control
- curtain walls
- design-build project delivery
- elevator design
- environmental context
- ethical standards
- financial management
- human resources
- integrated project delivery
- integrating building systems
- mechanical rooms
- office organization
- paving
- planning construction documentation
- plenum requirements
- post-occupancy evaluation
- practice methodologies
- project delivery methods, execution, follow-up, planning, and management
- quality control
- supplemental contract documentation
- sustainable materials
- value engineering
- weather barriers
- wood framing

The problems in this book reflect the most recent editions of a number of codes and standards, including

- 2007 AIA Contract Documents
- 2009 SectionFormat
- 2010 *Americans with Disabilities Act (ADA) Standards for Accessible Design*
- 2011 AISC *Steel Construction Manual*, 14th edition
- 2013 LEED Rating Systems
- 2014 ACI 318, *Building Code Requirements for Structural Concrete*
- 2014 *National Electrical Code* (NFPA 70)
- 2015 *International Building Code*

- 2015 *International Energy Conservation Code*
- 2015 *International Green Construction Code*
- 2015 *International Mechanical Code*
- 2015 *International Plumbing Code*
- 2015 *Life Safety Code* (NFPA 101)
- 2016 CSI MasterFormat

Although this book can be a valuable study aid in itself, it is designed to be used in conjunction with PPI's *ARE 5 Review Manual for the Architect Registration Exam* and *ARE 5 Practice Exam for the Architect Registration Exam*.

EXAM PROBLEM TYPES

There are several types of problems on the ARE 5 and in this book.

- multiple-choice problems
- check-all-that-apply problems
- fill-in-the-blank problems
- hot spot problems
- drag-and-place problems
- case study problems

Multiple-Choice Problems

Multiple-choice problems have two types. One type of multiple-choice problem is based on written, graphic, or photographic information. You will need to examine the information and select the correct answer from four given options. Some problems may require calculations. A second type of multiple-choice problem describes a situation that could be encountered in actual practice. Drawings, diagrams, photographs, forms, tables, or other data may also be given. The problem requires you to select the best answer from four options.

Multiple-choice problems often require you to do more than just select an answer based on memory. At times it will be necessary to combine several facts, analyze data, perform a calculation, or review a drawing.

Check-All-That-Apply Problems

Check-all-that-apply problems are a variation of a multiple-choice problem, where six options are given, and you must choose all the correct options. The problem tells how many of the options are correct, from two to four. You must choose all the correct options to receive credit; partial credit is not given.

Fill-in-the-Blank Problems

Fill-in-the-blank problems require you to fill in a blank with a value that you have derived from a table or a calculation.

Hot Spot Problems

Hot spot problems are used to assess visual judgment, evaluation, or prediction. Hot spot problems include the information needed to make a determination, along with an image (e.g., diagram, floor plan) and instructions on how to interact with the image. The problems will indicate that you should place a single target, also known as a hot spot icon, on the base image in the correct location or general area. On the exam, you will place the target on the image by moving the computer cursor to the correct location on the image and clicking on it. You will see crosshairs to help you position the point of click. You will be able to click on an alternate spot if you think your first choice is not correct. Your choice is not registered until you exit the problem. You can click anywhere within an acceptable area range and still be scored as correct.

Drag-and-Place Problems

Drag-and-place problems are similar to hot spot problems, but whereas hot spot problems involve placing just one target on the base image, drag-and-place problems involve placing two to six design elements on the base image. Drag-and-place problems are used to assess visual judgment or evaluation with multiple pieces of information. The problem statement describes what information is to be used to make the determination, and provides instructions on how to interact with the image or graphic item.

A drag-and-place problem, for example, may require you to drag and place design elements such as walls or beams onto the base image. On the exam, you will use the computer cursor to place the elements on the image by clicking and holding elements and dragging and releasing the elements on the correct location on the image. Depending on the question, you may use an element more than once or not at all. This type of question also provides an acceptable area range for placing the elements. The range may be small for questions about a detail or large for something like a site plan.

Case Study Problems

Each division's exam includes one to two case studies. Case studies are performance problem types comprising a scenario, a set of related resource documents (for example, code resources, drawings, and specifications), and a set of case study-specific problems. During the exam, you will be able to click on browser-like tabs at the top of the computer screen and flip back and forth between the case study scenario and resource documents. The case studies will test your ability to examine and use multiple pieces of information to make decisions about scenarios that could be encountered in the practice of architecture.

Case study problems may be multiple-choice, check-all-that-apply, fill-in-the-blank, hot spot, or drag-and-place.

HOW TO USE THIS BOOK

As you work the problems, you will prepare for the ARE 5 in the most effective way possible. The problems were written to highlight your areas of strength, as well as identify areas needing further study. Should you have difficulty with a topic, an explanation may be found in the corresponding chapter of the *ARE 5 Review Manual*. Incorrect answers enlighten by showing you common mistakes, and the steps necessary to arrive at correct answers are thoroughly documented. When you take full advantage of the practice problems and solutions, you will gain knowledge that is essential for peak performance on your exam.

If you are using this text to practice a particular area of study, go directly to the topic of interest and begin. Any weakness noted while attempting to solve the problems should prompt you to review the applicable material in the *ARE 5 Review Manual*. Keep in mind that the key to success on the exam is to practice solving problems.

Allow yourself time to prepare. You will get the most benefit out of your exam preparation efforts if you make a plan and stick to it. Make sure that as you review chapters in the accompanying *ARE 5 Review Manual*, that you also leave enough time to work the problems associated with those chapters. You should revisit practice problems during your exam preparation. Even if you successfully worked all the problems in a given chapter upon your initial review, you must maintain that knowledge as you work through unfamiliar or difficult material.

Although there is no substitute for a good formal education and the broad-based experience provided by your participation in the Architect Experience Program (AXP) with a practicing architect, this book, and the others in PPI's ARE 5 review series, will help you direct your study efforts to increase your chances of passing the ARE 5.

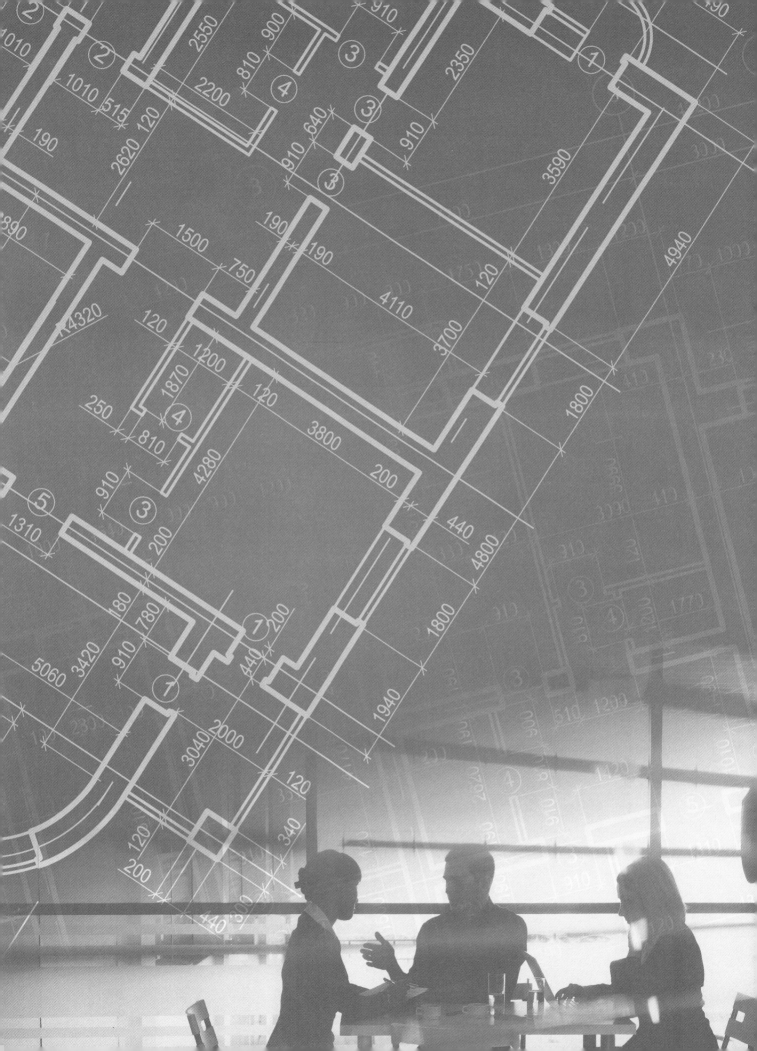

DIVISION 1: PRACTICE MANAGEMENT

1 Business Operations

1. The principal of a firm with 20 employees needs to hire additional staff to cover the workload of a newly awarded project. In order to maximize profitability, what is the most important issue that the principal should consider in deciding what type of staff to hire?

- (A) skills needed for the new project
- (B) potential billing rate for new hires
- (C) workload of existing staff on current projects
- (D) experience that new hires bring for future projects

2. In order to raise long-term productivity in a midsize firm, what changes to available resources might the firm make?

- (A) Hire experienced architects to replace newly licensed staff.
- (B) Relocate to new offices with less space and lower rent.
- (C) Invest in a new building information modeling (BIM) program instead of a current computer-aided drafting (CAD) system.
- (D) Require staff to work a minimum number of paid overtime hours.

3. Which of the following requirements apply to a professional architectural corporation? (Choose the three that apply.)

- (A) A certificate of authorization may be required in some states.
- (B) A formal agreement between directors is required by the state.
- (C) Articles of incorporation must be filed with the state's secretary of state.
- (D) A business license is required by the municipality where the firm is located.
- (E) Stockholders, directors, and officers must be licensed architects in the state in which they practice.
- (F) Duplicate filings of incorporation must be sent to the Internal Revenue Service (IRS).

4. An employer of an architectural firm can best prohibit moonlighting by employees by using a(n)

- (A) oral agreement
- (B) noncompete clause
- (C) at-will employment law
- (D) employment contract

5. An architectural firm with 36 employees is interviewing candidates for a project manager position. During the interview, which of the following questions can the interviewer ask?

- (A) What experience did you have when you worked with our competitor?

- (B) What is your age?

- (C) Do you have any physical problems that would prevent you from doing this work?

- (D) What is your national origin (in case we try to pursue work overseas)?

6. An architectural firm is preparing a proposal for a large mixed-use project for which other architectural firms are competing. One of the principals, an American Institute of Architects (AIA) member, formerly worked for one of the competing firms, where the principal was a project architect on similar mixed-use projects. The marketing manager wants to include two of the former projects the architect worked on as evidence of experience in the current proposal and feature the project with the firm's own photographs and project histories. Ethically, what is the best course of action for the firm?

- (A) Refuse to use the projects in the proposal.

- (B) Call the competing firm and request permission to use the photographs.

- (C) List the projects as experience and clearly state it was with the other firm.

- (D) Use the photographs and project histories, giving credit to the other firm.

7. A student is completing an architectural education interview for a part-time intern position at a firm. The student is willing to work without pay to get the job and gain experience. What should the architect's response be?

- (A) Agree to take on the student on a non-paid basis to see how the student performs.

- (B) Tell the student that the firm is obligated to pay him, but the student can otherwise compete for the job.

- (C) Hire the student on a non-paid basis, and express regret that the firm does not participate in the National Council of Architectural Registration Boards (NCARB) Architectural Experience Program (AXP).

- (D) Hire the student with pay, and advise the student to start the NCARB AXP.

8. A client with a new restaurant concept idea and accompanying program, who has worked with other architects to design restaurants in a large metropolitan area, hires a new firm to provide complete architectural services. After the restaurant has been operating for six months, the restaurant loses business and ultimately fails. The client notifies the architect that the client will sue because the architect did not provide the type of successful design that other architects did on previous projects. The architect should advise the lawyer and the client that the architect

- (A) met all the program requirements

- (B) met the profession's standard of care

- (C) designed the ideal restaurant for the new concept

- (D) did the best work possible with the untested concept

9. A large corporation that develops and maintains data centers across the country hires an architect to design a new facility and develop the necessary construction documents. The project proceeds through the design development phase and meets all the requirements of the developer and the program. It is then halted by the developer because of legal issues with the land purchase. The developer pays the architect for services rendered through the design development phase but tells the architect to keep all the design work and wait until the problems are resolved. After a year, the legal issues are resolved and the developer instructs the architect to resume work on the construction documents based on previous efforts. After the project is complete, the developer claims that the architect and the architect's consultants did not incorporate the latest technology into the data center. Regarding liability, the architect is probably

- (A) liable because the architect should have updated the contract documents to reflect new changes in technology

- (B) liable because the contract only called for completing the contract documents based on work in previous phases

- (C) not liable because the architect exercised the standard of care at the time the project was being designed

- (D) not liable because the developer gave the approval to continue work as the project was originally designed

10. A major architectural magazine has offered to publish an article with photographs of one of a firm's completed projects. In addition to the basic data about the project, including area, date of completion, consultants, and similar information, the magazine wants to publish the cost of the project. According to the American Institute of Architects (AIA) *Code of Ethics and Professional Conduct*, under what circumstances may an AIA architect provide this information after notifying the owner of the upcoming article?

(A)   The architect can provide the information unless requested not to do so by the owner.

(B)   The owner must give the architect permission to release any data.

(C)   The architect may publish the cost per square foot without releasing total cost.

(D)   The architect may provide whatever information the firm wishes to give.

11. A restrictive covenant in an architectural firm means that

(A)   the employer is limited in what it can require its employees to do

(B)   the architect's design must conform to any regulations of a homeowners' association

(C)   an employee that leaves the firm cannot set up a competing business in the same city

(D)   independent contractors working for the firm must abide by the rules of the firm

Solutions

1. There are several issues that any employer must consider in hiring. These include short-term needs to handle an immediate project and long-term requirements for the firm. In this case, the new project requires someone with specific skills.

The billing rate for the new hire will be sufficient to cover expenses and make a profit, so this is not a primary concern. If a new employee is needed, it is obvious that existing staff are busy. A person with broad experience would be valuable for future projects, but this would probably be a secondary concern when deciding whom to hire.

The answer is (A).

2. A basic measure of productivity in professional service firms is the ratio of output to input. In the case of an architecture firm, this means producing the most amount of work for the least amount of time and cost. This can be measured in ratios such as revenue per technical staff or total billings to total compensation, as well as other financial considerations. Investing in tools to make it easier for existing staff to do their work faster with a better product is the best change.

Replacing new staff with experienced architects is incorrect. In theory, more experienced staff could product the same amount of work more quickly and more cost effectively than newly licensed staff, but more experienced staff would also have to be paid more. Making this kind of transition is not cost-effective.

Relocating the office is incorrect because productivity in an architectural firm is dependent primarily on people. Minimizing overhead costs, such as rent, are important, but would not increase productivity.

Mandatory overtime is not a good general business decision and would be met with resistance from employees, even though it increases revenue for the same number of staff.

The answer is (C).

3. Some states require a separate certificate of authorization to allow the firm to conduct business. A formal agreement between the directors is not required by the state. Corporations, regardless of type, are governed at the state level and articles of incorporation must be filed with the state's secretary of state.

Municipal business licenses are not required.

For professional corporations, unlike subchapter C or subchapter S corporations, all the stockholders, directors, and officers must be licensed architects.

Duplicate filings of incorporation are not required by the IRS.

The answer is (A), (C), and (E).

4. Although an oral agreement legally can be considered a contract, it is not always effective at prohibiting moonlighting.

A noncompete clause in an employment contract means after leaving the firm, the employee cannot set up a competing business in the same geographical area, nor accept work from the previous employer's developers. It does not apply to moonlighting by current employees.

At-will employment is the informal method of working without a contract and does not prohibit moonlighting.

By using an employment contract, the firm can spell out exactly what is and is not allowed by the employee, which may include a prohibition of moonlighting or taking jobs outside the firm.

The answer is (D).

5. Equal employment opportunity laws prohibit employers from asking about age, marital status, race, or national origin.

The *Americans with Disabilities Act (ADA) Standards for Accessible Design* makes it illegal for firms with 15 or more employees to discriminate on the basis of disabilities. This includes asking questions during an interview about disabilities that might interfere with doing the job.

The firm is allowed to ask questions regarding work experience, including work experience gained while working with competitors.

The answer is (A).

6. According to the AIA document, *Code of Ethics and Professional Conduct*, Canon IV, AIA members should be honest about the scope of their responsibilities in connection to work for which they are claiming credit. It is acceptable for the architect to state that the architect has worked on the two projects as long as the extent of involvement was clearly stated in the proposal and that it was while working for the other firm. Featuring the projects with photographs, however, even with permission, could give the impression that the architect had more responsibility than actually existed. It could also be confusing to the potential client and embarrassing for the architect if same project appeared in two proposals.

The answer is (C).

7. According to the AIA document, *Code of Ethics and Professional Conduct*, Canon V, an architectural firm is obligated to compensate employees fairly and to nurture fellow professionals, including interns, as they progress through their careers. From a practical standpoint, if the student is interested in becoming an architect, the student must participate in the NCARB AXP and could begin the process while still in architecture school. The architect should say that the student would be paid if hired and that the student should start the AXP process.

The answer is (D).

8. In applying the standard of care, the architect only has to do what a reasonably prudent architect would do in the same locale, in the same time frame, given the same or similar facts or circumstances. In this case, the architect probably took the client's program and new idea and designed accordingly. In all likelihood, the client's new concept, which might have been untested, resulted in the business failure. It could be argued that the new concept idea does not constitute "similar circumstances" to the other restaurants, but the client should have had enough knowledge and experience of the restaurant business in the local area to provide the architect with a good program and sufficient guidance.

Meeting all the program requirements is important, but that is just part of the standard of care concept. If the architect claimed to have designed the ideal restaurant, this would raise unreasonable expectations and raise the standard of care, which could make him liable. Simply saying the architect did the best work possible is a weak argument by itself, but it is actually part of the standard of care that a reasonably prudent architect would practice.

The answer is (B).

9. The standard of care requires that an architect perform as a reasonably prudent architect would in the same time frame. In this instance, the architect and the consultants incorporated the latest technology available at the time and were instructed to proceed without notice by the developer that anything new was required; instead, they were told to proceed on the original design work. Although the architect might have asked the developer if

anything had changed in the intervening year, the architect was under no obligation to do so given the developer's instructions.

The answer is (C).

10. According to the AIA document *Code of Ethics and Professional Conduct*, Canon III, Obligations to the Client, states that AIA members should maintain the owner's confidentiality when requested. If the architect tells the owner of a potential article in a magazine, the owner has the opportunity to request that certain information, including photographs, not be published if there are security or proprietary concerns. The AIA member must follow that request. Related to this is a clause in AIA Document B141, *Standard Form of Agreement between Owner and Architect with Standard Form of Architect's Services*, which gives the architect the right to photograph the project and include photographs in promotional and professional materials unless it includes confidential or proprietary information and if the owner has previously told the architect, in writing, of what specific information is confidential or proprietary.

The answer is (A).

11. Restrictive covenants in an architectural firm, known more commonly as noncompete clauses, can be part of an employee contract with an employer and limit what the employee may do if the employee leaves the firm. Such covenants may restrict for whom the employee works for a specific amount of time, whether or not the employee can set up a competing business, whether or not the employee can work for the firm's clients, or restrictions on passing on confidential information.

An employee contract may limit what an employee can or cannot do while employed, so option (A) is incorrect. Option (B) describes restrictions on the design of houses or buildings in developments, and it is unrelated to restrictive covenants. Independent contractors may or may not have written agreements with a firm, but these are also unrelated to restrictive covenants.

The answer is (C).

2 Financial and Risk Management

1. The architect's role as the owner's agent is best described as

(A) acting on behalf of the owner, making decisions, expediting the work, and taking on responsibilities for which the owner is normally responsible

(B) mediating between the owner, the contractor, and vendors for the benefit of the owner

(C) balancing the needs of the contractor and the owner and being the principal of the relationship

(D) working for the owner in certain designated areas where the architect has been given the authority to act on the owner's behalf

2. During negotiations to develop a final, fixed construction cost with a preselected contractor, the owner wants to reduce the cost of construction suggested by the architect's original cost estimate. The architect should advise the owner to

(A) suggest that the project be put out to bid if the price is too high

(B) set a fixed limit on the construction cost, and negotiate directly with the subcontractors

(C) establish contractual penalties for exceeding the architect's original estimate

(D) consider the contractor's recommendations for alternate construction methods

3. Which type of architectural services fee structure is preferable when a client is embarking on his or her first architectural project and does not yet have a program?

(A) fixed sum

(B) multiple of direct personnel expense

(C) percentage of construction cost

(D) unit cost based on square footage

4. A common way of evaluating staff productivity in an architecture firm is to examine the

(A) direct salary expense

(B) time utilization ratio

(C) net multiplier

(D) direct personnel expense

5. An architecture firm is designing a tranquil, spa-like treatment center for cosmetic dentistry. The dental clinic will be housed within an existing building. The architect's scope of services includes space planning; detailing new partition walls; coordinating updates to the mechanical, electrical, data, and plumbing systems with appropriate consultants; and providing interior design services, including specification of furnishings for the suite. Which American Institute of Architects (AIA) document or documents are most appropriate for use as the owner-contractor agreements for this project?

(A) AIA Document A101, *Standard Form of Agreement Between Owner and Contractor where the basis of payment is a Stipulated Sum*, with AIA Document A201, *General Conditions of the Contract for Construction*

(B) AIA Document A107, *Standard Form of Agreement Between Owner and Contractor for a Project of Limited Scope*

(C) AIA Document A105, *Standard Form of Agreement Between Owner and Contractor for a Residential or Small Commercial Project*

(D) AIA Document A151, *Standard Form of Agreement Between Owner and Vendor for Furniture, Furnishings, and Equipment where the basis of payment is a Stipulated Sum*, with AIA Document A251, *General Conditions of the Contract for Furniture, Furnishings, and Equipment*, for purchase of the furniture; and A101, *Standard Form of Agreement Between Owner and Contractor where the basis of payment is a Stipulated Sum*, with AIA Document A201, *General Conditions of the Contract for Construction*, for construction work

6. A tort may arise from

(A) criminal activity of the architect

(B) unauthorized downloading of software

(C) negligence of the architect

(D) theft of building materials from the project site

7. Which of the following are <u>advantages</u> of a <u>sole proprietorship</u>? (Choose the three that apply.)

(A) ease of establishment

(B) management control by the owner

(C) liability is limited to the owner's investment

(D) tax advantages

(E) ability to raise capital

(F) ease of ownership transition

8. About one-third of the way through development of construction documents, a project architect notices that fee expenditures are about 15% over budget. What is the

first course of action that the architect should take to ensure that the project makes a profit?

(A) Determine what has caused the problem.

(B) Notify the client that fees may need to be increased.

(C) Alert the firm owners, and ask for direction to correct the problem.

(D) Modify the remainder of the project schedule and fee allocation.

9. Monitoring architectural fees and the percentage of project completion is most often done

(A) daily

(B) weekly

(C) biweekly

(D) monthly

10. An architecture firm is establishing billing rates for employees working on a large hotel project. The firm plans to propose a <u>cost plus fee compensation</u> method. Which of the following criteria would be factored into the calculation of each employee's billing rate? (Choose the <u>four</u> that apply.)

(A) direct salaries of employees

(B) cost of benefits such as insurance and vacation time

(C) profit allowance

(D) overhead of the architect's office

(E) taxes

(F) percentage of the construction cost

11. A utilization ratio is a

(A) measure of an employee's billable time versus overhead time

(B) comparison between programmed and nonprogrammed spaces

(C) calculation of the efficiency of a mechanical system

(D) way to express the buildable area of a site

12. When deciding on what to charge a developer on an hourly rate agreement, an architect should verify the

(A) quick ratio

(B) direct personnel expense numbers

(C) breakeven rate

(D) net multiplier

13. When evaluating the financial well-being of a firm, the owner or principal should always review the

(A) aged accounts receivable report

(B) direct personnel expense numbers

(C) time analysis report

(D) overhead rate

14. An architect is approached by a developer to design a small shopping strip mall. The architect has experience in this particular building type, but during preliminary discussions, the developer states that the strip mall must be designed and constructed within a very short time frame to make financing feasible. The architect knows the schedule is unreasonable. To minimize the architect's risk, the architect should

(A) tell the developer that the schedule could be met if a fast-track project delivery method is used

(B) explain that the schedule is impossible and that the developer must reduce its scope

(C) not accept the project that has such a short schedule and a developer with unreasonable expectations

(D) suggest that the developer consider splitting the project into two phases to shorten completion time

15. The architect can minimize exposure to claims by subcontractors by

(A) including an indemnification clause in the agreements

(B) having the general contractor include a claims-free clause in contracts with the subcontractors

(C) communicating only with subcontractors through the general contractor

(D) requiring that the developer approve any communications with the subcontractors

16. An architect accepts a job from a new developer. The architect is worried about being paid in a timely manner because of cash flow problems with the architect's other jobs. What course of action should the architect pursue?

(A) Require a retainer equal to 20% of the estimated fee before the project starts, and credit this to the final payment.

(B) Submit each invoice with a detailed itemization of work completed, who completed it, and the associated fee.

(C) State in the contract that a late payment fee will be applied to any invoice that is more than 30 days late.

(D) Include a contract provision stating that invoices will be sent every two weeks and work will stop after 45 days of nonpayment.

17. According to American Institute of Architects (AIA) Document B101, *Standard Form of Agreement Between Owner and Architect*, the architect is required to carry which types of insurance to minimize risk? (Choose the four that apply.)

(A) automobile

(B) general liability

(C) personal injury protection

(D) professional liability

(E) property

(F) workers' compensation

18. During the construction administration phase of a project, an architectural firm should

(A) leave the sequence, means, and methods of construction up to the contractor

(B) let the contractor identify potential safety problems

(C) ask the building official to notify the contractor of any building code violations

(D) let the owner coordinate all requirements of other contractors

19. What should an architectural firm do to ensure it has clear copyright claims to all of its work?

(A) During agreement negotiations, have the developer sign a separate agreement regarding copyright.

(B) Use the American Institute of Architects (AIA) standard form for architectural copyright protection.

(C) Develop a standard copyright notice that is printed on every drawing and project manual, and register all works with the U.S. Copyright Office.

(D) Nothing; upon publication, drawings and specifications are automatically subject to copyright protection under the Architectural Works Copyright Protection Act.

20. The balance sheet is an important tool to evaluate the financial well-being of an architectural firm because it

(A) lists the income and expenses of the business for a given time period

(B) shows a broad view of the firm's finances with assets and liabilities

(C) indicates the difference between technical and nontechnical staff salaries

(D) shows how employees are spending their time on billable work versus non-billable work

21. When reviewing the current ratio, a firm principal notices that the rate is 1.2. What should the principal do?

(A) Consider moving excess cash into an interest-bearing account.

(B) Examine ways to reduce fixed assets and minimize non-billable time.

(C) Work on reducing liabilities and increasing assets.

(D) Nothing; 1.2 is acceptable.

22. A firm with 18 employees discusses ways to improve its service. During the past year, there were problems with work being late, project fees being over budget, and contract documents being uncoordinated. What changes would have the most positive impact?

(A) Have the firm's management more closely monitor staff and develop proven standard details.

(B) Assign an experienced staff mentor to each project team and set limits on non-billable hours.

(C) Identify the causes for lateness and over-budget fees, and develop checklists for common tasks.

(D) Develop a quality control program, and more closely monitor project progress reports.

Solutions

1. An agent acts on behalf of another and assumes certain specified authority and duties but does not take on responsibilities that another person normally would have.

The answer is (D).

2. On a negotiated project, the contractor is in the best position to recommend alternate materials and construction methods that will lower costs while still meeting the owner's design requirements.

Bidding the project is no guarantee that the price will be lower; in fact, it may go up. The owner should not negotiate with subcontractors; that is the contractor's responsibility. Simply setting an arbitrary limit on construction cost does not encourage a lower price and is a punitive way to limit costs during negotiation.

The answer is (D).

3. It is very likely that clients undertaking their first construction project without a program would spend a great deal of their time and the architect's time determining needs and making decisions. Programming is not considered to be part of the architect's basic services. A cost plus fee method such as multiple of direct personnel expense would ensure that no matter how much time is spent on the project, the architect can still cover expenses and make a profit.

The answer is (B).

4. The net multiplier expresses the ratio of net revenues to direct salary expense.

$$\text{net multiplier} = \frac{\text{net revenues (\$)}}{\text{direct salary expense (\$)}}$$

The net multiplier, then, expresses how many dollars of revenue come into the firm for each dollar paid to employees. Employees must generate more revenue than their direct salary expense for the firm to continue to operate, pay for all indirect expenses (e.g., rent, insurance, benefits), and remain profitable.

Net revenues are the total amount of revenue generated by the firm's own forces. This excludes "pass-through" income such as consultant's fees and reimbursable expenses.

Direct salary expense is the amount paid to the firm's workforce, excluding the value of benefits such as insurance. Direct personnel expense includes the value of benefits.

The time utilization ratio compares the number of hours an employee charges to projects to the total number of hours for which that employee is compensated. Non-billable time is an overhead expense and must be controlled to keep the firm profitable.

Part 2 of *The Architect's Handbook of Professional Practice* discusses this and other financial and legal issues related to the establishment and management of architectural firms.

The answer is (C).

5. The most appropriate choice of owner-contractor contracts for this project is a combination of AIA Document A151: *Standard Form of Agreement Between Owner and Vendor for Furniture, Furnishings, and Equipment where the basis of payment is a Stipulated Sum,* with AIA Document A251, *General Conditions of the Contract for Furniture, Furnishings, and Equipment,* for purchase of the furniture; and AIA Document A101, *Standard Form of Agreement Between Owner and Contractor where the basis of payment is a Stipulated Sum,* with AIA Document A201, *General Conditions of the Contract for Construction,* for construction work. The contracts could be with the same contractor, with two different contractors, or with a contractor and a furniture dealer.

Most AIA documents deal with only the provision of "traditional" architectural and construction services. The exceptions are the interiors family, including AIA Document A151 and AIA Document A251, which were developed jointly by the AIA and the ASID (American Society of Interior Designers). It is important to keep the design contract separate from the FF&E (fixtures, furnishings, and equipment) contract to preserve the architect's independence from monetary interest in the sale of the goods that the architect has specified. It is advisable to use the Interiors family documents in situations where the scope of the project is limited to FF&E because these forms reference the *Uniform Commercial Code,* which provides rules for commerce in the United States.

Documents in the Interiors family are not suitable for construction work such as the major tenant improvement described in this problem or for projects with structural work or life safety systems. Therefore, portions of a project dealing with those issues should be covered under a separate agreement.

Although the Architect Registration Exam (ARE) focuses most on AIA Document A101 and AIA Document A201, architects should be familiar with the other AIA documents and the situations in which they are appropriate. Summaries of the documents are available on the AIA website at aia.org.

The answer is (D).

6. A tort is a civil wrong resulting from negligence as opposed to a criminal act. The other three choices are criminal acts.

The answer is (C).

7. A sole proprietorship has unlimited liability for negligence or other claims against the company, and it is subject to claims on personal property and other assets. In addition, it is often difficult to raise capital or establish credit unless the owner's personal credit rating is good. Because the business depends on the abilities and the reputation of the owner, it can be difficult to sell the business or make other ownership transition arrangements.

The answer is (A), (B), and (D).

8. Determining the cause of the problem should be the first step in reining in project fees. It may be that the client is indecisive or asking for work beyond the original scope of services. Personnel may be spending time developing unnecessary details. It may be possible to assign tasks to employees with lower billing rates to keep costs under control. In any event, this course of action would be a first step before the firm's owners are notified because they would want to know the cause of the problem.

The remainder of the design schedule may have to be modified but only after the root cause of the original problem is determined. If the problem was caused by the architectural firm, the client should not be asked for more money. However, if the client is requesting work beyond the original scope, the firm may be entitled to fees for additional services.

The answer is (A).

9. Most projects, large and small, are monitored on a weekly basis. This provides the opportunity to catch problems early enough to take corrective action and fits into the normal weekly cycle of office management, allowing employee assignments and deadlines to be made according to the project's status and the status of other work in the office.

Daily management would require too much time and would not give a broad enough view of the project as it progresses. Biweekly monitoring could be done for very large and lengthy jobs, but it might not allow corrections of problems to be made in time to be the most effective. Monitoring on a monthly basis would definitely allow problems to grow before being discovered.

The answer is (B).

10. There are a variety of compensation methods architects can propose when negotiating with a potential client. The most common methods are fixed fees, cost plus fees, percentage of construction cost, and unit cost.

The cost plus fee method compensates the architect for the actual cost of doing the work plus a fee for profit. Fees are generally billed at hourly rates, which are determined as a multiple of an employee's salary or salary plus benefits. The multiplier is adjusted based on overhead the firm must pay and profit levels the firm wishes to achieve; generally, multipliers range from 2 to 3.5. Calculations of appropriate billing rates must consider the employee's base salary, any benefits offered to that employee, and taxes.

A fixed fee is a stipulated sum of money that the client will pay the architect for services. The services are agreed upon in advance, and changes to the services made by the owner generally warrant additional compensation for the architect. The fees are determined by creating a list of tasks necessary to complete the project, assigning hours and personnel to each task, and multiplying the number of hours expected to complete the task by each person's hourly billing rate. The result is a ballpark fee based upon the personnel selected and the time the estimator thinks that it will take to complete the project. The estimate can then be adjusted to arrive at a fee that the estimator believes will allow the firm to make a profit on the project. If the estimator guesses incorrectly and it actually takes more time to complete the work, the firm may have to absorb the extra expenses.

The percentage of construction cost fee structure is not commonly used. With this method, the professional's fee is a percentage of the cost of project construction. However, with this method, a client may wonder if the architect will design a more expensive project to increase the design fee, or conversely, a relatively inexpensive project may be very complicated and the percentage of construction cost may not cover the architect's expenses to design the project.

The unit cost method bases fees upon some unit, such as square footage. This fee structure is sometimes used for projects such as a tenant space fit-out, where the scope of the work is relatively similar from one project to another.

The answer is (A), (B), (D), and (E).

11. A utilization ratio is used by firms to determine the amount of time spent on billable work as a percentage of total time for which an employee is compensated. A utilization ratio can be used in an analysis of the profitability and financial standing of a firm. It is calculated by dividing direct hours (or hours billed to projects) by total hours. Generally, employees at lower levels in the firm (e.g., drafters and interns) have higher utilization ratios than project architects and partners, who likely devote a portion of their time to overhead activities such as firm management and marketing.

The answer is (A).

12. The quick ratio is the ratio of the total current assets (including cash and equivalents plus accounts receivable) and revenue earned but not billed, divided by total current liabilities. This number is used to judge the financial health of the firm, but it is not directly related to billing rates.

Direct personnel expense numbers includes money needed for the actual salary of each employee, plus allowances for fringe benefits, taxes, and so forth. It is not directly related to billing rates.

The breakeven rate accounts for costs of personnel and overhead but not profit.

The net multiplier accounts for the costs of direct labor (direct personnel expense), indirect labor (like administrative assistants), overhead, and profit.

The answer is (D).

13. Direct personnel expense numbers is the cost of paying employees plus the cost of mandatory and discretionary expenses and benefits including taxes, health insurance, and similar employee-related costs.

The time analysis report shows how each employee is dividing his or her time between work, vacation time, sick leave, and other non-chargeable time. It is not as critical as the aged accounts receivable report for the overall financial health of the firm.

The overhead rate is the ratio of total firm overhead divided by total direct labor. It should not exceed a certain value (typically 1.3 to 1.5 of total direct labor), but it is not as critical as the aged accounts receivable report.

The aged accounts receivable report shows the status of all the invoices for all jobs in the firm and the time between the invoice date and the payment date. Getting paid in a timely manner is critical for cash flow and the overall financial health of the firm. Invoices that have not been paid within a certain time, generally 60 days, need the attention of the principals.

The answer is (A).

14. A developer with unreasonable expectations or lack of knowledge about construction can expose the architect to risk before a project gets started. The architect, knowing the schedule is unreasonable, should turn down the project unless the schedule is changed or the project is reduced in scope to fit within the available time.

The answer is (C).

15. There is no "claims-free" clause in subcontractor agreements.

Although the architect should always communicate with the subcontractors through the general contractor, it is not the main way to minimize risk.

The developer should not be communicating with the subcontractors; communication between the developer and subcontractors should be through the architect.

An indemnification clause attempts to hold harmless the owner and architect for any damages or claims resulting from the performance of the work by the contractor or others, including subcontractors, with whom the architect has no contractual relationship. This is a standard provision found in AIA Document A201, *General Conditions of the Contract for Construction*.

The answer is (A).

16. Retainers are a valid way to get money up front and cover any future nonpayment, but retainers are difficult to require of developers. A 20% retainer is considered excessive, whereas a 10% retainer is considered more reasonable.

Detailed invoices should be sent to all developers explaining what work was completed and its associated fee, but this alone is not enough to encourage payment.

Late payment fees can encourage payment, but many developers balk at this. Even with a late payment fee, developers still can delay payment and adversely affect the architect's cash flow.

The primary concern in this situation is cash flow, so the architect must take whatever action keeps the developer paying in a regular, timely manner. One way to do this is to send invoices more often to get a more frequent payment schedule and to enforce payment by making it clear that nonpayment will result in work stopping. Both of these provisions must be made clear to the developer before work starts and must be stated clearly in the contract.

The answer is (D).

17. Under AIA Document B101, Article 2, the architect is required to carry the following types of insurance: automobile, general liability, professional liability, and workers' compensation.

Automobile insurance covers liability and property damage to vehicles.

General liability insurance protects against claims of property damage, liability, and personal injury caused by the architect or employees, consultants, or other people hired by the architect.

Professional liability insurance protects the architect and employees against bodily injury, property damage, or other damage. It is often called errors and omissions insurance and protects against mistakes in the contract documents or other services the architect offers.

Workers' compensation is required by law and protects employees against injuries caused by work-related activities. Workers' compensation insurance is required in most states and covers medical costs and a portion of lost wages for employees who become ill or injured due to work-related activities.

The answer is (A), (B), (D), and (F).

18. Although the contractor is responsible for safety on the job, the architect should point out obvious safety problems instead of leaving the responsibility to the contractor. However, the contractor is responsible for taking the necessary action to remedy the problems.

The architect has the implied duty to inform the contractor of relevant information that may affect the progress of the work. The architect should not ask the building official to talk to the contractor. The architect can talk to the contractor directly regarding any observed building code violations. Waiting for the building inspector to identify building code violations could delay the project.

The architect has the duty to assist the owner in coordinating requirements and schedules of other contractors who are not under contract with the general contractor.

An implied duty of the architect is to cooperate with the contractor but not to interfere with the contractor's work. The contractor is ultimately responsible for sequencing and identifying the means and methods of construction.

The answer is (A).

19. A separate signed agreement is not required. The provisions for copyright are in AIA Document B101, *Standard Form of Agreement Between Owner and Architect.*

There is no AIA form for architectural copyright protection.

Printed material (e.g., drawings, specifications, and other pictorial or graphic representations of the architect's work) is automatically considered to have copyright protection when it is published. However, this is not the best way to ensure clear copyright claims.

The best way to ensure protection is to place a copyright notice on each printed item and register them with the U.S. Copyright Office. The Architectural Works Copyright Protection Act gives the architect the right to the actual building form, composition of spaces, and elements in the design, which prevents others from making an unauthorized copy or a derivative of a building.

The answer is (C).

20. Option (A) is incorrect because it describes a profit and loss statement; this is important to evaluate the financial well-being of a firm but provides different information. Option (C) describes information given on the profit and loss statement. Option (D) describes information found on a time analysis report, which is specific to individual staff members, but does not represent all the factors that affect the financial condition of the firm.

The balance sheet shows all the assets and liabilities of a firm and gives an overall view of the financial health of the firm, including its net worth. It can be used to evaluate the firm's financial condition at any time.

The answer is (B).

21. The current ratio is a value found by dividing current assets by total current liabilities. It is a measure of a firm's ability to meet current obligations and should be a minimum of 1.0 to 1.5, the higher the better. Option (A) is incorrect because a value of 1.2 does not indicate that the firm has extra cash to invest. Option (B) is incorrect because reducing fixed assets and minimizing non-billable time does not significantly change the current ratio. Option (D) is incorrect because a current ratio of 1.2 is lower than ideal, so doing nothing is not a prudent course of action.

A current ratio value of 1.2 indicates that there may be problems ahead in paying salaries and meeting other short- and long-term liabilities. The firm should try to increase assets by finding new jobs (or contracts) and reduce liabilities such as loans and uncollected fees.

The answer is (C).

22. While closer monitoring by the firm's management could catch mistakes and answer questions from less experienced staff, this is not the best use of their time. Standard details that have been proven to work are a good idea but would be part of a quality control program. Option (B) is incorrect because an experienced staff member should be part of every project, especially if there are many inexperienced staff members in the office. Setting limits on non-billable hours alone would not correct problems with scheduling and being over budget. Option (C) is incorrect because identifying causes and developing checklists, while necessary, are not definite suggested changes.

A well-implemented quality control program is an excellent way to minimize risks and establish consistent procedures for producing work. A quality control program could incorporate all the suggestions in the other options to produce good contract documents and help get projects completed on time. Monitoring project progress reports more closely would help project managers and firm management identify time and fee problems early enough to take corrective action.

The answer is (D).

3 Delivery of Services

1. The joinder provisions in American Institute of Architects (AIA) Document A201, *Contract General Conditions for Construction*, and AIA Document B101, *Standard Owner and Architect Agreement,*

(A) prohibit the architect from being involved in arbitration

(B) allow parties to consolidate arbitration conducted under the agreement

(C) allow two parties to "team up" against the other to share legal expenses

(D) prohibit a subcontractor from being called as a witness against the contractor

2. Which statements are true of a project alliance? (Choose the three that apply.)

(A) Non-owner parties receive payment of overhead costs, profit, and bonuses only upon successful completion of the work.

(B) The agreement among the parties establishes a new legal entity.

(C) All decisions are made by consensus.

(D) No mechanisms for dispute resolution are included in the agreement.

(E) Liability of one party to another is limited but not waived.

(F) A project alliance closely resembles the traditional design-build agreement.

3. Which party owns the copyright on a building?

(A) owner

(B) architect

(C) contractor

(D) construction manager

4. At the beginning of a project, the owner asks the architect to recommend the types of insurance the owner will need to carry for the duration of the project. Which of the following responses are appropriate? (Choose the two that apply.)

(A) Give the owner American Institute of Architects (AIA) Document G612, *Owner's Instructions to the Architect Regarding the Construction Contract.*

(B) Suggest the standard insurance types, and advise the owner about optional insurance.

(C) Tell the owner that the owner's insurance agent should make the recommendations.

(D) Arrange a meeting with the architect's insurance counselor and the owner.

(E) Call the owner's insurance agent and explain the owner's needs.

(F) Refer to AIA Document A201, *General Conditions of the Contract for Construction*, for a list of required insurance types.

5. Which office organization structure would give individual employees the most job satisfaction?

(A) departmental

(B) pyramidal

(C) sole proprietorship

(D) studio

6. An architect has been asked to develop a proposal to provide architectural services to design a small, speculative office building for a new client. To increase the likelihood of making a profit on the project, what method of determining compensation should the architect propose?

(A) rate per square foot

(B) stipulated sum

(C) percentage of the work

(D) multiple of direct personnel expense

7. When deciding whether to accept a project from a potential client, the architect should be most concerned with the

(A) architect's current level of staffing

(B) project's financial feasibility

(C) project's distance from the architect's office

(D) question of whether the client has worked with an architect before

8. During a construction project, the electrical contractor discovers a code violation error on the electrical engineer's drawings. Determining how to correct the problem and paying for any costs associated with the error is the responsibility of the

(A) architect

(B) electrical engineer

(C) electrical contractor

(D) general contractor

9. American Institute of Architects (AIA) documents concerning architect/consultant agreements are found in the

(A) C-series

(B) D-series

(C) E-series

(D) G-series

10. Which statement about construction managers is true?

(A) If an owner brings an independent construction manager into a project shortly before construction begins in order to help "value engineer" the project, the architect's responsibilities and fees are not affected.

(B) A construction manager is often hired when a project has fast-tracked multiple prime construction contracts rather than one general contract for construction.

(C) A construction manager serving as an adviser to an owner during the design development phase is responsible for estimating the construction cost and guaranteeing a maximum price for the work.

(D) American Institute of Architects (AIA) Document A101, *Standard Form of Agreement Between Owner and Architect*, and AIA Document A201, *General Conditions of the Contract for Construction*, can be used as the agreement between the owner and construction manager.

11. An architecture firm specializing in multi-family residential work is asked by a developer to submit a proposal for a high-rise apartment building. In the request for proposal, the developer states that the project will use a "construction manager as adviser" method of project delivery and that the developer insists on using standard ConsensusDOCS contract agreements. What should be the architect's response to this developer?

(A) Decline to submit a proposal and tell the developer that using the ConsensusDOCS agreements would put the firm at too much risk.

(B) Tell the developer that using a construction manager as adviser project delivery method would not be appropriate for this size and type of project with the ConsensusDOCS agreements.

(C) Insist that the ConsensusDOCS agreements be used only after review by the architect's attorney, who could modify provisions if necessary.

(D) Agree to using the ConsensusDOCS agreements but insist that the developer use a "construction manager as constructor" project delivery method.

12. The marketing department of a midsize architectural firm secured a request for proposal (RFP) for a very large mixed-use retail, residential, and commercial project in their city. Seven other firms, both locally and out of state, are receiving the RFP. This project would provide several years of work and enhance the firm's reputation. The firm does not have experience in this project type nor the staff to do the work. What response improves the firm's chances of securing the commission?

(A) Begin hiring the necessary professional staff with experience in this project type who could also work on other projects in the firm.

(B) Explore forming a joint venture with another firm with experience in the project type and the available staff to complete the project.

(C) Develop a limited partnership with a principal and professional staff who have experience in mixed-use developments.

(D) Politely decline the request for proposal, explaining to the developer that the firm would not be qualified.

13. The city council for a large city plans to construct a new civic center that will have several city administration buildings, a courthouse, and a museum. The city council announced an open competition to any architectural firm that wants to submit proposals for master planning. A growing firm sees this as an opportunity to expand the practice into urban planning and design. In deciding whether to enter the competition, what are the most important factors the principals should consider? (Choose the three that apply.)

(A) Does the firm have enough money to cover the cost of developing a viable proposal?

(B) Is it possible that being selected would also result in getting a commission for the buildings?

(C) Does the firm have enough experienced staff to work on the proposal?

(D) Can the firm hire temporary staff to help with the proposal and keep them if the proposal is accepted?

(E) What other projects are currently in the firm and when are they scheduled for completion?

(F) Is the city offering compensation for each firm and how much?

14. When a project is being designed and constructed using the American Institute of Architects (AIA) standard forms for a sustainable project, who is responsible for developing the sustainability plan?

(A) owner

(B) architect

(C) contractor

(D) certifying authority

15. The principals at an architecture firm accept a questionable project and developer because they need the work to maintain staff. The project initially proceeds well and the firm is paid for the first two months. After that, the developer stops paying but assures the firm that payment is coming. The developer then goes bankrupt, and the firm is never paid for the last two months. The greatest impact on the firm is the

(A) effect on the financial well-being of the firm

(B) principals foregoing part of their salary

(C) developers realizing they could get free work from the firm

(D) firm gaining a reputation for not wisely accepting developers

16. What is the most likely effect on an understaffed architectural firm that accepts a project with a large commission?

(A) The firm will not be able to complete the project to the developer's satisfaction.

(B) The human resources department will need to hire new staff too quickly, which may reduce the quality of the employees hired.

(C) The existing staff will have to work overtime, resulting in overwork and stress.

(D) The firm will need to hire new employees as needed.

17. The best time for an architectural firm to begin minimizing risk with clients is during

(A) marketing

(B) developer research

(C) developer interviews

(D) contract negotiating

18. A small but growing architecture firm with five employees is currently a sole proprietorship. The owner decides to change the firm's business structure to minimize risk to the owner and future principals. What type of business organization should the owner consider?

(A) limited partnership

(B) joint venture

(C) limited liability company

(D) professional corporation

19. Which project delivery method should an architect recommend to a client to minimize construction problems, disputes, and cost overruns?

(A)   design-bid-build

(B)   fast-track

(C)   standard design-build

(D)   integrated project delivery

20. A midsize architecture firm is planning to expand its services to include interior design and strategic planning. The firm currently operates on a studio basis, which works well for the firm. As the firm grows in both personnel and service offerings, what type of organization plan will be the most appropriate?

(A)   Maintain the current studio organization.

(B)   Develop studios with specialist departments.

(C)   Use studios with expertise in project types.

(D)   Change to a horizontal departmental structure.

21. To engage the client in early programming and design decisions more actively, which method will work best for the architect?

(A)   brainstorming

(B)   interactive PowerPoint

(C)   sketch meetings

(D)   squatters' session

22. Throughout the development of construction documents for a project, the architect and electrical engineer regularly exchanged computer-aided drafting (CAD) drawings. During construction, after the electrical contractor placed many of the luminaires and ran conduit, the general contractor noticed that the luminaire locations were different than noted on the architect's reflected ceiling plans and the engineer's lighting plans. American Institute of Architects (AIA) Document C401, *Standard Form of Agreement Between Architect and Consultant*, was used by the architect. Who is responsible for paying for the corrections?

(A)   architect

(B)   electrical contractor

(C)   electrical engineer

(D)   general contractor

23. What is the most efficient and cost-effective way for a general practice architecture firm with 20 employees to develop project manuals and specifications?

(A)   Use an in-house specification writer and develop office master specifications.

(B)   Subscribe to a master specification service and develop specifications in-house.

(C)   Hire a specification writing consultant on a project-by-project basis.

(D)   Have the senior project architect on each project write the specifications.

24. While designing a mid-rise city courthouse and detention facility, which person should the architect most actively involve in the vertical transportation solutions?

(A)   electrical engineer

(B)   elevator consultant

(C)   facility manager

(D)   security consultant

25. An experienced multi-family housing developer has approached an American Institute of Architects (AIA) architecture firm to commission the design for a 50-unit apartment building. In preliminary discussions, the developer says that a pro forma has been done and states the construction budget for the project, including architectural fees. Based on past experience, the architect realizes the budget is at least 20% under what is required for a building of the type and quality the developer has described and that the fees may be 10% too low. How should the architect respond to the offer?

(A)   Decline the offer, saying the budget is unrealistic and the building could not be constructed for the amount the developer has proposed.

(B)   Decline the offer, saying it would violate the AIA *Code of Ethics and Professional Conduct* to accept a job that was clearly unfeasible.

(C)   Accept the offer but insist that the proposed budget be increased or that the scope of the project be decreased.

(D)   Accept the offer and find ways to meet the budget, and require that the developer provide a retainer for services.

26. In order to minimize risks when taking on a project, what factors should an architect know about a potential owner who has previous building experience? (Choose the four that apply.)

(A) owner's preferred type of professional services agreement

(B) ease of discussing issues and problems with the owner

(C) financial ability of the owner to complete the project

(D) problems with past projects the owner has done

(E) project team that the owner has assembled

(F) owner's preconceived ideas of design

27. A midsize architecture firm is organized into departments to complete a variety of project types. The principals want to develop a way to do more design-build work in order to reduce the problems they have had with traditional design-bid-build projects and to reduce risk overall. They also want to market their expertise in their current building types. Which of the following approaches would best meet their goals?

(A) Look for one or more contractor-led design-build firms, and make agreements to be their consulting architect.

(B) Become a designer-led design-build firm, and hire contractors as consultants.

(C) Try to find a design-build firm that needs an in-house architect, and merge with it.

(D) Begin to market the firm as a "bridging expert" to work with the owner and design-build firms.

28. Design-assist contracting

(A) is a form of construction-manager-as-adviser project delivery

(B) provides architectural services to contractors on an as-needed basis

(C) can aid in the development of complex elements of a building design

(D) allows the architect to offer advice to subcontractors on their work

29. An architecture firm has been given a project for which the allowable time for design is very short. What design methodology should be used to develop a good schematic design solution?

(A) Give the task to the office's lead designer.

(B) Organize a charrette with the project team.

(C) Hold a brainstorming session with the principals.

(D) Ask everyone in the office to provide design ideas.

Solutions

1. The joinder provisions included in the AIA documents were substantially revised in 2007. Similar language is in all AIA documents that require arbitration, such as AIA Document A201, Sec. 15.4.4, and AIA Document B101, Sec. 8.3.4. While previous versions placed strict limitations on consolidation and joinder, the documents now allow either party to consolidate an arbitration (if certain criteria are met) and to include by joinder a third party.

The answer is (B).

2. A project alliance is a legal structure often associated with integrated project delivery (IPD). In IPD, the architect and contractor are not contractually bound to each other (as they are in design-build); each has a separate contract with the owner.

The architect is responsible for coordinating the team of design professionals and consultants best suited for the project, while the contractor maintains responsibility for hiring and coordinating the efforts of subcontractors and those involved with construction of the building.

There are a variety of legal structures and contracts that may be used to establish the relationships among the project participants.

- A project alliance allows for the payment of direct costs incurred by team members but ties additional compensation to performance; the payment of profit, overhead, and bonuses depends on the successful completion of the project's goals. This is intended to encourage team members to work together for a successful outcome to the project so that all may benefit. Participants waive their liability to one another. Mechanisms for dispute resolution are not part of the contract because all parties agree to comply with decisions that the team makes by consensus.

- A single purpose entity is an independent corporate structure that is newly formed specifically for a project. All implications of starting a new business (e.g., taxes, insurance, corporate structure, legal status, licensing) must be fully considered. As with a project alliance, the payment of direct costs is included in the base agreement, but additional compensation depends on successful completion of the project goals. Disputes (that cannot be resolved internally through negotiation) may be resolved through mediation, arbitration, or litigation.

- A relational contract is used to limit the parties' liability, but liability is not waived. In the absence of team consensus, the owner is charged with making final decisions. Compensation for direct costs, profit, and overhead is included in the agreement, but payment of

additional compensation or bonuses depends on the project results. Disputes that cannot be resolved through negotiation among the parties may be resolved through mediation, arbitration, or litigation.

Of these three structures, the relational contract is the most similar to the traditional design-build model of project delivery.

One way to form an IPD relationship is to use the model contracts offered by the AIA that are specifically written for IPD projects. These documents define the responsibilities of each party and offer guidance in specifying requirements for confidentiality agreements, compensation, dispute resolution, insurance, and the like.

- AIA Document A195, *Standard Form of Agreement Between Owner and Contractor for Integrated Project Delivery*

- AIA Document A295, *General Conditions of the Contract for Integrated Project Delivery*

- AIA Document B195, *Standard Form of Agreement Between Owner and Architect for Integrated Project Delivery*

- AIA Document C196, *Standard Form of Agreement Between Single Purpose Entity and Owner for Integrated Project Delivery*

- AIA Document C197, *Standard Form of Agreement Between Single Purpose Entity and Non-Owner Member for Integrated Project Delivery*

The AIA publication *Integrated Project Delivery: A Guide* is an excellent resource for understanding this approach to design and construction phase services. The document is available for download from the AIA website at aia.org (search for it by title).

The answer is (A), (C), and (D).

3. The architect owns the copyright on his or her work from the moment the ideas are expressed in a tangible form, such as sketches, CAD files, technical drawings, and models. These expressions that move a building from an idea to a built structure are known as instruments of service and are addressed in AIA Document B101, Article 7. AIA Document B101, Sec. 7.2 states that the architect retains ownership of the copyright. AIA Document A201, Sec. 1.5, informs the contractor of the architect's right to ownership and explains that although the contractor is permitted to use the instruments of service for the purposes of constructing that project, the contractor may not use them for any other purpose.

In response to feedback from owners, the intellectual property sections of the AIA documents were overhauled in 2007. AIA Document B101, Sec. 7.3.1, allows an owner to use the instruments of service for other projects, provided that the architect has been fully compensated. If the architect is not hired for the next project, the owner must indemnify the architect from all claims resulting from subsequent use. In addition, AIA Document B101, Sec. 11.9, requires the owner to pay a licensing fee to the architect to continue to use the documents.

The right to ownership of the instruments of service is of critical importance to architects, and all owner-architect agreements should contain language protecting this right. Architects bear responsibility for the way that these documents are used. AIA Document B101, Sec. 7.3, allows the owner a nonexclusive license to reproduce drawings for use on this project only. The owner does not own the design or the instruments of service, just the building that is constructed using them.

If the owner wishes to build another building using the same design, the architect's consent must be obtained. This protects the architect from circumstances where drawings are being used without the architect's knowledge and without proper payment for architectural services. It also guards against situations where the drawings prepared specifically for one project are being used under conditions not addressed by the original documents, which may expose the architect to liability.

The answer is (B).

4. An architect is not qualified to give insurance advice. The architect should inform the owner that insurance decisions should be made in consultation with the owner's insurance or legal advisers. AIA Document G612 may be provided as a guide.

The answer is (A) and (C).

5. A departmental structure often pigeonholes employees into doing only one type of job or task. While some employees like this, most architects and aspiring architects like variety. A pyramidal organization is a "top-down" type of structure where the principal makes decisions and hands off the work to subordinates who do not have the opportunity to get involved in all aspects of a business. Most sole proprietorships are small businesses where individual employees often get to do a variety of types of work but decisions regarding assignments are the responsibility of the principal.

The studio format of office organization gives individual employees the most job satisfaction.

The answer is (D).

6. There are at least 10 methods of calculating compensation for architectural services. Four are time-based: multiple of direct salary expense, multiple of direct personnel expense, professional fee plus expenses, and hourly billing rate. Other methods include stipulated sum, percentage of cost of the work, square footage, unit cost, multiple of consultants' billings, and royalty. In many cases, different methods of compensation are combined on the same project. Methods based on area are best used for repetitive types of projects for which the architect has good historical time and expense data. Work based on a stipulated sum may run over the originally allotted time, decreasing or eliminating any profit first estimated. With a percentage of the work method, a great deal of time may be expended even on a low-cost building, such as a speculative office.

The multiple of direct personnel expense includes the salaries of people working on the job and their required benefits, plus overhead and profit. Because this is a time based method of compensation, each hour spent working on the project includes a profit factor. For a new client wanting a speculative type of building, the architect should use the multiple of direct personnel expense method to increase the odds of getting paid for all services performed.

The answer is (D).

7. Although the architect should be concerned with all of the parameters listed, the financial feasibility of the project is the most important. Without a viable project, the architect may perform preliminary work without getting paid, and the project might never be completed.

The answer is (B).

8. AIA Document C401, *Standard Form of Agreement Between Architect and Consultant,* states that consultants are responsible for code compliance regarding their areas of the work. By signing their documents, the consultants become responsible for compliance with applicable codes and regulations.

Review AIA Document C401. Consultants are also responsible for the accurate production of their own drawings and specifications and should check their own documents for consistency. However, from a legal perspective, the architect as prime consultant is liable to the owner for the consultant's work.

The answer is (B).

9. AIA documents are clustered according to the type of agreements included, as follows.

A-series	owner/general contractor
B-series	owner/architect
C-series	other agreements (including architect/consultant and joint ventures)
D-series	miscellaneous documents
E-series	exhibits
F-series	(reserved for future use)
G-series	contract administration and project management forms (e.g., bid documents log, change order, construction change directive)

The answer is (A).

10. A construction manager (CM) is a benefit to a project with fast-tracked multiple prime contracts, particularly when the owner is not interested in or does not have the experience for coordinating all the parties working on site.

The *Architect's Handbook of Professional Practice* lists a variety of scenarios in which the use of a construction manager tends to be the most beneficial to the owner.

- projects with fast-tracked multiple prime contracts

- projects that the CM joins early in the design phase, so that the owner can take advantage of the CM's construction expertise while building details are being developed, minimizing the risk that major revisions will be needed to the construction documents later in the process

- projects in which the owner is willing to deal with multiple professionals

- projects in which the CM is sensitive to the relationship between the architect and owner and does not try to come between the two

A CM may act as either an adviser to the owner or as a construction contractor. The difference is significant. In the role of adviser, the CM has no direct financial responsibility for the project. In the role of construction contractor, however, the CM is responsible for delivering a finished product for the agreed-on price.

Bringing an independent construction manager into a project often changes the responsibilities of the architect. The CM may take on many of the construction administration tasks traditionally performed by the architect. In addition, the CM's suggestions for cost-cutting may involve revisions to the design and contract documents. When a new player is added to a project team, all people involved should reevaluate their lists of responsibilities

and proposed fees and clarify who is now responsible for each item.

The American Institute of Architects (AIA) publishes the CM-Adviser family of documents, which are for use when a CM serves as an adviser to the owner. The CM-Constructor family is for use when a CM is financially responsible for delivering the project within the guaranteed price.

The answer is (B).

11. The ConsensusDOCS standard contract documents are contract forms developed by a consortium of construction industry organizations including the Associated General Contractors of American, the Associated Builders and Contractors, the Mechanical Contractors Association of America, the Construction Specifications Institute, and nearly 40 other trade groups. ConsensusDOCS are a family of model contract documents developed primarily to compete with the standard family of AIA contract documents and to end a perceived architect bias in the AIA documents. The stated purpose was to take a balanced approach to defining the rights, obligations, and risks of the various parties involved in a construction project and to reduce the number and severity of disputes.

Declining to submit a proposal eliminates the possibility of getting a valuable commission.

Telling the developer that using a construction manager is not appropriate for this project is incorrect. Using a construction manager as adviser for this type of project is acceptable and should not affect the response to the developer.

Using the ConsensusDOCS unchanged would put the architect at risk because of the possible presence of unacceptable clauses in the agreement.

If the ConsensusDOCs can be reviewed by the architect's and owner's attorneys and insurance agents with the ability to modify unacceptable clauses, the ConsensusDOCs can be used for the project.

The answer is (C).

12. Hiring staff would be unwise as the firm may not get the project, and the firm would need additional work to keep the new staff busy.

Developing a limited partnerships is a long-term organizational strategy, not a way to compete for one project.

Declining the RFP is a realistic possibility and probably would not result in any harm, but if the principals determine that the project helps the firm, it should do what it can to get the project.

If the firm is intent on doing what it can to get the project, a joint venture is ideally suited to the situation. The firm must first establish a teaming agreement with the potential joint venture firm to include with their proposal. The teaming agreement includes the roles and responsibilities of the firms, along with other provisions that would go into a joint venture if they got the project. If the project was not awarded to them, the joint venture would not be formed, with no adverse effect to either firm.

The answer is (B).

13. Competitions can be either a good way to secure a commission or a real money loser. In deciding to enter any competition, a firm must primarily consider money and staffing. The principals must estimate how much it would cost to submit a proposal and be willing to forfeit that amount if they do not get the job. If the city provides a nominal compensation to each entrant, that might partially offset the office's cost, but this is uncommon. The principals also have to determine if the firm's current workload would allow the time commitment. The other options are also considerations, but they are not the most important factors.

The answer is (A), (C), and (F).

14. A project designed and constructed using the AIA standard forms for sustainable projects must use the following process.

The owner establishes a sustainable objective, which is the owner's reason for incorporating sustainable measures on the project (e.g., to achieve a sustainability certification).

A sustainability workshop is held to confirm the objectives, establish goals, discuss sustainability measures, and review feasibility and budget.

The architect prepares a sustainability plan, a contract document that defines the details of implementing the sustainability goals and objectives. If the owner wants the project to have some type of sustainability certification (e.g., LEED), the architect must provide the owner with copies of the necessary paperwork for registering the project with the appropriate certifying authority.

The answer is (B).

15. The principals foregoing part of their salary does not a have a direct impact on the firm. Clients taking advantage of free work and a tainted reputation for the firm are not likely impacts. It is doubtful that other developers will learn of the situation.

The greatest effect is the lost income. Depending on the size of the firm and its cash reserves, the impact could

have major consequences or be something the firm could absorb.

The answer is (A).

16. After a project has been awarded, a firm can hire new employees as required in order to complete the project. At the beginning stages of a project, the required project staffing level is usually at its lowest point, so overtime is not required. Additional staff can be hired as needed.

The answer is (D).

17. Minimizing risk begins with knowing the target market. Business development efforts should be directed at markets that the architect understands and deems to be good matches for the firm's goals, experience, capabilities, and values. For example, a speculative overseas developer is not a good prospect for a medium-size firm in the United States that does not have experience with foreign work. Similarly, an architect who believes strongly in sustainable design should not market to clients who do not share that value.

The answer is (A).

18. A limited partnership requires two or more people and the firm may not have two or more principals who would share the risks of the business.

A joint venture is a one-time relationship formed for a specific project and not for a general business organization.

Liability for malpractice with professional corporations, unlike a C corporation or subchapter S corporation, is usually limited to the person responsible, which could be one of the owners or a future principal.

In a limited liability company, members have no personal liability and liability is limited to each member's investment. In addition, limited liability companies are easier to set up and operate than a corporation.

The answer is (C).

19. Design-bid-build is not recommended because the low-bid contractor usually sets the price based on minimal labor and materials prices. Once the project begins, the contractor finds ways to get more money through change orders or claiming the architect's documents were not complete enough to accurately bid on. This can lead to disputes during construction and cost overruns.

Fast-track is not recommended because a fast-track method by itself does not guarantee an absence of problems or cost overruns. Fast-track delivery can be used with any type of project delivery method, including design-bid-build, so many of the same problems and cost overruns could occur. However, fast-track used with one of the construction manager delivery methods minimizes construction problems and cost overruns.

Standard design-build is not recommended because the owner does not have as much control over some aspects of design and quality of material, which can lead to disputes. This occurs even though the owner has a fixed price early in the planning process and the design-build entity is responsible for maintaining that price. Some of these problems can be alleviated by using the bridging method of design-build. In that method, the owner hires an architect to develop a more detailed set of owner's requirements than otherwise would be developed by the owner alone.

Of the choices given, integrated project delivery (IPD) is the method most likely to minimize problems. All the major participants are working together to give the client the best product at the lowest cost consistent with the owner's needs.

The answer is (D).

20. Maintaining the current studio organization is not appropriate because of a mismatch between the current staff and the type of service that studio would offer. For example, if the existing studio organization comprises only architects, it may not be able to complete a new commission for interior design or strategic planning services as the firm expands its services.

Studios with specialist departments such as design, construction documents, and contract administration require a very large staff and are thereby not suitable for a midsize firm.

A departmental structure is not appropriate because staff with particular experience with one service, such as interior design, would not be suited to complete work on another project type, such as strategic planning.

The firm should continue with the current studio organization if it works well but reorganize to have studios with different expertise such as architecture, interior design, and strategic planning. Initially, there could be one studio for each discipline, but as the firm grows, additional studios could be added, along with staff with different skills and experience.

The answer is (C).

21. Brainstorming can involve the client, but it is not focused or structured enough to find common ground for programming and design.

PowerPoint is mainly a presentation medium and does not engage the client.

Sketch meetings are mostly one-sided and are primarily a way to develop physical design solutions rather than developing programming requirements and general design ideas.

A squatters' session is an intense, multi-day group meeting with the architects, client, and users of the building being programmed and designed. The session takes place in or near the client's facility so the client and users are available for interaction and decision-making. The all-day meetings allow the architect to establish the parameters of the programming and design issues, interview the users of the facility, explore ideas, ask questions, record information, and allow the client to participate actively in the process. The use of squatters is described in the book *Problem Seeking, an Architectural Programming Primer* by William M. Pena and Steven A. Parshall.

The answer is (D).

22. The architect is not responsible because the architect and engineer were exchanging drawings, and the engineer should have taken the architect's reflected ceiling plan drawings as an indication of where the architect wanted the luminaires to be placed. If the engineer felt that the placement was not good from a lighting standpoint or for other reasons, the engineer should have worked with the architect to arrive at a resolution.

The electrical contractor fulfilled his duties by following the drawings given. While it is possible that the electrical contractor may have noticed the discrepancy, the electrical contractor is under no obligation to compare the reflected ceiling plan with the electrical engineer's lighting plan.

The general contractor is not responsible because the general contractor fulfilled the contractor's duty according to AIA Document A201, *General Conditions of the Contract for Construction.* These conditions state that the contractor must compare the documents, but only for the purposes of facilitating construction, not for the purpose of discovering errors, omissions, or inconsistencies in the contract documents.

According to AIA Document C401, *Standard Form of Agreement Between Architect and Consultant,* consultants such as electrical engineers must coordinate their services with the architect and other consultants as well as perform their services with the same standard of care as other professionals under the same or similar circumstances.

The answer is (C).

23. A dedicated in-house specification writer is not an efficient and cost-effective solution for a 20-person general practice firm.

Subscribing to a master specification service might be a viable alternative. However, these types of specifications require someone knowledgeable in material selection and installation methods, and these services are sometimes too general in their approach to work for every project. Using a subscription service still requires someone in the firm to modify the master specification and coordinate with the drawings.

Having several architects responsible for specifications is confusing and requires that each of these architects be experienced in developing project manuals and specifications.

A midsize general practice firm doing many project types is best served by hiring a competent specification writer who can work with the firm to customize the firm's own specifications or other master specifications to the specific needs of each project. The cost of the consultant could be passed on to the client with reasonable markup for coordination, and the firm would not have to pay the taxes and benefits for the consultant.

The answer is (C).

24. Although all of these people will be involved with vertical transportation, the elevator consultant is in the best position to give initial design advice as well as more detailed building solutions. The elevator consultant will help with the standard elevator-related issues that exist in any building and advise on any needed special security features available for the equipment and controls. The electrical engineer, facility manager, and security consultant would lend their advice and expertise, but only from their select points of view.

The answer is (B).

25. This is a situation with too much risk for the architect to take on in both construction budget and fees. If an experienced developer has underestimated the costs so much, the designer may want too much for too little. Even if the architect can convince the developer to increase the budget or decrease the scope, chances are good that financial problems would arise if the architect accepted the commission. However, there is nothing in the *Code of Ethics and Professional Conduct* prohibiting the architect from taking on the risk of a project with these parameters. Option (C) is incorrect because even with a reduced scope, the developer probably would not accept the idea or would try to minimize construction cost to the detriment of quality. It is doubtful that the costs could be decreased by 20%, and requiring a retainer would still not provide the architect with the fee necessary to do a good job.

The answer is (A).

26. While the process is made easier by an owner who can discuss issues as a project moves through the long process of design and construction, this is not the most important quality to evaluate when an architect decides to accept a commission. The owner may prefer a contract

type other than an AIA agreement that places the architect at risk. The owner's financial status is always important. Any problems with a past project may suggest there could be a problem with the current project. The project team that the owner uses for the project can be a help or hindrance to the architect, so this is an important factor to evaluate. While any preconceived ideas of design the owner may have may turn out to be frustrating to the architect, it is not a significant issue. All the other options are factors an architect should know about a potential owner.

The answer is (A), (C), (D), and (E).

27. Option (B) is not the best choice because the firm would have to become experts in design-build and take on the added burden and risk of finding and working with contracting firms. Option (C) is incorrect because this would negatively impact the architecture firm's independence and ability to market its services. It would also be difficult to merge a midsize firm with architects and support staff into an existing design-build firm. Option (D) is incorrect because most of the design work would be completed by the design-build organization. The architects could still market their criteria architect services for owners who are doing design-build projects, but acting solely as a criteria architect or architect/engineer/project manager (AE/PM) would reduce the firm's gross fees, as the firm would not be providing complete architectural services.

Being a consulting architect for a design-build firm would meet the stated goals. The firm could continue to do design work without the issues and problems that come with traditional project delivery methods. The contractor could provide advice on constructability and would take on the responsibility of cost control. At the same time, the architecture firm could continue to market its services in the traditional way or complete projects using other delivery methods.

The answer is (A).

28. Design-assist contracting is best suited for construction manager as constructor (CMc, sometimes called construction manager at risk (CM@R)) projects where the contractor is already providing constructability advice, so option (A) is incorrect. Option (B) is incorrect because this would better describe the architect acting as a consultant with a design-build contractor. Option (D) is incorrect because the subcontractor or product supplier would be offering advice to the architect.

Design-assist contracting is a project management method that includes specialty subcontractors or trades early in the design and construction document phases to assist with the development of complex or unique portions of the building. It is based on the assumption that some trades, subcontractors, or product suppliers are more knowledge-able about their portion of the work than the architect or the general contractor. For example, it could be used to help the architect design a unique and innovative exterior cladding system.

The answer is (C).

29. Giving the task to the lead designer could produce a viable solution, but it lacks the input of others, which takes additional time in a standard design process. Holding a brainstorming session with the principals has the advant-age of the decision-making authority but lacks important insights by designers and others on the team, including the owner; this approach also takes additional time. Ask-ing everyone in the office to provide ideas is unwieldy and takes more time than having the specific team members focus on the problem. This approach also requires staff to take time away from their other projects.

A charrette is an intense design session during which the participants come up with a solution to a problem in a short time. With the project team assembled, all points of view can be heard and various ideas explored. The owner may or may not be involved.

The answer is (B).

Case Studies

Case Study 1

A developer started the design of a three-story building with 60,000 ft^2 of usable space with an architectural firm but became dissatisfied with the firm's work. The developer is in the process of sending out requests for proposals to other architecture firms in the area.

The project must be completed in two years from the time of the requests for proposals and requires site planning, core and shell building design, and tenant improvements. The project's budget is not yet set, but costs should be minimized to maintain competitive lease rates. In particular, to minimize costs, the developer does not want extreme sustainability design features included in the project. The building will be leased to healthcare professions, including doctors and dentists, so all offices must be able to accommodate minor outpatient surgical procedures.

An architecture firm specializing in small, multi-family residential, restaurant, retail, and tenant development is interested in bidding on the project. The firm consists of 13 people including two principals, two project managers, five project architects, two CAD operators with building information modeling (BIM) experience, an administrative assistant, and a receptionist. There is just enough work to keep everyone busy at the firm, but a few projects are nearing completion. The firm is a limited liability company that operates using a loose studio organization and practice methodology based on the principals' design and management experience. Specifications are typically written by an outside firm, but the principals are planning to hire someone to write specifications in-house. Although the firm has limited experience with this project type, the principals would like to expand their practice to accommodate this type of project.

1. In reviewing the ethical issues involved with this potential project, with what should the principals be most concerned?

(A) obtaining permission from the previous architect to work on the project

(B) convincing the developer that sustainability issues are important

(C) providing new learning opportunities for firm employees

(D) overstating the qualifications of the firm for the proposed project type

2. The principals have read the project brief and are in discussions with the developer. How can the principals best convey to the developer that the project's standards of care will be met?

(A) Tell the developer that the firm will go "above and beyond" work done by other architectural firms.

(B) Tell the developer the firm will do whatever research is necessary to meet the developer's design and budget goals.

(C) Promise to meet all of the developer's design and budget goals.

(D) Allow the developer to include a contract provision that requires the firm to perform as the best healthcare architect would.

3. Which three questions would best help the principals determine whether or not their firm is capable of completing the developer's project requirements? (Choose the three that apply.)

(A) Will the firm be able to complete the project within the two-year requirement?

(B) Will the principals have enough time to devote to the project?

(C) Will the firm's current workload allow for another project?

(D) Will the project require documentation using building information modeling (BIM)?

(E) Will the firm's limited experience still be applicable to this new project type?

(F) Will the firm be able to establish a competitive fee and still make a profit?

4. The developer is creating a project cost pro forma and requests that the principals submit an estimate of their firm's fees for both tenant development and core and shell services. What type of fee would best ensure the firm makes a profit but is still competitively priced when its fees are compared to other firms bidding on the project?

(A) hourly, with a not-to-exceed amount for the core and shell and per-area cost for the tenant development

(B) cost-plus-fee for both core and shell and tenant development

(C) a percentage of construction costs for core and shell and hourly for tenant development

(D) a stipulated sum for core and shell and per square foot for tenant development

5. Before accepting the project, how can the firm minimize risk? (Choose the four that apply.)

(A) Research the developer's history with development projects.

(B) Suggest that a construction manager be retained by the developer.

(C) Request a firm budget figure from the developer.

(D) Propose the developer use a design-bid-build project delivery.

(E) Study the feasibility of designing the building the developer proposed.

(F) Use the developer's contract.

6. The principals want to win this bid so they can expand their firm's practice and diversify into other project types (e.g., healthcare facilities). What practice strategy should the principals implement to best meet their goals?

(A) Change to a departmental organization to anticipate growth and handle multiple project types more efficiently.

(B) Find a healthcare consultant to work with on this and future projects, and hire another architect to grow the staff and help with the current projects.

(C) Set their proposed fee low enough to secure the job, and then consider hiring an architect with health care experience.

(D) Establish a healthcare studio within the firm, and then staff the studio with an architect who has healthcare experience and a project architect.

7. What practice methodology is best for the project and the architecture firm?

(A) Hire a healthcare consultant to assist with preliminary design and design development. Have a project manager, project architect, and computer-aided drafting (CAD) operator assist.

(B) Have an experienced project architect do the preliminary design work at a lower billing rate with oversight by the design principal. Turn over production to another project architect and CAD operator.

(C) Use the design skills of the principal, and have a project manager and project architect do preliminary work through design development. Outsource document production and keep construction administration in-house.

(D) Assemble a team of a principal, project manager, one or two project architects, and a CAD operator. Hire consultants, a specification writer, and rendering services only as required.

8. While investigating the developer's reputation and during the initial interview, the principals learned that the developer frequently includes a "no extreme sustainable design" project requirement. However, the developer has a good reputation in the community. How should the principals respond to the developer's request for proposal?

(A) Decline to submit a proposal because of the developer's attitude toward sustainable design.

(B) Decline to submit a proposal because of their firm's lack of experience in this project type.

(C) Agree to submit a proposal, but investigate the feasibility of the project.

(D) Agree to submit a proposal but ask for a detailed program from the developer.

9. In discussing this project, the principals want to review the potential risks and rewards of the project and how the project might affect the firm. What issues should be given highest priority for discussion? (Choose the three that apply.)

(A) potential profit and fees

(B) reputation of the firm in the architectural community

(C) ability to retain employees

(D) likelihood of litigation by the developer

(E) budget overruns due to lack of experience

(F) chance to grow the firm

10. What are the firm's best documentation strategies for this project?

(A) Complete construction drawings in-house with building information modeling (BIM) software, and pay a specification writing firm to assemble the project manual.

(B) Hire a local drafting service to do construction drawings, and complete the project manual in-house using a master specification system.

(C) Draft the construction drawings with standard computer-aided drafting (CAD) software, and use a master specification system to complete the project manual.

(D) Outsource the construction drawings to an overseas service to save money, and pay a specification writing firm to assemble the project manual.

11. In addition to structural and mechanical engineers, what other consultants should the firm consider retaining for this project? (Choose the two that apply.)

(A) civil engineer

(B) landscape architect

(C) electrical engineer

(D) fire protection

(E) interior designer

(F) vertical transportation

Case Study 2

A 10-person architecture firm has been hired to renovate a three-story, 27,900 ft^2 warehouse that is located on a corner lot in a city's downtown district. The owner wants to remodel the warehouse to include retail stores on the first floor and offices on the upper two floors. Built in 1915, the warehouse includes heavy timber construction with masonry exterior walls. The warehouse does not qualify as a national historic landmark, but it may be eligible for state or local historic designation. If so, the owner wants to obtain tax credits for historic preservation by maintaining the existing exterior and the heavy timber construction. The first floor of the warehouse, approximately 9300 ft^2, is currently configured into some smaller rooms, with the second and third floors utilizing an open floor plan currently used for storage. There are outdated stairs between floors and a freight elevator near the back of the warehouse.

The firm has some experience with smaller renovation projects but is expanding into historic preservation projects. The firm is organized as a professional services corporation and consists of two principals, two project managers, four project architects, a CAD operator, and a receptionist/administrative assistant.

12. The firm's principals determine that current staffing is not sufficient to complete the work during the early phases of the project, which require historical research and preliminary design. What is the best course of action?

(A) Survey the current employees to see if they can work overtime early in the project.

(B) Reassign one of the firm's architects to this project, and hire a temporary employee to fill in for the architect.

(C) Retain a historical preservation consultant for research and a freelancer for schematic design.

(D) Hire a new full-time employee with historic preservation experience.

13. In order to satisfy the historic requirements for the project, the minimum standard of care requires the architect to

(A) conduct thorough historic research on the building before beginning design

(B) team with another architecture firm that has experience with historic preservation

(C) assure the owner that the project will receive tax credits for historic preservation

(D) follow the *Standards for Rehabilitation* of the Technical Preservation Services of the National Park Service

14. What practice strategy should the architect first adopt to assist the owner in obtaining tax credits, as well as position the firm for future historic preservation work?

(A) Research and understand state and local requirements for rehabilitation.

(B) Explore the resources of the Technical Preservation Services of the National Park Service.

(C) Understand the requirements of the National Park Service for historic preservation work.

(D) Develop a close working relationship with the state historic preservation officer.

15. In order to minimize risk and address staffing issues, what is the best project delivery method the architect could suggest to the owner?

(A) design-bid-build

(B) design-build with bridging

(C) construction manager as adviser

(D) integrated project delivery

16. The architect wants to develop accurate base sheets for starting construction documents. What technique is the most appropriate?

(A) sonic measuring

(B) orthophotography

(C) electromagnetic distance measurement

(D) laser scanning

Solutions

1. The principals do not need to obtain permission from the previous architect. The AIA document *Code of Ethics and Professional Conduct* does not prohibit an architect from supplanting other architects, especially in this case where the client has presumably severed the relationship with the previous architect.

Extreme sustainability measures are not required by the *Code of Ethics and Professional Conduct*. While the *Code of Ethics and Professional Conduct* requires that architects advocate for sustainable practices, the firm could forgo extreme sustainability measures that would increase the cost of the project by designing in a sustainable manner using features and techniques that would not increase the cost over a more conventional building.

Providing new learning opportunities for firm employees is not an ethical concern. Although the firm should be structured to nurture fellow professionals, this is not the primary concern in deciding to apply for and accept this project.

Overstating the firm's qualifications is an ethical issue. The principals must not say or give the impression that their firm is skilled in projects of this type. Instead, they could stress their firm's experience in tenant development and basic core and shell work for other building types.

The answer is (D).

2. According to the AIA, standard of care is defined as what a reasonably prudent architect would do in the same general circumstances and given the same or similar information. Therefore, saying the firm will go "above and beyond" expands the legal definition of the standard of care. Additionally, such a promise to the developer could expose the firm to future legal ramifications if their promise was not upheld.

Promising a specific result is incorrect because it also raises the standard of care beyond what is normally expected of an architect.

Putting anything in the contract that raises the normally agreed-upon standard of care is unwise. It also may make it impossible for the firm to obtain professional liability insurance or it may negate the insurance the firm already has.

Promising to meet all of the developer's design and budget goals meets the standard of care. The architect only has to present his or her qualifications and experience and suggest to the developer that, although the architect has not specialized in the developer's project type, the architect can perform standard, competent architectural services,

easily work with the developer to define needs, and do any necessary research.

The answer is (B).

3. Given the situation, the three issues that this firm should consider first are whether or not the rather small firm could complete the work given other commitments, whether or not the firm could successfully take on the job without having experience in this building type, and whether or not the firm could be competitive with fees, given that the client is interviewing other architects. Another office with healthcare experience might be able to do the job faster and for a lower fee.

Option (A), option (B), and option (D) are legitimate questions, but they are probably not the most critical for deciding whether or not to submit a proposal. Given the two-year time frame, there probably would be sufficient time to complete a project of this size and scope. Whether or not the principals have enough time would be included in the question of office workload in general. If the project did require BIM, the existing staff probably would be able to provide that service.

The answer is (C), (E), and (F).

4. As with most developers, the developer wants a good estimate of the cost for professional services, both as a good business practice and to include in his or her pro forma. A pro forma is a financial projection for a development project that includes the cost of developing the project and expected income. It is meant to determine if the project is feasible. Hourly, with a not-to-exceed amount for the core and shell and a per-area cost for tenant development would provide the developer with the requested information while still ensuring the firm is competitive in its fees and still can make a profit.

For this type of project, architectural fees are generally separated into site work (e.g., core and shell) and tenant development work. Both types of fees are spread over a longer period of time than a stand-alone project and usually are contracted into separate projects. Typically, after the site work is completed and the spaces are leased, the developer gives each tenant the choice to have either the developer's architect plan the tenant's space as part of the "bare bones" tenant allowance or to have the tenant hire a separate architect (e.g., if the tenant wants a more elaborate design than the developer's architect would develop).

A cost-plus-fee for development would compensate the firm for actual work done, even though the extent of the work is not yet known. However, this fee structure could put the firm at a disadvantage when the developer compares the firm's fees with other firms who give a fixed price or a not-to-exceed amount.

A percentage of construction cost plus hourly fees for tenant development is acceptable for the tenant development because the firm would be paid a fair amount regardless of the project's complexity or length. However, a percentage of construction cost is detrimental to the overall financial well-being of the firm because the scope of the work is unknown and the developer constantly would be trying to minimize costs, which minimizes the firm's fee.

A stipulated sum and per square foot rate for tenant development is not in the best interest of the firm because there are too many project unknowns. At this early stage of the project, it is not in the firm's financial interest to set a fixed price for services. However, the firm can estimate a reasonable cost for completing tenant development on a square foot basis.

The answer is (A).

5. Knowing the developer and the developer's history with construction and working with architects before accepting a project minimizes risk. The firm should verify that the developer is knowledgeable about construction, pays bills on time, is not prone to litigation, and does not make unreasonable requests of architects.

Retaining a construction manager does not necessarily lessen risk for the architect and is probably unnecessary for a project of this size.

The firm should request a firm budget to determine what work is required and evaluate whether the project is even feasible.

Because the developer wants to minimize costs, the architect should propose a design-bid-build delivery method. This method is typically less risky than other delivery methods and achieves the developer's goal of low costs.

A feasibility study identifies areas of risk to the firm in completing the project.

Architects should avoid using contracts other than the standard AIA documents because AIA agreements have been developed over many years to protect the architect.

The answer is (A), (C), (D), and (E).

6. Departmental organization is not advantageous for small firms because there is not enough professional personnel to staff a departmental organization.

Finding a healthcare consultant is not advisable even though a healthcare consultant might help market the firm for this particular project. Since the firm's goal is to grow and do more healthcare work, it should bring this expertise in-house.

Establishing a healthcare studio is not sensible for a small office because there would not be enough specialized work in this field to keep it busy. A studio could be considered later if the firm gets more work in this particular project type.

The firm does not have experience with healthcare facilities, so the principals should proceed on a conservative basis. The firm should first win the bid by proposing a low fee. If it gets the project, the firm can use it as a springboard to hire a new architect with healthcare experience to help the firm further expand their its marketability.

The answer is (C).

7. The nature of the project does not necessitate hiring a specialist. The firm could do the project even though it does not have healthcare experience. Much of the healthcare-related technical work of the base building would be the responsibility of the mechanical and electrical engineering consultants.

The firm's practice methodology is based on the design and management experience of the principals, and they should be directly involved rather than a project architect, even if their billing rates are a little higher.

Outsourcing is not necessary for a project of this scope, staff availability, and the two-year time frame for design and construction. This option also introduces coordination problems.

While all of these strategies could work, for a project of this size and complexity, it is best to use the firm's studio organization approach and keep as much of the work in-house as possible. Although the firm is small, a few projects are finishing, so the firm could do most of the work. This gives the firm better control, provides several employees with experience in healthcare, and keeps the profit in-house.

The answer is (D).

8. The firm wants to grow and expand its project type expertise, so the principals should submit a proposal (contrary to option (A) and option (B)). Although the developer has stated that no extreme sustainability measures should be included in order to save costs, the firm should question the developer about what he or she means by "extreme" so that the firm can determine whether some of the more cost-effective sustainable design strategies could be integrated into the project. The firm's lack of experience in this building type can be addressed in other ways once it gets the project.

Asking for a detailed program for this type of project is not needed because part of it is a basic core and shell development. For the tenant development portion, initial programming is not needed since this occurs as each tenant signs a lease and the architect conducts programming for each tenant's needs.

It is likely that the project is feasible; however, the developer has not given the firm a budget. The developer may have unreasonable expectations about development costs and the potential income from the project, so further investigation is needed to ensure the developer's expectations are in line with what the firm is planning on delivering. If the principals determine that the project is not feasible after learning more about the developer's expectation, they can always retract their bid.

The answer is (C).

9. Potential profit and fees is the first issue to review. This is important not only from a basic financial standpoint but also as a way to retain employees because work is slowing down for the firm.

The reputation of the firm is already established in the architectural community, so option (B) is not a high priority. Completing a new project type might improve that reputation, but it is not a primary concern. The ability to retain employees is already addressed by the additional income and work the project would provide. The likelihood of litigation should have been explored when the principals first investigated the developer. Before they decide to accept the job, they should feel comfortable in knowing that the developer would not likely make a claim against the firm.

Option (E) is a prime concern because the firm does not possess the expertise to execute this project without healthcare consultants or experienced employees, so the firm may not estimate costs accurately. A discussion of growth is important because the project provides the firm with new work, a new expertise, and potentially more employees.

The answer is (A), (E), and (F).

10. The firm should not hire a drafting service. The firm should keep the production of construction drawings in-house since it has experienced CAD operators and architects to direct the work. The firm has the personnel to work on the project, which would keep the fee income in-house.

Option (C), using standard CAD software or building information modeling (BIM), is a judgment call. Having CAD operators with BIM experience on a development project with leased space is a marketing point: the firm would give the BIM model to the developer for ongoing maintenance and management of the building.

The firm should not outsource the construction drawings for a project of this size. The firm has the staff to do the work and outsourcing would not be cost-effective.

Even though the firm eventually wants to write its own specifications, this may not be the time to make that transition. It does not have enough work to justify hiring a specification writer and it is too much work to add to the workload of one of its architects. From a business standpoint, it makes more sense to focus on expanding the firm's services and hiring architects who can complete design and administration work on a variety of project types. The firm should hire a specification writing firm for this small project, and the firm could add a nominal upcharge to the specification writing firm to cover coordination costs.

The answer is (A).

11. An architectural firm hires consultants to do work that the architect is not qualified to do or is so complex that specialized assistance is required. For a project of this size, type, and complexity, a civil engineer is necessary.

There is not enough information in the project brief about landscaping, so it is unknown whether a landscape architect is needed.

Even though the scope of this project is small in size and complexity, an electrical engineer is likely needed in addition to structural and mechanical engineers.

A fire protection consultant is not necessary because a mechanical engineer would have training in basic fire protection engineering.

Because the firm has experience in tenant development work and retail and restaurants, it is capable of doing the space planning and interior design of the individual tenants, so an interior designer is not necessary.

A vertical transportation specialist is not necessary for this small-scale project. Instead, the project would require only an elevator product representative to provide assistance in selecting the type and number of elevators required for a three-story building.

The answer is (A) and (C).

12. Option (A) is incorrect because overtime work does not necessarily solve the need for historic research or preliminary design if the existing staff do not have the experience. In addition, excessive overtime is costly. Option (B) is incorrect because reassigning someone from another job not only disrupts the continuity of that job, but also makes it difficult for a temporary employee, if one can be found, to fill in for the reassigned architect. Option (C) is a possible course of action that fulfills the immediate needs of the current project but does not provide the experienced staff necessary to market for any additional new historic preservation projects the firm might take on in the future.

If the firm needs additional staffing for historical research and design work and anticipates that additional historic work will be required in the future, hiring a new employee with historic preservation experience is the best approach.

The answer is (D).

13. Although the architect would want to know about the building's history prior to starting work, this is not the most important thing when discussing the legal concept of standard of care. In this case, it is not necessary for the architect to team with another architectural firm to meet the standard of care requirements. The architect should not assure the owner that the project will receive tax credits since this is determined by the local or state organization that certifies projects and grants credits.

To meet the standard of care for a project involving historic preservation and application for possible tax credits, the architect should know and follow the *Standards for Rehabilitation* of the Technical Preservation Services of the National Park Service.

The answer is (D).

14. Although all of the options are important practice strategies for doing historic preservation work, the first thing the architect should do is determine what state and local programs are available and what the particular requirements are for any given location in which the architect might work. This would enable the architect to speak intelligently to the current owner as well as potential clients when marketing. This determination would also direct the architect's subsequent efforts in researching historic preservation, understanding the Technical Preservation Service requirements, and developing knowledge of local and state requirements.

The answer is (A).

15. A traditional design-bid-build approach would put the architect more at risk to develop a design that meets cost and time constraints, as well as require that the architect's staff complete all the standard professional services, which could be problematic given the office's staffing situation. A construction manager as adviser (CMa) delivery method would relieve the architect of some risk concerning constructability, cost, and schedule. However, it would add another member to the team and still require the architect to produce design work and construction documents, as well as provide construction administration with the architect's staff. If a construction manager was considered, the construction manager as constructor (CMc) method should be considered instead because it would result in less risk to the architect.

Using the design-build with bridging approach would put nearly all the burden for detailed design, coordination, costs, schedule, and construction on the design-build firm. Using the bridging variation to the design-build approach, the architect could still be involved with initial design and the development of the project requirements. Depending on the level of involvement the architect wanted to or was able to have based on staffing, the owner and architect could look for a design-build firm with in-house architects, or they could explore having a contractor-led design-build firm hire the architect as a consultant.

The answer is (B).

16. Sonic measuring has limited range for this size of building and cannot distinguish between closely spaced elements. Orthophotography might work for the exterior but is not appropriate for interior measurements. Laser scanning would be the most accurate way to take measurements but is more expensive and more detailed than is necessary for the measurements needed for this project. For this particular building, electromagnetic distance measurement would likely yield the most accurate results at the lowest cost and effort.

The answer is (C).

DIVISION 2: PROJECT MANAGEMENT

4 Project Planning and Management

1. According to American Institute of Architects (AIA) Document B101, *Standard Form of Agreement Between Owner and Architect*, what are the architect's responsibilities regarding sustainable design practices?

(A) The architect must incorporate sustainable design practices in the project.

(B) The architect has no obligation to discuss or incorporate sustainable design practices unless the project program specifically states that the building is to be Leadership in Energy and Environmental Design (LEED) certified or recognized by another green building rating program.

(C) The architect should consider environmentally responsible design alternatives and discuss the feasibility of incorporating them with the owner. The owner is responsible for deciding which design approaches to incorporate.

(D) The architect is not responsible for the performance of innovative or untested technologies that the owner insists on including in a sustainable design project.

2. What distinguishes a critical path method (CPM) chart from other types of project planning tools?

(A) It represents time and tasks graphically.

(B) It is developed with the assistance of all team members.

(C) It shows interdependencies between activities.

(D) It assigns specific tasks to each team member.

3. According to American Institute of Architects (AIA) Document B101, *Standard Form of Agreement Between Owner and Architect*, the owner is responsible for providing

(A) professional liability insurance

(B) nonexclusive licenses for use of the instruments of service

(C) required safety equipment at the project site

(D) testing and inspections required by law

4. The architect can best chart the involvement and responsibilities of all members of the project team with a

(A) flow diagram meeting

(B) full wall schedule

(C) Gantt chart

(D) project monitoring chart

5. A project architect is developing a project work plan for the coming year. The firm is organized into studios, and the project team includes the project architect, two designers, and a draftsman, with annual salaries and utilization rates as shown.

staff member	salary	utilization rate
project architect	$100,000	40%
designer	$60,000	60%
designer	$60,000	60%
draftsman	$45,000	80%

The project architect estimates that the studio will gross $400,000 in annual revenue. The firm's break-even multiplier is 2.25. The actual annual revenue will exceed the estimated amount by what percentage?

- (A) 0%
- (B) 10%
- (C) 18%
- (D) 20%

6. Which of the following American Institute of Architects (AIA) documents is used to create a license to use computer-aided drafting (CAD) files and building information models (BIM)?

- (A) AIA Document C106, *Digital Data Licensing Agreement*
- (B) AIA Document E201, *Digital Data Protocol Exhibit*
- (C) AIA Document E203, *Building Information Modeling and Digital Data Exhibit*
- (D) AIA Document G808, *Project Data*

7. During preparation of construction drawings, the architect should coordinate with the structural engineer by

- (A) requiring the engineer to submit progress drawings when changes are made
- (B) conducting weekly meetings with the engineer and exchanging progress copies of drawings
- (C) holding conference calls between staff at both offices at times required by the work progress
- (D) submitting weekly written memos to the engineer describing the architectural requirements

8. An architect has been hired to design an addition to a building of historical significance, and the owner wishes to incorporate sustainable design technologies. Part of the project includes renovating and remodeling a portion of the existing building. The architect suggests that the owner retain the services of a historic preservation consultant. In order for the architect to make optimal use of the consultant's work, the owner should hire the consultant

- (A) as soon as possible
- (B) after schematic design work has been completed
- (C) after the design development phase
- (D) on an as-needed basis for technical questions

9. Which of the following are likely results of shortening the critical path of a construction schedule? (Choose the two that apply.)

- (A) Direct costs will increase.
- (B) Direct costs will decrease.
- (C) Overhead costs will increase.
- (D) Overhead costs will decrease.
- (E) Quality control will increase.
- (F) Activities on float paths will be delayed.

10. Which of the following influence the architect's design schedule? (Choose the four that apply.)

- (A) architect's available staff
- (B) client's decision-making and approval process
- (C) structural consultant's workload
- (D) size of the project
- (E) building code in effect in the project jurisdiction
- (F) owner's proposed construction timeframe

11. An architecture firm is commissioned to remodel a large warehouse building into a multiscreen cinema complex. During the pre-design phase, the architect tells the client that the existing structure must be reviewed and surveyed by the consultants on the design team. Which consultant should evaluate the building first?

- (A) civil engineer
- (B) structural engineer
- (C) mechanical engineer
- (D) electrical engineer

12. An electrical engineer would typically perform load calculations and develop panel schedules in which phase of basic services?

   (A)   pre-design

   (B)   schematic design

   (C)   design development

   (D)   construction documents

Solutions

1. The guidelines for sustainable design practice are discussed in AIA Document B101, Sec. 3.2, Subparagraph 3.2.3 and Subparagraph 3.2.5.1. These guidelines state that the architect must consider environmentally responsible design alternatives as part of basic services and assess the feasibility of incorporating them in the schematic design phase. The impact of these strategies on the project program, schedule, and budgets should be discussed with the owner. The owner then determines the type and extent of the sustainable technologies that are to be incorporated into the project design.

The sustainable strategies that the owner can choose to accept or eliminate are only those that go above and beyond the requirements for code compliance. Some approaches that improve the building's energy efficiency and sustainability are also mandatory code requirements. For example, if the local jurisdiction requires compliance with a standard to satisfy the requirements of the energy code, the owner may not disregard this requirement. In this case, the architect or the architect's consultant should not consider designing for compliance to be an additional service. However, if the owner decides to incorporate other sustainable design approaches that are not normally included or are not required for local code compliance, it is appropriate for the architect to provide this work as an additional service and indicate this as such in AIA Document B101, Article 4, Additional Services.

The answer is (C).

2. The CPM is a planning tool used to develop a schedule for large projects that require the participation of many team members. A CPM chart differs from other types of planning tools, such as a full wall schedule, milestone chart, or Gantt chart, because it considers the interdependence of activities.

The answer is (C).

3. The agreement requires the architect to carry professional liability insurance and other types of insurance, and it sets the agreed-upon minimums. This agreement does not impose specific insurance requirements on the owner, but it encourages the owner to seek appropriate legal, accounting, and insurance advice. The architect holds the rights to the instruments of services. The owner is granted a nonexclusive license to use these documents for this project only. Safety procedures and equipment at the project site are the responsibility of the contractor.

AIA Document B101, Article 5, defines the owner's responsibilities. Subparagraph 5.7 requires the owner to provide tests, inspections, and reports required by law or the contract documents.

The answer is (D).

4. The full wall schedule technique requires everyone on the project to work on developing the project schedule. This facilitates discussion about work tasks, responsibilities, and project deadlines. Participation of all team members is encouraged, and as a result, everyone has a vested interest in the final schedule.

The answer is (B).

5. Calculate direct labor costs using the information provided about the employees' salaries and their utilization rates. The utilization rate is the percentage of work time that is billable to projects. It is clearest to put this in table format.

staff member	salary	utilization rate	direct labor cost
project architect	$100,000	40%	$40,000
designer	$60,000	60%	$36,000
designer	$60,000	60%	$36,000
draftsman	$45,000	80%	$36,000
total	$265,000		$148,000

Determine the amount of profit that will be earned if the department brings in revenue of $400,000 by calculating the break-even amount using the multiplier and the table's direct labor costs.

$$\text{break-even amount} = (\text{direct labor costs})(\text{multiplier})$$
$$= (\$148,000)(2.25)$$
$$= \$333,000$$

Determine the amount of actual revenue earned.

$$\text{actual revenue} = \text{estimated revenue} - \text{break-even amount}$$
$$= \$400,000 - \$330,000$$
$$= \$70,000$$

Finally, calculate the percentage.

$$\text{percentage} = \frac{\text{actual revenue}}{\text{estimated revenue}}$$
$$= \frac{\$70,000}{\$400,000}$$
$$= 17.5\% \quad (18\%)$$

The answer is (C).

6. AIA Document E201 and AIA Document E203 define the terms of use of contract documents and are designed to be used as exhibits to a prime agreement, such as AIA Document A101, *Standard Form of Agreement Between Owner and Contractor where the basis of payment is a Stipulated Sum*, or AIA Document B101, *Standard Form of Agreement Between Owner and Architect*. They are not intended to be used independently. AIA Document G808 is a project management tool that can be used to record regulatory information about the project, such as zoning approvals and resolution of code issues.

AIA Document C106 is a stand-alone document that can be used by an architect to allow firms that do not have a pre-existing contract with the architecture firm to use the CAD or BIM files prepared by the architecture firm.

The answer is (A).

7. Submission of engineering progress drawings implies only a one-way exchange of information. Conference calls alone cannot fully describe the visual information being developed during production of construction documents. Telephone calls or emails must be supplemented with some type of exchange of visual information through computer networking, faxes, or a physical exchange of printed drawings. The written word is not sufficient to describe drawings, and tends to be a one-way method of communication. Two-way communication of graphic information is critical to the success of the complex coordination required between consultants and the architect. Regularly scheduled meetings and the exchange of progress documents achieve this goal.

The answer is (B).

8. In general, project consultants should be hired as soon as possible on a project so they can advise on initial scope and design direction as well as on more technical questions.

The answer is (A).

9. Overhead costs decrease when a schedule is shortened. Each day that the contractor must rent an office trailer, pay a superintendent's salary, or cover other overhead expenses costs a fixed amount of money. If the construction period is shortened, the contractor incurs fewer expenses and the total overhead decreases. Activities on float paths may have to be completed more quickly to finish a project on time, but a change in the critical path schedule would not delay these tasks. If the critical path is shortened, direct costs will increase. A shorter construction period requires more equipment and more worker-hours to accomplish the same amount of work in a reduced amount of time. As the labor force is increased or work hours are extended, workers tend to become less efficient and supervision becomes more difficult. Quality control levels often decrease because workers trying to work quickly are more likely to make errors.

The answer is (A) and (D).

10. The architect does not have direct control over the consultants' workload or ability to complete a given job at a specific time. The building code in effect at the location of the project would not affect the schedule for design or for construction.

The design schedule is impacted by the size and complexity of the project, the number of people available to work on the project, and how quickly the client can make required decisions and approve the architect's work during the various stages of the design. In addition, the abilities and design methodology of the architect's team can affect the time it takes to produce a job. The owner's proposed construction timeframe can suggest a deadline for the design work, but the architect must determine if the owner's projection is realistic.

The answer is (A), (B), (D), and (F).

11. The condition of the building structure is the primary concern during the preliminary examination of the building proposed for remodeling. Once the structure of the building is determined to be in good condition, mechanical and electrical engineers can evaluate the condition of the existing building systems to determine the extent of the work necessary to upgrade these systems for the building's proposed use. Any civil engineering work, such as site grading, drainage, and the like, can wait until a later time.

The answer is (B).

12. Prior to doing load calculations and developing the specific panel schedules, the electrical engineer will need specific information from the architect concerning power outlet locations and service needs of the equipment the client plans on using. This information is developed during the pre-design (programming), schematic design, and design development phases and would then be available to the electrical engineer for design development. The final checking and drafting would be done during the construction documents phase.

The answer is (C).

5 Contracts

1. An architect is designing a nursing home with 150 beds. The patients have varying levels of mobility and independence. The building manager requests a heating, ventilating, and air conditioning (HVAC) system that permits patients to control the temperature in their own rooms, is quiet, and requires minimal maintenance. Which type of system is the most appropriate recommendation?

    (A)   packaged terminal units

    (B)   fan coil terminals

    (C)   variable air volume

    (D)   single duct, constant air volume

2. A building manager uses a group of consultants for most of the tenant fit-out projects in an office complex. He issues separate contracts to the building systems engineering firm, the contractor, and the architect. The building systems engineering firm provides plumbing, electrical, mechanical, and fire protection design. The contractor provides cost estimating services during the design phase and is responsible for building the project. The architect prepares a blank reflected ceiling plan showing the suspended ceiling grid and sends it to the owner and engineer for use in placing light fixtures, diffusers, and sprinkler heads. During construction, an existing beam is discovered, which was previously unknown to exist above the ceiling. The beam conflicts with the light fixture locations, and the ceiling layout must be redesigned. Which

party is responsible for the cost of this additional design and installation work?

    (A)   architect

    (B)   building manager

    (C)   building systems engineering firm

    (D)   contractor

3. At the start of construction, the owner requests that the architect provide a full-time staff member on the job site. The agreement between the architect and owner was developed using American Institute of Architects (AIA) Document B101, *Standard Form of Agreement Between Owner and Architect*. Which of the following is true?

    (A)   On-site project representation is already required by the owner-architect agreement as a basic service.

    (B)   The architect may amend the owner-architect agreement to include descriptions and fees for additional services.

    (C)   Additional services cannot be added after the owner-architect agreement is developed because changes to the scope of the work may delay the project schedule.

    (D)   Although this service was not identified in the owner-architect agreement, the architect must provide on-site project representation without additional cost.

4. American Institute of Architects (AIA) Document B101, *Standard Form of Agreement Between Owner and Architect*, separates the architect from the contractor with

(A) agency

(B) privity

(C) mediation

(D) indemnification

5. A performance bond

(A) ensures that subcontractors complete their work

(B) guarantees that the contractor will finish on time

(C) covers any possible liens that may be filed on the building

(D) protects the owner by having a third party responsible for completing the work if the contractor does not

6. Under the provisions of American Institute of Architects (AIA) Document B101, *Standard Form of Agreement Between Owner and Architect*, the owner is required to

(A) review laws and regulations applicable to the project

(B) commission tests for possible groundwater pollution

(C) develop a schedule of performance for architectural services

(D) name a designated representative to act on the architect's behalf

7. For the remodeling and renovation of an 1850s church, the architect retains the services of a historic preservation consultant using American Institute of Architects (AIA) Document C401, *Standard Form of Agreement Between Architect and Consultant*. The consultant's services include developing drawings showing the repair and anchoring of existing stonework. During construction, the contractor discovers that the anchoring methods specified by the consultant violate the local building code and have to be

modified at additional cost. The party responsible for the cost of the modifications is the

(A) architect

(B) consultant

(C) contractor

(D) owner

8. Furnishing a site survey is the responsibility of the

(A) architect

(B) civil engineer

(C) contractor

(D) owner

9. The type of foundation system to be used on a construction project should be determined by a(n)

(A) structural engineer

(B) geotechnical engineer

(C) civil engineer

(D) architect

10. An architect may suggest that the client contract directly with the structural engineering consultant because this

(A) gives the architect more control over the consultant's work

(B) permits the consultant to start work earlier

(C) permits the owner to coordinate the efforts of the project team better

(D) relieves the architect of responsibility for paying the consultant

Solutions

1. Packaged terminal units and fan coil terminals permit control over the temperatures of individual spaces but do not operate as quietly or require as little maintenance as variable air volume (VAV) systems.

Single duct, constant air volume (CAV) units are relatively inexpensive to install and maintain but do not offer occupants the ability to control the temperatures of individual spaces.

A VAV system is the best choice for this application. VAV systems allow for individual control of temperature, quiet operation, and minimal maintenance.

The answer is (C).

2. Since the building manager issued separate contracts to each of the consultants, the building manager is acting as the construction manager. Construction managers are responsible for the coordination of the separate contracts that have been issued. Because this coordination was not performed during the design phase, the construction manager is responsible for the cost of the additional design and installation work required to remedy the issue.

The answer is (B).

3. AIA Document B101 may be used to define the terms of the agreement between the owner and architect. Basic services are defined in Article 3 of the document. AIA Document B101, Article 4, establishes the architect's responsibilities beyond basic services. On-site project representation is included in the table in AIA Document B101, Sec. 4.1, as a responsibility excluded from basic services.

The architect and owner should complete the table indicating which, if any, of the services listed are to be the responsibility of the architect. The additional services to be provided should be described in an exhibit attached to the agreement so that the scope of the work and compensation for the architect's effort is clear.

Additional services also may be requested after the agreement is developed and the project is underway. They should be defined in an amendment exhibit to the agreement after the architect and owner agree upon the scope of services and fee for the additional work. If any adjustment to the agreement time or schedule is necessary to accommodate the request, it should be negotiated at that time and included in the amendment to the original owner-architect agreement.

The answer is (B).

4. AIA Document B101 states that nothing in that agreement will create a contractual relationship with a third party against either the architect or the owner. This reinforces the idea of privity—two parties to a contract are not liable to a third party.

The answer is (B).

5. A labor and material payment bond is designed to pay liens if they occur. Other provisions of the owner-contractor agreement, such as liquidated damages, are designed to encourage the contractor to finish on time. The general contractor is responsible for the performance of the subcontractors under provisions of American Institute of Architects (AIA) Document A201, *General Conditions of the Contract for Construction.*

A performance bond purchased by the contractor from a surety company obligates the company to ensure the project is finished should the contractor default. If the contractor does not complete the work, the surety would hire another firm to finish the project in accordance with the requirements of the contract documents.

The answer is (D).

6. AIA Document B101, Sec. 5.7, states that one of the responsibilities of the owner is to furnish tests, inspections, and reports required by law or by the contract documents. These include structural, mechanical, and chemical tests for air and water pollution or for hazardous materials.

The answer is (B).

7. Under the provisions of AIA Document C401, consultants are responsible for code compliance regarding their area of work and for the accurate production of their drawings.

The answer is (B).

8. The owner is required to furnish and pay for site surveys according to both American Institute of Architects (AIA) Document B101, *Standard Form of Agreement Between Owner and Architect,* Sec. 5.4, and AIA Document A201, *General Conditions of the Contract for Construction,* Sec. 2.2.3.

The answer is (D).

9. The geotechnical engineer makes the various soil tests required for a particular site and suggests the type of foundation based on the bearing capacity of the soil and other factors. However, responsibilty for the design of the foundation and type of system employed is ultimately the structural engineer's.

Typically, the geotechnical engineer's report is contracted and paid for by the client, and the services of the structural engineer are included in the architect's scope of services.

The answer is (A).

10. When an owner contracts directly with a consultant, the architect is not involved with contract provisions, contract disputes, or payment to the consultant. However, the architect sacrifices some control over the consultant's services by not contracting directly with the consultant.

The answer is (D).

6 Project Execution and Quality Control

1. In order to build a commercial building in a residential neighborhood, what must be obtained first from the local zoning jurisdiction?

    (A)   joint use easement

    (B)   variance

    (C)   conditional use permit

    (D)   restrictive covenant

2. An architectural review board is appointed by the city council to review and approve all proposed additions, renovations, and new construction along the waterfront where development of the city began. The city council has designated this area as a historic preservation district and has established guidelines that require the use of authentic materials, historically appropriate color schemes, and construction designed to fit into the context of the existing area. This is an example of

    (A)   inclusionary zoning

    (B)   cluster development

    (C)   planned unit development

    (D)   overlay zoning

3. As part of developing a building design, an architect needs to perform a building code analysis. The first step in this analysis is to determine the

    (A)   occupancy (use group)

    (B)   building's allowable height and area

    (C)   allowable construction types

    (D)   local regulations including the adopted version of the building code and any local modifications

4. An architecture firm will employ a quality circle in order to

    (A)   gather feedback from employees informally

    (B)   bring together employees from different departments

    (C)   develop strategic and financial plans

    (D)   identify and address work-related problems

5. What is an example of contemporaneous documentation?

    (A)   submittals log

    (B)   change order

    (C)   meeting minutes

    (D)   phone log

6. What quality assurance program or methods allow a firm's design and production process to be certified as compliant by a third-party auditor?

- (A) Six Sigma
- (B) ISO 9001
- (C) AIA Quality Management Phase Checklists
- (D) total quality management

7. Developing typical construction details, boilerplate language for general notes, project checklists, and master specifications are techniques used by architecture firms to

- (A) maintain project files
- (B) document corporate knowledge
- (C) conduct quality assurance reviews
- (D) communicate with team members

8. Which statement about standard of care is true?

- (A) Standard of care allows an architect practicing in accordance with it to forego professional liability insurance.
- (B) Standard of care is defined in American Institute of Architects (AIA) Document B101, *Standard Form of Agreement Between Owner and Architect.*
- (C) Standard of care is equivalent to a warranty statement.
- (D) Standard of care protects an architect from litigation.

9. Information regarding the minimum number of plumbing fixtures required for various occupancies may be found in which of the following sources?

- (A) building codes
- (B) plumbing codes
- (C) both building and plumbing codes
- (D) the local authority having jurisdiction

10. According to American Institute of Architects (AIA) Document A201, *General Conditions of the Contract for Construction*, the contractor may reasonably ask for an extension in the contract time without penalty for which of the following reasons? (Choose the four that apply.)

- (A) the owner's stop work order
- (B) slow work by a subcontractor
- (C) the architect's delay in approving shop drawings
- (D) labor disputes
- (E) normal winter weather conditions
- (F) change order requested by the owner

11. According to American Institute of Architects (AIA) Document B101, *Standard Form of Agreement Between Owner and Architect*, the architect must prepare cost estimates for the project during the

- (A) schematic design phase
- (B) design development phase
- (C) schematic and design development phases
- (D) schematic, design development, and construction documents phases

12. When deciding on the types and amounts of insurance needed for a project, on which of the following professionals should the owner rely? (Choose the two that apply.)

- (A) architect
- (B) contractor
- (C) owner's attorney
- (D) owner's insurance agent
- (E) insurance requirements stated in the sample American Institute of Architects (AIA) documents
- (F) architect's insurance adviser

13. In the renovation of a historic structure, the treatment approach that attempts to retain the most historic materials and spaces while allowing replacement of damaged exterior materials is

- (A) preservation
- (B) rehabilitation
- (C) restoration
- (D) reconstruction

Solutions

1. A joint use easement allows two or more property owners to share a common feature, such as a driveway. A variance is a deviation from the zoning regulations. Restrictive covenants are provisions that restrict the use of the property by the buyer. A conditional use permit (CUP) is a permit issued by the zoning jurisdiction for a proposed use that is not otherwise allowed in a particular zoning district. Of the options listed, only a CUP allows a commercial building to be built in a residential neighborhood.

The answer is (C).

2. A planned unit development is an area set aside for a specific use, such as a residential subdivision or a mix of commercial and residential uses. Cluster zoning allows structures to be grouped on one part of a site to preserve open space on other parts. Inclusionary zoning requires construction of low-income housing as a condition of approval.

A historic preservation district is an example of overlay zoning. The primary zoning designation for the properties in the historic district might be commercial, residential, or some other category, but all improvements to the properties in this area are subject to the approval of the architectural review board. The board's goal is to protect areas of architectural or cultural distinction from decay due to demolition or neglect or to encourage development complementary to the area's existing character.

The answer is (D).

3. At the beginning of the building code analysis, the architect must determine the local regulations, which include the type and edition of adopted building codes (e.g., the *International Building Code, International Mechanical Code, National Electrical Code*), as well as modifications adopted by the local jurisdiction that add, delete, or modify parts of the building codes. After determining the local regulations, other building factors can be considered.

The answer is (D).

4. A quality circle is a participatory management technique that brings employees who do the same, or similar, work into formal, small groups in order to identify and address work-related problems. Solutions to problems are then presented to management. The quality circle identifies those problems that affect day-to-day work. A steering committee may be appointed to coordinate the efforts of multiple quality circles focusing on various issues. The steering committee then vets ideas to be passed along to the firm's management. Management issues such as developing strategic and financial plans are outside of the scope of work performed by a quality circle.

The answer is (D).

5. Contemporaneous documentation is a written record of verbal or informal communications which is kept in real time and is generally not issued to other project participants in a standard form. This type of documentation could include the project manager's daily journal, notes from telephone conversations or conversations on site, or email and text messages. Along with providing a record of the project's progress and the project manager's day-to-day activities, contemporaneous documentation may be admissible in court in the case of a claim under the business-entry exception to the hearsay rule. To be eligible as evidence, the record must be prepared at the time of the event and it must be representative of a regular activity that is a part of the firm's normal course of business.

The answer is (D).

6. ISO 9000, which was established by the International Standards Organization (ISO), refers to a quality assurance program that can be applied to a variety of processes and industries, including service providers, manufacturing, management, and design. The seven quality management principles on which all ISO 9000 standards are based are as follows.

- *customer focus:* meeting customer expectations and objectives

- *leadership:* all employees are working toward a common purpose

- *engagement of people:* the skills of all employees are being utilized and recognized appropriately

- *process approach:* the company has established clear guidelines for systems and processes

- *improvement:* organization reacts to successes and failures in a proactive way

- *evidence-based decision making:* choices are made after thorough investigation of objective data

- *relationship management:* maintain open communication with all parties with whom the company interacts

ISO 9000 is an umbrella term that refers to a number of quality standards; ISO 9001 applies to architectural design processes. To participate, a design firm must develop and implement programs that satisfy the requirements of each section of the standard; all aspects of practice are evaluated, including purchasing procedures (including the qualifications of consultants that a firm employs), record keeping, systems for preparing and checking work, and financial management. An organization's process can be certified to an ISO standard if it complies with the program requirements, and compliance is validated by frequent third-party audits of the company's policies and practices.

The answer is (B).

7. Project files are notes specific to an individual project. Quality assurance reviews are conducted periodically to ensure that design elements have been correctly detailed and coordinated for the project. Communication among team members may be facilitated by using a standard detail as a starting point for the discussion.

One of the most important assets of an architecture firm is the corporate knowledge amassed by firm employees. Often, corporate knowledge exists only in employees' memories, which can be lost when an employee leaves. Therefore, it is valuable to document that information in a written or digital archive for use or reference on future projects. This may include setting up a file of typical construction details, writing guide specifications, creating a template for completing a code review, or developing general notes that can be edited to suit the project.

The answer is (B).

8. AIA Document B101, Sec. 2.2, includes a statement defining standard of care.

> "The Architect shall perform its services consistent with the professional skill and care ordinarily provided by architects practicing in the same or similar locality under the same or similar circumstances. The Architect shall perform its services as expeditiously as is consistent with such professional skill and care and the orderly progress of the project."

Architects practicing according to the customary standard of care are still open to litigation and need to carry professional liability insurance. Even if a lawsuit is unfounded, the insurance can offset the costs of defending the firm against the claim.

Architects should be careful not to make any statements in contracts or correspondence that could be interpreted as a warranty statement. Practicing in accordance with the standard of care is not a guarantee that there will be no errors or omissions in the contract documents. The standard of care expected of architects applies to all activities that the architect undertakes, whether or not the agreement includes a definition of what this level of care entails.

The answer is (B).

9. The required number of plumbing fixtures is given in plumbing codes. Often, these requirements are also reproduced in the building codes.

The answer is (C).

10. AIA Document A201, Sec. 8.3, states valid reasons for an extension to the contract time. The contractor may request an extension if the owner issues a stop work order and the contractor needs more time to restart work at the site, if the architect causes a delay by failing to approve shop drawings within the allotted time, if labor unions call a strike during the course of construction, or if the owner issues a change order that requires additional time to complete. Slow work by a subcontractor and normal winter weather conditions are not valid reasons for requesting an extension of time.

The answer is (A), (C), (D), and (F).

11. AIA Document B101 requires the architect to develop a preliminary cost estimate based on area, volume, or a similar conceptual estimating technique, and subsequently update it at each phase through to the construction documents phase.

The answer is (D).

12. The owner should seek advice from his or her legal counsel and insurance agent on matters of insurance.

The architect should not give insurance advice, and the architect's insurance adviser should not be responsible for providing advice to the owner. The architect can assist the owner and insurance agent by providing American Institute of Architects (AIA) Document G612, *Owner's Instructions to the Architect*. This document provides a framework for the discussion between the owner and his or her advisers so that all of the relevant requirements can be determined. The limits determined by the owner and advisers can then be incorporated into the contract. The contractor should be involved with only the various types of insurance that contractors must carry for the project.

The answer is (C) and (D).

13. Four basic types of treatments can be applied to historic structures, as defined in the Secretary of the Interior's *Standards for the Treatment of Historic Properties*. Preservation is the most historically accurate and requires keeping existing elements in situ. Restoration returns a building to its appearance at a particular point in time. Reconstruction is building based on documentation (e.g., photographs and historical records) that recreates elements of the building that have been demolished or lost to time. Rehabilitation emphasizes the retention and repair of historic materials but gives some latitude for replacement of damaged materials.

The answer is (B).

Case Studies

Case Study 1

Two firms, SKEG Architecture and League Library Consultants, have been awarded a joint contract to provide design services to create a new building for the Capstan Community Library.

League Library Consultants is a small consulting firm of five employees with two principals: an architect and interior designer with years of library design experience and her business partner, a librarian. They plan to analyze the library's current collection, resources, and facilities; estimate the library's future needs; and work with the library board and SKEG Architecture to develop the preliminary building program. They will also be responsible for selecting and specifying the furniture, shelving, and checkout and security equipment.

The contract between the library board and the architecture firm is based on AIA Document B101, *Standard Form of Agreement Between Owner and Architect*. SKEG Architecture's in-house staff will provide architecture, interior design, and structural engineering services. SKEG's mechanical and electrical consultant is Cog Engineering Group; this firm also offers civil engineering services and will be responsible for the site design. The contract between SKEG and Cog Engineering, and the contract between SKEG and League Library Consultants, are both based on AIA Document C401, *Standard Form of Agreement Between Architect and Consultant*.

The library board intends to award separate contracts for general construction and for furniture, furnishings, and equipment. They will bid both contracts and will use AIA Document A101, *Standard Form of Agreement Between Owner and Contractor where the basis of payment is a Stipulated Sum*; AIA Document A201, *General Conditions of the Contract for Construction*, for the general construction contract; AIA Document A151, *Standard Form of Agreement Between Owner and Vendor for Furniture, Furnishings and Equipment where the basis of payment is a Stipulated Sum*; and AIA Document A251, *General Conditions of the Contract for Furniture, Furnishings and Equipment*, for the FF&E.

Resource 2.1 Preliminary Programming Worksheet

Project: Capstan Community Library

Prepared by: League Library Consultants & SKEG Architecture

space description	area (ft^2)	required adjacencies	floor
entrance, lobby and circulation desk	750		1
circulation work area	500	circulation desk	1
new materials and periodicals	650	lobby	1
café	250	lobby	1
adult computer lab	1000	adult section	1
adult non-fiction stack area	1200	adult section	1
adult fiction stack area	1200	adult section	1
quiet reading rooms (2)	250	adult section	1
community meeting room	1000	lobby	1
storage and receiving	500		1
audio-visual materials and non-print media	500		2
reference desk and reading room	900		2
local history archives and display	500		2
young adult stack area	750	youth section	2
youth computer lab	600	youth section	2
children's stack area	1500	youth section	2
multipurpose classrooms (3)	750		2
conference room	300	near stairs and elevator	2
library director's office	200	conference room	2
administrative assistant	150	library director's office	2
staff break room	200		2
custodial area	150 (per floor)		1 and 2
mechanical and electrical rooms[a]	–		1 and 2
restrooms[b]	–		1 and 2
circulation areas[c]	–		1 and 2, stairs per code requirements and elevator

[a]The size of the mechanical and electrical rooms on a floor will be 10% of the total net programmed area of that floor.
[b]The area is based on the required fixture counts per plumbing code requirements.
[c]Assume 65% efficiency; restrooms and custodial areas are included in this number.

Resource 2.2 Maximum Floor Area Allowances per Occupant

function of space	maximum floor area allowance (ft^2/occupant)
accessory storage areas, mechanical equipment room	300
assembly with fixed seats	number of fixed seats installed within
assembly without fixed seats	
concentrated (chairs only, not fixed)	7 net
standing space	5 net
unconcentrated (tables and chairs)	15 net
business areas	100 gross
library	
reading rooms	50 net
stack area	100 gross

Resource 2.3 Minimum Number of Required Plumbing Fixtures*

classification	occupancy category	description	water closets male	water closets female	lavatories male	lavatories female
assembly	A-3	auditoriums without permanent seating, lecture halls, libraries	1 per 125	1 per 65	1 per 200	
business	B	transaction of business or professional services	1 per 25 for first 50 and 1 per 50 for the remainder exceeding 50		1 per 40 for first 80 and 1 per 40 for the remainder exceeding 80	
storage	S-1 and S-2	low and moderate hazard storage	1 per 100		1 per 100	

*The fixtures given are based on one fixture being the minimum required for the number of persons indicated or any fraction of the number of persons indicated. Where plumbing fixtures are required, separate facilities must be provided for male and female. Separate facilities are not required in structures with a total occupant load of 15 or less. To determine the male and female occupant load, the total occupant load is divided in half.

1. Which of the following deliverables will the architect and other members of the design team provide to the owner in the schematic design phase submission? (Choose the four that apply.)

(A) geotechnical report

(B) correspondence with utility companies to confirm availability of services at project site

(C) conceptual sketches

(D) zoning research

(E) site survey

(F) construction cost projection

2. The mechanical engineer, architect, and owner agree that the new library building should be commissioned before it is opened to the public. Which of the following is true?

(A) Commissioning begins near the end of the construction phase.

(B) The commissioning agent is responsible for programming the building control systems.

(C) All commissioning activities can be completed within a month or two after the construction is complete.

(D) The scope of the commissioning activities depends on the owner's building performance objectives.

3. Based on their evaluation of the library's existing resources and projected growth, League Library Consultants developed the preliminary programming worksheet included in Resource 2.1. Required setbacks on the project site will limit the width of the building to 75 ft. Estimate the first floor footprint so the civil engineer can begin the site design.

(A) 75 ft × 144 ft

(B) 75 ft × 150 ft

(C) 75 ft × 157 ft

(D) 75 ft × 165 ft

4. The design team decides to build the community meeting room and restrooms in a separate wing of the new building so they can be used when the library is closed. The community meeting room will be an open space without fixed seating and will utilize an operable partition to divide the space into two rooms when needed. How many plumbing fixtures will be required to serve this meeting room?

(A) two unisex restrooms, with one lavatory and one water closet in each

(B) one water closet and one lavatory for males, one water closet and one lavatory for females

(C) one water closet and one lavatory for males, two water closets and one lavatory for females

(D) two water closets and one lavatory for males, two water closets and one lavatory for females

5. SKEG Architecture and League Library Consultants are pleased with their collaboration on this project and decide to pursue future projects as a team. As this project winds down, they are invited to submit a proposal for a school library renovation in a neighboring county and investigate forming a joint venture. Which statements about joint ventures are correct? (Choose the three that apply.)

(A) A joint venture does not pay income taxes.

(B) The architecture firm's professional liability insurance will cover both firms in the joint venture; it is not necessary for each party to purchase its own policy.

(C) One party would be liable for errors or omissions of the other party's employees and vice versa.

(D) American Institute of Architects (AIA) Document C101, *Joint Venture Agreement for Professional Services*, can only be used to form a joint venture between two architecture firms.

(E) AIA Document C101, *Joint Venture Agreement for Professional Services,* requires the firms to decide between two methods of compensation.

(F) The AIA's sample joint venture agreement includes a requirement that the parties establish a policy board responsible for managing the joint venture.

6. Which of the following provisions are included in the agreement between SKEG Architecture and Cog Engineering Group, which is based on American Institute of Architects (AIA) Document C401, *Standard Form of Agreement Between Architect and Consultant*? (Choose the four that apply.)

(A) SKEG Architecture's agreement with the owner is attached as an exhibit to the architect-consultant agreement.

(B) Cog Engineering Group is required to develop a schedule for the firm's work and is obligated to abide by that schedule unless both the architect and the consultant agree to modify it.

(C) SKEG Architecture assumes toward Cog Engineering Group the same obligations and responsibilities that the owner assumes toward the architect.

(D) The agreement between SKEG Architecture and Cog Engineering Group creates a contract between Cog Engineering Group and the library board.

(E) SKEG Architecture is required to pay Cog Engineering Group within 10 days of receipt of the consultant's invoice for services rendered.

(F) Communications between Cog Engineering Group and the library board must route through SKEG Architecture.

7. Which statements are true? (Choose the two that apply.)

(A) When the construction and furniture, fixtures, and equipment (FF&E) contracts are finalized, SKEG Architecture and the furniture vendor will have a contractual relationship.

(B) SKEG Architecture will be assigned construction administration responsibilities in American Institute of Architects (AIA) Document A251, *General Conditions of the Contract for Furniture, Furnishings and Equipment*.

(C) The agreement between SKEG Architecture and the library board states that "time is of the essence" in the design phase.

(D) Time limits stated in the contract documents are of the essence of the contract between Capstan Community Library and the selected furniture vendor.

(E) League Library Consultants acts as an agent of SKEG Architecture.

8. League Library Consultants will provide programming services and prepare the specifications for the furniture, fixtures, and equipment (FF&E) for this project. Which statement is correct?

(A) Programming is a part of the architect's basic services as defined in the American Institute of Architects (AIA) owner-architect agreement.

(B) FF&E design is a part of the architect's basic services as defined in the AIA owner-architect agreement.

(C) Both programming and FF&E design are additional services according to the AIA owner-architect agreement.

(D) AIA Document B253, *Standard Form of Architect's Services: Furniture, Furnishings, and Equipment Design*, may be used as a stand-alone agreement for these services.

9. The original agreement between SKEG Architecture and the library board did not include specifying the equipment for the computer labs because the library's IT manager agreed to accept this responsibility. However, during the schematic design phase and unbeknownst to the design team, this IT manager quit. How should League Library Consultants react when it realizes no one has been assigned this responsibility?

(A) Contact SKEG Architecture and notify the architect that additional work will be required.

(B) Prepare the specifications for the computer equipment and include this documentation in the furniture, fixtures, and equipment package.

(C) Notify the electrical engineer at Cog Engineering Group and ask for the computer equipment to be specified.

(D) Send a letter to the library board requesting that they decide who will be assigned this task.

10. Which of the following techniques could SKEG Architecture use to determine the project schedule and set dates for their design review submissions to the library board?

(A) project monitoring chart

(B) Gantt chart

(C) full-wall schedule

(D) flow diagram

Case Study 2

Jane Wythe is a principal architect at JLT Architects, a 10-person firm that has been involved with the design and construction of several private elementary schools and early childhood education centers. The firm has been awarded a contract to provide architectural design services for a new day care facility on the campus of Mountain College. The center will provide care for the preschool-age children of staff and students and serve as a hands-on training site for upperclassmen enrolled in the college's early childhood education program.

The project parameters are given in the request for proposal (RFP) issued by the college. JLT is preparing for initial design meetings with the college's representatives, and Jane is working on structuring their agreements with consultants.

The firm's staff includes the following employees.

- Jane, a principal architect, will serve as the client liaison. She is currently supervising three other design projects in various stages of completion, so she will delegate many of the day-to-day design and project development responsibilities to Catherine.

- Catherine is a registered architect who has been practicing for 15 years. She joined the firm four years ago and is a capable and efficient project manager.

- Linda is one of Jane's partners in the firm and a registered architect who has been practicing for 25 years. Linda's specialty is code review and compliance. She performs quality assurance reviews and writes most of the firm's specifications. She has been busy as the project manager for a small hotel project, which is nearing the end of the construction documents phase.

- Tom is Linda and Jane's partner. Tom is a structural engineer and coordinates many of the firm's business activities, such as invoicing and day-to-day financial management. His background in the construction industry allows him to prepare cost estimates for projects in design and to manage the firm's construction administration activities.

- Chris is a newly licensed architect who has been with the firm since graduating from college four years ago.

- John is the firm's interior designer. When the firm does not have projects requiring interior design services, he assists with production of working drawings and other drafting tasks.

- Dave is a recent architecture school graduate working on his internship and preparing for the Architect Registration Exam (ARE).

- Maria, who has a degree in architectural engineering, is an excellent drafter. She has a knack for organizing information and has been working closely with Tom on projects in construction.

- Dana is the firm's office manager who has worked at JLT for a few months. She was previously employed in a similar role at a very large engineering firm and has experience with marketing and proposal preparation.

- Adam is a student at Mountain College who works part-time as a CAD operator when his course schedule allows.

Resource 2.4 Request for Proposal for Architectural/Engineering Services

Mountain College Child Care Center
MC Project #50-98372MC

Project Description

Mountain College (MC) is soliciting proposals for architectural/engineering (A/E) services for the design of a new child care center. The facility will offer daytime care for children of Mountain College faculty, staff and students, and will be the primary practicum site for students in MC's early childhood education curriculum. The facility will be located on campus and will accommodate approximately 50 children (ages 6 weeks–kindergarten) and approximately 20 staff members and student teachers. Seminar rooms will accommodate 24–30 additional college students taking courses in the education department.

The design of this facility shall comply with all applicable building codes, the requirements of the state Departments of Health and Education, and the guidelines established by the National Association for the Education of Young Children (NAEYC).

Scope of Services

The firm selected will assume full responsibility for design and preparation of construction documents for the building, which may require specialized consultants to be a part of the proposed project team. Design and documentation shall comply with the guidelines in Mountain College's *Building Standards Manual*. The A/E firm will be responsible for administering the bidding process with the assistance of the college's procurement staff and will have typical construction administration duties as defined in the contract. Mountain College uses AIA Document B101, *Standard Form of Agreement Between Owner and Architect*, for owner/architect agreements; AIA Document A101, *Standard Form of Agreement Between Owner and Contractor where the basis of payment is a Stipulated Sum*; and A201, *General Conditions of the Contract for Construction*, for owner/contractor agreements. The college intends to utilize a design-bid-build project delivery method.

Program

Mountain College has completed a preliminary feasibility study, which produced the program included in this RFP, but will rely upon the architecture firm to develop the final program (which shall include determination of requirements for service spaces, circulation, restrooms, and the like). The building will be occupied from 6 AM to 6 PM each day. The design of the building exterior shall be complementary to the existing campus context. The college wishes to incorporate sustainable technologies as the project budget will allow, but it does not intend to seek certification from a green building rating program.

Preliminary Project Program

space description	quantity	approximate area (ft^2)	requirements
infant classrooms	2	300	Each infant classroom will be divided into a play area and a rest area. Both areas must be visible from all locations in the room. The classroom shall include eight lineal feet of lockable storage cabinets, one sink in the classroom area, and 15 open storage cubbies. The two classrooms will share one boys' restroom and one girls' restroom. Storage space will be provided for diapers and extra clothing. All classrooms should have windows and exterior views.
toddler and preschool classrooms	4	250	Each toddler/preschool classroom will include eight lineal feet of lockable storage cabinets, one 5 ft by 3 ft closet for stacking cot storage, one sink in the classroom area, and 15 open storage cubbies. Restrooms should be as determined by code requirements. All classrooms should have windows and exterior views.
indoor play area/ multipurpose space	1	1200	The multipurpose space should have a half-court basketball court configuration, plus storage space for riding toys, other physical education equipment, lunch tables and chairs. The space will contain a movable partition that can be used to divide the room into two equal spaces. There should also be a pass-through to the kitchen. This space will be used for free play, serving lunch daily, and occasional parent events.
nursing mothers' rooms	2	75 (minimum)	Each nursing mothers' room should be private, with a lockable door, counter/changing surface, accessible outlet, small sink, and chair. These rooms should be near the center entrance and infant classrooms.
kitchen	1	250	Includes refrigeration/freezer area, warming equipment, dry goods storage for nonperishable snacks. Adjacent to multipurpose space. Meals will be prepared at a nearby dining hall but served from this space.
office/security desk	1	300	At main entrance. Includes check-in desk, parent notice board, and two modular furniture workspaces. The entrance to children's spaces from this area must be secured.
conference room	1	100	The conference room should have seating for six and be adjacent to office. Access to conference room should be from the reception area only.
seminar rooms	2	250	The seminar rooms are classrooms for early childhood development courses. Each room should seat 12–15 college students. Access to the child care areas from the seminar rooms must be secured.
student/staff lounge	1	200	Adjacent to seminar rooms and men's and women's restrooms. Should contain 25 lockers and 4 study carrels.

Resource 2.4 (continued)

space description	quantity	approximate area (ft²)	requirements
central resource room	1	100	Storage for shared and surplus curriculum materials and audio/visual equipment, office supplies, copier, etc. Should contain open shelving, work counter, and lockable cabinets. Adjacent to student/staff lounge.
outdoor play area	1	500	Must be enclosed by the building on at least 70% of perimeter, and fenced/gated on no more than 30% of perimeter. Includes play equipment and resilient ground surfaces. Half of the space should be shaded during operating hours. All landscaping materials must be non-toxic.
delivery area	1	50	Adjacent to kitchen storage room. Public access from the delivery area to any other areas is prohibited.
laundry	1	TBD	Should contain two residential washing machines and two residential dryers, folding space, and locked storage cabinets for supplies.
janitorial room	1	TBD	Should contain a service sink and locked storage for supplies.
mechanical/ electrical rooms	2	TBD	As required for building systems equipment.

Security Considerations

Mountain College contracts with SecureSafety Corporation for all security system components and maintenance and design services for this project will be provided by the College under an existing open-ended contract. The biometric access system used elsewhere on campus should be incorporated at all entrances and exits. All entrances and child care spaces must be equipped with closed circuit cameras.

Building Systems Considerations

The child care center will be connected to the college's campus-wide geothermal heating and cooling system. Natural daylight should be provided in each classroom, with indirect, full spectrum, artificial lighting, and task lighting as required. Lighting design must be in compliance with the guidelines published by the state Department of Education. Automatic sprinkler and fire alarm systems must be installed throughout. The mechanical and electrical systems design and installation will be reviewed by the college's commissioning agent; this review will be coordinated by the college's facilities department under separate contract. Plumbing fixtures/restrooms will be included per code requirements.

Site Design Considerations

Provide short-term parking for drop off and pickup. The pedestrian path from parked vehicles to the building entrance should not cross the vehicular path. The building entrance should be covered and have a thermal vestibule. Long-term parking for staff and students will be provided at the campus parking garage.

Interior Finishes Considerations

All products specified for use within the building envelope must be formaldehyde-free and zero-VOC. Recycled content and rapidly renewable materials are encouraged. Finish materials should have a life expectancy of at least seven years.

Project Budget and Schedule

This project is a component of the college's *Vision for the Future* master plan. Mountain College has allocated a budget of $2.25 million, which will include construction costs, professional fees, and related expenses. There will be no land acquisition costs associated with this work, as the property is already part of the college's campus. Utility mains (water, sewer, electricity, data/phone, natural gas, and access to the geothermal system) are located within 100 yards of the building site. Mountain College's facilities department will coordinate and provide site surveying services for the project.

Extensive geotechnical investigation has not yet been performed, but it is anticipated that the subsurface conditions at this location will be similar to those discovered during construction of the science center across the street. This portion of the college's campus was constructed on a reclaimed strip mine. During the construction of the other science center, areas of poorly compacted fill were found throughout the site. Mountain College requests that the A/E firm engage a geotechnical engineer to perform test borings and consult with the designer to develop the foundation system design.

A/E firms will develop a project schedule for Mountain College's review and approval. Consider the following requirements when preparing the schedule.

- The college plans to open the facility within 2.5 years (30 months).

- The construction period may not exceed 16 months.

- Commissioning must be complete before a certificate of occupancy will be issued and the building will be permitted to be opened to the public. It will take about one month to perform the commissioning review and correct any issues.

- The college anticipates a two-month bidding period. This includes advertising the project, distributing the documents, responding to requests for information, issuing addenda, and receiving and evaluating bids. The college intends to award the project before the end of the two months. The college customarily allows one month between project award and the start of construction for mobilization.

RFP Response Requirements

The A/E firm for this project will be selected based on qualifications and experience with projects of similar size, scope, and type. Proposers shall complete the professional qualifications form on the college's website; resumes and supplemental materials may be uploaded to accompany the online form. Proposals must be submitted electronically.

11. JLT Architects is developing a project schedule for Mountain College's review. Some of the information that should be included in this schedule remains incomplete in the draft shown.

anticipated schedule

month	task
month 1 (*weeks 1–4*)	initial client meetings and confirm programmatic requirements
month 2 (*weeks 5–8*)	schematic design phase
month 3 (*weeks 9–12*)	
month 4 (*weeks 13–16*)	design development phase
month 5 (*weeks 17–20*)	
month 6 (*weeks 21–24*)	construction documents phase
month 7 (*weeks 25–28*)	
month 8 (*weeks 29–32*)	
month 9 (*weeks 33–36*)	
month 10 (*weeks 37–40*)	bidding and notification of award
month 11 (*weeks 41–44*)	
month 12 (*weeks 45–48*)	
months 13–29	construction period (16 months)
month 30	

Using the information given in the RFP, which of the following statements are true? (Choose the three that apply.)

(A) Commissioning of the mechanical and electrical systems must be complete before a certificate of substantial completion is issued.

(B) Contractors must begin work on the site within one week of notification of award.

(C) JLT's schedule should include time for code review and approval before the documents are released for bid.

(D) The schematic design phase is expected to comprise more than than 25% of the total time allotted for design.

(E) The bidding period will be one month.

(F) The architecture firm plans to complete the design development phase in three months.

12. Considering the information given in the case study about JLT Architects' employees and capabilities and the responsibilities outlined in the RFP, which of the following services must be provided by consultants to the architecture firm? (Choose the four that apply.)

(A) geotechnical engineering

(B) landscape architecture

(C) security consulting

(D) commissioning

(E) lighting design

(F) mechanical engineering

13. The mechanical engineer is reviewing the contract proposed by the architecture firm and has a question about the term "prime agreement." To which of the following American Institute of Architects (AIA) documents does the term "prime agreement" refer?

(A) AIA Document C401, *Standard Form of Agreement Between Architect and Consultant*

(B) AIA Document C422, *Service Order for use with Master Agreement Between Architect and Consultant*

(C) AIA Document A101, *Standard Form of Agreement Between Owner and Contractor where the basis of payment is a Stipulated Sum*

(D) AIA Document B101, *Standard Form of Agreement Between Owner and Architect*

14. Which of the following are examples of scope creep? (Choose the three that apply.)

(A) revising the interior finish selections because the original choices do not meet the life expectancy requirement

(B) developing an additional scheme for the preschool rooms because this year's class is exceptionally large

(C) revising the interior finish selections because one of the teachers does not like the colors that were chosen

(D) changing the custom cabinetry specification so that prefabricated cabinets may be used instead to minimize installation time and accommodate the contractor's schedule

(E) reviewing structural steel shop drawings

(F) developing the hardware schedule

15. As the firm is completing the schematic design submission, the early childhood education department of Mountain College learns that it can receive additional grant funding for their programs if the building is certified through the United States Green Building Council's Leadership in Energy and Environmental Design (LEED) program. The college asks the architect to proceed with obtaining LEED certification as soon as possible. How should the architect respond?

(A) Begin review of the schematic design documents to determine where it may be possible to earn LEED points, and present a summary of this review to the college.

(B) Submit a proposal for a feasibility study to the college, prepare an amendment to the owner/architect agreement for additional services, and notify the owner that this change may require adjustment of the design schedule and project budget.

(C) Start the design development phase, and instruct consultants to begin making changes to the design to allow for certification.

(D) Notify the owner that the budget will not allow for certification and continue with the project as planned.

16. Which change to the project requirements would have the greatest impact on the preliminary code analysis?

(A) Eliminate the multipurpose room.

(B) Make the building two stories.

(C) Relocate the building to the other side of campus.

(D) Eliminate the fire suppression system.

17. Which of the following documents is the most likely to be included in the bid package for this project?

(A) National Association for the Education of Young Children (NAEYC) *Design Guidelines*

(B) Mountain College's *Building Standards Manual*

(C) American Institute of Architects (AIA) Document G710, *Architect's Supplemental Instructions*

(D) supplementary conditions

18. Which diagram accurately illustrates the layout that best meets the adjacencies required by the preliminary project program?

(A)

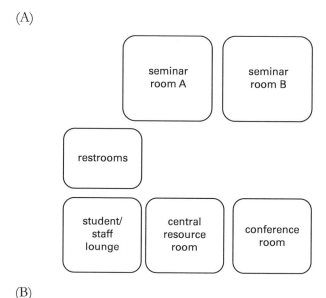

(B)

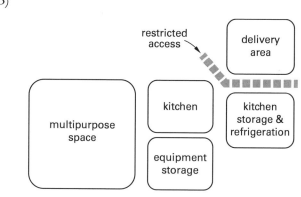

(C)

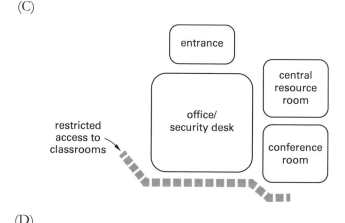

(D)

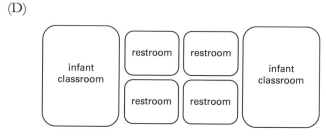

Project Management

19. To encourage competitive bidding, the college's procurement guidelines require the architect to write specifications that allow numerous manufacturers' products to be incorporated into the work, provided that they meet the specification requirements. To comply with the owner's requirements, what kind of specification will Linda need to write?

(A) performance

(B) descriptive

(C) proprietary

(D) reference standard

20. The School of Education learns that it can receive a higher score on its upcoming reaccreditation review if its new facility is available for use by the time of the review early next year. The education department is an important source of revenue for the college, and achieving a higher level of certification will help attract new students to the school. For this reason, the Board of Trustees grants permission to fast track the project and changes the delivery method to a construction manager at risk (CM@R). A CM@R is hired with a contract based on American Institute of Architects (AIA) Document A133, *Standard Form of Agreement Between Owner and Construction Manager as Constructor where the basis of payment is the Cost of the Work Plus a Fee with a Guaranteed Maximum Price.* The architecture firm has just completed the design development phase and made its submission to Mountain College. How will the architect's responsibilities be affected?

(A) The college will compensate the architect for work performed to date, but it will terminate the design contract because further project development will become the construction manager's responsibility.

(B) The architect will continue with the project, but the scope of services will be modified so that cost estimating and constructability reviews will be removed from the architect's scope and transferred to the construction manager. The contract should be revised or amended accordingly.

(C) The architect will be required to sign a contract with the construction management firm.

(D) During the construction phase, the architect will not need to review submittals or process change orders because the CM@R will have had the opportunity to be involved during the design phase.

21. The college requires the architecture firm to submit documents for review by college facilities staff three times during the design process: at the end of the schematic design phase, the design development phase, and the construction documents phase. The requirements for each submission are outlined in the owner/architect agreement. Which statement is true about the design development submission?

(A) The design development submission cannot be approved if the cost estimate submitted with the design development documents exceeds the project budget.

(B) The design development submission includes fully developed specification sections.

(C) The design development documents do not contain enough information to obtain a negotiated price from a contractor.

(D) The architect must wait for approval of the design development submission before beginning work on the construction documents phase.

22. Which statement best describes effective quality control?

(A) Catherine reviews the work prepared by the production team, redlines it, and makes corrections. Then Jane or Linda reviews the complete set of drawings before sending them to the college for review.

(B) To give consultants as much time as possible to coordinate their work, the consultants email their drawings to Catherine the day before the submission is due to the college.

(C) The college's facilities staff reviews and marks up the submission and then approves the submission with comments.

(D) The architecture firm hires a third-party peer reviewer to identify necessary corrections to the documents.

23. At the end of each month, Catherine reviews her team's time sheets and prepares the information Tom will need for invoicing. The project report generated by the accounting software for time accrued in January is shown.

The total fee for architectural/engineering (A/E) services is 15% of the overall project budget. Of this, 40% has been earmarked for consultant services and the remainder is for the architectural services. The cost for the architectural services will be divided evenly between the design and construction administration phases. If the firm assumes that the architectural service costs will be evenly divided among the nine months in the design phase, was the time expended in January within the budgeted amount?

(A) Yes, January's fees are within the budgeted amount.

(B) Yes, the architecture firm's fees are within budget, but the consultants' fees exceed their budgets.

(C) No, the time accrued exceeds the budgeted amount for January.

(D) Additional data are necessary to answer this question.

name	task description	hours	rate	amount
Jane	client meeting and follow-up correspondence and travel	8	$150	$1200
Linda	design development code review and compile table for cover sheet	6	$150	$900
Tom	design development constructability review and cost estimating	16	$150	$2400
Catherine	client meeting and travel and prepare minutes; sketch wall section and window details and hand off to production; teleconference with mechanical engineer; review kitchen equipment with college staff; review finish selections and sample boards	50	$125	$6250
John	select finishes/specification research, obtain samples and prepare sample boards for meeting with client	20	$100	$2000
Chris	research exterior envelope materials and requirements and draft wall section details; prepare reflected ceiling plan backgrounds and send to electrical engineer	30	$85	$2550
Maria	drafting—notes on floor plans, prepare window head/jamb/sill details, schedules	42	$70	$2940
total in-house		172		$18,240
invoice received from mechanical, electrical, and plumbing services engineering firm				$6530
invoice from kitchen consultant				$1500
total invoiced for January				$26,270

Solutions

1. The owner is responsible for providing the geotechnical report and the site survey to the design team at the beginning of the project. The schematic design submission should include documentation of correspondence with utility companies to confirm the availability of services at the project site (or, if they are not currently available, information on extending those services to the site and the associated cost). The schematic design submission should also include zoning research documenting the requirements pertaining to the site and building design, conceptual sketches showing the preliminary layout of the building and its appearance, and a construction cost projection based on the schematic design documents.

The answer is (B), (C), (D), and (F).

2. Commissioning is the process of verifying that the building's systems are installed and operate as the designer intended and that the performance of the systems is in accordance with the design intent. The design intent is a statement developed by the engineer based on the owner's operational objectives. The scope of the commissioning activities to be performed depends on the achievable goals and building performance objectives identified by the owner and the design team.

Ideally, commissioning begins in the design phase when input from a third-party reviewer may be used to improve the design. The contractor is responsible for providing and installing the building control systems as they are specified, but the commissioning agent confirms that they are installed properly and function as intended. Commissioning may take up to a year to complete, so that the systems' performances can be tested during all seasons and phases of operation.

The answer is (D).

3. The gross area of a space represents the total area: programmed spaces, or net area, plus circulation and support spaces needed to allow the building to function properly, as well as the thicknesses of the exterior walls. The gross area can be estimated during programming and the early parts of the design phase by calculating the total of the net areas, as listed in the program document, and then by increasing this number by a factor representing a reasonable efficiency for the specified building type.

Many programming decisions play into the efficiency of a building, including the following.

- type of construction and building's use

- size and occupant load of the building and correlating requirements for egress systems, restroom facilities, and the like

- type of mechanical and electrical systems selected and the equipment's location and distribution requirements

- whether the project is a new building designed specifically to accommodate the program, or a retrofit of an existing building, where the program may not fit as neatly

- individual offices versus large open work areas partitioned with systems furniture

- open spaces within the building such as two or more story atria

The information given in the project description states the efficiency of this building is projected to be 65%. This means that 65% of the total building area will be programmed space, and the other 35% of the building area will be dedicated to circulation or services.

To calculate the gross area of the first floor, begin by totaling the net areas included in the program.

space description	area (ft^2)
entrance, lobby and circulation desk	750
circulation work area	500
new materials and periodicals	650
café	250
adult computer lab	1000
adult non-fiction stack area	1200
adult fiction stack area	1200
quiet reading room	250
community meeting room	1000
storage and receiving	500
total	7300

The program states that the custodial areas and the restrooms are included in the allowance for circulation area. The space allocated for mechanical and electrical rooms is not included in this number and must be calculated and added to the total. The program states that the size of the mechanical and electrical rooms on a floor will be 10% of the total net programmed area of that floor.

$$
\begin{aligned}
A_{\text{rooms}} &= \left(A_{\text{programmed,total net}} \right)(10\%) \\
&= (7300 \text{ ft}^2)(10\%) \\
&= 730 \text{ ft}^2
\end{aligned}
$$

Add the total net area and the area calculated for mechanical and electrical rooms on this floor. This sum is the total programmed area for the first floor.

$$A_{\text{programmed, first floor}} = A_{\text{programmed,total net}} + A_{\text{rooms}}$$
$$= 7300 \text{ ft}^2 + 730 \text{ ft}^2$$
$$= 8030 \text{ ft}^2$$

The program says to assume 65% efficiency for the circulation areas. Divide the total programmed area for the first floor by the efficiency to determine the gross area of the building.

$$A_{\text{gross}} = \frac{A_{\text{programmed,first floor}}}{\eta} = \frac{8030 \text{ ft}^2}{65\%}$$
$$= 12{,}353.84 \text{ ft}^2$$

The problem states that the maximum width of the building should be 75 ft. To determine the other dimension of the building footprint, divide the gross area by the maximum width.

$$\frac{A_{\text{gross}}}{w_{\text{max}}} = \frac{12{,}353.84 \text{ ft}^2}{75 \text{ ft}}$$
$$= 164.74 \text{ ft} \quad (165 \text{ ft})$$

As the details of the design are refined, the tabulations of gross area, net area, and the resulting efficiency calculation will need to be revisited periodically. They will change as the building layout is determined, the adjacencies between spaces are better defined, and details regarding the building's envelope and internal systems are developed. As the design progresses, the methodology for calculating net area, gross area, and efficiency becomes more complex and includes additional measuring conventions (e.g., area factors for open interior spaces or covered exterior spaces). In the early part of design, however, this calculation will provide the information necessary to allow the consultants to begin their work.

The answer is (D).

4. To determine the number of plumbing fixtures required for a corresponding space, first calculate the occupant load. A community meeting room is an assembly occupancy. Resource 2.1 states that the meeting room is 1000 ft^2. Resource 2.2 indicates that the occupant load for an assembly occupancy without fixed seats can be calculated in multiple ways depending on how the space will be used.

Configurations will vary depending on function. To plan for the maximum number of occupants that will be allowed in this space, use the value given for standing space in an assembly without fixed seats: 5 ft^2 net per person.

$$\frac{A}{\text{occupant load factor}} = \frac{1000 \text{ ft}^2}{5 \dfrac{\text{ft}^2}{\text{occupant}}} = 200 \text{ occupants}$$

The building code allows the assumption that because half of the occupants are male and half are female, there are 100 male occupants and 100 female occupants.

Resource 2.3 provides the information necessary to determine the number of fixtures that will be required for males and females. In an assembly, there must be one water closet for every 125 male occupants and one for every 65 female occupants. There must be one lavatory for every 200 male occupants and one for every 200 female occupants.

Calculate the requirements for male occupants.

$$\frac{100 \text{ male occupants}}{125 \dfrac{\text{occupants}}{\text{fixture}}} = 0.8 \text{ fixture} \quad (1 \text{ fixture}) \quad [\text{water closet}]$$

$$\frac{100 \text{ male occupants}}{200 \dfrac{\text{occupants}}{\text{fixture}}} = 0.5 \text{ fixture} \quad (1 \text{ fixture}) \quad [\text{lavatory}]$$

Calculate the requirements for female occupants.

$$\frac{100 \text{ female occupants}}{65 \dfrac{\text{occupants}}{\text{fixture}}} = 1.54 \text{ fixture} \quad (2 \text{ fixtures}) \quad [\text{water closet}]$$

$$\frac{100 \text{ female occupants}}{200 \dfrac{\text{occupants}}{\text{fixture}}} = 0.5 \text{ fixture} \quad (1 \text{ fixture}) \quad [\text{lavatory}]$$

The answer is (C).

5. Although an architecture firm's professional liability insurance will cover non-negligent actions relative to projects, it will not cover the actions of the other party. The AIA joint venture agreement, AIA Document C101, *Joint Venture Agreement for Professional Services*, establishes the amounts and types of insurance that each of the firms is required to carry and also gives the firms the option to purchase joint policies on behalf of the joint venture for this specific project.

A joint venture is a new business entity formed by two or more existing firms to provide professional services for a specific project. The profits, losses, and tax liabilities of the joint venture are passed through to the constituent firms, which are then responsible for paying taxes on their share of the earnings.

The AIA's joint venture agreement can be used to establish a joint venture between various types of professional firms, including architects, engineers, or other consultants. This document offers the choice of organizing the joint venture according to a division of compensation or a division of profit and loss. With the first method, payments to the firm are split according to pre-determined proportions based on each firm's scope of work. With the second method, the firms are compensated for their efforts throughout the project (e.g., through a time-and-materials based invoice prepared monthly), and share the risk or reward at the end of the work.

The document also requires the parties to create a policy board comprised of representatives of both firms. These representatives are responsible for project administration and assigning project responsibilities.

The answer is (A), (E), and (F).

6. The agreement between SKEG Architecture and their engineering consultant, Cog Engineering Group, has been formed using AIA Document C401.

The architect is required to notify the consultant of any questions or issues with an invoice within 10 days of receipt according to AIA Document C401, Sec. 11.6.1. However, this is a pay-when-paid agreement as explained in AIA Document C401, Sec. 11.6.2, which means that the consultant will be paid after the architect has received funds from the owner.

Cog Engineering Group and the owner do not have a contractual relationship. However, the agreement between the architect and the owner is attached to the architect-consultant agreement as an exhibit according to AIA Document C401, Sec. 1.1. AIA Document C401, Sec. 1.3, states that the obligations of the architect to the consultant are to be the same as those that the owner has to the architect.

Communications between Cog Engineering Group and the library board should be through SKEG Architecture, so that the architecture firm is apprised of all discussion and decisions about the project.

The architect-consultant agreement requires the consultant to develop a schedule for their firm's work and is obligated to abide by that schedule unless both the architect and the consultant agree to modify it. The requirements for this schedule are outlined in AIA Document C401, Sec. 2.7.

The answer is (A), (B), (C), and (F).

7. AIA Document A251 is a contract between the owner and the furniture vendor, but it assigns tasks to the architect during the installation phase. The architect does not have a contractual relationship with the furniture vendor.

Because of the nature of the architect's work, the phrase "time is of the essence" is not used in the AIA owner-architect agreement.

The AIA architect-consultant agreement specifically states that the consultant is an independent contractor and does not act as an agent of the architect.

The architect is responsible for reviewing submittals, visiting the site to evaluate progress, and provide other contract administration services; the activities are similar to the construction phase tasks performed by the architect under the typical owner-contractor agreement.

Both the owner-vendor and owner-contractor agreements include time limits that are of the essence of the contract. The performance requirement in this agreement is that the architect will provide services in an expeditious manner. This recognizes that the architect may have to obtain information from a variety of sources to coordinate and advance the project, and may not have control over the timeframe in which all of this information can be obtained.

The answer is (B) and (D).

8. Programming and furniture, fixtures, and equipment (FF&E) design are both additional services as described in AIA Document B101, *Standard Form of Agreement Between Owner and Architect.* AIA Document B253, *Standard Form of Architect's Services: Furniture, Furnishings, and Equipment Design,* may only be used as a supplement to the primary agreement between the owner and the architect, not as a stand-alone contract.

Programming and FF&E design services can be included in the contract at the beginning of the project by noting them in AIA Document B101, Article 4, Additional Services, and defining the scope of the additional work. If it becomes evident that the additional services are necessary after the main agreement has been finalized, the services can be incorporated into the contract by using AIA Document G802, *Amendment to the Professional Services Agreement,* and one of the B-series *Standard Form of Architect's Services* documents to describe the scope.

The answer is (C).

9. The agreement between SKEG Architecture and League Library Consultants requires the consultant to notify the architect if the consultant becomes aware of a need to perform additional services. American Institute of Architects (AIA) Document C401, *Standard Form of Agreement Between Architect and Consultant,* Sec. 4.1, states that the consultant "shall not proceed to provide such services until the Consultant receives the Architect's written authorization."

Upon receipt of the consultant's notification, the architect can discuss the issue with the owner and determine how the owner wishes to proceed. The owner may choose to hire an independent consultant or may request that the design team perform these services. The architect would then determine which of the consultants would most appropriately be assigned this task and issue an amendment to that contract authorizing the additional work.

The answer is (A).

10. A Gantt chart is a bar chart that graphically illustrates a project schedule. This scheduling tool ties activities to their beginning and completion dates, and it can be used to project how long each required activity will take to achieve.

The answer is (B).

11. The RFP states that the college allows contractors one month between the notification of award and the start of construction for mobilization. This information has not yet been incorporated into the schedule, but this should take place in month 12. The commissioning of the mechanical and electrical systems must be completed before the building is opened to the public.

The draft schedule does not currently include time for code review and approval before the documents are released, which is necessary to protect the firm from liability.

The schematic design phase should comprise more than 25% of the total time allotted for design.

The bidding period will be more than one month, and the construction documents phase will be more than three months.

The answer is (A), (C), and (D).

12. The RFP provides the design firms with general information about the owner's requirements and how the project will be structured, including which responsibilities the architecture firm will assume and which tasks will be managed by the owner.

The security equipment specified for this project must be compatible with the security systems used at other campus facilities. The RFP states that security system design services will be provided under the college's existing open-end contract with SafetySecurity Corporation, so it is not necessary for the firm to provide security consulting services. The RFP also states that the owner will provide commissioning services.

American Institute of Architects (AIA) Document B101, *Standard Form of Agreement Between Owner and Architect*, Subparagraph 5.5, states that the owner will provide geotechnical services. In this case, however, the RFP assigns this

responsibility to the architect. The project description calls for an outdoor play area landscaped with non-toxic plant materials. None of the firm's employees have the skills necessary to select appropriate play area materials, so a consulting landscape architect should be hired. The architecture firm will also need to hire consultants to provide lighting design and mechanical engineering services.

The answer is (A), (B), (E), and (F).

13. The AIA offers standard forms and documents that may be used in drafting contracts, service orders, etc. A consultant's contract with the architect references the prime agreement to ensure that the consultant's responsibilities to the architect align with the architect's responsibilities to the owner.

The prime agreement is the contract between the owner and the architect. In this case, the prime agreement is AIA Document B101. If another type of agreement is used, the architect should ensure that both the owner-architect and architect-consultant agreements include similar language to ensure that the rights and responsibilities defined in the two contracts are aligned.

The answer is (D).

14. The revision of the finish specifications so that the selected products meet the life expectancy requirements is not an example of scope creep. The original project scope requires that the finishes be designed to last at least seven years, so the architect is obligated to make this change to fulfill the contract requirements. Reviewing structural steel shop drawings and preparing hardware schedules are also part of basic design services.

Scope creep occurs when tasks not originally included in the project scope are added into the project, typically without additional compensation or additional time allowed for the designer. These requests may seem small individually, but when many pile up, they can be the difference between meeting the project's budget and schedule and losing money on the job. As the scope expands, it requires the architect to assume responsibility and accept liability for the extra services that are provided.

Scope creep can be the fault of either the owner or the designer. Sometimes it can be attributed to a lack of understanding of the project scope, which is why it is important for all members of the team to be familiar with the contract requirements and frequently check that the tasks being performed are in agreement with this description.

It is the architect's responsibility to understand the agreed upon scope of work and to recognize when requests fall outside of the original parameters. The architect may take on these additional tasks but should notify the owner that this work is an additional service. The owner and architect should agree upon an adjustment to the fee, project budget, or schedule as necessary before beginning the work.

The answer is (B), (C), and (D).

15. The college's request to design a LEED-certified building is a change to the architect's original scope of work, so the architect should bring this to the owner's attention and suggest that the owner/architect contract be modified to reflect this change. American Institute of Architects (AIA) Document G802, *Amendment to the Professional Services Agreement*, and AIA Document B214, *Standard Form of Architect's Services: LEED Certification*, can be used to make this change.

Second, it may not be possible to achieve certification within the existing budget and schedule, particularly when the change to the scope is made late in the schematic design phase and a preliminary scheme has already been developed. A feasibility study can be a useful tool for determining whether the change is reasonable and what adjustments to budget and schedule would be required. This is an additional service for which the architect should be compensated. The design phase will probably need to be put on hold while these decisions are made, so it is important that the architect communicate these effects to the owner in a timely manner.

Finally, when the impact of the change has been determined, the budget and schedule can be adjusted by the owner to accomplish the new goal, and the owner/architect and architect/consultant agreements can be modified to compensate the architect and consultants fairly for the additional work.

The answer is (B).

16. Eliminating the fire suppression system would have the greatest effect on the preliminary code analysis. Including sprinklers allows the designer more flexibility in the design. When sprinklers are provided, height and area allowances and fire separation distances are increased, longer exit access travel distances are permitted, fire separation requirements between spaces are reduced, and incidental occupancies are permitted without fire-rated separation.

The answer is (D).

17. The NAEYC Guidelines and Mountain College's *Building Standards Manual* are not part of the contract and would not be a part of the bidding documents. These documents are reference materials used by the architect to develop the design documents. AIA Document G710 is used by the architect during the construction phase to provide additional information to the contractor.

Supplementary conditions are attached to a standard AIA document, such as AIA Document A101, *Standard Form of Agreement Between Owner and Contractor where the basis of payment is a Stipulated Sum*, to add, delete, or modify statements in the standard contract and customize it for a particular project. It allows the owner to edit the contract without taking out any of the standard material. It also makes the changes to the standard contract obvious. AIA Document A503, *Guide for Supplementary Conditions*, can be used to help the owner or the owner's attorney to develop this addendum. Because the supplementary conditions modify the agreement between the owner and the contractor, the architect should advise the owner to seek independent legal counsel before including this document.

The answer is (D).

18. Option (A) shows the conference room in the same area as the seminar rooms, which is incorrect; the conference room must be adjacent to the office.

Option (C) shows the central resource room adjacent to the office; this space is for storage of curriculum materials and should be adjacent to the student and staff lounge.

Option (D) shows two restrooms for each infant classroom. The program states that the two classrooms are permitted to share one boys' and one girls' restroom.

Option (B) shows the information given in the project program correctly. The program requires the delivery area to be separated from all other areas in the building to prevent unauthorized access to the facility. The delivery area is adjacent to the storage area so that it is convenient for a staff member to bring deliveries into the storage room at a later time; it also protects this area from exterior access by suppliers. The program requires the multipurpose space to be adjacent to the storage area for equipment such as chairs, tables, and riding toys, and requires a method of egress between the kitchen and the multipurpose space.

The answer is (B).

19. The specifications for this project will be descriptive. Descriptive specifications outline the requirements for each product to be incorporated into the work, but they do not list the brand names of products that meet the requirements. The specification writer must ensure that products that possess all of the characteristics that the specification requires are available in the marketplace, even if they are not specifically cited in the specification. The specification must also be written in a way that does not exclude products that may otherwise be acceptable for use. For example, a specification may require that a product be tested according to specific ASTM test and be of a certain thickness. If three products pass the requirements of a reference standard test but only one of them complies with the requirement for thickness, this specification does not allow competitive bidding and use of more than one product.

The answer is (B).

20. The architect's scope of services is changed because the owner decided to switch from a design-bid-build delivery method to a CM@R delivery method. For the CM@R delivery method, a contracting firm is brought into the project in the design phase to estimate cost, review constructability, and provide the owner with a guaranteed maximum price for the work. The construction management (CM) firm becomes the general contractor responsible for building the facility. The CM@R delivery method allows a project to progress more quickly because the design phase and the construction phase can overlap. For example, the CM can obtain the foundation permit and begin construction of the subgrade work while the superstructure's design is being finalized.

In this case, the architect has an existing agreement with the owner that specifies that the delivery method will be design-bid-build. The agreement should be revised to reflect the change to the delivery method. This can be accomplished by amending the original agreement (e.g., writing an addendum using AIA Document B503, *Guide for Amendments to AIA Owner-Architect Agreements*). Alternatively, it may be advisable to terminate the original agreement and establish a new agreement that more clearly defines the architect's new responsibilities in the design and construction phases now that the structure of the project has changed. If this is done, AIA Document B133, *Standard Form of Agreement Between Owner and Architect, Construction Manager as Constructor Edition*, may be a more appropriate template. The architecture firm may then need to modify its agreements with its consultants to reflect this new approach.

The answer is (B).

21. The design development submission is an important step in the design process because the documents prepared at this stage define the shape, size, materials, and configuration of the building components and allow the owner the opportunity to review and comment on the progress of the work. Ideally, the owner will have been a part of the decision-making process and will have already been consulted about the decisions, so the information in the design development submission should not be completely new to the owner. However, this submission may be the first time that the owner will see all of the decisions to date in a coordinated package that includes both drawings and outline specifications.

The design development submission may be approved even if the cost estimate exceeds the budget, but with the provision that changes be made so the final design will comply with the cost parameters.

Usually when the architect submits the design development documents, many decisions about the materials still need to be made and many properties of materials must be specified; therefore the specifications will not be fully developed. Some firms choose to submit outline specifications with their design development submissions; others submit a draft of the full specification marked where information still needs to be completed or confirmed.

The information included in a design development submission may be complete enough to allow the owner to negotiate a price for the project from a contractor. However, it would not be developed to the point that the project could be competitively bid.

The owner/architect agreement for this project is American Institute of Architects (AIA) Document B101, *Standard Form of Agreement Between Owner and Architect*, which requires that the architect obtain approval of the design development submission before proceeding with the construction documents phase. This ensures that the owner has the opportunity to review and comment on the progress of the work before moving forward.

The answer is (D).

22. Option (B), option (C), and option (D) rely on others to catch mistakes. If there is no time for the consultant's drawings to be coordinated with the architectural work, there is a greater probability of conflicts and errors. Similarly, it is the firm's responsibility to spot conflicts, not the owner's. The submission drawings are a reflection of the architect's work and should be as well coordinated as possible. The owner's comments may include items that the owner wishes to change, comments or questions about the design, and so on, but the owner is not responsible for detecting conflicts. It reflects poorly on the designer if such errors are present.

Using a third-party peer reviewer is an effective way to ensure the quality of the documents, but often this reviewer is not as familiar with the work as the project team and may not be aware of all of the factors influencing a detail or selection. The comments and questions raised by the peer review must be evaluated and considered by the project manager before the changes are incorporated into the documents. Reviewers should not make the changes.

The most effective quality control method is to plan for a series of coordination reviews, both by a person intimately familiar with the project (Catherine) and someone with knowledge of the project but who can review the work with "fresh eyes" (Jane or Linda, in this example). This is an example of a first-party peer review.

The answer is (A).

23. The overall project budget given in the request from proposal (RFP) is $2,250,000. The total architectural/engineering (A/E) services fee is

$$(\$2{,}250{,}000)(0.15) = \$337{,}500$$

The consultants' portion of the A/E services fee is

$$(\$337{,}500)(0.40) = \$135{,}000$$

The remaining A/E services fee is the architecture firm's portion.

$$\$337{,}500 - \$135{,}000 = \$202{,}500$$

The architecture firm's budget of $202,500 is divided into two halves of $101,250 for the design and construction administration budgets. If the design budget is spread over a period of 9 months, the allocation for each month is

$$\frac{\$101{,}250}{9 \text{ mo}} = \$11{,}250/\text{mo}$$

Because the architecture firm billed $18,240 for January, the time expended for this month exceeds the budgeted amount for January.

The answer is (C).

Project Management

DIVISION 3: PROGRAMMING & ANALYSIS

7 Building Context

1. If a soil is analyzed as being primarily silty, how should it be characterized?

(A) very fine material of organic matter

(B) rigid particles with moderately high bearing capacity

(C) particles with some cohesion and plasticity in their behavior

(D) smaller particles with occasional plastic behavior

2. A portion of a recreation area is shown. Which location would be the best site for a restaurant and visitor's center?

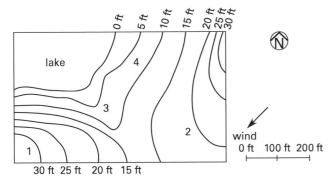

(A) location 1

(B) location 2

(C) location 3

(D) location 4

3. A speculative office building probably would not be built if the developer discovered that

(A) all of the catchment area was not served by arterial streets

(B) the site consisted of mostly sandy soil with a 6 ft top layer of expansive clay

(C) the vacancy rate of office space in the city was three times the national average

(D) the neighborhood community objected to the sight of parking lots

4. A client wants to obtain federal tax credits for rehabilitation of an old building that has been designated as a state historic landmark. The architect should inform the client that

(A) new additions or exterior alterations cannot vary from the historic character

(B) a thorough historic survey is required to verify conformity to federal standards

(C) the Secretary of the Interior's *Standards for Rehabilitation* must be met

(D) the cost might exceed the client's budget because state standards must be used

5. Which of the automobile entrances to the site shown is most desirable?

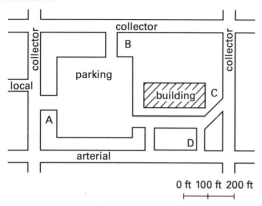

(A)   entrance A

(B)   entrance B

(C)   entrance C

(D)   entrance D

6. Four possible locations for a one-story building on a given site are shown, along with the site contours.

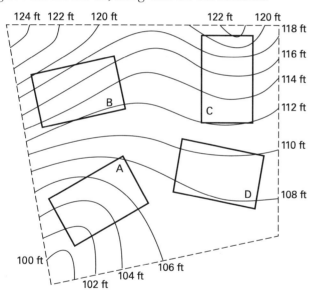

Which of the locations would offer the greatest construction cost savings?

(A)   location A

(B)   location B

(C)   location C

(D)   location D

7. Which of the following contour line signatures represents a ridge?

(A)

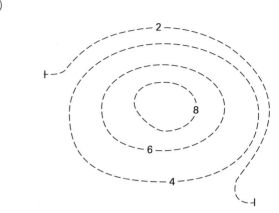

(B)

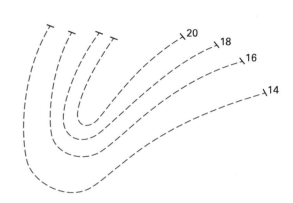

(C)

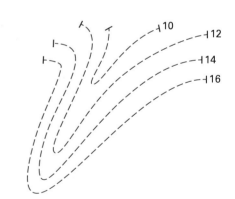

(D)

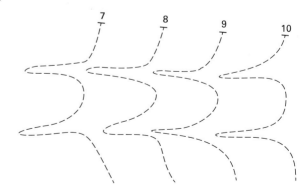

8. The construction of a large general hospital is being planned for a neighborhood that lies between an outer edge of a downtown area and a medium- to high-density housing area. There are already smaller clinics and doctors' offices in the area. The following concerns have been addressed in the design of the hospital building. In presenting the project to the city planning board, which concern should the architect emphasize?

(A) The proposed street closure, planned in order to expand the building site, will not affect traffic.

(B) Sufficient parking will be made available on the project site.

(C) The bulk of the building design will not block sunlight from the housing.

(D) Sewer and water services will not have to be expanded to serve the building.

9. An architect is developing a site plan for a building that is adjacent to a highway. Which of the following strategies is best for attenuating noise?

(A) Maximize the distance between the new building and the highway.

(B) Construct a masonry wall as high as possible next to the highway.

(C) Plant a combination of deciduous and evergreen trees 100 ft deep.

(D) Locate the building as far from the highway as possible and plant a row of evergreen trees.

10. In order to strengthen the sense of neighborhood and community, a developer constructs a public square in the middle of a housing development. The public square is an example of a(n)

(A) landmark

(B) edge

(C) district

(D) node

11. According to the principles of crime prevention through environmental design (CPTED), which of the following are the most useful strategies? (Choose the four that apply.)

(A) adding security guards at critical points

(B) using territorial reinforcement

(C) placing bars on ground floor windows

(D) employing electronic methods of protection

(E) requiring the use of keypad locks

(F) locating windows to overlook public areas

Solutions

1. Option (A) describes organic material, option (B) describes gravels, and option (C) describes clays.

The answer is (D).

2. Location 1 has a good view, but at the top of a hill it would be very windy. In addition, access to the lake would be difficult due to the steep slope from this site to the water. Location 3 is in a drainage pattern; this alone makes it unsuitable for development, but this area would also be cool due to its position at the bottom of two slopes and in the path of wind coming through the valley. Location 4 has a good view, has easy access to the lake, and could be used for development, but the slightly steeper slope might complicate grading and site work. Location 2 has level ground and a good view of and access to the lake, and its location on a south-facing slope would capture the sun and minimize the detrimental effects of the wind.

The answer is (B).

3. The vacancy rate in the region or community is the one factor that would most affect the financial success of the project and the decision to build.

A speculative office building depends on a wide catchment area, and a lack of arterial roads in some portions of it would most likely not affect the marketability of the project. If there was strong objection to parking lots, the visual impact could be minimized through landscaping, or parking could be placed underground or in a well-designed parking structure.

Either a relatively thin layer of clay only 6 ft thick could be removed and replaced with better soil, or the foundations could be placed on the good underlying layer of sandy soil.

The answer is (C).

4. The Secretary of the Interior's *Standards for Rehabilitation* developed by the Heritage Preservation Services branch of the National Park Service must be met if federal investment tax credits are to be used. These standards take precedence over any state or local requirements.

The standards do allow for new additions and alterations to be differentiated from the old while still being compatible in massing, size, scale, and architectural features. A survey and study of the subject property in itself does not guarantee conformance with the federal standards. A cost higher than the budget is not related to the ability to receive a federal tax credit.

The answer is (C).

5. The most desirable entrance location is the one located in the collector street, entrance B. Entrance A is too close to another intersecting street. Entrance C intersects the street at an angle that is unsafe. Entrance D intersects an arterial street. Although sometimes possible, this situation should be avoided, especially if it is as close to an intersection as is this one.

The answer is (B).

6. There are two considerations in this problem: the amount of grading required to provide a level pad for the building, and the grading required to establish good drainage away from the building. Because location D is on the shallowest portion of the site, it would require the least cut-and-fill work to provide a level site, and drainage could be accomplished easily, both resulting in cost savings.

Location A is in a valley (i.e., it is a drainage swale), and it would be difficult to resolve the drainage problems here. Location B is on a steep slope and would need extensive cut-and-fill work to provide a level pad. Since location C is on a ridge, severe cutting would be required to level the site, although drainage would be accomplished easily.

This is a common type of problem designed to test knowledge and understanding of how topography affects site selection and building planning. You may be given a single site with a topography and asked to select the best location for a given use, or you may be given four different topographic layouts and asked which is best suited for a particular project. The problem may focus on how topography affects the cost of moving earth, drainage, solar access, road planning, aesthetics, or some combination of these.

The answer is (D).

7. Contours are used to represent three-dimensional landforms in a two-dimensional drawing. Ridges and valleys are frequently confused; the contours point toward the lower elevation for a ridge and toward the higher elevation for a valley.

Hills are generally easy to spot as they are represented with concentric circles (or near circles), but the elevations must be checked to determine whether the landform is a hill or a depression. The elevations near the center are higher for a hill and lower for a depression.

Contours with very regular spacing usually represent some human-made element on the site, such as a street with a curb and gutter.

The answer is (B).

8. All these issues are important, but the architect wants to tailor the presentation toward the key concerns of the planning board and the community at large. In this type of neighborhood, parking already would be in short supply considering the number of downtown workers, housing, and the high-traffic needs of clinics and doctors' offices. Therefore, parking likely would be the most important concern to the community.

This problem requires an understanding of all the major elements of planning a project and their effect on transportation services, traffic, utilities, ecology, drainage, and aesthetics. You may be asked questions about what types of drawings or other documentation could best show a proposed project in its neighborhood context. In general, know how the surroundings affect the project and how the project affects the surrounding community.

The following terms are important to know.

catchment area: The area surrounding a land development site, encompassing the population base that the development is meant to serve.

contextualism: The belief that new buildings should be designed to harmonize with other buildings and elements in the vicinity.

demographics: The statistical data of a population, such as age, income, and so forth.

personal space (personal distance): The subjective distance or area surrounding a person's body into which a person feels comfortable allowing others to intrude, depending on the situation. Psychologist Robert Sommer developed a theory that there are four distances of personal space, including intimate distance, personal distance, social distance, and public distance—all of which vary by culture and specific situation.

planned unit development (PUD): A large parcel of land, typically with a mix of uses, that has been designed and laid out according to principles approved by the local planning authority and often with citizen input. A PUD is commonly used to develop land in a way that ordinarily would not be allowed based on normal planning and zoning restrictions of a jurisdiction.

proxemics: A term coined by anthropologist Edward T. Hall and now used to describe the study of the spatial requirements of humans and the effects of population density on behavior, communication, and social interaction.

superblock: A large parcel of land designed to minimize the impact of the automobile on residential development in which access to interior lots is provided by cul-de-sacs branching from surrounding streets and providing one or more open spaces.

tax base: The object on which a tax is calculated. For example, property is the tax base of a property tax.

The answer is (B).

9. All of the strategies listed would help mitigate the noise problem, but building a solid, high mass wall would be the most effective.

Although increasing the distance between a noise source and the receiver helps to reduce the sound level, it would not make a significant difference in this case. Even though noise from a point source decreases as the square of the distance increases, noise from a linear source, such as a highway, only decreases directly as the distance increases. Doubling the distance would only decrease the sound level by about three decibels, which is barely noticeable.

Trees help attenuate sound, but only if they are planted in a deep row and if a combination of deciduous and evergreen trees is used. A deep row of trees consists of several rows perpendicular to the direction of the sound. The greater the number of rows, the better the sound attenuation will be. Planting a combination of deciduous and evergreen trees is helpful because their different densities attenuate different sound frequencies. However, trees are most effective in attenuating sound at higher frequencies and may not be very useful in dealing with the low frequencies of highway noise.

The answer is (B).

10. A node is a center of interest that people can enter, such as a plaza, a public square, or the intersection of paths. A node is smaller than a district and may be the center of a district.

A landmark is a point reference and a device for wayfinding and symbolic identification of an area. A district is a two-dimensional area that people perceive as having a common, identifying character and that is critical to the sense of neighborhood. An edge is a linear element other than a path that forms a boundary between two districts or that breaks continuity.

This question requires an understanding of the ideas of Kevin Lynch as described in his book, *The Image of the City*.

The answer is (D).

11. Of the options listed, simply placing bars on windows would be the least effective crime prevention technique, according to the principles of CPTED. CPTED is the process of designing security into architecture. The various strategies it uses are implemented through architectural design, electronic methods, and organizational methods. Architectural design methods include the use of defensible space concepts that deny admission to a target and create a perception that there is a risk in selecting a target; such concepts include natural access control, natural surveillance, territorial reinforcement, and legitimate activity support. Mechanical access control including locks and window bars supplement natural and electronic access-control measures. Natural access control elements include fences, hedges, and gates, which create the perception that selecting the target is a risk. Electronic methods include the use of locks, alarms, access control, electronic surveillance, and similar techniques. Organizational methods include the use of human resources such as guards, door attendants, receptionists, and the like.

The answer is (A), (B), (D), and (F).

8 Codes and Regulations During Programming

1. Place new contour lines between A and B to create a swale that will channel runoff between the 6 in high curb of the existing road and the sidewalk to create a uniform wash off the sidewalk into the swale. The sidewalk is several inches higher than the adjacent ground.

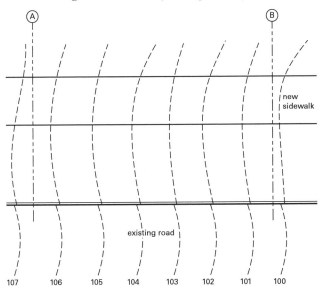

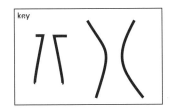

2. Which of the following building types would have the most stringent requirements for fire alarm and fire suppression systems?

    (A)   motel

    (B)   nursing home

    (C)   office building

    (D)   print shop

3. A building in Gettysburg, Pennsylvania, figured prominently in the Civil War and is now used as a small private museum. The brick structure is adjacent to a battlefield and has been maintained largely as it was in 1863, with the exception of a small wood frame addition built in the 1960s. The addition is deteriorating and will be removed. This project is an example of which historic building treatment approach?

    (A)   rehabilitation

    (B)   restoration

    (C)   reconstruction

    (D)   preservation

4. The owner of the lot shown wants to develop a building with the maximum allowable gross square footage.

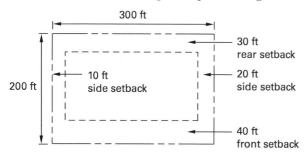

If the floor area ratio (FAR) is 2.0 and the owner builds only full stories to the setback lines, how high will the building be?

(A)   two stories

(B)   three stories

(C)   four stories

(D)   five stories

5. Which of these can zoning ordinances do? (Choose the four that apply.)

(A)   influence building form

(B)   determine the allowable flooring loading based on occupancy

(C)   stabilize property values

(D)   determine required amounts of parking

(E)   allow city governments to predict infrastructure needs

(F)   establish the required number of toilet facilities at a municipal stadium

6. Which of the following are required components of an incentive zoning plan? (Choose the three that apply.)

(A)   base floor area ratio

(B)   bonus ratio

(C)   specific plan for development

(D)   floor area ratio (FAR) cap

(E)   floor area ratio cap

(F)   bonus cap

7. Which of the following would be included in a zoning ordinance? (Choose the four that apply.)

(A)   maximum building heights

(B)   maximum numbers of occupants

(C)   minimum parking requirements

(D)   minimum setbacks from property lines

(E)   minimum width for utility easements

(F)   minimum number of loading spaces

8. Each area listed below is included in the plans for the construction of a new high school. Which areas must comply with the *ADA Accessibility Guidelines*? (Choose the four that apply.)

(A)   copy room designated "faculty only"

(B)   temporary passageway during construction for pedestrian access to the football field

(C)   lifeguard tower within the indoor pool area

(D)   special collections area in the library

(E)   additional bleachers constructed for a weekend football game

(F)   contractor's on-site construction trailer

9. Through which of the following areas may exits pass? (Choose the four that apply.)

(A)   office reception areas

(B)   building lobbies

(C)   unoccupied storage areas

(D)   apartment entries

(E)   kitchens

(F)   stairwells

10. What standard test is used to determine the optimum compaction of site fill?

(A)   Proctor test

(B)   pit test

(C)   dry sample boring test

(D)   soil load test

11. An architect is planning a 30 ft by 35 ft addition to a community library. The entire addition will be a single large meeting room. This room will be used for "story hour" and other library programs and will also be made available to community organizations for meetings and presentations. The space will be open with no fixed seating. Using the information in the table shown, what is the maximum occupancy of this space?

function of space	floor area per occupant (ft²)
assembly without fixed seats	
concentrated (chairs only—not fixed)	7 net
standing space	5 net
unconcentrated (tables and chairs)	15 net
business area	100 gross
library	
reading room	50 net
stack area	100 gross

(A) 30 occupants

(B) 70 occupants

(C) 150 occupants

(D) 210 occupants

12. During the design of a small retail building, an architect discovers that the building design exceeds the maximum height allowed by 18 in and that reducing the building's height is impossible. The architect should suggest that the owner apply for a(n)

(A) conditional use permit

(B) easement

(C) PUD

(D) variance

13. Which of the following is used to prevent sediment runoff during construction?

(A) bioswale

(B) riprap

(C) screen grating

(D) silt fence

14. To determine the minimum parking requirements for site development, the architect should first consult

(A) the *ADA Accessibility Guidelines*

(B) development covenants

(C) the local building code

(D) zoning regulations

15. Which of the following would have the least effect on the maximum height of a building?

(A) bulk plane restrictions

(B) floor area ratios (FARs)

(C) zoning setbacks

(D) occupancy groups

16. Which of the following are typically regulated by zoning ordinances? (Choose the four that apply.)

(A) how a property is used

(B) types of exterior materials

(C) floor area ratios

(D) number of loading spaces

(E) minimum amount of window exposure

(F) distances from property line to building

17. Setback distances are determined by a city's

(A) building code

(B) zoning code

(C) development agency

(D) planning office

Solutions

1. To channel the runoff between the road and sidewalk, create a valley between the two. Contour lines of a valley "point" upslope, so use the C-shaped contour as shown.

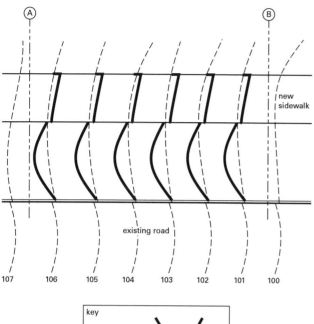

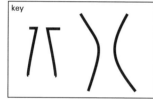

Because the curb is higher than the road, the new contour lines would be added downslope of the highest point. To create sheet flow off the sidewalk into the swale, the contours of the sidewalk need to face toward the swale. Because the sidewalk will be higher than the ground, the new sidewalk contours at the swale will be slightly offset (in plan view) in the direction of the downward slope and must jog back along the raised edge of the sidewalk on the other side.

2. As a Group I (institutional) occupancy, a nursing home would be required to have extensive alarm systems and be sprinklered throughout. Occupants of institutional buildings, such as hospitals, prisons, and nursing homes, often have limited mobility and require more warning and time to evacuate the building in case of fire.

Group B (business) occupancies, such as office buildings and print shops, are not required to be equipped with automatic sprinkler systems, and small Group B occupancies are not required to have alarm systems if the occupant load is low or if the sprinkler system is equipped with flow valves that activate an alarm when sprinkler water flows. Although a motel would be required to have smoke alarms, it probably would not be required to have a sprinkler system since motels are typically one or two stories high and each guest room has a doorway leading directly to an exterior exit access.

The answer is (B).

3. Restoration focuses on the most important time period in the life of a structure. In this case, the most significant time was the Battle of Gettysburg, July 1 through 3, 1863. Therefore, any additions built at other times could be removed. The materials and character of the original structure should be repaired.

Rehabilitation is often used when the property is being converted to a use other than its historical function. It allows more flexibility in the materials and methods of construction that can be used to repair the building, as long as the historic character of the building is maintained.

Reconstruction is the process of rebuilding a lost structure based on historical documentation. One of the most familiar examples of this approach is the buildings and environs at Colonial Williamsburg.

Preservation is the most historically accurate approach. It maintains additions made over time and chronicles the history of the building through the modifications.

The answer is (B).

4. The area of the lot is 60,000 ft². If the floor area ratio is 2, the maximum amount of floor area that can be built is 120,000 ft². The available ground area that can be covered within the setbacks is 270 ft × 130 ft, or 35,100 ft². Dividing this figure into 120,000 gives 3.42 stories, which indicates that three full stories can be built.

The answer is (B).

5. Zoning ordinances are enacted in municipalities to control what types of structures are built in certain locations. Zoning requirements such as setbacks, floor area ratios, and height limitations influence the form of the building that can be constructed on a site and consequently influence the appearance of a neighborhood. Zoning regulations prohibit construction of incongruent building types within a specific area; for example, zoning ordinances would likely separate residential neighborhoods from heavy industrial uses, helping to stabilize property values. Zoning also helps governments plan for the future by restricting the capacity of the land and helping predict the types and capacities of utility systems necessary in a specific area.

The answer is (A), (C), (D), and (E).

6. Incentive zoning is a way to encourage private developers to provide amenities for public use in exchange for the opportunity to build a larger or taller structure on a site. An example of incentive zoning is the bonus floor area given to developers of skyscrapers in New York City, New York, who include a public plaza on the ground floor level.

Incentive zoning plans must include a base floor area ratio (the standard against which to compare) and a bonus ratio—the FAR that is provided if the public space is a part of the design, along with a specific plan for the development that will trigger the bonus. The plans may include caps on the FAR and the bonus FAR—for example, a bonus may be given for providing public parking in an underground garage to increase from the base FAR of 1.5, but the bonus FAR may not exceed 2. For incentive zoning to be a true incentive, the value of the additional (leasable) floor area must exceed the cost of providing the public amenity.

The answer is (A), (B), and (C).

7. A zoning ordinance is a set of rules enacted by a local governing body or by a board that the governing body has designated, such as a zoning or planning commission. This set of rules regulates the types of building and development that are permitted in certain areas of a jurisdiction.

Zoning ordinances specify what uses are permitted in certain areas and may separate the land within the jurisdiction into commercial, industrial, and residential zones. In addition, zoning ordinances typically dictate how a site may be developed by establishing floor area ratios, minimum lot sizes and dimensions, maximum lot coverage requirements, maximum building heights, minimum setbacks from property lines, and parking requirements, including minimum number and sizes of loading spaces.

Sometimes a zoning ordinance gives different requirements from the building code in effect in the same region. This often happens, for example, with requirements for maximum height and area. Building codes determine these maximums on the basis of occupancy groups and types of construction, which are modified by factors such as whether the building will be sprinklered and whether access for firefighting equipment will be provided. If the local zoning ordinance and the building code give different maximum heights or areas, the lower of the two takes precedence.

A zoning ordinance would not determine the maximum number of occupants permitted in a structure. This requirement is established by the building code in the jurisdiction, in accordance with the occupancy group and type of construction of the building. In addition, a zoning

ordinance would not include requirements for or widths of utility easements.

The answer is (A), (C), (D), and (F).

8. The *ADA Accessibility Guidelines* state that all newly designed or newly constructed areas must meet accessibility requirements. This includes all employee work areas and all temporary construction that is open to the public (such as a protected walkway, temporary seating for a special event, and so forth).

The following areas are not required to be accessible.

- temporary facilities associated with the process of construction (job site trailer, scaffolding)

- raised areas used primarily for security or life safety (lifeguard tower, security guard tower)

- non-occupiable service areas accessed infrequently for maintenance or monitoring (catwalks, penthouses, pump rooms)

- single occupant structures accessed from above or below grade (such as a tollbooth accessed through an underground tunnel)

- raised structures for officiating sporting events

- water slides

- nonpublic animal containment areas

- raised boxing and wrestling rings

The answer is (A), (B), (D), and (E).

9. The *International Building Code* (IBC) specifically states that exits cannot pass through kitchens; through storerooms, closets, or other spaces used for similar purposes; or through rooms that can be locked to prevent egress. Lobbies, reception areas, entries, and stairwells may all be parts of the path of egress. However, to be part of an exit, a space is not permitted to be locked from the inside under any circumstances.

The answer is (A), (B), (D), and (F).

10. The Proctor test determines the optimum compaction of site fill based on its density and optimum moisture content.

A pit test is simply a pit dug in the soil to allow visual inspection of the soil.

A dry sample boring is not a test but a method of extracting soil samples.

A soil load test determines the design load of soil by

Programming & Analysis

applying steadily increasing loads on a platform placed on the site.

The answer is (A).

11. A library or community hall is classified as an A-3 (Assembly) occupancy according to the *International Building Code* (IBC). If fixed seating is provided, the number of occupants equals the number of seats. Where no fixed seating is provided, the designer must refer to IBC Table 1004.1.1 to calculate the occupancy of a space.

The maximum occupancy of the space is the greatest possible number of occupants as calculated using the IBC table. If tables and chairs are provided, each occupant is allocated 15 ft^2. If the room will be arranged with rows of seating, each person occupies 7 ft^2. If occupants are standing, each is allocated 5 ft^2 of standing space.

The usage that allocates the least space per occupant will give the greatest occupancy, so dividing the area of the room by 5 ft^2 gives in the maximum occupancy of this space.

$$(30 \text{ ft})(35 \text{ ft}) = 1050 \text{ ft}^2$$

$$\frac{1050 \text{ ft}^2}{5 \dfrac{\text{ft}^2}{\text{occupant}}} = 210 \text{ occupants}$$

The answer is (D).

12. When a building design exceeds the maximum height allowance and the building height cannot be reduced, the owner should apply for a variance. A variance is an allowed deviation from zoning regulations. They are often granted where it is impossible or difficult to meet a zoning requirement or where a zoning ordinance does not completely cover unusual conditions.

A conditional use permit is given by a city or zoning jurisdiction to allow, if certain conditions are met, an otherwise prohibited use. This would not be appropriate for a situation where the allowed building height was exceeded.

An easement is the right to use a portion of land owned by another for a specific purpose.

A planned unit development (PUD) is a planning tool for large tracts of land that gives a developer discretion in how the land is developed. Aspects of the plan must comply with standards and restrictions determined by the local planning agency.

The answer is (D).

13. A silt fence is a temporary construction designed to filter water runoff from a construction site and trap sediment before it is washed into drains or nearby bodies of water.

A bioswale is a shallow ditch lined with grass or other ground cover. Like a silt fence, it is designed to slow storm runoff and remove sediments, but it is a permanent construction. Riprap is rock along a watercourse or drainage area designed to prevent erosion. Screen grating would not prevent sediment runoff.

The answer is (D).

14. Zoning regulations typically govern the minimum number of parking and loading spaces required on a site. This should be the first requirement that the architect researches. The *ADA/ABA Accessibility Guidelines* give requirements for the number, size, and configuration of accessible spaces, but this information can only be determined after the total number of parking spaces is established. Although not common, there may be additional requirements in covenants, but these would be determined after zoning regulations were determined. The building code in effect within a jurisdiction does not determine the required number of parking spaces.

The answer is (D).

15. Although zoning setbacks may indirectly influence building height, they have the least effect of the four answer choices. FARs limit the total gross buildable area based on lot size, but when the maximum buildable area is placed within the restriction of zoning setbacks, the building height is thus determined. Bulk plane restrictions limit the area beyond which a building can pass, which often limits the total height.

In the building codes, a building's occupancy group and construction type determine the maximum building area, the maximum height in feet, and the maximum number of stories.

The answer is (D).

16. Exterior material types are not regulated by zoning ordinances, though they may be governed by covenants, development restrictions, and to some extent by building codes. Zoning ordinances do not regulate either minimum or maximum window area.

The answer is (A), (C), (D), and (F).

17. Setbacks are established by the zoning code of a city or county. Zoning controls the various aspects of land use, including allowable uses, the amount of land that can be covered with buildings, bulk of structures, setback distances, and parking and loading space requirements.

The answer is (B).

9 Site Analysis

1. A house is being designed for a new development in a suburban location. The nearest water main is one block away, about 300 ft, and the city currently has no plans to extend the line in the near future. City and county regulations do permit the drilling of wells. What action should the architect recommend to the client regarding the water supply?

(A) Estimate the cost of extending the municipal line, since the water quality is known and it would ensure a long-term supply. Consult with nearby property owners who plan to build in the area to see if they would be willing to share the cost of extending the line.

(B) Drill a test bore to determine the depth, potential yield, and water quality of a well, and compare this information with the cost of extending the municipal line.

(C) Assist the owner in petitioning the city to accelerate its plans for extending the water line to serve new development.

(D) Consult with nearby property owners who use wells and with well drillers to estimate the depth and yield of wells in the area. Compare the estimated cost and feasibility of drilling with the feasibility of extending the municipal line at the owner's cost.

2. In the terminology of Kevin Lynch's 1960 book, *The Image of the City*, an area that is perceived as a symbol of a part of a city is a

(A) node

(B) landmark

(C) district

(D) core

3. Which of these is true of a vegetated roof? (Choose the four that apply.)

(A) It reduces the amount of stormwater runoff on a site.

(B) It reduces the impervious surface area on a site.

(C) It increases the amount of water that can be harvested for nonpotable uses such as landscape irrigation and flushing toilets.

(D) It will have a longer lifespan than a conventional membrane roofing system.

(E) It can minimize heat island effects.

(F) It is more expensive to maintain than a traditional roofing system.

4. A developer plans to construct an office building on a previously undisturbed site. Each of the buildings shown has the same gross square footage. Which of the following diagrams represents the best planning approach?

(A)

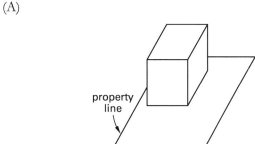

(B)

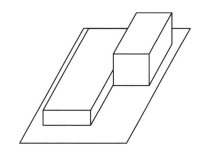

(C)

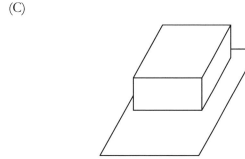

(D)

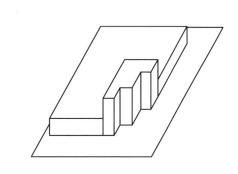

5. A building site with the dimensions shown has setbacks of 25 ft on all four sides. If the allowable FAR is 3.0, which building footprint would be best for sustainable design?

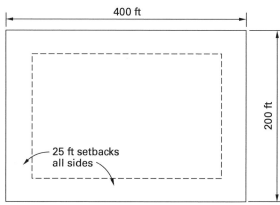

(A)

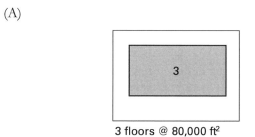

3 floors @ 80,000 ft^2

(B)

6 floors @ 40,000 ft^2

(C)

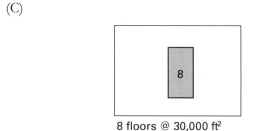

8 floors @ 30,000 ft^2

(D)

10 floors @ 24,000 ft^2

6. An architect is planning an infill building in an urban setting. To maintain the continuity of the public space enclosure defined by the other buildings, the architect should be most sensitive to the

(A) building height

(B) recess line

(C) setback

(D) transition line

7. An architect plans a large building on an urban site. The length of the building is placed along the property line at the sidewalk and aligned with the street's other buildings. This is an example of creating a(n)

(A) path

(B) district

(C) node

(D) edge

8. An architect is studying several sites for possible development by a client. Of the following sites, the one most likely to be buildable is

(A) a designated wetland

(B) a brownfield

(C) in a floodplain

(D) an endangered species habitat

9. Information about the elevations or contours of a building site is found in a

(A) deed of trust

(B) metes and bounds description

(C) plat

(D) survey

10. Information about street drainage in a city would be obtained by contacting the city's

(A) public works department

(B) building department

(C) planning department

(D) department of highways

11. In a dense urban context, site analysis prior to design should include studies of which of the following? (Choose the four that apply.)

(A) solar shading

(B) drainage

(C) imageability

(D) surrounding historical context

(E) land values

(F) views

12. During the evaluation of a proposed construction site, the architect sketched the property lines, building location, existing sewer line in the adjacent street, and proposed location of the sanitary sewer connecting the building to the main line, as shown.

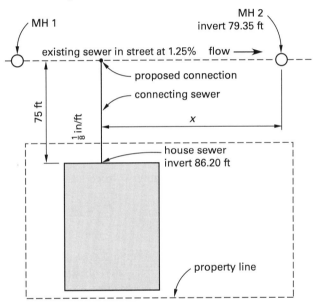

In order to determine if this site and building location are feasible for a sewer connection, what additional piece of information does the architect need?

(A) distance between MH 1 and MH 2

(B) distance x between MH 2 and the connection point

(C) size of the connecting sewer line

(D) invert elevation of MH 1

13. If land is limited, which of the following is the best way to plan parking lots?

(A) two-way circulation with 90° parking on both sides of a drive

(B) 30° parking on both sides of a one-way loop system

(C) combining service circulation with parking at a 45° angle

(D) 90° parking on one side of a one-way circulation drive

14. The fraction of radiant energy reflected from a surface relative to the total radiant energy received by the surface is called

(A) albedo

(B) conductivity

(C) insolation

(D) radiant fraction

15. In the Northern Hemisphere, the optimum tilt angle of an active solar collector for year-round use is approximately equal to the

(A) solar altitude on the spring and fall equinoxes

(B) solar altitude on the winter solstice

(C) building's latitude

(D) building's latitude plus 15°

16. For overall energy conservation and cost-effectiveness in a temperate climate, the most advantageous type of earth-sheltered building would be one that is

(A) built into the side of a south-facing hill

(B) above ground with earth bermed against all sides

(C) above ground with a thick covering of earth and vegetation on the roof

(D) completely underground with a central court that is open to the sky

17. A small, three-story rectangular office building in a temperate climatic region is planned for the site shown.

To simplify grading, the long dimension of the building will be placed parallel to the contour lines.

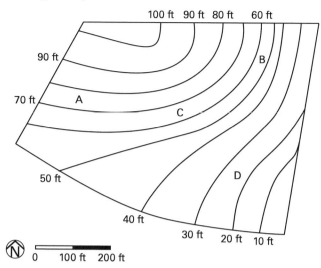

Which of the four locations indicated would be best suited for a building designed to demonstrate the application of passive solar heating?

(A) location A

(B) location B

(C) location C

(D) location D

18. Contour lines are shown.

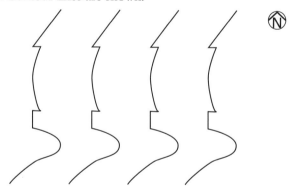

These contour lines typically indicate a

(A) sidewalk sloping down from east to west with a berm on the south side

(B) road with drainage in the middle and a sidewalk and berm on the south

(C) swale adjacent to a walking path sloping from northeast to southwest

(D) curbed street sloping up from west to east next to a drainage ditch

19. An architect is planning a site for a complex of office buildings and wishes to specify ground surface materials that will help to moderate the microclimate. To meet this goal, the architect should specify materials with

(A) high albedo and high conductivity

(B) low albedo and low conductivity

(C) high albedo and low conductivity

(D) low albedo and high conductivity

20. Which of the following statements are correct about site slopes? (Choose the four that apply.)

(A) Roads in northern climates can safely have up to a 12% grade.

(B) A 1.5% slope is suitable for rough paving.

(C) Landscaped areas near buildings should have at least a 2% slope away from the structure.

(D) A safe sidewalk slopes in the direction of travel no more than 2.5%.

(E) Sidewalk cross slopes must be a maximum of 2%.

(F) Slopes for grass for recreational use can have up to a 5% slope.

21. A topographic survey of a small office building indicates that the east side yard has a horizontal to vertical slope of 40% along a 30 ft length between the property line and the elevation at which the grade must contact the proposed building. To be compatible with the adjacent property landscaping, the owner wants to put in mowed grass landscaping. What is the least expensive way of reworking this area to make this possible?

(A) Build a 5 ft high retaining wall at the property line, and regrade between the wall and the building.

(B) Build one 4 ft high retaining wall midway between the property line and the building.

(C) Build two 4 ft high retaining walls at the third points between the property line and the building.

(D) Terrace the slope with three short retaining walls and four strips of grass.

22. The building site shown is surrounded on four sides by city streets. Which building and road layout is most appropriate for the site topography?

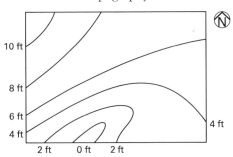

(A)

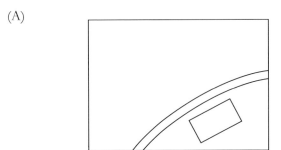

(B)

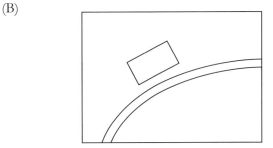

(C)

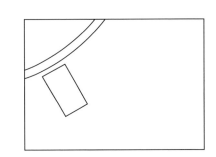

(D)

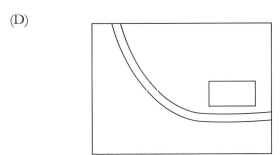

23. The plan shown links a restaurant deck with a patio area below the restaurant and adjacent to a pond. Using the maximum allowable slope for the ramps and the given slopes for the concrete walk and patio area, place the given elevations in the boxes provided to establish the lowest possible elevation of the deck. The lowest portion of the patio must be at least 4 ft higher than the pond.

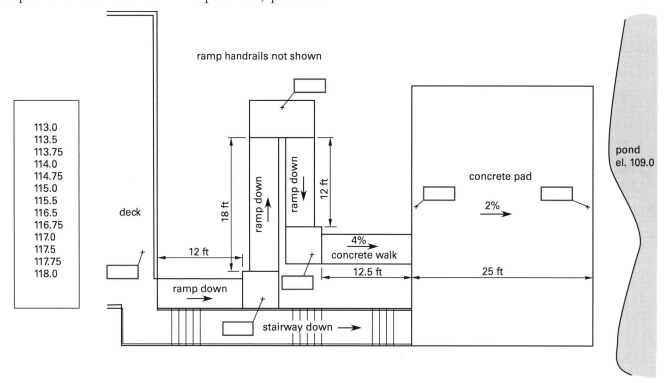

Solutions

1. Even though the nearest water line is 300 ft away, the best recommendation would be to use city water, where the quality and quantity are known and a long-term supply is assured. Although nearby property owners might or might not be willing to share the cost, the owner still would be best advised to extend the line.

Drilling a test bore could help determine the depth, potential yield, and water quality, but that would cost almost as much as drilling a well.

Petitioning the city to extend the line would be time-consuming and probably not successful if the city had already decided against it.

Asking nearby property owners who use wells about their experience would yield useful information, but even if the cost and water quality were acceptable, extending the municipal line would still be the preferred course of action.

The answer is (A).

2. A core is the focus of a district that may be perceived as a symbol of that part of the city. The core is often located at the junction of primary paths, or it could be an element or feature that influences the rest of the area. For example, a core might be a large open air market, a baseball stadium, or a street with lots of shops and restaurants. A core attracts people to the area, is served by the major transportation paths, and is the first image that most people associate with that part of the city.

The Image of the City discusses the legibility of cities and ways to "read" them. It also focuses on the mental images of cities that people use to find their way. There are five elements in Lynch's city; in Lynch's words, these are

- *paths*: "channels along which the observer customarily, occasionally, or potentially moves"

- *edges*: "linear elements not used or considered paths by the observer"

- *districts*: "sections of the city which the observer mentally enters 'inside of' and which are recognizable as having some common, identifying character"

- *nodes*: "points, the strategic spots in a city into which an observer can enter, and which are the intensive foci to and from which he is traveling"

- *landmarks*: "another type of point reference, but in this case, the observer does not enter within them, they are external"

The answer is (D).

3. A vegetated roof is a roofing system that consists of a layer of plants and soil contained within an impermeable plastic liner on top of the structural roof assembly. Captured rainwater is used to irrigate the plants, and the moisture is released back into the atmosphere through evapotranspiration. Because the rainwater is used for irrigation of the plants on the roof, this technique reduces the amount of water that can be harvested for other non-potable uses.

A vegetated roof reduces the impervious surface area on a site; as the depth of the pan holding the soil and plants increases, the runoff coefficient of the surface decreases. Garden roofs have the added advantage of minimizing heat island effects. The roofs may be designed as active gardens requiring tending and watering, or may contain plants that require little to no maintenance. Generally, the lifespan of a vegetated roof is longer and overall maintenance costs are less than would be incurred with a conventional roof system because the roofing membrane is protected from ultraviolet radiation by the layers of organic material.

The answer is (A), (B), (D), and (E).

4. Designing a taller building with a smaller footprint to minimize site disturbance is the best approach to development on a previously undisturbed, or greenfield, site. A smaller footprint results in less area of impervious surfaces (which minimizes runoff) and limits the disturbance to existing landscaping and wildlife habitats. A smaller footprint generally results in a more energy- and resource-efficient building as well, with lower long-term maintenance costs.

The answer is (A).

5. The floor area ratio (FAR) is the total floor area of the building divided by the total site area. Based on the given building site, the total site area is 80,000 ft^2. The total floor area of the buildings in each option is 240,000 ft^2, so all options have a FAR of 3.0.

For sustainable design, the footprint of the building should be minimized to reduce disturbance of the natural landscaping and to minimize the impervious area. Although not part of the question, the parking, walks, grading, and other site development should also be minimized.

The answer is (D).

6. To maintain the continuity of the public space enclosure defined by the other buildings, an architect should be most sensitive to the recess line. In urban site planning, the recess line is the top of the full-width plane of a building facade, which effectively defines the enclosure of public space relative to the distance between it and an opposite facade. If there is any portion of the building above the recess line, it is set back to provide daylighting or views, so it does not affect the sense of enclosure of the public space. The building height and the recess line are not necessarily at the same elevation.

A setback is simply the minimum horizontal distance between the property line and the building. The transition line is a line running the full width of the facade and that may be expressed as a change of material or limited projection. The transition line may divide the facade somewhere below the recess line without altering the overall composition of the public space.

The answer is (B).

7. An edge is a linear element other than a path that forms a boundary between two districts or that breaks some type of continuity. A solid wall of a building (even if penetrated by doors and windows) aligned with other buildings on the same street would form an edge. In this situation, the edge of the building would break the continuity of the street and open space. It would not be a path because it cannot be traveled on. A district is a two-dimensional area, and a node is a strategic center of interest that people can enter.

The answer is (D).

8. Each option listed has its own disadvantages. However, a brownfield probably would be the most buildable because, although it would take additional money and time, contaminates could be removed or otherwise mitigated. In addition, federal tax credits and incentive programs may be available to encourage the use of a brownfield site.

A floodplain would be very difficult to build on, assuming that the local, state, and federal regulations allowed it at all, because increased construction costs and continuing insurance costs could make it economically infeasible. Wetlands and endangered species habitats could not be used for development.

The answer is (B).

9. Of the choices given, a survey is the only document that includes information on land elevations, which are indicated either with spot elevations or continuous contours.

A deed of trust is a written document that primarily describes the owner of the property and from whom it was purchased. A deed includes a description of the property, either by address or lot description, but it does not include land elevation information. A metes and bounds description is a written description of the boundaries of a

parcel of land. It defines the perimeter of the site by using a starting point and describing each boundary line by angle of bearing and length. A plat is a legal description of a subdivided piece of property that includes information on lots, streets, rights-of-way, and easements, among other items.

The answer is (D).

10. The public works department (or a similarly named department) would be responsible for design and maintenance of a city's road drainage, which would be part of the storm sewage system.

The department of highways would most likely be the state agency responsible for design and construction of the roads themselves. Building departments and planning departments are not directly involved in wastewater drainage.

The answer is (A).

11. A solar shading study would show how the proposed building would block sunlight on other buildings as well as on the streets and outdoor areas. An imageability study determines how existing buildings, streets, and public spaces contribute to the neighborhood's image; that is, those elements defined by Kevin Lynch in his book, *The Image of the City*. This information could then be used to suggest ways that the proposed building could reinforce the existing urban context.

A study of the neighborhood's historic context would reveal significant historic structures and influences and may suggest how the proposed building could better fit into the community. A view analysis would show the significant views from the site and indicate where windows, entries, and how other features on the proposed building should be positioned.

In a dense urban area, drainage would not be an important consideration for early site analysis, as most of the site would be taken up with buildings. Land values would have already had an effect on the decision to purchase the site and is not critical for site analysis prior to design.

The answer is (A), (C), (D), and (F).

12. To calculate the invert elevation of the connection point to see if the connecting line would fall above or below the main line, determine the distance x and then work backward from the invert elevation of manhole (MH) 2 using the slope of 1.25%. This will give the invert elevation of the main line where the connection will be made. The lowest point of the connecting sewer line can be calculated using the house sewer invert elevation, the $1/8$ in/ft slope, and the 75 ft distance.

The distance between MH 1 and MH 2 is irrelevant because the slope and one invert elevation are known. An invert is the low point or bottom of a pipe or manhole in a sewage system. The size of the connecting sewer line does affect the minimum slope, but the slope is already given as $\frac{1}{8}$ in/ft. The invert elevation of MH 1 is also irrelevant because the slope and invert of MH 2 are known.

This problem requires an understanding of the importance of gravity flow in drainage and how to calculate slopes. Although this problem does not require calculation of the invert elevation at the point of connection, it assumes a knowledge of what is required. The information needed is either the distance between two points and the elevation of the two points, or the elevation of one point, the slope, and the distance to the second point.

Be aware that a 1% slope is approximately $\frac{1}{8}$ in/ft and a 2% slope is approximately $\frac{1}{4}$ in/ft.

The answer is (B).

13. 90° parking layouts are always the most efficient if space is limited. A single-loaded circulation drive providing access to parking is not as efficient as two rows of parking sharing one drive.

The answer is (A).

14. A surface's albedo is calculated as the reflected radiant energy divided by the total (received) radiant energy. Albedo can range from zero to 1.0. A surface with an albedo of 1.0 is a perfect mirror (i.e., all energy is reflected). A surface with an albedo of zero is a perfect black matte surface (i.e., all energy, or radiant heat, is absorbed).

Conductivity is the rate at which heat flows through a material. Insolation is the total solar radiation on a horizontal surface. Radiant fraction is not a real term.

The answer is (A).

15. The best orientation of solar panels, either for heating or photovoltaics, is approximately the latitude of the building location or slightly greater. For space heating systems, an angle of the latitude plus 15 degrees is optimum for the winter heating season.

The answer is (C).

16. A building built into a south-facing slope gains the advantages of an earth-sheltered structure (stable earth temperature, protection from cold north winds, and natural soundproofing), while keeping the south side open for passive solar energy use and minimizing the costs of earth moving.

Providing earth berms against four sides of an above-ground building increases costs for earth moving and

decreases the opportunity to use the south facade for solar heat gain. A building with a vegetated roof cover, or "green roof," does reduce both heat gain and heat loss over the roof, but it costs more to build and does not help protect the sides of the building. Underground buildings with courtyards have the advantage of stable earth temperature but are expensive to build and have little window area.

The answer is (A).

17. For solar heating in a temperate climate, the best orientation for a rectangular building is with the long side positioned about 17° east of south. This orientation provides maximum radiant heat gain. Assuming that the building will be oriented parallel to the contours as stated in the problem, the other locations on the site would tend to position the building in other directions.

It is important to understand the basic planning guidelines for the four general climatic regions of the United States: cold or cool, temperate, hot-arid, and hot-humid. Most questions concerning climate refer to the temperate region, but an understanding of the design principles for any region is essential. Many of these principles are described in *Design with Climate* by Victor Olgyay.

The answer is (C).

18. This pattern is characteristic of roads with a crown in the middle sloping toward curbs on either side. As with any contour map, contour lines representing a ridge (which is what a crown of a road is in miniature) point in the direction of the downslope, so this road slopes down from east to west (or up from west to east as the answer choice states). The contours pointing in the other direction represent a ditch. Just as with any valley on a contour map, the lines point in the direction of the upslope.

The answer is (D).

19. Specifying materials with low albedo and high conductivity will help to moderate the microclimate. Albedo is a measurement of a material's solar reflectance: the higher the number, the more reflective the surface. Conductivity measures the speed with which heat travels through a material.

Examples of materials with low albedo are traditional concrete and dark-colored gravel. Materials with high conductivity include sand and soil.

The answer is (D).

20. Most roads should be kept at a grade of less than 10%; very short roads and parking garage ramps are exceptions. In northern climates, where snow and ice are a problem, it is even more important to maintain gentle slopes. A 12% grade would not be safe and could make driving difficult. Grass slopes for grass for recreation should have a maximum 3% slope. Table 9.3 in the *ARE5 Review Manual* lists recommended slopes for various uses.

The answer is (B), (C), (D), and (E).

21. Building a 5 ft wall is more expensive and does not achieve the owner's goal of being compatible with the neighboring landscaping. Building two or three retaining walls also works but is more expensive.

In order to landscape with mowed grass, a maximum slope of 3:1, or about 33%, is required. The current slope is 40%, so it will have to be reduced. Because the grade at the property line cannot be changed and the grading at the building is fixed, one or more retaining walls will be required.

To analyze how this might be accomplished, determine the elevation distance between the property line and the proposed building. The elevation distance, d, is calculated using horizontal distance, L, and slope, G.

$$G = \left(\frac{d}{L}\right) \times 100\%$$

$$d = \frac{GL}{100\%} = (40\%)(30 \text{ ft})$$

$$= 12 \text{ ft}$$

To minimize cost, the number of retaining walls should be kept to a minimum, and each retaining wall should be 4 ft or less in height. This height can be constructed without extensive engineering work or extensive footing construction.

As shown in the retaining wall study, if one 4 ft wall is constructed midway between the property line and the building, the resulting slope is 27.6%.

$$G = \left(\frac{d}{L}\right) \times 100\% = \left(\frac{4 \text{ ft}}{14.6 \text{ ft}}\right) \times 100\%$$

$$= 27.6\%$$

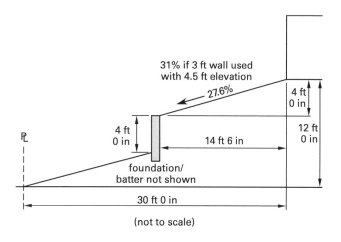

(not to scale)

This slope is within the 33% maximum slope necessary for mowed grass. In order to minimize costs even more, constructing a 3 ft retaining wall would make the slope about 31%, which is still within the acceptable range for mowed grass.

The answer is (B).

22. Without knowing other conditions of the site, the best placement of the building and road is based on road grading and building construction on the existing topography. Roads should cut across slopes gradually to minimize steep grades, so this eliminates option (D) where the road runs perpendicular to the slope. The road is well placed in option (C), but the length of the building runs perpendicular to the slope, which would make construction more difficult and expensive. Option (A) works fairly well, with a gradual slope for the road and the building on level ground, but the road is in a valley and on the north side of the building. Option (B) places the building parallel to the contour lines, is on a south-facing slope, and has a road gently rising across the grade with curves following the direction of the contours, so this is the best choice.

The answer is (B).

23. To determine the lowest possible elevation, start with the pond elevation, H_1, and use the maximum allowable accessible slope of 1:12, to find the lowest elevations, H_2 and H_3, of the concrete patio and pad.

$$H_2 = H_1 + 4 \text{ ft}$$

$$= 109 \text{ ft} + 4 \text{ ft}$$

$$= 113 \text{ ft}$$

The high point of the pad is a 2% grade, or 2 ft per 100 ft.

$$H_3 = H_2 + (0.02)(25 \text{ ft})$$

$$= 113 \text{ ft} + 0.5 \text{ ft}$$

$$= 113.5 \text{ ft}$$

The elevation for the landing between the ramp and the concrete walk, H_4, which is a 4% percent grade, is

$$H_4 = H_3 + (\%\text{grade})(\text{concrete walk})$$

$$= 113.5 \text{ ft} + (0.04)(12.5)$$

$$= 114 \text{ ft}$$

Working upward using a 1:12 maximum slope, the elevation of the landing between the ramp down and ramp up, H_5, is

$$H_5 = H_4 + \left(\frac{1 \text{ ft}}{12 \text{ ft}}\right)(12 \text{ ft})$$

$$= 114 \text{ ft} + 1 \text{ ft}$$

$$= 115 \text{ ft}$$

At the intersection of the ramps down, in an 18 ft distance, the elevation of the ramp landing, H_6, is

$$H_6 = H_5 + \left(\frac{1 \text{ ft}}{12 \text{ ft}}\right)(18 \text{ ft})$$
$$= 115 \text{ ft} + 1.5 \text{ ft}$$
$$= 116.5 \text{ ft}$$

The minimum deck elevation, H_7, across another 12 ft horizontal distance is

$$H_7 = H_6 + \left(\frac{1 \text{ ft}}{12 \text{ ft}}\right)(12 \text{ ft})$$
$$= 116.5 \text{ ft} + 1 \text{ ft}$$
$$= 117.5 \text{ ft}$$

Illustration for Sol. 23

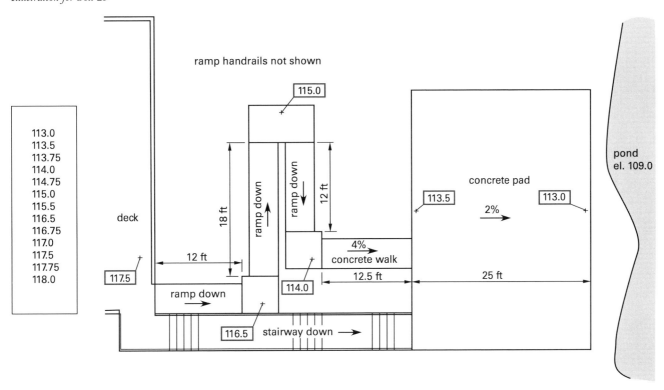

10 Building Analysis

1. A graywater system would be integrated most appropriately into a(n)

(A) laundromat

(B) office building

(C) residence

(D) restaurant

2. Which of the following energy sources would be the most economical option for heating a small retail building in Washington state?

(A) electricity

(B) natural gas

(C) oil

(D) steam

3. What combination of lighting would be the most appropriate choice for a women's clothing store?

(A) color-improved mercury lamps with metal halide accent lighting

(B) limited natural daylight, warm white deluxe fluorescent for general illumination, and tungsten halogen for accent lighting

(C) incandescent general lighting with low-voltage accent lighting on displays

(D) daylighting for general illumination and incandescent fixtures for dressing areas and display lighting

4. During strategic facility planning, an affinity is identified between two functions that will occur within the facility. For this reason, the facility must be planned so that the spaces in which these two functions will occur

(A) are in the same position on different floors

(B) will not both be inaccessible to occupants at any time

(C) are the same in size, furnishings, and equipment

(D) are physically near each other

5. Which of the following are typically part of the project schedule developed by the architect during the programming process? (Choose the four that apply.)

(A) architectural services negotiation

(B) pre-design phase

(C) bidding time

(D) construction

(E) commissioning

(F) construction schedule

6. Analyze the adjacency diagram and resulting block plan shown.

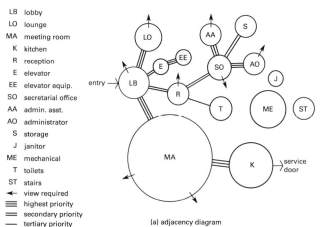

What is its most significant weakness?

- (A) The secretarial office is not adjacent to the reception room.
- (B) The storage space is not near the secretarial office.
- (C) janitor's room is not near the toilet rooms.
- (D) The lounge is too far from the lobby.

7. Which of the following building types would probably have the lowest efficiency?

- (A) shoe store in a shopping mall
- (B) community library
- (C) hospital
- (D) college chemistry building

8. Which of the water heaters shown would be the least efficient for domestic use?

(A)

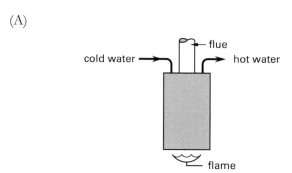

(B)

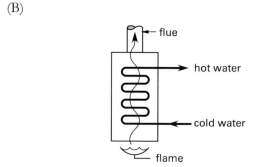

(C)

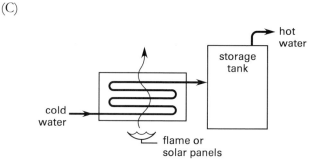

(D)

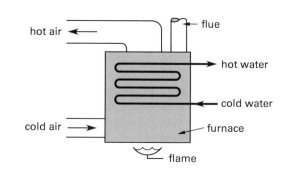

9. Which is the most accurate method of determining the value of a property?

(A) development method

(B) comparison method

(C) income approach method

(D) allocation method

10. The net-to-gross ratio for a small retail store has been estimated by the architect to be 80%. The client has told the architect that 60,000 ft^2 of sales and storage space are required. The architect should plan for a building area of ___ ft^2. (Fill in the blank.)

11. While developing the preliminary project schedule during the programming phase, which would be the most reliable sources of information about construction time? (Choose the three that apply.)

(A) historical documents on similar projects from the architect's office

(B) annually published cost and scheduling book

(C) the construction manager whom the client has hired for the job

(D) a contracting firm that has done work for the architect in the past

(E) other architects who have completed similar projects

(F) architectural and construction magazine articles on similar projects

12. A small medical clinic is being planned for a suburban location on an open, level site. It is to include services of general practice, obstetrics/family planning, testing and laboratories and dental offices, along with medical offices and an administration area. All together the building will have a net area of about 70,000 ft^2. Access to the building is primarily by automobile. The group developing the project wants the facility to be a comfortable, friendly place that minimizes the anxiety of a visit to the doctor and that makes it as easy as possible to get around. It expects the venture to be successful and each department to grow as the catchment area grows.

In order to meet the goals of the client, which of the following design responses would be most appropriate? (Choose the four that apply.)

(A) Group the waiting areas and the reception area together to encourage social interaction.

(B) Specify furniture that is attached to the floor to maintain organized seating.

(C) Base the size of the waiting rooms on a behavior setting where establishing territory should be encouraged.

(D) Develop a different color scheme for each of the separate services.

(E) Design a children's play area in one corner of waiting areas.

(F) Arrange individual chair seating against walls and other objects so it faces room entries.

13. A medical facility will be located on large, flat site. It consists of several departments, each of which is expected to expand but at different times. Which of the following organizational concepts would be the most appropriate for such a medical facility?

(A) grid

(B) axial

(C) central

(D) radial

14. A high-tech, startup, computer company with several divisions has hired an architect to do programming for a new facility. The client wants to place all divisions in one building in the first phase but expects each division to grow at six-month intervals. Which of the following aspects of flexibility related to this facility is the most important in developing the structural framing concept?

(A) convertibility

(B) versatility

(C) expandability

(D) accessibility

15. A large company is planning to construct new corporate headquarters. The vice president of operations presents a list of personnel, their positions in the firm, and company-mandated space standards to the architect. This list would be described as a

(A) facilities program

(B) functional program

(C) firm program

(D) component program

16. A 50-year-old warehouse that shows no obvious signs of deterioration is to be remodeled as an office building. Which of the following areas should be most carefully evaluated at the start to help determine the project's feasibility? (Choose the four that apply.)

(A) ceiling heights

(B) fire protection systems

(C) foundation

(D) roof

(E) structural framework

(F) windows

17. In order to gather and document information quickly for the restoration of a historic building with a large interior dome, the architect should recommend that the client use

(A) field measurements

(B) false-color imaging

(C) photogrammetry

(D) laser scanning

18. Social contact and interaction in a picnic pavilion would be promoted most by

(A) making the dimensions of the pavilion small enough that the anticipated number of users would cross into each other's "personal distance"

(B) designing benches around the support columns so people would have a place to sit and talk

(C) separating the cooking and serving area from the dining area and entrance

(D) providing a variety of informal spaces of different sizes, locations, and uses

19. An architect is asked to calculate the rentable area of the following office space according to ANSI/BOMA Z65.1, *Office Buildings: Standard Methods of Measurement.* The columns are 1 ft by 1 ft. The exterior walls are 1 ft thick and the inside face of the glass is 6 in from the inside face

of the interior wall. The corridor walls and demising walls are 4 in thick. Which of the measurement procedures would result in an undersized rentable area?

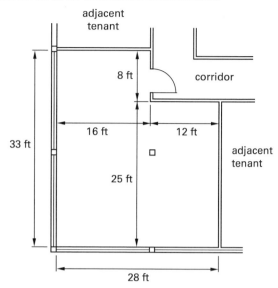

(A) Take the width of the office as 28 ft 8 in.

(B) Use 33 ft as the length of the office.

(C) Deduct the area of the column.

(D) Include a portion of the common restrooms and corridors.

20. The process of strategic facility planning begins with the analysis of three basic business drivers. What are they? (Choose the three that apply.)

(A) company's geographic location

(B) company's overall sales

(C) company's revenue

(D) local business regulations

(E) market volatility

(F) number of employees in the company

21. During the programming process for a building project, the client asks the architect to diffuse costs by building in stages. The architect should identify this requirement as which of the following programming concepts?

(A) flexibility

(B) phasing

(C) expansibility

(D) priority

22. A developer who is purchasing farmland to convert to a housing development would most likely finance the project with a

    (A)   bridge loan

    (B)   mezzanine loan

    (C)   blanket loan

    (D)   conventional mortgage

23. On average, where do construction costs tend to be lowest?

    (A)   in urban areas

    (B)   in suburbs

    (C)   in rural areas

    (D)   construction costs for a project are the same regardless of the locale

24. An accessible route must serve

    (A)   all accessible spaces and parts of a building

    (B)   the corridors, stairs, elevators, and toilet rooms of a building

    (C)   entrances, parking, toilet rooms, corridors, and drinking fountains

    (D)   those areas where physically disabled people are likely to need access

25. Which of the following areas of a building are considered parts of the means of egress? (Choose the four that apply.)

    (A)   storeroom

    (B)   corridor

    (C)   public sidewalk

    (D)   exterior courtyard

    (E)   city roadway

    (F)   enclosed stairway

Programming & Analysis

Solutions

1. Graywater systems, when allowed by local building and health departments, are most appropriately used where the ratio of nonpotable to potable water needs is relatively high. A laundromat would produce a great amount of wastewater that could be captured for other purposes. A graywater system captures wastewater—for example, from lavatories, washing machines, and other fixtures—that does not contain organic waste. The system then uses the water for irrigation or for nonpotable uses like flushing toilets.

The answer is (A).

2. In the northwestern part of the United States, electrical generating facilities are plentiful and provide a relatively low-cost way to heat buildings.

Natural gas is popular in the Midwest, while oil is commonly used in the northeastern part of the United States. Steam is not economical unless it is produced in a central facility for use in an urban area or is a by-product of other types of power generation.

The answer is (A).

3. The combination of limited natural light, warm white fluorescent general illumination, and tungsten halogen accent lighting offers the best balance of appropriate color rendering and energy efficiency. Daylighting would provide natural light for viewing clothes and excellent color rendering, but would need to be limited in order to prevent damage to delicate fabrics. Warm white deluxe lamps would be energy efficient and provide a pleasant, overall light. The tungsten halogen accent lights will provide sparkle to jewelry displays and highlight featured merchandise.

Mercury lamps and metal halide lighting have cooler tones which may render colors inappropriately. Incandescent fixtures throughout would not be energy efficient. Using daylighting for general illumination could damage fabrics and would limit the store's hours of operation to daylight hours.

The answer is (B).

4. Affinity describes the relationship between two functions that are interdependent or need to be in physical proximity to each other. Another term used to express this relationship is adjacency.

The answer is (D).

5. The architect's involvement in scheduling the overall project timeframe begins only after the architect is hired, which occurs after negotiating for the architect's services. The architect cannot schedule construction—only the contractor can do that—although the architect may estimate the time required to help establish what type of project delivery method the client should consider.

Know the different types of scheduling techniques, such as the Gantt schedule (or bar chart) and the critical path method (CPM).

The answer is (B), (C), (D), and (E).

6. The secretarial office has a secondary priority so it does not have to be adjacent to the reception room, just near it. The more important adjacency is the administrative assistant's office and the administrator's office on either side of the secretarial office. Although the storage room is not close to the secretarial office, this is a secondary adjacency and can be easily reached through the corridor. The janitor's space has no adjacency indicated so presumably it can be located anywhere. The adjacency diagram indicates that the lounge should be immediately adjacent to the lobby but some distance away via the corridor.

The answer is (D).

7. Efficiency, also called the net-to-gross ratio, expresses the relationship of programmed spaces to circulation, structural, and utility spaces. It is calculated by dividing the sum of the programmed spaces (the net floor area) by the total building area (the gross floor area), and is expressed as a percentage.

Buildings with heavy mechanical and circulation requirements, like hospitals, often have much lower efficiencies than buildings such as offices and retail stores. Buildings that allocate a great deal of floor space to housing the structural system (e.g., large columns, thick masonry walls) are generally less efficient than those that do not have these features. Although efficiency is determined in part by the building type, it is also dependent on the designer's skill in creating a layout with a circulation plan that occupies a minimum amount of space, so that the majority of the building's floor area can be allocated to programmed uses.

A hospital would have the lowest efficiency of the building types listed because of the space occupied by specialized mechanical systems, the wide clearances needed in hallways, and the complex circulation paths.

The answer is (C).

8. Option (D) illustrates an indirect, tankless type of water heating system. Water is heated in a furnace or boiler whose primary purpose is to provide space heating for the building. Therefore, to maintain desired quantities of hot water at all times, the furnace would have to operate during warm periods when space heating is not required. Generally, this type of heating system is used in conjunction with another source of heating for the water only. The furnace only provides hot water when it is operating to heat the building.

The answer is (D).

9. The comparison method, or market data approach, uses information on similar-sized properties with similar amenities that are for sale in the area at the time of valuation to determine the value of a property. An investor considering the purchase of undeveloped property for commercial use would consider the prices of other similar parcels in the area, but may need to adjust the valuation to reflect other factors, such as location or access to existing utilities. If market data is available, the comparison method is the most accurate way to determine the value of all types of properties.

If market data is not available, one of the other three methods listed may be used. The development method, or anticipated use method, is used when the property may be subdivided for residential or commercial use. For example, a developer purchasing a large amount of farmland with the intention of converting it to a residential subdivision would consider the costs required for development, the physical attributes of the property and how they may affect costs (e.g., soil quality), the amount of time it will take to sell the lots, and the anticipated selling prices. The costs of development would be deducted from the projected sales prices to determine a value for the land.

The income approach method, also called the residual method, may be used for properties in areas where there is no unimproved land and no market data against which to compare. The income that will be generated by the property is estimated and compared against the cost of the site improvements. The income generated by the improvements determines the value. This method, like all valuation methods, makes the assumption that the improvements represent the highest and best use of the property.

The allocation method is used to determine the value of improved properties. This method determines the land value by deducting the value of site improvements from the total value of the property (which is equal to buildings plus land). The remainder is the value of the land.

The answer is (B).

10. The net-to-gross ratio is found by dividing the net usable area by the gross area, which includes circulation areas, mechanical rooms, and similar ancillary areas. The desired net usable area is given and the net-to-gross ratio

is known, so the needed gross area can be estimated by dividing the net area by the ratio expressed as a decimal.

$$\text{gross area} = \frac{\text{net usable area}}{\text{net-to-gross ratio}}$$
$$= \frac{60,000 \text{ ft}^2}{0.80}$$
$$= 75,000 \text{ ft}^2$$

The answer is 75,000 ft².

11. Records of similar projects that the architect has maintained would be a fairly accurate source of information about the time required to build. From this historical data, the architect could factor in any unique elements of the new project to arrive at a preliminary schedule that would work reasonably well for programming. The best source of current information would be the construction manager who is part of the building team because that person would have a great deal of experience with managing construction schedules. Other architects who have done similar projects would also be able to offer valuable information on construction time, including any problems they encountered related to completion time.

Annually published cost and scheduling books would not be a good choice because the scheduling information they contain is typically based on number of hours or manpower required to complete individual aspects of construction. Such books would be more useful for estimating time required to complete components of the overall project. Asking a contractor who previously worked with the architect would not be a good choice because, without assurances that they would be awarded the job, the contractor might not be inclined to give accurate information. Magazines are poor sources of information on construction time because they seldom include such information and the projects would be in different geographical locations, making any information unreliable.

The answer is (A), (C), and (E).

12. Grouping the waiting areas and the reception area to encourage interaction would probably be the least desirable option for two reasons. People are usually a little nervous while waiting with strangers and prefer the option to avoid contact in sociofugal space. In addition, because there are different departments in a medium-sized facility, having everyone in one space would be inefficient as well as uncomfortable. One large waiting area would make people feel less at ease and therefore would be counterproductive to the client's goals. Seating that is attached to the floor would seem unfriendly and would not allow for a small amount of personalization or for two or more people waiting together to adjust positions to make the experience more comfortable.

The answer is (C), (D), (E), and (F).

13. On an ample and flat site, terrain probably would not restrict this type of organizational pattern. Because such a facility may grow, but at different times, and because there are several distinct departments, a radial organization would work for each phase and allow for easy growth. An axial pattern might work, but because everyone enters in one place for directions and orientation in a medical facility, the central focus of a radial pattern probably would be preferable.

The answer is (D).

14. For the first phase of this type of building, most functions probably would be fixed, requiring little need for convertibility in the future or multiple use initially. The primary need of expandability would determine the structural framing system employed so that the building could be added onto easily.

The answer is (C).

15. A functional program provides raw data for analysis and development of a facilities program, which considers scope, area requirements, adjacencies, costs, and site analysis. The functional program is usually used to make the case for a new facility by demonstrating that a current facility no longer meets the inhabitants' needs. The owner prepares a functional program (but may be assisted by an architect or programmer) because preparation of this type of program requires an in-depth understanding of the operations of the company.

The answer is (B).

16. The foundation, roof, structural framework, and windows represent major components of a building. If they are inadequate or in poor condition, they could be too expensive to repair or replace while maintaining project feasibility.

The ceiling heights of a warehouse would be sufficient for an office. Fire protection systems would probably be non-existent or would have to be upgraded in any event, so this would be less of an initial concern.

The answer is (C), (D), (E), and (F).

17. Laser scanning would be the best choice because this method could quickly make the required remote measurements from just a few points (or possibly even one). Physical access to any part of the dome would not be required.

Photogrammetry would take more time and might require that control points be placed on the dome and hand surveyed to establish a base coordinate system. Standard field

measurements taken by hand would be very slow, would not be very accurate, and would require extensive scaffolding. False-color imaging would not be at all appropriate because this type of analysis provides no information on field measurements.

The answer is (D).

18. A variety of informal spaces would promote social contact. Forcing too many people within close, personal space would be counterproductive. People would become uncomfortable and defensive. The orientation of the benches would be sociofugal, requiring that people face away from each other. The cooking and serving area would be one of the most popular gathering spaces and a destination for people. Here, people could watch food being prepared, serve themselves, and informally meet other people.

The answer is (D).

19. Calculations of the rentable area of an office follow different rules from calculations of the architectural area of a space. To calculate the rentable area of a space, use the following guidelines.

- When measuring from an exterior wall in which more than 50% of the wall is glass, measure from the inside face of the glass.

- Measure to the inside face of walls between the office and the corridor.

- Measure to the centerline of demising walls, or walls between tenants.

- The rentable area would also include a share of common restrooms and corridors.

- No deductions are made for columns or projections necessary to the building.

The length of the office must include half of the demising partition and the distance to the inside face of the glass.

The answer is (B).

20. Strategic facility planning is a niche service that some architectural firms offer. These firms have expanded the traditional definition of architectural programming to include market analysis and business planning for their clients. Architects who offer this specialty often team with professionals in allied fields such as business, law, industrial engineering, or real estate to offer a comprehensive package of services.

The process of strategic facility planning begins with the analysis of business drivers. Three basic business drivers are considered: the company's revenue, its number of employees, and its overall sales. These data give the analysts a sense of where the company stands in relationship to its competitors.

The team then considers the type and goals of the organization. Corporate clients have a different approach to decision making than nonprofit and government sector clients, and the issues of greatest importance to each must be understood before a particular client can be advised. Demand-side factors (those that benefit the end user) and supply-side factors (those that benefit the landlord) are weighed as well. Depending on the client, these factors may or may not include geographic location, local business regulations, and market volatility. Finally, all these factors are considered in the development of a plan for space utilization and possible growth.

The answer is (B), (C), and (F).

21. The concept of phasing states that a project must be completed in stages to accommodate cost or time constraints.

Refer to all 24 programmatic concepts listed in the book *Problem Seeking* by William M. Peña.

The answer is (B).

22. A blanket loan is a common tool of developers and is used for the purchase of land that a developer intends to subdivide and resell. Generally it includes a clause that releases each subdivided plot from the loan as it is purchased and a portion of the debt is repaid.

A bridge loan is a short-term loan used to close quickly on a property or to finance a project that must begin immediately while waiting for another lender to approve a long-term loan. A hard money loan is similar and is based on the value of the property against which the loan is made. The amount of the loan depends on the quick-sale value of the property or the loan-to-value ratio.

Mezzanine loans, which are often used by developers, are large loans with a variable interest rate that increases substantially near the time that the repayment is due. Stock in the developer's company is used as collateral, as opposed to a conventional loan, where the property itself would serve as collateral. The loan requires a gamble that the property will produce enough revenue to repay the loan when the interest rates escalate.

A conventional mortgage, which may have either a fixed or adjustable interest rate, is secured by the property purchased. The party borrowing the money agrees to repay the loan over a period of time, and when the debt is repaid, the borrower has clear title to the property. If the borrower defaults, the lender may begin foreclosure and seize the property.

The answer is (C).

23. Construction costs tend to be lowest in suburban areas. Workers in urban areas tend to demand higher wage rates, escalating the cost, while access and transportation to remote rural areas can also force the cost to rise. Suburban areas are generally well connected to urban areas by major transportation routes, but they are not so remote that the cost of transporting materials from the city to the site becomes prohibitive.

The answer is (B).

24. By definition, any part of a building that is required to be accessible must be accessible from the entrance of the building.

The answer is (A).

25. Public sidewalks and city roadways are not part of the means of egress because they are examples of the public way. All of the other building areas listed are part of the exit access, the exit, or the exit discharge.

The answer is (A), (B), (D), and (F).

Programming & Analysis

11 Selection of Structural Systems

1. To support the roof of a building with an extra-long span, the most economical steel structural system is

(A) trusses

(B) arches

(C) rigid frames

(D) steel cables

2. For spans of 300 ft or more, the most appropriate steel structural system generally consists of

(A) a skeleton frame comprising beams, girders, and columns

(B) steel trusses

(C) steel rigid frames

(D) steel arches

3. A reinforced concrete slab is generally considered a one-way slab when the ratio of long span to short span is

(A) 1.0

(B) 2.0 or more

(C) 3.0 or more

(D) 4.0 or more

4. In lateral load resisting systems, a steel frame is often used in conjunction with concrete shear walls. What type of load does each component of this system carry?

(A) The steel frame carries most of the vertical gravity load, and the concrete shear walls carry the lateral load.

(B) The steel frame carries the lateral load, and the concrete shear walls carry most of the vertical gravity load.

(C) Both components carry the vertical and lateral loads equally.

(D) The steel frame carries most of the vertical and lateral loads.

5. In wood construction, what is the main benefit of using platform framing as opposed to balloon framing?

(A) reduced vertical shrinkage

(B) increased fire resistance

(C) better resistance for lateral loads

(D) ease of construction

6. A building in an earthquake-prone area is designed to have an open front and shear walls around the other three sides. This constitutes an irregularity. What is the correct and most practical solution in this case?

- (A) Add drag struts to the front.

- (B) Provide a moment-resisting frame in the front.

- (C) Increase the safety factors in the design calculations.

- (D) Change the entire design and close the front with a shear wall.

7. Which of the following statements about concrete walls are true? (Choose the four that apply.)

- (A) Concrete has replaced stone and brick for foundation walls because it is more economical and more watertight.

- (B) Concrete foundation walls are often reinforced at a large reinforcement ratio.

- (C) Plain (unreinforced) concrete foundation walls withstand uneven settlement without serious cracking better than brick masonry walls do.

- (D) Columns may rest on a concrete bearing wall.

- (E) Foundation walls must resist vertical loads and lateral earth pressure.

- (F) Reinforcement in concrete foundation walls is necessary for temperature, shrinkage and uneven settlement.

Solutions

1. For the roof of a building with an extra-long span, the most economical steel structural system is a cable system. The cost of roof support per square foot using cables is generally lower than the cost of using other rigid steel structural systems.

It is estimated that based on normal allowable working stresses and a 10% sag for a suspended cable, a 36 in W-shaped beam can carry its own weight for about 220 ft, while a steel cable can carry its own weight for about 3.3 mi.

The answer is (D).

2. For spans of 300 ft or more, the most appropriate steel structural system generally consists of steel arches. Steel arches are used extensively to support roofs covering large unobstructed floor areas in structures such as hangars, field houses, and exhibition halls with spans often exceeding 300 ft. Rigid frames are generally preferred for intermediate spans.

The answer is (D).

3. A reinforced concrete slab is generally considered a one-way slab when the ratio of long span to short span is 2.0 or more, and it is considered a two-way slab when the ratio is less than 2.0. A one-way slab is reinforced for bending moment in the short direction, and for temperature and shrinkage stresses at the minimum ratio in the long direction. A two-way slab is reinforced for bending moment in both directions.

The answer is (B).

4. The steel frame carries most of the vertical gravity load, and the concrete shear walls carry the lateral load. This system is commonly used, and the concrete shear walls are often placed around the building's mechanical core, enclosing elevators and stairways. The shear walls transmit the lateral forces to the foundation and must be continuous.

The answer is (A).

5. The main benefit of using platform framing is the ease of construction resulting from utilizing the platform in each story for wall and partition frame preassembly.

The answer is (D).

6. The correct and most practical solution is to provide a moment-resisting frame in the front. The rear is rigid and the front is open, so it is flexible. Providing a moment-resisting frame in the front will make the front as rigid as possible while maintaining the possibility of an opening there.

Drag struts will not solve the problem in this case, so option (A) is incorrect. Increasing the safety factors in the design calculations is not a solution. Safety factors are normally given by building codes; designers do not select their own factors.

Also, increasing the safety factors does not resolve the irregularity resulting from a flexible front and a rigid rear. Changing the entire design and eliminating the opening would generally not be a practical solution, so option (D) is incorrect.

The answer is (B).

7. Option (B) is false. Concrete foundation walls are frequently reinforced to better withstand temperature change, shrinkage, and uneven settlement, though reinforcement may be minimal.

Option (C) is also false. Brick masonry foundation walls withstand uneven settlement without serious cracking better than plain concrete.

The answer is (A), (D), (E), and (F).

Case Studies

Case Study 1

A retail client has hired an architect to develop a site located in a northern climate. The site will have a building that houses a small group of boutique shops and a freestanding restaurant, as shown in Resource 3.1. Both the shops and restaurant will be in one-story buildings. The property is approximately 123,000 ft^2, and the topography gently slopes approximately 12 ft from the northeast corner toward a wetlands area in the southwest corner.

As a pedestrian-oriented neighborhood center, the entrances to the shops should face either 5th Avenue or Stuart Street. The restaurant should be accessible from the street, as well as from the parking area. The main facade should face 5th Avenue.

The architect is studying various options to meet the requirements of the client's program, site conditions, and code requirements, while also applying sustainability concepts. To begin preliminary planning, the client has given the architect a summary of the pertinent programming requirements and local regulations, as shown in Resource 3.2. The options the architect has sketched are shown in Resource 3.3.

Resource 3.1 Site Plan

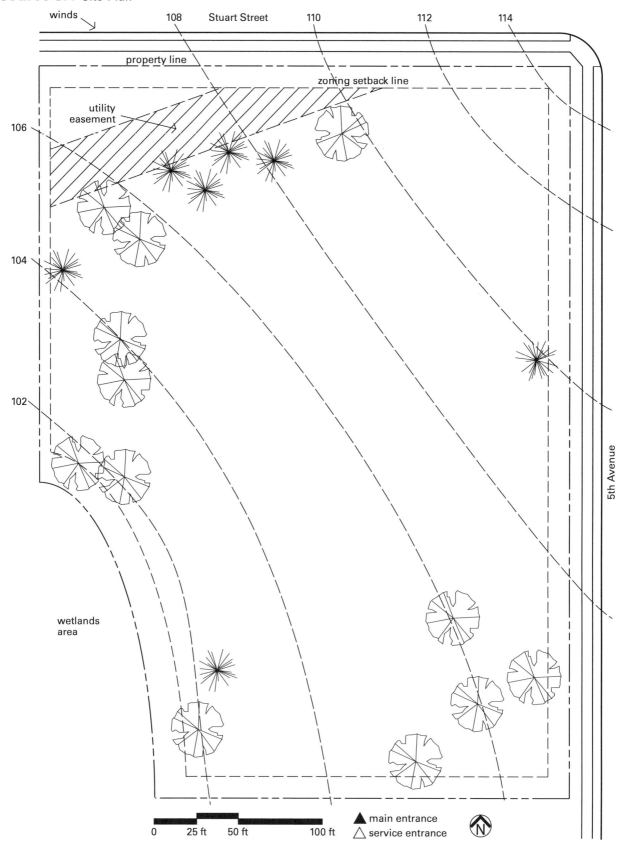

Resource 3.2 Program and Regulation Requirements

	requirements	comments
shops	approximately 7500 ft^2 for inline stores ability to expand by a minimum of 1500 ft^2 parking provided at a ratio of 4 spaces per 1000 gross ft^2 visual impact of parking from the street should be minimized	greater expansion desired
restaurant	approximately 5000 ft^2 access provided from parking as well as from 5th Avenue outdoor deck with a view of the wetlands parking provided at a ratio of 6 spaces per 1000 gross ft^2 separate service drive required	important client gives this a high priority may be minimal drive
codes and regulations	all construction subject to the *International Building Code* (IBC) no building improvement within setbacks except drives and sidewalks no permanent structures in utility easement except drives and sidewalks no building or site development within 50 ft of wetlands no curb cut closer than 200 ft from intersection parking limited to 90° configuration	

Programming & Analysis

Resource 3.3 Alternative Sketches

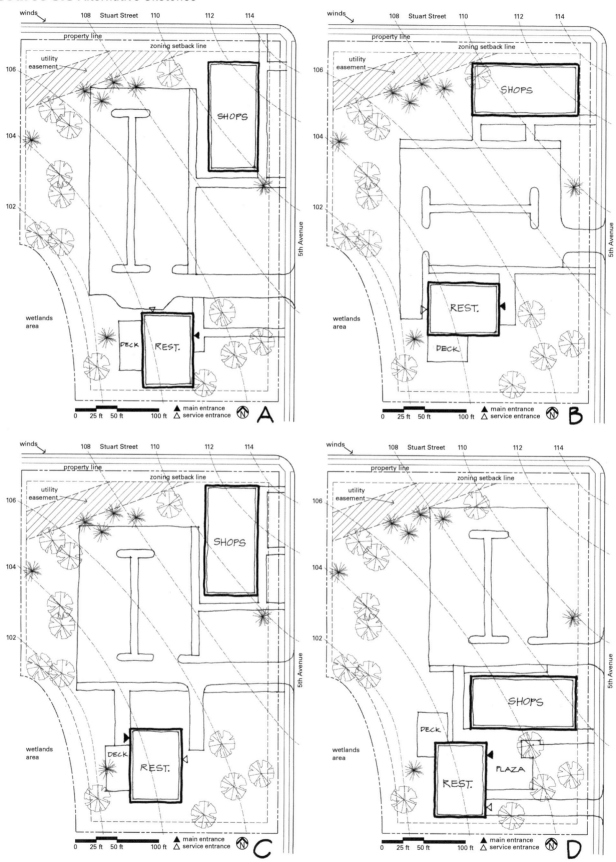

1. What strategy could be used to improve sustainability of the proposed development?

(A) Use permeable paving for the parking lot.

(B) Create a bioswale in the southwest portion of the site.

(C) Locate catch basins at critical points near storm sewers.

(D) Engineer an infiltration basin to catch runoff from the site.

2. What site restriction will have the greatest influence on site planning?

(A) easement restrictions

(B) direction and degree of slope

(C) setback requirements from the wetlands

(D) minimum curb cut location from intersection

3. As shown in Resource 3.3, what inherent quality of the site would most influence the choice of one of the site plans over another?

(A) southern exposure

(B) existing trees

(C) slope

(D) wind direction

4. What is the total site area required for parking, drives, and parking landscaping?

(A) 12,000 ft^2

(B) 18,000 ft^2

(C) 24,000 ft^2

(D) 30,000 ft^2

5. In Resource 3.3, the architect has sketched four possible site plans for the overall layout of the buildings and parking area. Which site plan best satisfies the program requirement of shop expandability?

(A) site plan A

(B) site plan B

(C) site plan C

(D) site plan D

6. Which site plan in Resource 3.3 best satisfies the priorities listed in the building program and regulation requirements of Resource 3.2?

(A) site plan A

(B) site plan B

(C) site plan C

(D) site plan D

7. Analyze the site plans shown in Resource 3.3. Which site plan provides the best pedestrian circulation and urban connection to the neighborhood?

(A) site plan A

(B) site plan B

(C) site plan C

(D) site plan D

8. Analyze the site plans shown in Resource 3.3. Which site plan provides the best relationship between the buildings and parking?

(A) site plan A

(B) site plan B

(C) site plan C

(D) site plan D

9. An alternative layout to the standard inline stores is shown. (See *Illustration for Prob. 9.*)

From an urban planning standpoint, what is the main advantage to this alternative layout?

(A) The shops can be accessed from the street or the plaza.

(B) Parking is near the street and close to the buildings.

(C) Land is available for expansion on the south end.

(D) The shops and restaurant are near each other.

Illustration for Prob. 9

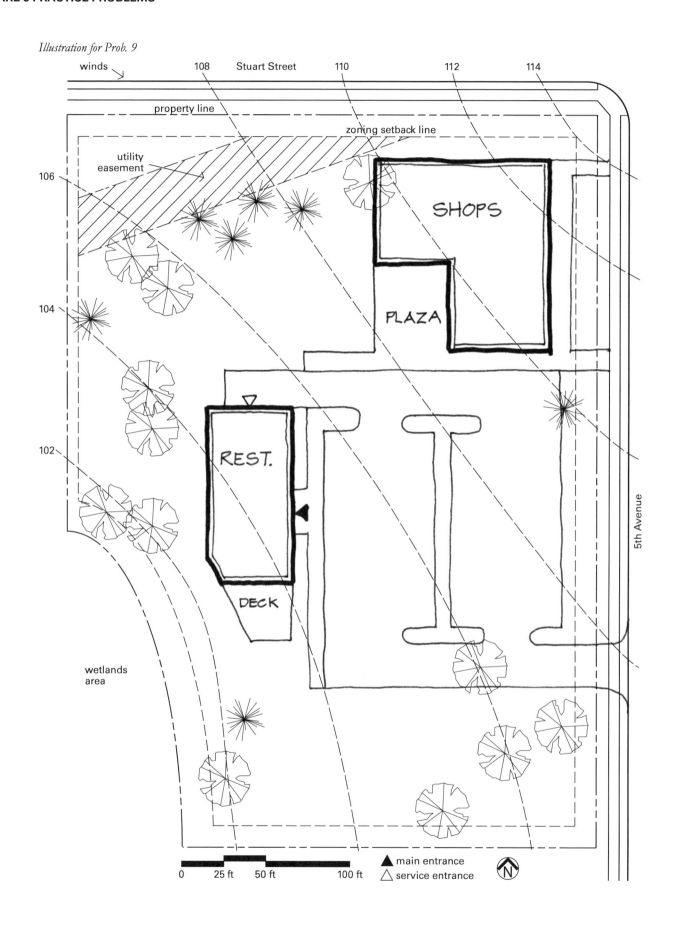

10. The client asked the architect to develop one more alternative layout, which is shown. (See *Illustration for Prob. 10.*)

What are the biggest problems with this alternative layout? (Choose the four that apply).

(A) The expansion of the shops is limited.

(B) The parking lot uses both a single- and double-loaded aisle.

(C) The shops' entrances are not accessible from the parking lot.

(D) The restaurant entrance is not accessible from the street.

(E) The restaurant deck is oriented to the southwest.

(F) The service driveway is improperly located.

Illustration for Prob. 10

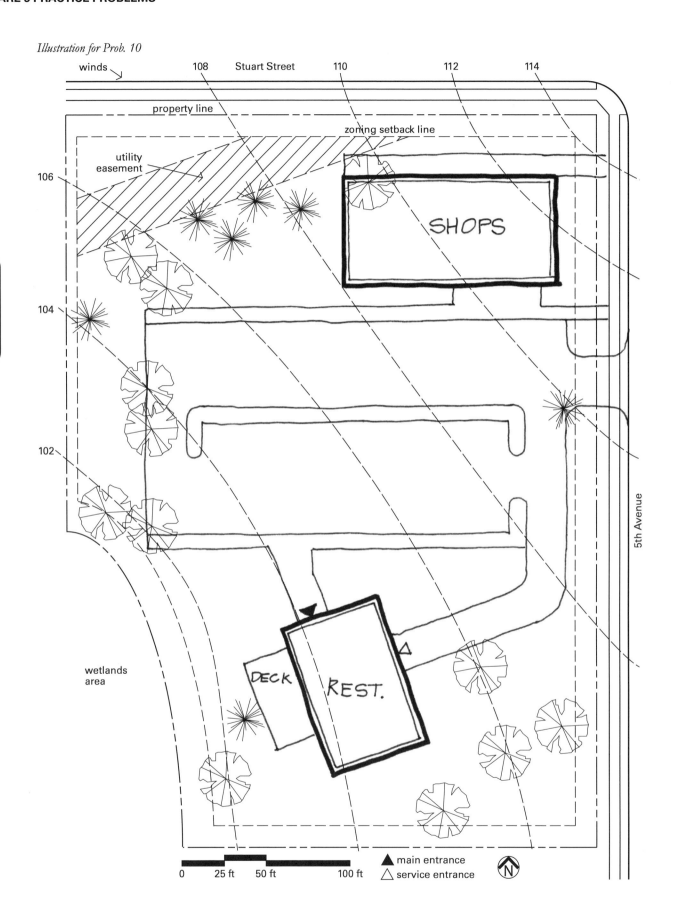

Case Study 2

The county of Lakeland is beginning preliminary planning for a county recreation center, which will include an outdoor amphitheater, a concession building, restrooms, smaller concrete pads, and kiosks for vending and merchandise sales. The recreation center is being funded through a combination of state and county resources. The site is located in a developing semirural area near a large city where most of the new development is single-family homes on one-acre lots. The climate is mild with prevailing winds from the northwest.

The county has retained an architect to review a preliminary block layout of the proposal.

The seating area will be arranged in a series of semicircular terraces, each retained by a low wall at seating height. The space between walls will have a hard surface for seating and a grass surface wide enough for viewers to place lawn chairs or spread blankets. Concrete pads will be located throughout the seating area for accessible seating. There is concern that concerts played at the amphitheater will generate excessive sound, so measures need to be taken to mitigate noise.

The amphitheater will use existing parking to the north of the proposed amphitheater. Two new parking lots will be constructed, one to the west and one to the east. The parking capacity will be 1800 cars in lot A and 925 cars in lot B.

Parking spaces will be provided in accordance with *ADA Accessibility Guidelines* Table 208.

Where more than one parking facility is provided on a site, the number of accessible spaces provided on the site will be calculated according to the number of spaces required for each parking facility.

Resource 3.4 Amphitheater Summary Program and Accessible Parking Requirements

space	area (ft^2)	notes
seating area	50,000	capacity 5000 on stepped platforms
stage	3200	
performers' support	4500	directly behind stage
stage storage	1000	
concession/restrooms	4000	at top of amphitheater
restrooms (2 @ 1000)	2000	1 on each side of amphitheater

Resource 3.5 Parking Spaces in Accordance with *ADA Accessibility Guidelines* Table 208

total number of parking spaces provided in parking facility	minimum number of required accessible parking spaces
1–25	1
26–50	2
51–75	3
76–100	4
101–150	5
151–200	6
201–300	7
301–400	8
401–500	9
501–1000	2% of total
1001 and over	20, plus 1 for each 100 or fraction thereof over 1000

Resource 3.6 Amphitheater Site Plan

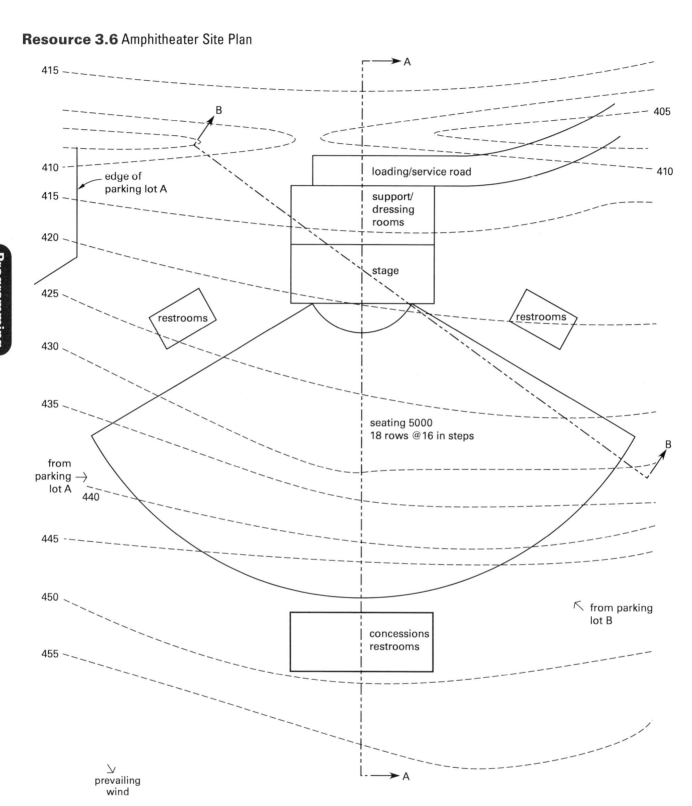

Resource 3.7 Amphitheater Site Cross-Sections

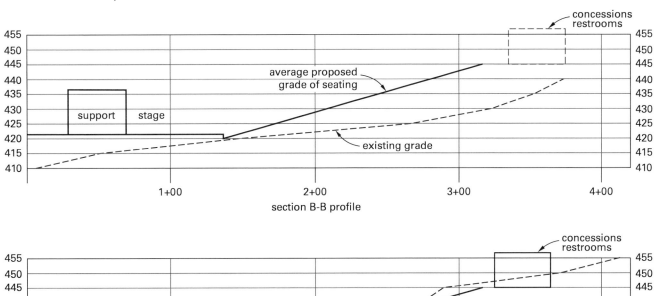

section B-B profile

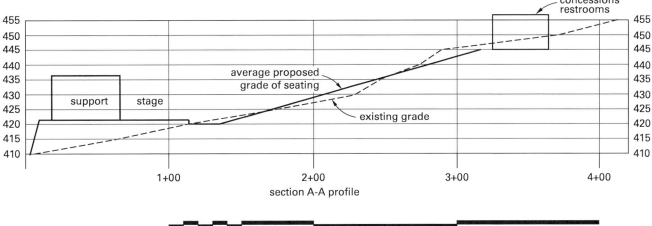

section A-A profile

vertical scale = 2x horizontal scale

11. A total of _____ accessible parking spaces will be required on the site with the construction of the new lot A and new lot B. (Fill in the blank.)

12. According to the site plan in Resource 3.6 and the section profiles in Resource 3.7, what section of the amphitheater will require the most imported fill?

(A) front of the theater near the stage

(B) along the west edge of the theater

(C) along the east edge of the theater

(D) area under the stage and support building

13. The site selected for the amphitheater is subject to prevailing breezes from the northwest, which can be cool in the spring and fall months. On the *Illustration for Prob. 13*, place three groups of landscaping to mitigate the effects of the wind. Each group may be used more than once, and tree groups may overlap slightly.

Illustration for Prob. 13

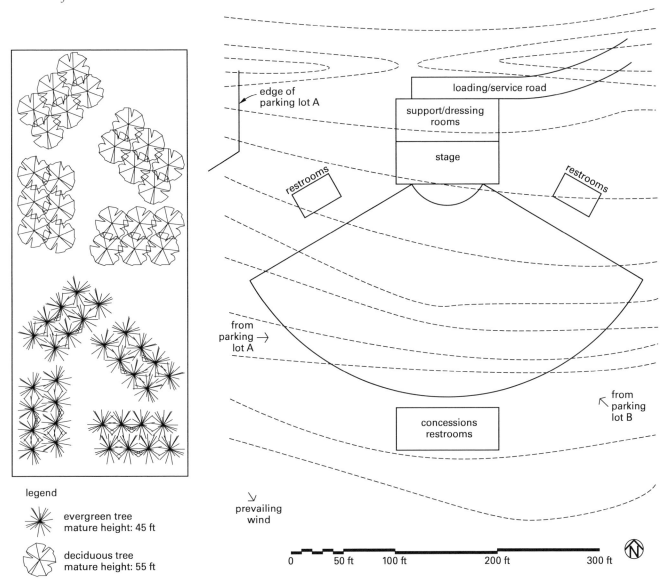

legend

evergreen tree
mature height: 45 ft

deciduous tree
mature height: 55 ft

14. As planning begins for required new grading on the existing site, the architect notices some definite problem areas. On the *Illustration for Prob. 14*, place the hot spot marker in the location where a swale will be necessary.

Illustration for Prob. 14

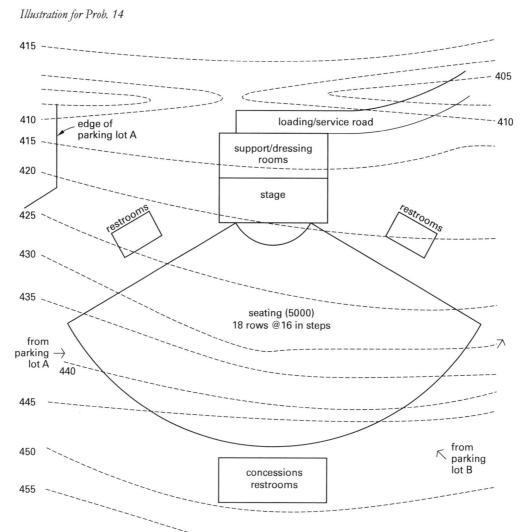

15. Although there will be a reflective canopy above the stage, the architect recognizes that the current schematic site plan needs to be modified to improve acoustics. On the *Illustration for Prob. 15*, place two hard surface walls where they will be the most effective.

Illustration for Prob. 15

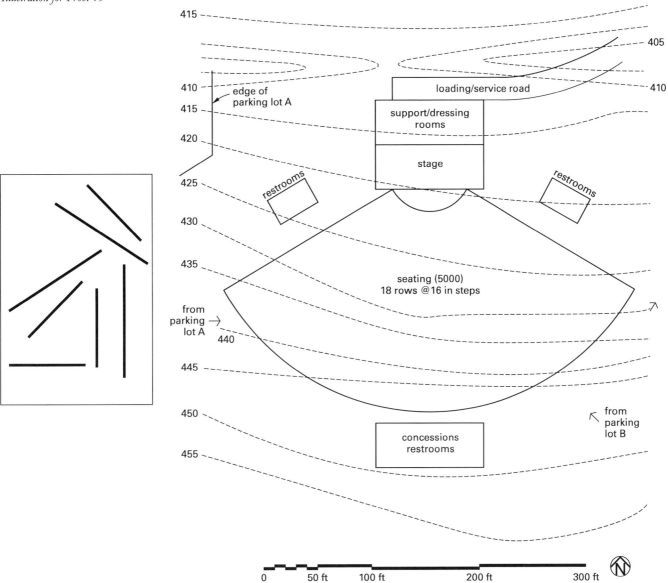

16. The county suggests that some type of cover should be placed over the seating area. Based on the program and site plan, which type of structure will have the lowest cost?

(A) steel arch

(B) open web steel joists

(C) steel space frame

(D) suspended steel cable

Solutions

1. Either a bioswale or infiltration basin would have to be constructed on the southwest portion of the site, which could interfere with the location of the restaurant and its deck. A catch basin is designed to hold runoff until it can be released into the storm sewer system, but it is not a preferable solution because it only delays runoff rather than reducing it.

For this development, the parking lot will occupy a large portion of the site, so permeable paving would reduce the runoff and be more efficient than the other options.

The answer is (A).

2. The easement restrictions can be incorporated easily into the larger site plan because the utility easement occupies just a small portion of the site. The slope across the entire site ranges from approximately 3–4%, which will not affect building or site planning. Because the site is fairly large, the requirement for the curb cut location would not significantly affect driveway access to the parking lot. The setback requirement from the wetlands, coupled with the programming requirement that the restaurant deck overlook the wetlands, will have the greatest influence on site planning because it affects both the location of the restaurant and access to parking and the restaurant.

The answer is (C).

3. The site is in a northern climate, so wind direction and southern exposure are important but could be mitigated by the design approach. The slope is very gentle, and it will neither greatly affect planning, nor serve as a significant asset for creating view planes. Mature, existing trees are a valuable resource when developing a site plan. A design alternative that saves as many trees as possible is preferable if other programmatic and code requirements are satisfied.

The answer is (B).

4. To estimate the size of the parking area and drives, first determine the number of parking spaces required. According to Resource 3.2, the shops require four parking spaces per 1000 ft^2.

$$\text{required spaces}_{\text{shop}} = A_{\text{shop}}\left(\frac{4 \text{ spaces}}{1000 \text{ ft}^2}\right)$$
$$= (7500 \text{ ft}^2)\left(\frac{4 \text{ spaces}}{1000 \text{ ft}^2}\right)$$
$$= 30 \text{ spaces}$$

Determine the required spaces for the restaurant. The restaurant requires six spaces per 1000 ft^2.

$$\text{required spaces}_{\text{restaurant}} = A_{\text{restaurant}}\left(\frac{6 \text{ spaces}}{1000 \text{ ft}^2}\right)$$
$$= (5000 \text{ ft}^2)\left(\frac{6 \text{ spaces}}{1000 \text{ ft}^2}\right)$$
$$= 30 \text{ spaces}$$

Use a value of 400 ft^2 per car to estimate the total square footage for parking, aisles, landscaping, and drives.

$$A_{\text{total}} = \left(\frac{\text{ft}^2}{\text{car}}\right)(\text{required spaces}_{\text{total}})$$
$$= \left(400 \frac{\text{ft}^2}{\text{car}}\right)(60 \text{ spaces})$$
$$= 24{,}000 \text{ ft}^2$$

The size of the space can be estimated using the program requirements and a two-aisle, double-loaded, 90° parking layout. A generous estimate for blocking out enough space is to assume a 65 ft width for a double-loaded parking aisle (i.e., a 25 ft aisle and two 20 ft parking rows). The space would be slightly less in a detailed layout using a 19 ft long parking row and allowing for some compact spaces. This would have a total width of approximately 140 ft (i.e., two 65 ft wide parking areas with a 10 ft landscaping island). Dividing 140 ft into 24,000 ft^2 would give an approximate length of 180 ft. Allowing for accessible parking spaces and access drives from the street would affect this area, but 180 ft is an adequate place to begin blocking out the necessary site area.

The answer is (C).

5. The shops in site plan B can be extended to the west, but they will need to be set back or angled to avoid the utility easement and will require the removal of existing trees. Expansion of the shops in site plan D is hindered by the pedestrian access from the parking lot to the restaurant and by the restaurant deck.

Site plan A allows for easy expansion of the shops to the south, well beyond the minimum requirements of 1500 ft^2. The sidewalk from 5th Avenue could be easily moved and the expansion would have direct access to parking as well as access from the street. The shops in site plan C could also be extended to the south, but the location of the access drive limits the area for expansion more than site A does.

The answer is (A).

6. The comments for the program and regulation requirements in Resource 3.2 include having the ability to expand the shops, minimizing the visual impact of parking, establishing shop entrances on one of the streets, having access to the front of the restaurant from 5th Avenue, and having the restaurant deck face the wetlands. Although site plan B provides direct access to parking, its shop entrances face south, which violates the programming requirement. Entrances oriented along Stuart Street would not create as strong a retail presence as entrances along 5th Avenue, as shown in site plan A. In addition, the service drive encroaches into the required wetlands setback. Site plan C fails to meet the requirement that the restaurant's facade face 5th Avenue and have direct pedestrian access from the street. Although site plan D presents an interesting plaza-oriented development it places the parking lot in a prominent location right on the corner of the property, emphasizing rather than minimizing the visual impact of parking as required by the program. It also requires a lengthy service drive.

Site A meets all of the requirements. In addition, it provides for an efficient service drive for the restaurant and a separate pedestrian access from 5th Avenue. Although it uses a slightly less efficient combination of a single- and double-loaded parking scheme, there is space on the west side of the parking lotto add parking spaces if required by any expansion of the shops. The only problem with site plan A is that a corner of the parking encroaches into the wetlands setback. However, this parking problem could be easily corrected by a slight reconfiguration of the parking aisle and landscaping island.

The answer is (A).

7. The development is in a pedestrian-oriented neighborhood so building entrances should be near the street. Walking from the neighborhood and within the development should be direct and easy. In site plan B, shop entrances do not face the street, and pedestrians must traverse the entire parking lot to walk from the shops to the restaurant. Site plan C requires a long, awkward path from the shop to the restaurant entrance, and there is no direct access from the street. Site plan D provides a pedestrian-oriented grouping of buildings and direct access from 5th Avenue, but it does not meet the requirement that the shops face 5th Avenue and allow for expansion. Site plan A satisfies all the requirements and leaves room for expansion to the south.

The answer is (A).

8. Site plan A, site plan C, and site plan D require patrons to traverse parking aisles, creating a longer and more indirect path for someone arriving by car. Site plan B places the parking between the two buildings, so both shop and restaurant patrons can park close to their destinations.

The answer is (B).

9. Although the shops can be accessed from the street or the plaza, requiring dual access makes it difficult to plan shops' storerooms, offices, and similar spaces. Parking is conveniently located, but there is little advantage to doing so. Although the land on the south end is available for development, if the shops needed to expand, the parking lot must be moved. From an urban planning standpoint, this is not as advantageous as locating the buildings near each other. Placing the two buildings close together encourages those shopping to eat at the restaurant and the restaurant customers to visit the shops. The south-facing plaza creates a comfortable, small-scale urban space. The configuration of the shops also creates a strong urban edge along the two streets.

The answer is (D).

10. The shops can be expanded only if the building line angled to follow the easement, which would significantly affect store planning and the total amount of expansion that could take place. In addition, existing trees would have to be removed with an expansion. There is no side-walk access to the front of the shops along Stuart Street from the parking lot. Although there is a sidewalk from 5th Avenue along the parking lot to the restaurant, the sidewalk is long and awkward. Furthermore, the service entrance of the restaurant faces the street. Even though somewhat shielded by distance and landscaping, the driveway is closer than the minimum 200 ft.

Although a single-aisle parking layout is not as efficient as a double-loaded aisle, a single-aisle parking layout is preferable if the total width of the parking lot is limited and allows only three rows of parking. The restaurant deck's southwest orientation would be advantageous in a cooler northern climate; it also faces the wetlands, as required by the program.

The answer is (A), (C), (D), and (F).

11. To calculate the total number of accessible parking spaces required on a site with multiple facilities (parking lots or garages), first calculate the required number for each facility and then add them together.

According to the case study scenario, lot A will have 1800 parking spaces. Lots with more than 1001 parking spaces require 20 accessible parking spaces plus 1 space for each additional 100 parking spaces over 1000.

$$20 + \frac{800}{100} = 28$$

Lot A requires 28 spaces.

Lot B will have 925 parking spaces. Lots with 501–1000 parking spaces are required to have 2% of the total parking spaces be accessible.

$$(925)(0.02) = 18.5 \quad (19)$$

Lot B requires 19 spaces.

The total number of required accessible parking spaces is

$$19 + 28 = 47$$

The answer is 47.

12. In Resource 3.7, the section A-A profile shows the existing grade mostly following the proposed grade. Although the area under the stage and support building will require imported fill, some of this will be foundation and flooring work, so there is less required as indicated on the single line profiles shown in Resource 3.7.

Find the elevation of the top of the amphitheater. For 18 rows of 16 in high steps, this elevation is 288 in or 24 ft. The lowest level of the theater, the pit in front of the stage, is at an elevation of approximately 420 ft, as shown in the Resource 3.7 section A-A profile. Therefore, the top of the amphitheater is at an elevation of 444 ft.

Compare this with the approximate existing elevations shown in the Resource 3.6 site plan. There is a difference of about 17 ft under the easternmost corner of the seating.

$$444 \text{ ft} - 427 \text{ ft} = 17 \text{ ft}$$

This is also indicated in the Resource 3.7 section B-B profile. There is a difference of about 7 ft under the western most corner of the seating.

$$444 \text{ ft} - 437 \text{ ft} = 7 \text{ ft}$$

Of the two, the east edge of the theater will require the most imported fill.

The answer is (C).

13. A single or double row of trees can reduce wind velocity from 30–60% at a distance of about five times the height of the trees. A multi-row of trees from 50–150 ft deep can reduce wind velocity by 30–60% at a distance of about 10 times the height of the trees and about 15–30% at a distance of about 20 times the tree height. It is better to plant the trees as deep as possible. In this case, evergreen trees will be better than deciduous trees for the spring and fall months, although they tend to grow slower and take longer to become effective.

The best approach to mitigating the winds is to plant evergreen trees on the northwest side of the amphitheater in as many rows as possible to create a deep windbreak. If the evergreen trees have a mature height of 45 ft, the wind will decrease for a distance of about 225 ft from the leeward side of the trees, which is almost the entire width of the amphitheater. There are several configurations of the given groups of trees that can be used. One possibility is shown.

The shaded area indicates the margin for error for locating the required elements. The location for any tree grouping is limited by the sightline from the extreme western corner of the seating area, the support building, the edge of parking lot A, and the access point from parking lot A. Trees can be placed farther to the north and west than indicated by the shaded area but this placement will negate their effect. (See *Illustration for Sol. 13*.)

14. Although extensive regrading will be required in most portions of the site, a swale will be necessary on the south side of the concession/restrooms building because the existing topography drains water directly into the building. Elsewhere, the existing topography is relatively compatible with the new structures. The shaded area in the illustration indicates the margin of error for placing the hot spot marker. (See *Illustration for Sol. 14*.)

15. Considering a plan view only, the reflective surfaces should be placed at the stage, one on each side, to reflect sound toward the audience. The shaded area indicates the margin of error for placing the walls. (See *Illustration for Sol. 15*.)

16. For the roof of a building with an extra-long span, the most economical steel structural system is a cable system. The cost of roof support per square foot using cables is generally lower than the cost of using other rigid steel structural systems. The cable system could then support a lightweight fabric covering.

The answer is (D).

Illustration for Sol. 13

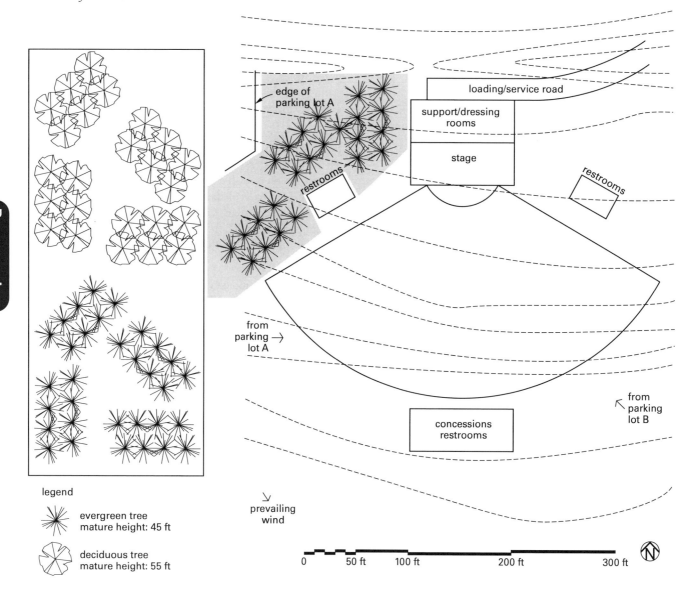

legend

evergreen tree
mature height: 45 ft

deciduous tree
mature height: 55 ft

edge of
parking lot A

loading/service road

support/dressing
rooms

stage

restrooms

restrooms

from
parking →
lot A

from
← parking
lot B

concessions
restrooms

↘
prevailing
wind

0   50 ft   100 ft   200 ft   300 ft

N

Illustration for Sol. 14

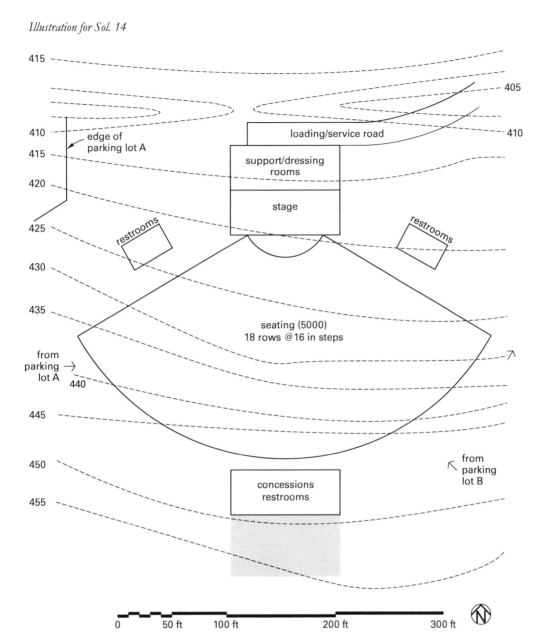

Illustration for Sol. 15

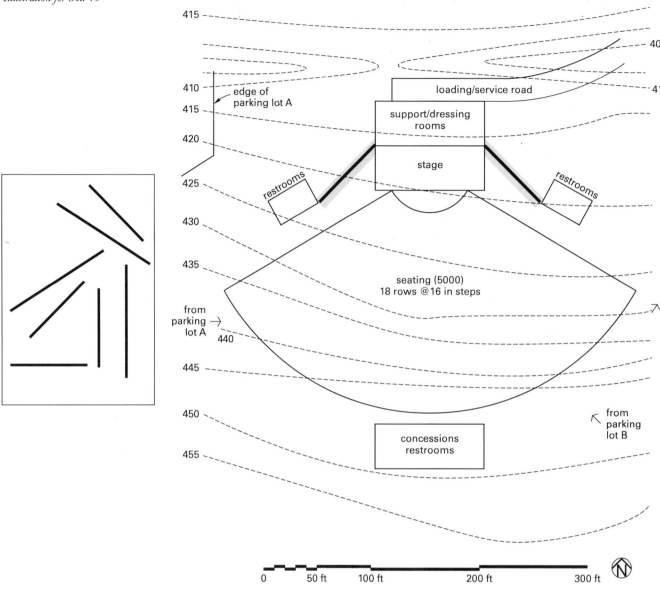

DIVISION 4: PROJECT PLANNING & DESIGN

12 Site Work Design Development

1. A soils report has indicated that the water table is 5 ft 0 in above the basement level of a planned three-story building. What type of construction technique most likely will be required?

- (A) dampproofing
- (B) surcharging
- (C) waterproofing
- (D) waterstopping

2. A deep excavation for a high-rise building in an urban area would require

- (A) battered walls
- (B) needle beams
- (C) steel sheeting
- (D) tiebacks

3. A soils report indicates that bentonite is present below the site of a proposed two-story manufacturing building. What type of foundation system should be used?

- (A) drilled piers with grade beams
- (B) raft foundation
- (C) caissons with pile caps
- (D) extended spread footings

4. For a large building being planned with a two-level basement used for meeting rooms, which of these water-related soil problems would be the most important to solve?

- (A) uplift pressure on the lowest slab
- (B) moisture penetration caused by hydrostatic pressure
- (C) deterioration of foundation insulation
- (D) reduced load-carrying capacity of the soil

5. Which parking configuration is most difficult for a driver to maneuver within?

- (A) 90°
- (B) 60°
- (C) 45°
- (D) 30°

6. A retention pond manages stormwater runoff by

(A) slowing it and allowing sediments to settle while letting the water seep into the ground

(B) holding the excess until it can discharge at a controlled rate into the storm sewer system

(C) preventing it from contaminating other portions of the site

(D) retaining it until it can seep into the ground

7. On a site with extensive development of buildings, roads, and parking, which change in drainage would have the most significant negative impact?

(A) decrease in pervious paving

(B) increase in water held on site

(C) increase in the number of drainage grates

(D) increase in the overall runoff coefficient

8. Several sites are being considered for the construction of a new community college. The most appropriate site would be the one adjacent to

(A) two major intersecting highways

(B) libraries and shopping

(C) a technology-oriented office campus

(D) a residential neighborhood and public transportation

9. Which of the following design features would have the most detrimental effect on the environment of the surrounding neighborhood in an urban setting?

(A) square building shape

(B) dark exterior colors

(C) extensive exterior paving

(D) reflective glass

10. The recommended minimum width for a sidewalk is _____ ft. (Fill in the blank.)

11. With regard to the theories of proxemics, which approach to the design of a plaza would probably accommodate the most people while allowing individuals to maintain comfortable personal space distances?

(A) large, flat, open space with trees defining the perimeter

(B) heavily landscaped area with areas of lawn

(C) amphitheater with bench-type seating in raised tiers

(D) space with various levels, benches, and spaces defined by low walls

12. The development of a middle-school campus is planned for a sparsely populated but growing suburban residential location. The city is planning new streets and property layouts around the school site, as shown. Two existing arterial streets border the site on the north and west as shown, and two new streets are proposed for the south (Evans Avenue) and east (10th Street) borders.

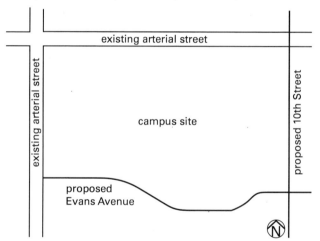

The school architect should recommend to the local planning board that the proposed streets be of which types?

(A) Evans Avenue: local

    10th Street: local

(B) Evans Avenue: local

    10th Street: collector

(C) Evans Avenue: collector

    10th Street: collector

(D) Evans Avenue: collector

    10th Street: arterial

Project Planning

13. Which of the intersections shown would be best for laying out a two-way site access road?

(A)

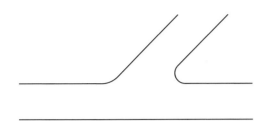

(B)

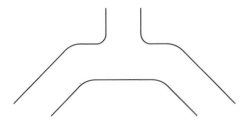

(C)

(D)

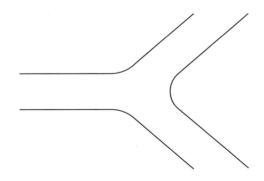

14. An architect can best discourage criminal activity in a street-level apartment lobby by applying which of the following design strategies?

(A)   separating the lobby and the street with a large expanse of glass

(B)   changing the paving texture at the property line

(C)   clearly marking the entrance with a "Residents Only" sign

(D)   adding a bright light over the entrance door

15. In regard to blast security, the space between a building and the outermost secured perimeter is called the

(A)   blast reduction zone

(B)   perimeter defense area

(C)   security setback

(D)   standoff distance

16. An architect is developing a site plan for a developed property with an existing building. The building is in good condition and was used for the same purpose as the client's proposed use of the site. Which of the following four strategies would earn the greatest number of points within the Leadership in Energy and Environmental Design (LEED) 2009 for New Construction rating system?

(A)   Maintain at least 50% of the interior nonstructural elements.

(B)   Remove the building and recycle and/or salvage at least 50% of construction and demolition debris.

(C)   Maintain at least 95% of the existing walls, floors, and roof.

(D)   Reuse materials from the site that amount to 5%, by cost, of the total value of materials on the project.

17. In the diagrammatic section shown, it is important to keep angles A and B within certain limits so as to

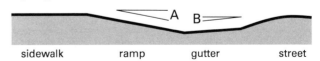

(A)   allow for accessibility

(B)   keep stormwater runoff within acceptable limits

(C)   provide an easy transition for pedestrians

(D)   allow bicycles to use the sidewalk

18. A condominium building and a parking area are to be developed on the site shown. (See *Illustration for Prob. 18.*)

A curb cut must be added to allow for street access to the parking area. Local zoning restrictions state that curb cuts cannot be closer than 75 ft to any intersection, and the local planning commission requires that no trees be removed to accommodate the new construction.

Place one condominium building, one parking area, and one curb cut on the site plan shown to make the best use of the site, topography, and views, as well as to minimize cost and site disruption. The ends of the curb cuts do not have to connect directly to the parking area outline.

Illustration for Prob. 18

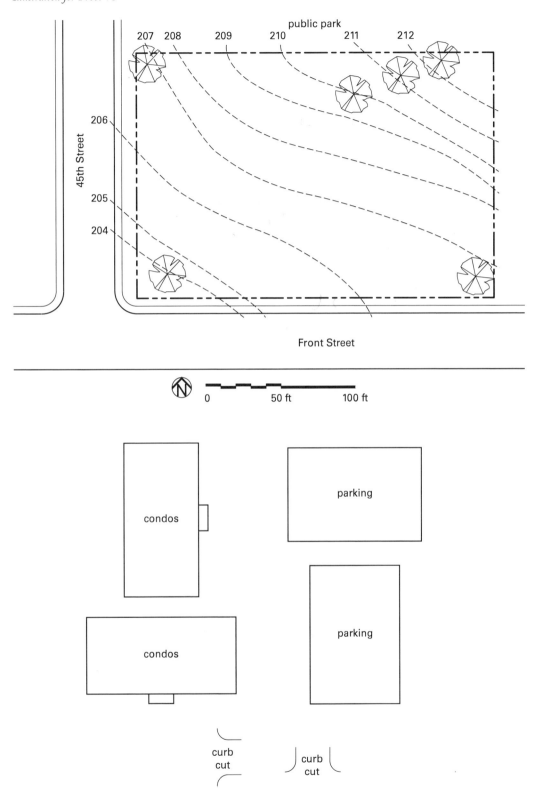

Solutions

1. Waterproofing is the control of water and moisture that is subject to hydrostatic pressure. It can refer to the application of watertight membranes, waterstops, or bentonite panels when building below the water table.

Dampproofing is the control of water and moisture when hydrostatic pressure is not present. Surcharging is the preloading of the ground with fill material to cause consolidation and settlement of the underlying soil. Surcharging is used to increase the bearing capacity of soil or to decrease possible settlement, or both. A waterstop is a preformed piece of material used to seal construction joints. Although waterstops would be used in this situation, they are a subset of the larger requirement to waterproof the entire basement slab and a portion of the basement walls.

The answer is (C).

2. A deep excavation would require the use of vertical soldier beams supporting horizontal timber breast boards or cribbing. The vertical soldier beams must be anchored into the adjacent earth with grouted tieback rods. Even steel sheeting would require tiebacks for support.

A battered wall is simply a type of retaining wall using a material, such as stones or brick, slightly angled to support the adjacent earth. It is not appropriate for a deep excavation wall in an urban area where space is limited. Needle beams are used to temporarily support a structure when its foundation is repaired or deepened. Steel sheeting requires the use of rakers that extend into the excavation site, limiting the depth of the excavation and interfering with construction activities in the excavated area.

The answer is (D).

3. Bentonite is an expansive type of clay that can push foundations and floor slabs upward when it gets wet. To prevent this, drilled piers are used to support the building weight on bedrock or stable soil below the bentonite. Grade beams span continuously between the piers and transmit building loads from the superstructure to the piers. Voids are left below the grade beams to allow the bentonite to expand without transmitting uplift forces.

A raft foundation is used to distribute a building load over a large area of low-bearing capacity soil. Caissons with pile caps are used to distribute a load from one column to two or more caissons or piers and would only be appropriate if there was a void below the pile cap. Spread footings placed on bentonite would be subject to the uplift of the swelling clay soil and would not be appropriate.

The answer is (A).

4. All of the answer options listed would need to be addressed, but because the problem asks which is most important, a judgment call is required. Option (D) is unlikely because a large building would probably utilize piers or caissons for the foundation, so the load-carrying capacity of the soil would not be as critical. Foundation insulation could be easily selected to avoid deterioration problems, so option (C) is an unlikely answer. Of the two remaining answers, hydrostatic pressure could cause the most problems, so this is the primary problem to be solved.

The answer is (B).

5. The most difficult parking configuration for a driver to maneuver within is a 90° angle arrangement. This is the only parking configuration listed that allows a two-way travel lane, and it is the most efficient of the four choices, allowing about 11 cars to park for each 100 lineal ft of curb. However, as a driver is pulling in or backing out of the space, he or she must be aware of traffic coming from either direction, and drivers must make a 90° turn into the parking space.

Both 45° angle and 60° angle configurations are relatively economical and allow easy access to and from parking spaces. They permit only one-way traffic aisles. A 45° angle configuration will allow approximately eight cars to park for each 100 lineal ft of curb. A 60° angle configuration allows about nine cars to park for each 100 lineal ft of curb.

30° angle configurations are the least efficient, allowing only about five cars to park within each 100 lineal ft of curb. They permit only a one-way traffic lane and are seldom used because they are uneconomical.

The answer is (A).

6. A retention pond, also called a holding pond or catch basin, prevents excessive stormwater runoff on a site from overloading the storm sewer system by temporarily holding the water and releasing it at a controlled rate.

Construction that is designed to allow sediment to settle while water drains into the ground is called a bioswale. Construction designed to retain stormwater until it can seep into the ground is called an infiltration basin.

The term catch basin sometimes also refers to a storm drainage structure that is designed to collect grit and trash while allowing the stormwater to flow out the drainage pipes.

The answer is (B).

7. The runoff coefficient is the fraction of total precipitation falling on a surface that runs off the surface or is not absorbed into the ground. Although the runoff coefficients may vary slightly depending on the types of paving materials used, on a site with a great deal of hard-surface development, more stormwater would have to be diverted to a storm drainage system or to natural waterways. It is preferable to minimize the amount of water allowed to run off a site.

From the information given in the problem statement, it is not clear whether or not pervious paving would be used. With a large amount of hard-surface development, the amount of water held on site would decrease, rather than increase. The number of drainage grates would most likely increase, but this is not the most significant problem.

The runoff coefficient is used to calculate the amount of runoff in cubic feet per second on a site. The calculation takes into account the rainfall intensity and the area of the site. The runoff coefficient value ranges from almost zero for wooded areas with spongy soil to 1.0 for totally waterproof surfaces. The formula is $Q = CIA$, where C is the runoff coefficient, I is the rainfall intensity in inches per hour, and A is the area of the surface in acres.

The answer is (D).

8. A community college is a regional resource and would benefit from easy access to transportation sources encompassing a wide area, which two highways would provide.

Although public transportation is also a requirement, a large-scale development like a community college would not be appropriate for a residential neighborhood.

This problem requires an understanding of whether the proposed land use is local, district, or regional in nature and what the compatible uses are. A locally based project, such as a branch library or church, is compatible with residential uses and pedestrian transportation, while regionally based projects require public or vehicular transportation.

The answer is (A).

9. Reflective glass would subject the surrounding buildings, streets, and pedestrian areas to harsh reflective light and heat during most of the day. Moreover, it would affect the surrounding areas throughout the day and during all times of the year.

A square building shape would not have much of an effect other than to cast a shadow during the day. Dark colors would generally absorb heat and affect the building itself more than the surrounding environment or microclimate. Extensive exterior paving would tend to absorb heat and affect the microclimate, but primarily in the immediate area of the paving.

The answer is (D).

10. A 5 ft width allows two wheelchairs to pass traveling in opposite directions, provides for the minimum 5 ft turning diameter for wheelchairs, and generally allows other common types of use, such as two people walking side by side, people passing in opposite directions, and comfortable use of walkers and other mobility aids.

The answer is 5 ft.

11. Proxemics is a term used by Edward T. Hall for his theory of cultural use of space. Proxemics deals with issues of territoriality, spacing and positioning between people, and how the organization of the environment can affect these issues.

When designing a plaza that could accommodate a large number of closely spaced people, the designer may incorporate features that provide a sense of territoriality, encourage actual or imagined separation, and offer a choice of varying spatial positions. These elements could be provided by using design features such as changes of level; juxtaposition of open spaces and spaces defined by street furniture, landscaping, and low walls; landscaped areas not intended for occupancy; and individual seating. This design could be flexible enough to accommodate a large number of people when required for large events, or could be used for individual groupings of people.

A large, open space would encourage individuals and small groups to spread out rather than feel at ease nearer together. A heavily landscaped area would be attractive and would help define separate spaces for people to gather, but may limit the greatest number of people from assembling. An amphitheater would accommodate a large number of people but would be limited in flexibility for other types of informal uses.

The answer is (D).

12. Local streets are intended to give direct access to building sites and are often curvilinear. At least one of these characteristics would be desirable for this property, and the street to the south (Evans Avenue) meets this requirement. In addition, Evans Avenue serves the longer dimension of the site, so there would be more opportunities to access the site from a local street on the south side of the property. Collector streets connect local streets and arterial streets, so 10th Street would best serve as a collector.

The answer is (B).

13. Intersections should always be laid out as simply as possible. When two roads intersect, a 90° angle is best.

When one road intersects another at an angle, the minimum angle is 80°.

The angle shown in option (A) is too acute. The angled roads shown in option (B) are too close to the intersecting road, which would make waiting and turning dangerous. Option (D) is incorrect because two-way Y-intersections are inherently dangerous.

The answer is (C).

14. Although all these design features would help discourage criminal activity, the best approach would be to make activity inside the lobby visible from the street. This employs the principle of natural surveillance.

Changing the texture of the flooring between the sidewalk and the private property, using a sign, and adding a light are methods of territorial reinforcement, but they would not be as effective as opening the lobby to public view.

Review the theories of defensible space, which include the basic concepts of surveillance, territoriality, and symbolic barriers. These were originally described by Oscar Newman in *Defensible Space* and later expanded in *Creating Defensible Space*. Some of the concepts are summarized in the section on "Crime Prevention through Environmental Design" in *Architectural Graphic Standards* by Charles George Ramsey, et al. Refer to the Recommended Reading list for additional resources. The ideas of defensible space have spawned the newer term "crime prevention through environmental design" (CPTED).

The answer is (A).

15. The standoff distance is the space between a building and the potential location of a blast threat. For blast protection, this distance should be maximized because blast energy decreases exponentially with increased distance between the source of the blast and the building.

The answer is (D).

16. If 95% or more of the existing building's structure, exterior walls, and roof are reused, the LEED 2009 NC rating system awards three points, one point each for reaching levels of 55%, 75%, and 95% (MR Credits 1.1 through 1.3). Window assemblies and nonstructural roofing material are excluded from these calculations.

(Under the older LEED NC rating system v2.2, two points were awarded, for 75% and 95%.)

In the LEED 2009 NC rating system, each of the other three strategies—maintaining 50% of the interior nonstructural elements (MR Credit 1.4), recycling and/or salvaging 50% of debris (MR Credit 2.1), and reusing materials from the site worth 5%, by cost, of the total value of materials (MR Credit 3.1)—would earn only one point.

The answer is (C).

17. The relationship between these two angles is important because if the transition between one slope and an opposing counterslope is too great, wheelchair users will have difficulty moving across them. In extreme cases, the footrests or anti-tip wheels on the wheelchair may not clear the surface, or the user could flip over backwards. The *ADA Accessibility Guidelines* limit the slope of curb ramps to 1:12 and the slope of counterslopes to 1:20.

The answer is (A).

18. The planning commission restriction on tree removal prevents any construction in the northeast corner of the site, so the condominium building and parking area must be placed in the southeast, southwest, or northwest corner.

The curb cut should be placed as far away from the intersection as possible and such that cars can enter the parking area from it, both for safety reasons and to minimize traffic conflicts. This eliminates the southwest corner as a location, even though the topography would work well for a paved parking area. The curb cut could be placed in the northwest corner, but this would require the parking to be placed on a steeper slope, making the grading a little more difficult and increasing costs. If the curb cut is placed in the southeast corner and the parking area is placed just above it oriented in a north-south direction, there is direct access from the parking area to the curb cut and street, minimizing costs and possibly decreasing the needed size of the parking area.

It would be best to locate the condominium building as far away from the street as possible to minimize noise. It is best oriented east-west to maximize the views toward the park and to provide a south-facing entry. Placing the condominium building in the northwest corner provides direct access between the parking area and the building, and creates a desirable open space on the south side of the building.

The shaded areas on the illustration shown represent the margin of error for placing the three required items. (See *Illustration for Sol. 18.*)

Illustration for Sol. 18

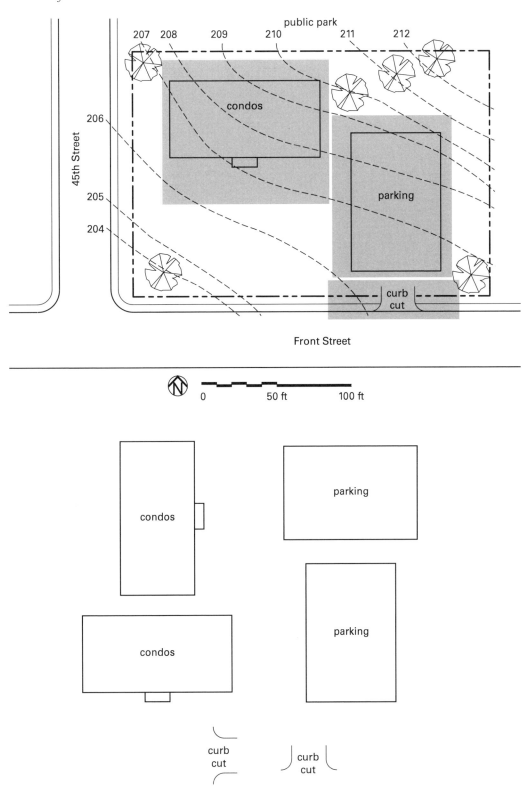

13 Sustainable Design

1. Certified contractors are required for handling or abatement of which of the following hazardous materials? (Choose the four that apply.)

(A)   asbestos

(B)   lead

(C)   polyvinyl chloride (PVC)

(D)   polychlorinated biphenyls (PCBs)

(E)   radon

(F)   vermiculite

2. Storm runoff is best minimized with the use of

(A)   cisterns

(B)   pervious paving

(C)   riprap

(D)   silt fences

3. An architect is evaluating the attributes of a particular building product as they relate to sustainability. The architect would most likely use a(n)

(A)   environmental impact study

(B)   life-cycle assessment

(C)   impact assessment

(D)   matrix comparison chart

4. A small building is being designed for a site in Minnesota. If it is desired to minimize reliance on mechanical systems, which of the following design strategies should be incorporated? (Choose the three that apply.)

(A)   maximize south-facing windows

(B)   incorporate high ceilings

(C)   design a compact form

(D)   use dark colors for the building exterior

(E)   minimize interior thermal mass

(F)   use evergreen trees on the south side of the building

5. A row of trees of moderate density will reduce the wind velocity on the leeward side by about 30–40% up to about

(A)   three times the height of the trees

(B)   five times the height of the trees

(C)   seven times the height of the trees

(D)   nine times the height of the trees

Project Planning

6. Potential overheating of a medical clinic in a temperate climate could be minimized by

(A) designing an overhang for the west and east sides of the building

(B) planning a building shape to minimize the surface area of south-facing walls

(C) having a landscape architect specify deciduous trees near the south elevation

(D) using reflective glass on the west side of the building

Project Planning

Solutions

1. Radon detection and remediation can be done by anyone, from homeowners to specialty contractors. PVC can be removed by anyone. Asbestos, lead, PCBs, and vermiculite all must be handled by a certified contractor.

The answer is (A), (B), (D), and (F).

2. Pervious paving allows rainwater to soak into the ground while providing support for parking or other outdoor activities.

Cisterns are designed for holding rainwater for further use, not to minimize the runoff. Riprap is stone reinforcement for the banks of rivers or lakes. Silt fences are used to prevent erosion and sediment runoff during construction.

The answer is (B).

3. A life-cycle assessment evaluates the environmental impact of a particular material over its entire useful life, including disposal. It could be used to compare the impacts of two or more materials so the architect could select the most sustainable one.

An environmental impact study (EIS), is used to evaluate the impact of a development on the environment. An impact assessment is one phase of a life-cycle assessment. There is no sustainability evaluation method by the name "matrix comparison chart."

The answer is (B).

4. Minnesota has a cool to cold climate. South-facing windows are good for passive solar heat gain. A compact form minimizes the surface area to reduce heat loss during the winter. Dark colors absorb more solar radiation than light colors.

Option (B) is incorrect because, used with natural ventilation, high ceilings are more appropriate for a hot-humid climate. Option (E) is incorrect because thermal mass should be maximized to take advantage of solar heat gain. In a cold climate it is desirable to have as much mass as possible to absorb and store the heat gathered during daylight hours for use at night.

Option (F) is incorrect because deciduous trees, not evergreen, are desirable on the south side of the building to let in the sun during the winter.

The answer is (A), (C), and (D).

5. For a row of trees of moderate density, wind speed is reduced about 30–40% on the leeward side up to a distance of about five times the tree height.

The answer is (B).

6. Option (A) is incorrect because overhangs are not effective on the west and east sides of a building due to the low sun angle. Vertical louvers, or fins, are more effective in these locations. Option (B) is incorrect because the south side actually receives less solar radiation than the east or west sides because the sun is high during the middle of the day. It would be more effective to minimize the roof area to cut down on solar radiation. Option (D) is incorrect because although reflective glass would reduce heat gain, it reflects sunlight on neighboring buildings and the landscape.

The answer is (C).

14 Codes and Regulations During Design Development

1. According to model codes, the minimum width of an office exit corridor serving an occupant load of 55 is

(A)   36 in

(B)   42 in

(C)   44 in

(D)   48 in

2. Which of the following would have the greatest impact on the size and configuration of an accessible restroom?

(A)   5 ft clear circular turnaround space

(B)   maneuvering space on the outside of the entry door to the room

(C)   clear space at towel dispensers and full-height mirrors

(D)   minimum 36 in access route into and through the room

3. An office in a non-sprinklered building has an occupant load of 290. In a non-sprinklered building, the *International Building Code* (IBC) requires a minimum exit width of 0.2 in per person based on the occupant load. Which of the following exit door combinations would most minimally meet the exit width required by the IBC?

(A)   a pair of 30 in entry doors and a 36 in door remotely located

(B)   two 36 in doors on opposite sides of the building

(C)   three 32 in doors remotely located

(D)   three 36 in doors remotely located from each other

4. A three-story speculative office building has a footprint of 6724 ft^2. The floors are equal in size. The building is sited on a 1.5 ac parcel. The floor area ratio is approximately

(A)   0.1:1

(B)   0.3:1

(C)   0.6:1

(D)   1:1

5. The abbreviated table shown includes requirements for occupancy loads.

use	occupant load factor $(ft^2/\text{occupant})$
assembly areas, concentrated use	7
(without fixed seats)	
auditoriums	
dance floors	
lodge rooms	
assembly areas, less-concentrated use	15
conference rooms	
dining rooms	
drinking establishments	
exhibit rooms	
lounges	
stages	
hotels and apartments	200
kitchens—commercial	200
offices	100
stores, ground floor	30

A restaurant on the ground floor contains 3500 ft^2 of dining area, a 1000 ft^2 kitchen, and a 1200 ft^2 bar area. What is the total occupant load?

(A)   202 occupants

(B)   319 occupants

(C)   380 occupants

(D)   409 occupants

6. The owner of the lot shown wants to develop a building with the maximum allowable gross area.

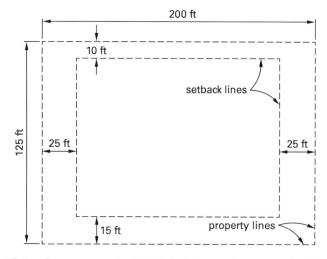

If the floor area ratio (FAR) is 3.0 and the owner builds each story to the setback lines shown, the building will be _____ stories. (Fill in the blank.)

7. The maximum allowable area of a building is limited by a combination of

(A)   floor area ratio and construction type

(B)   occupancy group and setback requirements

(C)   bulk plane limits and floor area ratio

(D)   construction type and setback requirements

8. For use in designing buildings and structures for wind forces, the ASCE/SEI7 standard defines three different wind exposure categories. In which category is the wind most severe?

(A)   category A

(B)   category B

(C)   category C

(D)   category D

9. The maximum allowable floor area of a building is primarily determined by the

(A)   city planning board

(B)   *International Building Code* (IBC)

(C)   *Life Safety Code*

(D)   zoning ordinance

10. To determine the required fire resistance for an exterior, nonbearing wall, which factors must an architect consider? (Choose the three that apply.)

(A)   construction type

(B)   size of openings in the wall

(C)   fire resistance rating of wall materials

(D)   percentage of opening area to total area

(E)   occupancy

(F)   distance from property lines

11. The corridor and exit stair shown in the partial plan are on the second floor of a non-sprinklered building and serve 10,800 ft^2 of retail space. Using the partial occupant load table and the building code excerpt, determine the minimum required egress widths, and write them in the boxes provided on the partial plan.

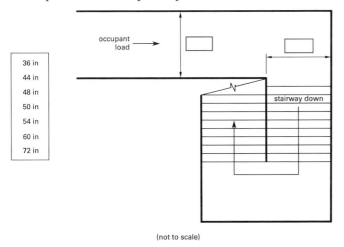

(not to scale)

Partial Occupant Load

function of space	floor area per occupant (ft²)
accessory storage areas, mechanical equipment rooms	300 gross
assembly without fixed seats	
concentrated (chairs only, not fixed)	7 net
standing space	5 net
unconcentrated (tables and chairs)	15 net
business areas	100 gross
education	
classroom area	20 net
shops and other vocational room areas	50 net
exercise rooms	50 gross
kitchens, commercial	200 gross
mercantile	
sales areas	60 gross
storage, stock, shipping areas	300 gross
residential	200 gross (two persons per sleeping room)

Building Code Excerpt

1. The capacity in inches of a means of egress for stairways shall be calculated by multiplying the occupant load served by a factor of 0.2 in per occupant for sprinklered buildings and by a factor of 0.3 in for non-sprinklered buildings. The capacity for other egress components shall be calculated by multiplying the occupant load served by a factor of 0.15 per occupant for sprinklered buildings and by a factor of 0.2 in for non-sprinklered buildings. However, the minimum width of

any component shall not be less than that required elsewhere in this code.

2. The minimum interior corridor width must be 44 in when the occupant load served is 50 or more or not less than 36 in when the occupant load served is less than 50. In Group E occupancies with an occupant load greater than 100, the minimum width shall be a minimum of 72 in.

3. The width of exit stairways, in inches, shall be determined as given in item no. 1 but in no case may stairways be less than 36 in when serving an occupant load of less than 50 or 44 in when serving an occupant load of 50 or more.

4. Stairways shall have a maximum riser height of 7 in and a minimum tread width of 11 in.

5. The width of landings in the direction of travel shall be no less than the required width of the stairway but need be no wider than 48 in.

12. Which person or entity generally has the final approval in determining where exit signs are located in a building?

(A) *International Building Code* (IBC)

(B) field inspector

(C) Occupationsal Safety and Health Administration (OSHA)

(D) city code plan checker

13. The partial plan shown is for a new training room that is to be added to an existing, fully sprinklered office building. (See *Illustration for Prob. 13.*) The room will contain an instructor's station (shown) and individual tables and chairs (not shown). Exit access corridors adjoin the north and east sides of the room.

Using the information in the building code excerpt and partial occupant load table, place the required door(s) in the position(s) that meet all code requirements and are appropriate for good planning practices. The same door may be used more than once, and door locations do not necessarily have to be located on the room outline.

Building Code Excerpt: Exit Access Doors, Doorways, Door Hardware, and Windows

1. Two (2) exit access doorways must be provided from any space in occupancy group A (assembly), B (business), or M (mercantile) where the occupancy load is greater than 49, or any space in occupancy group S (storage) where the occupancy load is greater than 29.

2. Doors opening from occupied spaces into the path of egress travel shall not project more than 7 in into the required width.

3. Exit access doorways must open in the direction of exit travel when the occupant load is greater than 50.

4. Exit access doorways must be placed at a distance that is equal to or greater than $\frac{1}{2}$ the length of the maximum overall diagonal dimension of the area being served, measured in a straight line between exit doors or exit access doorways, when the building is not sprinklered; or $\frac{1}{3}$ the length of the maximum overall diagonal dimension of the area being served, measured in a straight line between exit doors or exit access doorways, when the building is sprinklered

5. Separation distance shall be measured to any point along the width of the doorway.

Partial Occupant Load

function of space	floor area per occupant (ft^2)
accessory storage areas, mechanical equipment rooms	300 gross
assembly without fixed seats	
concentrated (chairs only—not fixed)	7 net
standing space	5 net
unconcentrated (tables and chairs)	15 net
business areas	100 gross
education	
classroom area	20 net
shops and other vocational room areas	50 net

Illustration for Prob. 13

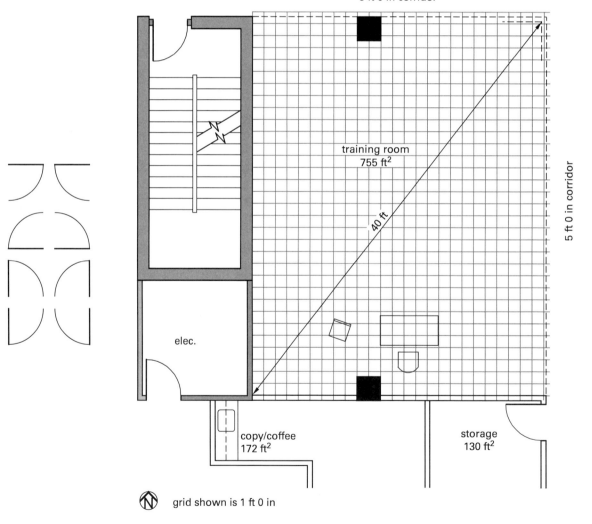

grid shown is 1 ft 0 in

Solutions

1. Model codes prescribe a minimum corridor width of 44 in, with various exceptions. Corridors in residential occupancies or those serving an occupant load of less than 50 may be 36 in wide. Other occupancies require wider corridors, but B occupancies (offices) require the 44 in width.

Model codes also require that the minimum width of an exit corridor be calculated by multiplying the occupant load by a factor given in the codes, which varies depending on the occupancy, the interior area of the building, and whether the building is sprinklered. Both requirements must be checked, and the larger of the two should be used. If this calculation results in a number larger than other minimum requirements given in the code (such as for corridors), then the larger dimension must be used.

The answer is (C).

2. Providing for a 5 ft turning circle requires the most space of the four choices listed. If the turning circle is provided, it is very likely that a 36 in access space and clear space at the towel dispensers will also be available. The manuevering space on the outside of the entry door is irrelevent to the interior dimensions of the restroom.

The answer is (A).

3. Find the total exit width required.

$$
\begin{aligned}
W_{\text{exit}} &= (\text{occupant load})\left(0.2 \ \frac{\text{ft}}{\text{person}}\right) \\
&= (290 \ \text{people})\left(0.2 \ \frac{\text{in}}{\text{person}}\right) \\
&= 58 \ \text{in}
\end{aligned}
$$

Any exit door must provide a clear width of at least 32 in, so option (A) and option (C) cannot be correct because their clear widths would be less than 32 in. Three 36 in doors would be acceptable, but the question asks for the minimally acceptable solution, which is two 36 in doors; this would provide approximately 66 in of width (considering the clear width of the door to be from the doorstop to the face of the door when open).

The answer is (B).

4. The floor area ratio expresses the relationship between the square footage of the building and the area of the site on which it is constructed. Zoning ordinances often set limits on the maximum floor area ratio allowed within a region as a means of controlling development density.

$$
\begin{aligned}
\text{FAR} &= \frac{A_{\text{building}}}{A_{\text{site}}} \\
&= \frac{(3 \ \text{floors})\left(6724 \ \dfrac{\text{ft}^2}{\text{floor}}\right)}{(1.5 \ \text{ac})\left(43{,}560 \ \dfrac{\text{ft}^2}{\text{ac}}\right)} \\
&= 0.31 \quad (0.3{:}1)
\end{aligned}
$$

The answer is (B).

5. From the table, assembly areas, including restaurants and bars, have an occupant load of 15. Commercial kitchens have an occupant load of 200. Therefore,

$$
\begin{aligned}
\text{dining area} &= \frac{3500 \ \text{ft}^2}{15 \ \dfrac{\text{ft}^2}{\text{occupant}}} = 234 \ \text{occupants} \\
\text{kitchen} &= \frac{1000 \ \text{ft}^2}{200 \ \dfrac{\text{ft}^2}{\text{occupant}}} = 5 \ \text{occupants} \\
\text{bar} &= \frac{1200 \ \text{ft}^2}{15 \ \dfrac{\text{ft}^2}{\text{occupant}}} = 80 \ \text{occupants} \\
\text{total} &= 319 \ \text{occupants}
\end{aligned}
$$

The answer is (B).

6. If the floor area ratio (FAR) is 3.0, the maximum amount of floor area that can be built is three times the area of the lot. To find the allowable number of stories, divide the available ground area, A, within the setbacks into the maximum allowable floor area.

First, find the maximum building floor area allowed by the floor area ratio.

$$
\begin{aligned}
A_{\text{building floor,max}} &= A_{\text{lot}}(\text{FAR}) \\
&= (25{,}000 \ \text{ft}^2)(3.0) \\
&= 75{,}000 \ \text{ft}^2
\end{aligned}
$$

Project Planning

Next, determine the available ground area within the setbacks that can be used for building.

$$A = W_{\text{between side setbacks}}$$
$$\times W_{\text{between front and rear setbacks}}$$
$$= (150 \text{ ft})(100 \text{ ft})$$
$$= 15{,}000 \text{ ft}^2$$

Finally, find the allowable number of stories by dividing the maximum building floor area by the available ground area.

$$\text{no. of stories} = \frac{A_{\text{building floor,max}}}{A}$$
$$= \frac{75{,}000 \text{ ft}^2}{15{,}000 \dfrac{\text{ft}^2}{\text{story}}}$$
$$= 5 \text{ stories}$$

The answer is 5 stories.

7. Zoning regulations limit total building area based on floor area ratio and setbacks, while building codes limit building area by construction type and occupancy group. Bulk plane limits may affect the area by limiting height in some cases, but they are not a primary determinant. Of the options given, the floor area ratio (from zoning codes) and construction type (from building codes) is the combination that limits maximum area.

The answer is (A).

8. The three wind exposure categories are labeled B, C, and D. The most severe wind exposure is in category D, which refers to flat and unobstructed terrain near large bodies of water. Category B refers to urban and suburban wooded areas and terrain with obstructions. Category C refers to open terrain, such as in a desert area. There is no category A.

The answer is (D).

9. A local city planning board may have requirements for building sizes, but the requirements are not a primary determinant. The IBC limits the maximum allowable floor area of a building based on occupancy, building construction type, frontage, and whether the building is sprinklered, all of which may set a limit more or less than a zoning ordinance. For example, a zoning ordinance may set a maximum limit of 200,000 ft² but using a Type IIA construction with no frontage may limit the area to 150,000 ft². The *Life Safety Code* also places restrictions on building area; however, like the IBC, it is not the primary determinant until occupancy and building type are determined. A zoning ordinance sets limits on the floor area ratio based on lot size, setbacks, maximum height, and solar access, among other possible

parameters. A combination of these factors will determine the maximum allowable floor area.

The answer is (D).

10. Once the architect uses an *International Building Code* (IBC) table to determine the hourly fire-resistance rating, the required fire-resistance rating of windows and doors also can be determined. For example, fire-protection-rated glazing is not even permitted in a 2-hr rated exterior wall, and doors must have a 1½-hr fire resistance rating. However, fire-resistance-rated glazing can be used if it has a 2-hr rating for the maximum size tested. The required fire resistance rating of the wall must first be determined before selecting building materials and assemblies to meet the rating. The percentage of opening area has nothing to do with fire resistance of an exterior wall. The fire-resistance rating depends on the construction type, occupancy, and separation of the building from the property line.

The answer is (A), (E), and (F).

11. Calculate the occupant load that the egress components must accommodate. In the partial occupant load table, a retail or mercantile occupancy has an occupant load factor of 60 ft² per occupant. Divide this into 10,800 ft² to arrive at 180 occupants.

$$\text{occupant load} = \frac{A_{\text{retail}}}{\text{occupant load factor}} = \frac{10{,}800 \text{ ft}^2}{60 \dfrac{\text{ft}^2}{\text{occupant}}}$$
$$= 180 \text{ occupants}$$

Two aspects of exit width must be determined, in addition to the capacity for stairs and other components, as well as the minimum required width of components. Because this is a non-sprinklered building, the required width for the corridor must be calculated by multiplying the occupant load by a factor of 0.2, as stated in the building code excerpt item no. 1.

$$W = (\text{occupant load})(0.2)$$
$$= (180 \text{ occupants})(0.2)$$
$$= 36 \text{ in}$$

As stated in the building code excerpt item no. 2, the minimum width is 44 in when the occupant load is 50 or more.

The required width for the stairway is calculated by multiplying the occupant load by a factor of 0.3 for non-sprinklered buildings.

$$W_{\text{stairway}} = (\text{occupant load})(0.3) = (180 \text{ occupants})(0.3) = 54 \text{ in}$$

This is more than the minimum width of 44 in for

stairways serving an occupant load of 50 or more, so the 54 in dimension takes precedence.

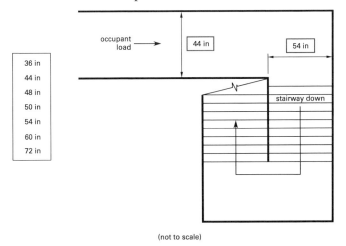

(not to scale)

12. Although the IBC gives specific requirements for exit sign placement and exceptions for where they are not required, the local building inspector usually has the final say in where they are required. This is because only when the actual conditions of construction are observed can an assessment be made of how well or even if the exit signs are visible. Even though the placement of exit signs by the architect and the electrical engineer may meet the letter of the IBC, in the field there may be areas where the signs are not visible. OSHA only gives testing requirements for exit signs. The city code plan checker may have an opinion about the exit sign location but the final responsibility rests with the building department.

The answer is (B).

13. There are four mandatory building code provisions that apply in this situation: the number of exit access doorways required, their separation distance, the direction of door swing, and how far the doors may project into the path of egress travel. Although this room is in a business occupancy, the *International Building Code* (IBC) allows a small assembly space to be classified as a B occupancy only if the occupant load is less than 50 and less than 750 ft^2.

Calculate the occupant load for the training room. Because this room will have tables and chairs the occupant load factor is 15 ft^2 per person according to the table.

$$\text{occupant load} = \frac{755 \ ft^2}{15 \ \dfrac{ft^2}{\text{occupants}}}$$

$$= 50.33 \text{ occupants} \quad (51 \text{ occupants})$$

More than 50 occupants makes this an assembly (A) occupancy, which also requires two egress doors. The room is also larger than 750 ft^2.

The doors serve an occupant load greater than 50, so they must swing in the direction of egress travel. Either left-hand reverse or right-hand reverse doors can be used. When fully open, they cannot project more than 7 in into the corridor. In order to fulfill this requirement, the doors must be recessed into an inset in the corridor wall.

In a sprinklered building, the doors must be placed a minimum distance of $\frac{1}{3}$ of the diagonal dimension of the room (40 ft) or, in this case, at least 13.33 ft apart.

Each door can be located anywhere along the corridor wall, but good planning practice is to locate one at the end of the room where the instructor will be. The second exit can be located as close as 13.33 feet from the first one, but the best location is somewhere in the back of the room to allow for unobtrusive entry and exit when class is in session and for better separation for safe egress. The shaded areas indicate the margin of error in placing the doors.

Illustration for Sol. 13

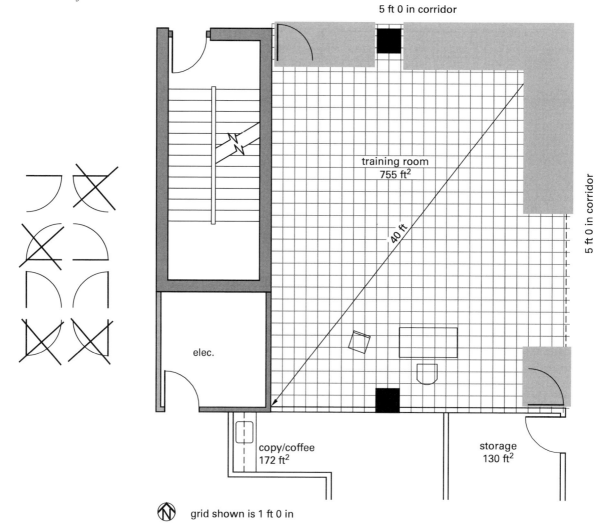

grid shown is 1 ft 0 in

15 Barrier-Free Design

1. An architect has been hired to prepare a design for remodeling toilet rooms to make them accessible. The architect finds it is impossible to provide adequate clearance on one side of an entrance door. What is the most economical course of action?

(A) Apply to the building department for a hardship exemption because compliance is not readily achievable.

(B) Tell the client that walls should be demolished and the toilet rooms replanned to provide the necessary clearances.

(C) Specify a power-assisted door opener that meets accessibility standards for the noncompliant door.

(D) Plan for accessible toilet rooms in another location in the building where all requirements can be adequately met.

2. For accessible doors, the minimum dimension of the distance, x, as indicated in the drawing, is ___ in. (Fill in the blank.)

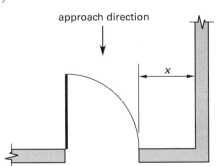

3. In the diagram shown, what is the minimum distance, x, between two entry doors in the vestibule?

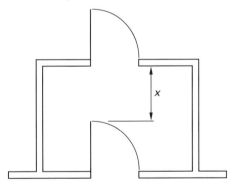

(A) 36 in

(B) 42 in

(C) 48 in

(D) 60 in

4. Identify the following critical dimensions as required by the *ADA Accessibility Guidelines.*

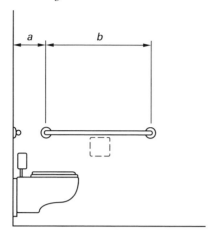

(A) $a = 6$ in minimum, $b = 42$ in minimum

(B) $a = 12$ in maximum, $b = 42$ in minimum

(C) $a = 12$ in maximum, $b = 48$ in minimum

(D) $a = 6$ in minimum, $b = 48$ in minimum

Project
Planning

Solutions

1. A power-assisted door would be the least expensive option and require the least construction time. It would be possible to solve the problem by demolishing the existing restrooms and rebuilding them to comply with accessibility standards, or meet the requirement for accessible facilities in another location in the building, but both of these options are likely to be less economical than the door opener.

The answer is (C).

2. For a front approach to an in-swinging door (pull side), there must be a minimum of 18 in on the latch side of the door. For an out-swinging door (push side), 12 in are required on the latch side of the door.

The answer is 18 in.

3. According to both *ADA Accessibility Guidelines*, Sec. 4.13.7, and *International Building Code* (IBC), Sec. 1008.1.8, the minimum distance between two entry doors forming a vestibule when one opens out and one opens in is 48 in.

The answer is (C).

4. The dimensions given in option (B) are the correct dimensions for a toilet-stall configuration according to the *ADA Accessibility Guidelines*.

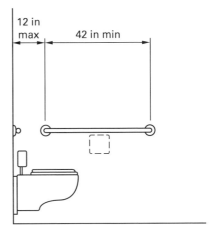

The answer is (B).

16 Human Comfort and Mechanical System Fundamentals

1. In a large single-tenant building, a LAN system would most commonly serve

- (A) building automation
- (B) computers
- (C) security
- (D) telephones

2. When designing a research laboratory building, how might an architect provide for extensive mechanical system requirements as well as a programmed requirement for flexibility in changing the layout of the laboratories over time?

- (A) Use interstitial spaces.
- (B) Locate mechanical risers on the outside of the building.
- (C) Distribute mechanical rooms throughout the building.
- (D) Design a compact, multistory structure.

3. Which type of heating, ventilating, and air conditioning (HVAC) system would be the best choice for a large building where a need for simultaneous heating and cooling is expected?

- (A) direct expansion
- (B) variable air volume
- (C) dual duct
- (D) reheat system

Solutions

1. LAN is an acronym for local area network, which is a system of individual computers, computer servers, and wired or wireless connections that allows all the users in an individual building or complex of buildings to share data on a nonpublic network.

A WAN is a wide area network, which is a system that connects computers at widely spaced locations to a private network. The locations can be in different cities or different states. Although both systems are intended for private use, they can be, and commonly are, connected with the internet.

The answer is (B).

2. Mechanical risers on the outside of the building would not provide for changes to the distribution network within the building. Distributing mechanical rooms might allow for one to be upgraded as necessary without disturbing other parts of the building, but would not provide for easy modification of mechanical and electrical services to individual rooms. Although a compact building would reduce the length of service runs for mechanical and electrical systems, it would still require disruption of occupied spaces while changes were being made.

Interstitial space is intermediate space between floors of a building used for mechanical, plumbing, and electrical systems. Interstitial space allows for the installation and modification of mechanical systems independent from the usable floors in between. It is often used for laboratory buildings and hospitals where the requirements for mechanical and electrical systems are extensive and often require changes and additions as the needs of the building and technology change. Although it increases initial cost, the inclusion of interstitial spaces provides the most flexibility for accommodating changes.

The answer is (A).

3. Hot and cool air are both constantly available in a dual duct system; it can provide heating and cooling simultaneously. (A multizone system also has the capability.) However, the dual duct system has some drawbacks: It is relatively expensive, requires a lot of ductwork (two runs to each space), and is not very energy efficient. Direct expansion, variable air volume, and reheat systems provide heating and cooling but cannot do both at the same time.

The answer is (C).

17 Mechanical, Electrical, and Plumbing Systems

1. A drainage system for a small two-story building is shown.

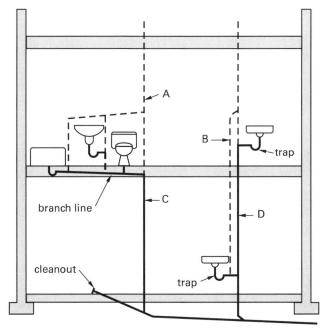

Which of the following components of the diagram is the stack vent?

(A) component A

(B) component B

(C) component C

(D) component D

2. Which of the following domestic water heating systems would yield the lowest operating costs for a duplex residential unit?

(A) active closed-loop solar

(B) direct-fired storage tank

(C) ground-source heat pump

(D) tankless instantaneous

3. Which of these is the most important concern in relation to a private water supply?

(A) fixture pressure

(B) hardness

(C) friction loss

(D) yield

4. Which heating, ventilating, and air conditioning (HVAC) system would be the most appropriate choice for a hospital?

(A) multizone

(B) high-velocity dual duct

(C) variable air volume

(D) fan coil with supplementary air

5. Which of the following have a significant effect on heat gain? (Choose the four that apply.)

(A) sunlight

(B) humidity

(C) motors and equipment

(D) air movement

(E) people

(F) fluorescent lighting

6. A building in a temperate climate will have some areas that require cooling and others that require heating at the same time. To minimize energy use, the best devices to employ are

(A) energy recovery ventilators

(B) heat pipes

(C) recuperative fuel economizers

(D) water-loop heat pumps

7. A seven-story office building is to have a variable air volume system. The building will have 105,000 ft^2 of net space and an estimated 126,000 ft^2 of gross area. About how much space should be the minimum area allowed for heating, ventilating, and air conditioning (HVAC) systems?

(A) 2500 ft^2

(B) 3800 ft^2

(C) 6300 ft^2

(D) 7600 ft^2

8. Air barriers are designed to stop infiltration and exfiltration caused by which of the following? (Choose the four that apply.)

(A) stack effect

(B) vapor pressure

(C) heating, ventilating, and air conditioning (HVAC) fan pressure

(D) wind pressure

(E) temperature differentials

(F) exhaust vents

9. A power distribution system is to be specified for an open office area. Which of the following is the most flexible and economical alternative?

(A) access floor system

(B) underfloor raceway system

(C) cellular metal floor raceways

(D) ceiling raceway system with pole raceways

10. Electrical operating costs in a single-tenant commercial building can be minimized by using which of the following techniques? (Choose the four that apply.)

(A) daylighting

(B) indirect lighting

(C) load control

(D) multiple metering

(E) occupancy sensors

(F) light emitting diode (LED) lamps

11. High voltages are used in commercial buildings because

(A) conductors and conduit can be smaller

(B) a wider variety of loads can be accommodated

(C) commercial buildings require more power

(D) transformers can step down the voltages to whatever is required

12. Which would be the best location for a transformer for a large school building?

(A) on the power pole serving the building

(B) in a separate room near the exterior wall

(C) outside, on a transformer pad close to the main switchgear

(D) in a protective shed where power from the utility company enters the property

Solutions

1. The stack vent is the vent through the roof that connects directly to the uppermost part of a soil stack or a waste stack. Generally, other vent lines are connected to it above the branch line from the highest fixtures in the building.

The answer is (A).

2. A solar water heating system would have the lowest long-term operating cost because no fuel costs would be involved.

A standard direct-fired storage tank unit would require purchasing gas, oil, or some other type of fuel to heat the water. A ground-source heat pump would not be able to supply water hot enough for domestic use and is inappropriate for this application; ground-source heat pumps are used for heating the home, not water. A tankless instantaneous unit would incur ongoing expenses due to its use of electricity and is not appropriate for general household domestic hot water generation.

The answer is (A).

3. Hardness affects the quality and taste of water as well as the longevity of the plumbing system. Very hard water can deposit minerals that build up in pipes and on plumbing fixtures. The taste may be objectionable, requiring installation of a water-softening or filtration system.

The answer is (B).

4. A system that exhausts all return air would be the best choice to maintain the quantities of fresh air needed in a hospital. A fan coil with supplementary air would satisfy this requirement.

All of the other systems listed return room air to the main air handling unit, where some of it is reused in the system.

The answer is (D).

5. Humidity and air movement do not affect heat gain. Although the effect of motors and equipment, people, and lighting may vary in different types of occupancies, they all produce heat.

The answer is (A), (C), (E), and (F).

6. Water-loop heat pumps use a continuous flow of temperate water to extract heat from areas that need to be cooled and add heat to other areas requiring heating using very little, if any, additional energy input.

Energy recovery ventilators work best in climates where the difference between indoor and outdoor air temperature is high. Heat pipes are not appropriate for this use because they would simply pre-warm cool outdoor air. A

recuperative fuel economizer is another type of system that simply uses hot exhaust gas to preheat incoming air or water. This type of equipment would save energy by increasing the efficiency of the heating plant but would not be as effective as the water-loop heat pump system.

The answer is (D).

7. For most midsize buildings, an all-air or air-water system needs about 3–9% of the gross area for HVAC system mechanical space. Office buildings fall somewhere near the midpoint of the range, so use 6% for this question. 6% of the estimated 126,000 ft^2 gross area is 7560 ft^2. This is rounded up to 7600 ft^2, so option (D) is correct as a minimum estimated area.

The answer is (D).

8. Wind pressure, stack pressure, and HVAC fan pressure all can influence infiltration and exfiltration rates. Vapor pressure does not cause air movement; rather, vapor pressure is a movement of moisture. Temperature differentials have little effect on infiltration or exfiltration.

The answer is (A), (C), (D), and (F).

9. Any of the options would allow flexibility, but the ceiling raceway system with pole raceways would be the least expensive.

An access floor system consists of individual panels, typically 24 in square, supported on adjustable pedestals above the structural floor. These systems provide unlimited flexibility for routing power, communications, and air supply, but are expensive and not justified unless a great deal of cabling is involved or future changes will be extensive (such as in a computer room.) An underfloor raceway system consists of a series of parallel rectangular metal raceways laid on the structural slab and covered with concrete. A cellular metal floor raceway is similar in concept, but is part of the structure. Raceways are similar to standard metal decking and serve as conduits for power and communication cabling. In both underfloor and cellular metal floor systems, the raceways are tapped when power and communication outlets are required.

The answer is (D).

10. Daylighting can be used to reduce electrical lighting requirements. Load control is a way of avoiding peak-demand electrical charges by automatically or manually shutting off nonessential electrical loads before the peak demand is reached. Occupancy sensors automatically turn light on or off depending on whether a space or room is occupied. LED lamps can minimize the power required for lighting compared with compact fluorescent or incandescent lamps.

Indirect lighting alone probably would not reduce power use; in fact, it may even increase power use because more wattage might be needed to achieve the required lighting level than would be needed with direct or task lighting. Multiple metering is used for multi-tenant spaces only and would not result in an overall cost savings for a commercial building.

The answer is (A), (C), (E), and (F).

11. As voltages increase, current may be decreased and the system will still provide the same amount of power. Lower currents require smaller conductors. For large commercial buildings, smaller conductors translate to less expense in conductors and conduit, as well as easier installation of smaller wires.

The answer is (A).

12. A transformer vault near the exterior wall would be the best choice for protection, ventilation, and ease of installation and removal. A large school building would require high voltage service from the utility company and step-down transformers provided by the owner. This type of transformer could not be installed on a pole. Although the transformer could be placed on a pad outside the building, this would leave it exposed to possible vandalism and might present a danger to the students.

The answer is (B).

18 Structural Systems

1. What type of irregularity is illustrated in the building elevation shown?

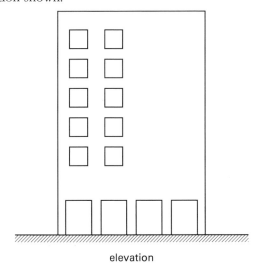

elevation

(A) stiffness irregularity

(B) diaphragm discontinuity

(C) torsional irregularity

(D) column stiffness variation

2. The roof of a building generally subject to what type of wind pressure?

(A) direct (positive) pressure

(B) uplift, or suction

(C) drag forces

(D) combination of direct (positive) pressure and suction

3. Which of the following structures require some complex wind calculations and possibly some wind tunnel testing? (Choose the three that apply.)

(A) commercial building with a total height of 50 ft

(B) residential building with a height of 200 ft

(C) office building with a height of 450 ft

(D) building with a height-to-width ratio of 3

(E) building with a height-to-width ratio of 7

(F) extra-long span suspension bridge

Project Planning

Solutions

1. The building elevation illustrates stiffness irregularity. The first story is a "soft story" because it is supported on columns, which creates a difference in stiffness from the rest of the building above. Bracing the columns would improve the condition.

A column stiffness variation results when the supporting columns on the first floor have different heights, as may be the case on a sloped site.

The answer is (A).

2. The roof of a building is generally subject to uplift, or suction. This is why roofs are often blown off during hurricanes and tornadoes.

The answer is (B).

3. An office building with a height of 450 ft, a building with a height-to-width ratio of 7, and an extra-long span suspension bridge would require some complex wind calculations and possibly some wind tunnel testing.

Generally, complex wind calculations and wind tunnel testing are required for buildings with heights exceeding 400 ft, for buildings subject to dynamic effects, those sensitive to wind vibrations, and for buildings with a height-to-width ratio of 5 or more. Wind tunnel testing is also often carried out on reduced-scale models of long-span suspension bridges.

The answer is (C), (E), and (F).

Project
Planning

19 Fundamentals of Lighting and Acoustics

1. Which of the following types of lamps provides the best color rendition of skin tones?

- (A) cool-white fluorescent
- (B) incandescent
- (C) mercury vapor
- (D) metal halide

2. The zonal cavity method of calculating average illumination on the work surface for a given number of luminaires depends on which of the following variables? (Choose the four that apply.)

- (A) angle of light
- (B) dirt accumulation
- (C) efficacy of the lamp
- (D) lumens per lamp
- (E) room size
- (F) wall reflectance

3. Problems with veiling reflections in a general-purpose workroom could best be reduced by

- (A) substituting ambient light for direct light fixtures
- (B) repositioning the light fixtures
- (C) reducing the brightness of the light fixtures
- (D) changing the type of lamps

4. Variables that must be considered when designing for daylighting include which of the following? (Choose the four that apply.)

- (A) longitude of the site
- (B) glass transmittance
- (C) height of the head of the glass
- (D) height of space above ground level
- (E) outdoor surface reflection
- (F) room surface reflection

5. Which of the following would an architect be most concerned about when designing the lighting for an office space with computer workstations and standard desks? (Choose the three that apply.)

   (A)   color rendering index

   (B)   visual comfort probability

   (C)   task/surrounds brightness ratio

   (D)   veiling reflections

   (E)   reflected glare

   (F)   lighting uniformity

6. Why would high-pressure sodium lamps be favored over low-pressure sodium lamps in a storage warehouse?

   (A)   They are less expensive.

   (B)   They have a longer lamp life.

   (C)   They can operate at higher, more efficient voltages.

   (D)   They have better color-rendering properties.

7. A material supplier states that adding a certain product to a wall assembly in a critical acoustical situation will increase the noise reduction (STC rating) between two spaces by 3 dB. What is the most appropriate response?

   (A)   Determine the additional cost and then decide whether or not to use the product.

   (B)   Thank the supplier for stopping by but explain that the architectural firm probably will not be using the product because that amount of noise reduction does not make it worth the effort or cost.

   (C)   Specify the product as long as it does not affect the design or construction cost by more than 5%.

   (D)   Inquire whether some modification can be made to the product to increase its rating to 6 dB and say that then the architectural firm might consider it.

Project Planning

Solutions

1. An incandescent lamp has a high color rendering index (CRI) and low color temperature, with a predominance of light in the red range. These characteristics give a complimentary rendering to skin tones.

A cool white fluorescent lamp has more blue and green light in its spectral distribution and makes skin tones appear more gray and washed out. Both mercury vapor and metal halide lamps have poor color rendering indexes and are not appropriate for lighting areas where skin tone rendition is important.

The answer is (B).

2. The zonal cavity method is used to calculate the total number of luminaires required to achieve the desired average illumination on the work surface, which is assumed to be 30 in above the floor. The variables considered in the calculation include the level of illumination desired, the area of the room, the number of lamps in each luminaire, the lumen output of each lamp, the coefficient of utilization, the light loss factor, wall reflectance, and the gradual loss of light due to dirt accumulation.

The coefficient of utilization (CU) is a measure of the efficiency of a particular luminaire in outputting light and is based on the design of the luminaire itself, the reflectance of the room, and the size of the room. The light loss factor represents a degradation of ideal light output due to aging of the lamp and gradual dirt accumulation on the lamp.

The answer is (B), (D), (E), and (F).

3. A veiling reflection is glare caused when the image of a light source is reflected from a viewing surface into the eye. The best way to reduce it is to provide general background illumination (ambient lighting) so the light sources are not concentrated in the area of the lamp.

Repositioning the luminaires (or the task) can reduce veiling reflections, but only when the task is in a specific location in relation to the light source. In a general-purpose workroom this would not be feasible. Reducing the brightness of the light source would help, but would also reduce the illumination provided for the task. Changing the type of lamps would have little effect on reflected glare.

The answer is (A).

4. The longitude of the site is not a factor in daylighting design. The latitude of the site might have a minor influence on how a daylighting design is implemented, but this is not a critical variable. The height of the space above ground level does not have a direct influence on daylighting except that it may affect tree obstructions and outdoor surface reflection.

Variables that affect daylighting include the brightness of the sky (which is affected by solar altitude, cloud conditions, and time of day), the area of the glass, the height of the head of the glass, the transmittance of the glass, the reflectance of surfaces within the rooms and nearby outdoor surfaces, and obstructions such as overhangs and trees.

The answer is (B), (C), (E), and (F).

5. In an office space where computer monitors and standard office tasks are present, the architect should be concerned with two results of glare. Veiling reflection would be of concern for standard office tasks such as writing and reading, whereas reflected glare would be critical in using the monitors. The brightness ratios between the tasks and their surroundings are important, especially when employees spend hours in front of a computer monitor. The color rendering index, visual comfort probability, and lighting uniformity are less important.

The answer is (C), (D), and (E).

6. Low-pressure sodium lamps produce a monochromatic yellow light that would not be appropriate in a storage warehouse where people may have to discriminate between colors.

The answer is (D).

7. Because a change in intensity level of 3 dB is considered "just perceptible," it would probably be better not to use the material regardless of how low the added cost was. Trying to modify the material to 6 dB would also probably not be worth the trouble. To achieve an STC rating 6 dB higher, it would be better to look at another type of construction assembly instead of trying to make do with a modified material. Option (D) could be correct if the material was such that simply doubling it rather than modifying it would result in a 6 dB increase.

The answer is (B).

20 Vertical Transportation

1. Which of the following types of elevators is used for high-rise office buildings?

(A) standard hydraulic

(B) high-speed hydraulic

(C) geared traction

(D) gearless traction

2. For a three-story department store, the most important variable for selecting an elevator would be its

(A) speed

(B) capacity

(C) control method

(D) machine room location

3. A geared traction elevator would be most appropriate for a(n)

(A) 5-story medical office building

(B) 16-story office building

(C) 4-story department store

(D) 8-story apartment building

4. What is the optimal location for an elevator machine room?

(A) beside the elevator on the lowest level of the building

(B) adjacent to the electrical room

(C) above the hoistway

(D) adjacent to the mechanical room

Solutions

1. Gearless traction is one type of mechanism used for high-speed elevators, which a high-rise building would require.

Geared traction elevators are used for low speed and high capacity. Hydraulic elevators are not appropriate for high-rise buildings; they are used for buildings from two to five stories, or up to about 50 ft.

The answer is (D).

2. A department store requires elevators with capacity. The capacity is the amount of weight that the elevators can carry, which translates into the allowable number of people that can be on the elevator at any one time.

For a three-story building, speed is not critical, and the control method and machine room location would be secondary considerations.

It is important to understand the different elevator control methods available. These include the single automatic, selective collective, and group automatic. A single automatic system answers only one call at a time, and the user has exclusive control of the car until the trip is complete. With a selective collective system, the elevator answers all calls in one direction and then reverses direction and answers all calls in the opposite direction. With a group automatic system, a computer controls two or more elevators and dispatches and operates all the elevators in the most efficient manner possible.

The answer is (B).

3. Geared traction elevators can be designed to serve a wide variety of slower speeds and high capacities, so they are ideal for low-rise buildings with heavy loads, such as department stores. A geared traction elevator could be used for a small medical office building, but a higher speed would offer better service. A 16-story office building would need a high-speed, moderate-capacity elevator, so a geared traction type would be inappropriate. An apartment building would require a low capacity but higher speeds.

The answer is (C).

4. Ideally, elevator mechanical rooms should be placed above the hoistway. They must be at least as wide as the elevator shaft and generally need to be more than 12 ft deeper than the hoistway, but the exact size of the space should be calculated considering the type of elevator specified, the sizes of all the equipment to be housed in the space, and the required servicing clearances.

The answer is (C).

21 Site Work

1. A client who has recently moved from New York to southern California has hired an architect to design a new house in the colonial revival style, which is similar to a former home. The architect should recognize that this building configuration request may be influenced by

(A) cultural attitudes

(B) status seeking

(C) symbolism

(D) regionalism

2. In the design of a manufacturing plant and its associated office space, the primary form determinant is most likely

(A) construction schedule

(B) mechanical systems

(C) structure

(D) sustainability

3. A small office building is being planned for the site shown.

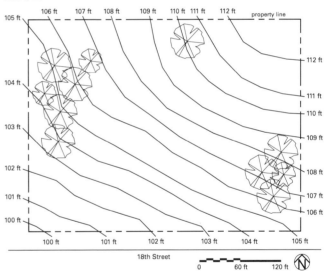

The architect has suggested that passive and active solar features be incorporated into the design. What feature will have the most influence on the solar design in the overall building configuration?

(A) existing landscaping

(B) geographic location of the site

(C) topography

(D) vehicular access

4. A client wants a museum to be built with two identically sized stories. The museum must have 74,800 ft^2 net assignable area, with a minimum of 15% of the space dedicated to circulation. The architect estimates the planned efficiency ratio to be 85%. The architect should plan for a building footprint of _____ ft^2 of when doing initial site planning. (Fill in the blank.)

5. The site shown is to be developed in accordance with local zoning and environmental requirements. (See *Illustration for Prob. 5.*)

The site is in zoning district R-2. Refer to the zoning ordinance excerpt in the table. (See *Table for Prob. 5.*)

The environmental requirements are as follows.

- There must be a minimum 20 ft setback from the edge of the wetlands.

- The utility company prohibits any site development within the easement and any building improvements within 5 ft of any easement.

- Solar access requirements prohibit any structures within 25 ft of the north property line in residential districts.

- On the plan, place the lines given to indicate the limits of the buildable area on the site. As many lines may be used as required, and the lines may overlap or cross.

Table for Prob. 5

zoning district[a]	setbacks			height limits		per gross floor area or unit parking[c]
	front	side	rear	feet	stories	
R-1[b]	25	15	15	30[d]	2	2 spaces and 350 ft^2
R-2[b]	25	10	5	45	3	2 spaces/unit
R-3	10	5	10	65	5	1.25 spaces/unit
M-1	5	5	5	70	5	1/1000 ft^2
M-2	0	0	5	110	8	2/1000 ft^2
B-1	10	0	5	110	8	1/1000 ft^2
B-2	10	0	0	150	12	1/guest room or unit
B-3	5	0	0	250	20	2/1000 ft^2

[a]R: residential, M: mixed use, B: business

[b]Maximum height can be increased 1 ft for every 5 ft increase in lot width over 50 ft up to a max. of 35 ft.

[c]See specific zoning district requirements for additional information.

[d]Bulk plane limit is required for side setbacks beginning on the property line at a point 10 ft above grade and extending at an angle of 45°. Upper story setback of 15 ft is required above 30 ft.

Illustration for Prob. 5

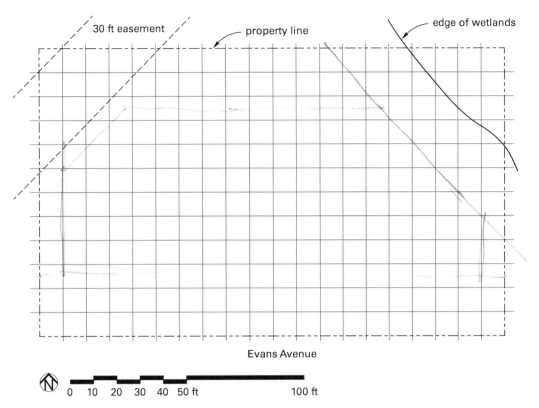

30 ft easement   property line   edge of wetlands

Evans Avenue

0 10 20 30 40 50 ft   100 ft

Note: 10 ft grid shown for reference only

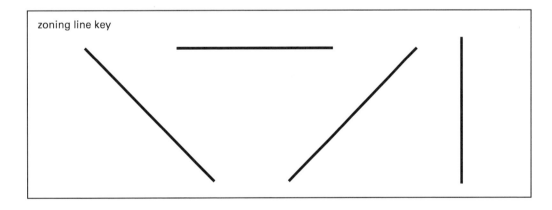

zoning line key

Project Planning

Solutions

1. The client's cultural upbringing is not known, so cultural attitudes cannot fully account for the client's style preference. The client, as well as the architect, would probably see the cultural setting of California as very different from New York. Building a house, even a very large mansion, probably would not convey an image of status in southern California. It is more likely that if the client wanted status, the architect should design a large, unique house in a contemporary style. Regionalism is not a factor because the architectural styles of contemporary southern California are typically quite different from the northeast United States. Such a request is an example of how a certain style of building symbolizes what a home should look like, so the factor most likely driving the client's request is symbolism.

The answer is (C).

2. When considering just form, the most likely parameter driving a manufacturing plant's building configuration is structure due to the need to have large, open spaces. This requirement would translate into a design of a simple post-and-beam system of widely spaced columns or a long-span structure, such as an arch or space frame. The other options are secondary influences because scheduling, mechanical systems, and sustainability measures easily can be integrated once the basic structure is determined. Even visible sustainability features, such as natural lighting or solar panels, would have to be designed in response to the size and shape of the manufacturing area.

The answer is (C).

3. While landscaping, topography, and vehicular access needs all affect building configuration, they do not directly impact the placement of solar features. Placement of solar features is most affected by where in the world the building is located. Passive solar features should be placed facing the side of the building that will get the most sun: the south in the northern hemisphere, and the north in the southern hemisphere. Geographic location influences a variety of building elements, including building orientation, passive heating, shading, daylighting, and photovoltaic panels.

The answer is (B).

4. The net assignable area includes space used for specific functions such as gallery space, receiving rooms, offices, work rooms, and similar spaces. It does not account for circulation, toilet rooms, mechanical rooms, space for walls, and the like. The 15% minimum circulation space is part of the 85% efficiency ratio and does not need to be included in the calculation. To determine the total gross area required, divide the net assignable area by the efficiency ratio.

$$\text{gross area} = \frac{\text{net assignable area}}{\text{efficiency ratio}}$$
$$= \frac{74{,}800 \text{ ft}^2}{0.85}$$
$$= 88{,}000 \text{ ft}^2$$

The museum will have two stories of identical size, so the footprint should be half the gross area.

$$\frac{88{,}000 \text{ ft}^2}{2} = 44{,}000 \text{ ft}^2$$

The answer is 44,000 ft².

5. In addition to the front, side and rear setbacks required by the zoning ordinance, the definition of the buildable area is restricted by the 20 ft wetlands setback, the 5 ft setback from the easement, and the 25 ft solar access requirement. The front and side setbacks determine the buildable area on the south, east, and west sides. The solar access restriction determines the building line on the north side. These are both modified by diagonal lines, one 5 ft from the southeast edge of the easement and one 20 ft from the wetlands area. Although technically the northeast building line would exactly follow the irregular line of the wetlands, for this problem it is placed 20 ft from the southwesterly limit of the wetlands.

On the illustration shown, the shaded area indicates the margin of error when placing the lines, as the limits are estimated by using the grid provided. (See *Illustration for Sol. 5.*)

Illustration for Sol. 5

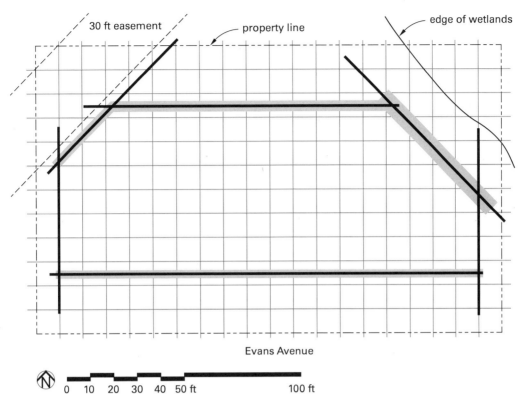

30 ft easement property line edge of wetlands

Evans Avenue

0 10 20 30 40 50 ft   100 ft

Note: 10 ft grid shown for reference only

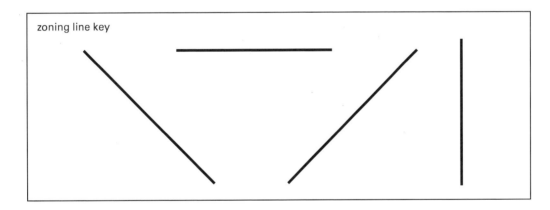

zoning line key

Project
Planning

22 Concrete

1. In the partial plan of a concrete basement shown, what would be the best way to improve the economy of the concrete formwork?

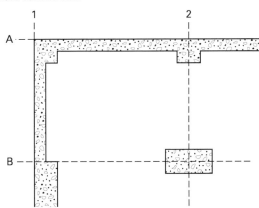

(A) Make the column square.

(B) Separate the pilaster at A2 from the wall.

(C) Form the pilaster at A1 with a diagonal.

(D) Make the wall along grid line 1 a uniform thickness.

2. A building is being planned for the storage of industrial equipment and machinery. What is the most appropriate reinforced concrete slab system for this building?

(A) flat slab on columns

(B) flat slab on columns equipped with shearheads

(C) flat slab on beams on all four sides

(D) pan joist concrete deck system

3. A section of a precast concrete panel attached to a cast-in-place concrete structure is shown.

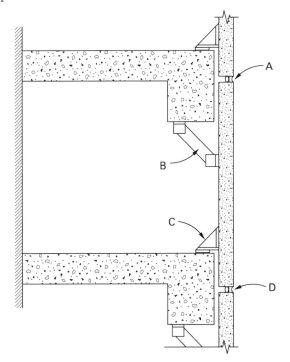

Which connection point should allow for both vertical and lateral movement?

(A) point A

(B) point B

(C) point C

(D) point D

4. Four vertical joints are shown.

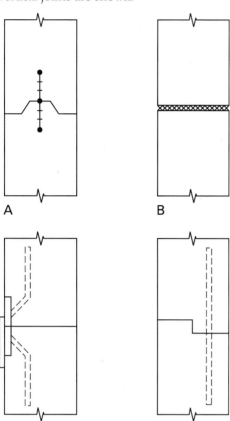

A

B

C

D

Which of the vertical joints would be appropriate for a concrete basement wall?

(A) A

(B) B

(C) C

(D) D

5. What is the primary purpose of the voids in a cored slab?

(A) to allow electrical services to be concealed in the slab

(B) to make a more efficient load-carrying member

(C) to make erection easier

(D) to minimize weight

Solutions

1. Forming corners in concrete always adds to the cost, so making the wall a uniform thickness would be most economical even though more concrete would be required. Making the column square would decrease the amount of concrete but would still require the same amount of forming. Separating the pilaster from the wall would actually increase the cost of formwork. Forming the pilaster with a diagonal would not be appropriate because of the structural problems caused by decreasing the column area and placing reinforcement.

The answer is (D).

2. The most appropriate reinforced concrete slab system for this building is a pan joist system. A flat slab on columns is generally used for light loads such as in residential buildings. Adding shearheads or beams on all four sides of the flat slab resolves the punching shear problem around the columns, and allows the system to be used for slightly longer spans and heavier loads, but would still be insufficient for storing industrial equipment and machinery. A pan joist system is the strongest system of the options listed, and it is the best suited for the heavy live loads of industrial and storage buildings.

The answer is (D).

3. A precast panel should have only two points of bearing on the structure. These are indicated at point C. One point should be a rigid connection and the other should provide for lateral movement. The remaining points of connection to the structure, or tiebacks as they are often called, should allow for both vertical and lateral movement of the panel due to differential movement of the structure and panel, and due to expansion and contraction caused by temperature differences.

The answer is (C).

4. Option (A) shows a strong keyed joint with a waterstop to prevent water penetration. The other selections show joints that are weak structurally or that do not provide for adequate waterproofing.

The answer is (A).

5. As with any beam, the deeper the member, the more efficient the beam. Using a cored slab rather than a solid slab allows the depth to be increased without increasing the weight in the center of the beam where it is not needed. Option (A) and option (D) are partially correct, but option (B) is the best choice.

The answer is (B).

Project Planning

23 Masonry

1. What is a requirement for a door opening in a masonry partition?

  (A) bond beam

  (B) arch action

  (C) weep holes

  (D) flashing

2. What type of brick would most likely be specified for an eastern exposure in New Hampshire?

  (A) NW

  (B) FBX

  (C) MW

  (D) SW

3. Which mortar joint is recommended for exterior use?

  (A) concave

  (B) trowel struck

  (C) weather struck

  (D) raked

4. Where should weep holes be located in a brick wall? (Choose the three that apply.)

  (A) at the lowest course of brick

  (B) above windows

  (C) above shelf angles

  (D) below window sills

  (E) under copings

  (F) every 15 ft vertically

5. Which of the following statements is true?

  (A) Spalling occurs when water-soluble salts in masonry units or mortar leach out of the brick.

  (B) Tuck pointing is used to finish mortar joints during construction of a new brick wall.

  (C) Flashing in a masonry wall should be terminated just before the face of the brick for best appearance.

  (D) A concealed flashing in a masonry wall with a concrete backup should terminate in a reglet.

Solutions

1. A bond beam is a masonry unit made to accommodate reinforcing and grout to span openings in masonry walls. These are often used in place of steel lintels.

The answer is (A).

2. SW stands for severe weathering and would be the type that should be specified for the northeastern United States. NW is normal weathering, and MW is moderate weathering. FBX refers to the finish appearance.

The answer is (D).

3. Trowel struck joints are not recommended because water can accumulate on top of the brick and seep into the joint. A weather struck joint is sometimes used, but water running down the brick above the joint may not drip off and may instead run horizontally under the brick. Raked joints are not recommended because water can pool in the tiny void between bricks, seep into the pores of the materials, and eventually damage the masonry and mortar. A concave joint avoids all these problems and has the added advantage of being easily tooled, which compresses the mortar.

The answer is (A).

4. Weep holes should be located at any location where water may accumulate within a multi-wythe, cavity, or veneer wall. The weep holes allow the water to drain or be wicked out of the wall cavity. Water tends to accumulate at the bottom of a wall or where any penetration through the wall creates a "shelf," such as above a window or at a steel angle. Both flashing and weep holes at 24 in on center, minimum, should be provided at each of the locations listed.

Weep holes are formed by placing short pieces of rope or plastic units in the mortar joint as it is being laid. The spacer is then removed after the mortar hardens, leaving a small hole. Alternatively, some masons choose to simply leave a portion of the bed joint unmortared. Either way, the opening gives water a way to escape from the wall assembly and helps to prevent condensation from accumulating within.

The answer is (A), (B), and (C).

5. Reglets are horizontal grooves cast into concrete that allow a piece of flashing to be slipped inside and then carried across the airspace and through the brick for proper drainage and moisture control.

Efflorescence (not spalling) occurs when salts leach out of a masonry assembly. This produces a white powdery substance that stains the face of the brick.

Tuck pointing is a process used to repair failing mortar joints. It involves removing the deteriorated mortar to a certain depth and inserting new, compatible mortar into the space, then striking it with a new, water-resistant edge treatment.

Flashing should always be extended at least $3/4$ in beyond the face of the brick and turned down at a 45° angle for proper drainage. If the flashing is terminated before the face of the brick, the moisture will seep into the brick and mortar and can cause damage. The 45° bend provides a drip edge that leads the moisture away from the face of the brick.

The answer is (D).

Project Planning

24 Metals

1. For short spans and in relatively small openings in 8 in and 12 in thick brick walls, the most commonly used steel lintels are

(A) angles placed back to back

(B) channels or C-shapes

(C) W-shapes used for beams

(D) structural T-shapes

2. Which of the following statements about steel connections are true? (Choose the four that apply.)

(A) Bolts are easily installed, inexpensive, and can be visually checked.

(B) One of the advantages of using welded studs is a reduction in the number of holes to be punched.

(C) The overall cost of riveted construction is usually lower than the cost of using bolted connections.

(D) Welding is more practical for moment connections.

(E) Rivets are still fabricated on a limited basis.

(F) Welding is less efficient than bolted construction.

3. In the detail shown, what is the purpose of the item labeled *x*?

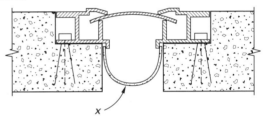

(A) to allow for vertical movement

(B) to collect condensation

(C) to provide a fire rating

(D) to create a sound seal

4. Galvanic action can be avoided by

(A) using neoprene spacers

(B) increasing the thickness of the materials

(C) reducing contact with dripping water

(D) using a third metal spacer

5. Which of the following would help to minimize oil canning? (Choose the three that apply.)

(A) Design attachment hardware that allows panels to move in response to expansion and contraction caused by changes in temperature.

(B) Include information in the specifications that requires the installer to transport panels vertically rather than horizontally.

(C) Specify a high-gloss painted finish on the panels.

(D) Carefully coordinate the design of the supporting structure to ensure that it is level and plumb.

(E) Design the panels to allow for a slight bend in the metal.

(F) Specify a thicker panel than would be normally required.

Solutions

1. In short spans and relatively small openings in 8 in and 12 in thick brick walls, the most commonly used steel lintels are angles placed back to back. Three steel angles are sometimes used. The W-shape beam is often used for longer spans or thicker walls.

The answer is (A).

2. Bolts are relatively inexpensive and easy to install. Welded studs, in which one end of a bolt is welded to one piece of steel, minimize the number of holes that must be punched for bolts. Moment connections require a continuous connection between two pieces of steel, and welding achieves that continuous connection better than than the use of bolts.

Rivets, though once popular, are not often used today, but they are still fabricated on a limited basis. A rivet has a cylindrical shank with a head at one end and excess metal at the other end. The shank extends through the parts to be connected and the remaining metal is compressed to form the other head. The head end is backed up by a pneumatic jackhammer. A second pneumatic hammer with a head-shaped die is used to form the second head. The overall cost of riveted construction is usually higher than the cost of construction using bolted or welded because of increased labor and equipment requirements. Welding is often more efficient than bolted construction because there are no angles, bolts, or washers to deal with and no clearance problems with wrenches.

The answer is (A), (B), (D), and (E).

3. The detail shows a building separation joint at the floor line. Fire protection is provided by one or more layers of fire-resistive material draped below the finish cover plate, which is directly above it.

The answer is (C).

4. Dissimilar metals should be physically separated by nonconducting materials such as neoprene in order to prevent galvanic action.

Increasing the thickness of the materials may postpone their complete deterioration but will not prevent it, so option (B) is incorrect. Direct contact with water will speed up galvanic action, but even moisture in the air is sufficient to cause it, so option (C) is incorrect.

Adding a third metal would still create the possibility of galvanic action, so option (D) is incorrect.

The answer is (A).

5. Oil canning gives a metal siding panel a wavy appearance. Generally, it is not a structural issue, just an aesthetic one. However, it can be minimized through careful design of the panels, attachment hardware, and supporting structure. For example, a textured, ribbed, or matte finish will minimize the appearance of waviness more than a smooth, glossy finish. Allowing space at the hardware connections for expansion and contraction will also help to minimize the waviness.

Most of the things that can be done to minimize oil canning fall under the responsibility of the contractor in the field, but the techniques can be written into the architect's specifications to ensure proper handling of materials and installation. Panels should always be transported vertically rather than horizontally, and care should be taken not to twist them. The supporting structure should be as flat, or planar, as possible.

The answer is (A), (B), and (D).

Project Planning

25 Structural and Rough Carpentry

1. Which of the following statements about sawn lumber joists in wood-framed buildings are true? (Choose the four that apply.)

(A) Joists often have a nominal width of 2 in.

(B) Joists often have a nominal depth of 6 in to 28 in.

(C) For heavy loads, joists may have a nominal width of 3 in to 4 in.

(D) Double joists must be provided under partitions parallel to the joists.

(E) Joists are often spaced at 12 in or 16 in on center.

(F) Joists rarely span more than 10 ft.

2. Fire-cut joists are required in

(A) platform framing

(B) heavy timber framing

(C) concrete walls

(D) masonry walls

3. Which of the following defects would most affect a wood joist's ability to resist horizontal shear?

(A) knot

(B) split

(C) wane

(D) warp

4. Which of the following engineered products would be best to use in place of traditional wood joists for spans from 16 ft to 20 ft?

(A) wood I-joists

(B) glued-laminated members

(C) medium-density fiberboard

(D) parallel-chord wood trusses

5. In order to minimize the space required for wood floor framing, the architect would most likely detail the connections to show the use of

(A) hurricane straps

(B) post caps

(C) saddle hangers

(D) splice plates

6. A structural member is shown.

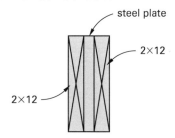

This structural member is known as a

(A)   composite beam

(B)   flitch beam

(C)   built-up beam

(D)   sistered beam

Solutions

1. Option (B) and option (F) are both false. Lumber joists often have nominal depths of 6 in to 14 in. The depth of 28 in is not included in the table of standard sizes for sawn lumber joists. Lumber joists often span 15 ft to 20 ft, and sometimes more.

The answer is (A), (C), (D), and (E).

2. A fire-cut joist is one with the ends cut at an angle such that the longer end rests on a masonry bearing wall and the shorter end is flush with the inside face of the wall. Fire-cut joists are required in masonry walls to prevent the masonry from being pushed up and out if the wood member should collapse during a fire.

The answer is (D).

3. A split is a separation of the wood fibers along the grain that extends through the piece of lumber. Because the value of horizontal shear depends on the integrity of the wood along its grain, any break would reduce the ability of the wood to resist horizontal shear.

The answer is (B).

4. Wood I-joists are designed to replace standard solid wood joists and rafters and would be very efficient, in terms of both cost and structure, for the spans indicated.

Glued-laminated (glulam) members would be more expensive and heavier than necessary for standard floor or roof framing in these span ranges. Medium-density fiberboard is a panel product and is not designed for structural uses such as beams or joists. Parallel-chord wood trusses could be used, but they are more efficiently used for longer spans.

The answer is (A).

5. Saddle hangers are pieces of preformed metal, designed to fit over a beam, that provide support for joists framed perpendicularly to the beam. This type of connection hardware allows the joists to be installed with their top edges flush with the top edges of the beams. It avoids the requirement that the joists be placed over the beams, which would increase the total depth required for the floor structure.

The answer is (C).

6. A flitch beam combines wood and steel into one member with load-carrying capacity far exceeding that of wood alone. Flitch beams are sometimes referred to as sandwich beams.

The answer is (B).

Project Planning

26 Finish Carpentry and Architectural Woodwork

1. The straightest, most uniform grain appearance in board lumber is achieved by specifying

- (A) plain sawing
- (B) quarter sawing
- (C) rift sawing
- (D) rotary sawing

2. In order to get a countertop or cabinet to fit snugly against a slightly irregular partition, which of the following should be specified or called out on the drawings?

- (A) astragal
- (B) extended frame
- (C) scribe
- (D) shoe molding

3. A detail is shown.

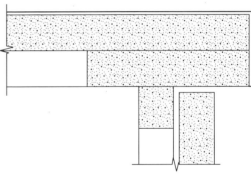

The detail illustrates the

- (A) top of a bookcase
- (B) edge of a cabinet countertop
- (C) front of a closet
- (D) edge of a display cabinet

4. Which diagram represents flush overlay cabinet construction?

(A)

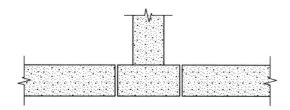

(B)

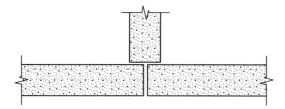

(C)

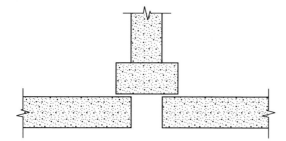

(D)

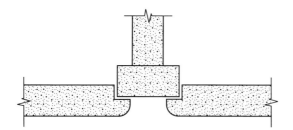

Solutions

1. With the rift sawing method, each cut for a board is made by sawing a quarter section of log radially toward the center point of the tree. This requires the quarter section of log being sawn to be shifted slightly for each cut. The grain in the resulting boards is nearly perpendicular to the face of the board. This gives the straightest grain pattern. Rift sawing is normally reserved for oak, to reduce the appearance of flaking, which is caused by medullary cells in the oak.

Quarter sawing is similar to rift sawing except that the quartered log is held in a stationary position as the cuts are made toward the center point of the tree. Yields for this type of sawing are higher than those for rift sawing, but boards made by cutting away from the center will have grains at a slight angle to the face of the board. Plain sawing cuts an entire log in one direction. Although plain sawing makes the most efficient use of the tree, boards cut near the tree edges will have a less uniform grain pattern. Rotary sawing is not an accurate term; rotary slicing is used only for veneer, not boards.

The answer is (C).

2. A scribe is an integral part of woodwork or a separate piece of trim that is cut, sanded, or otherwise shaped on the jobsite to exactly match the irregularities of an adjacent material.

The answer is (C).

3. The detail shows the built-up top of a countertop, as well as a frame and the top portion of a cabinet door. This would most likely be a countertop edge.

Option (A) is incorrect because a bookcase would not have the thicker, built-up top or a frame piece and probably would not have a door. Option (C) is incorrect because the framing for a closet either would be adjacent to a ceiling or would not include the thicker, built-up top piece. Option (D) is incorrect because a display cabinet would probably not have a door.

The answer is (B).

4. Flush overlay cabinet construction consists of drawer and door fronts aligned flush with each other with only a slight gap between them. As shown in the diagram, there is generally no face frame.

Option (A) represents flush construction. Option (C) represents reveal overlay construction, and option (D) represents lipped overlay construction.

The answer is (B).

Project Planning

27 Moisture Protection and Thermal Insulation

1. Many problems associated with exterior insulation and finish systems (EIFS) can be solved using which of the following design techniques?

(A) Design the wall using the rain screen principle.

(B) Use expansion joints at a maximum spacing of 10 ft 0 in.

(C) Increase the thickness of the finish coat.

(D) Provide extra flashing at window and door joints.

2. Which of the following materials provides the highest insulation value (R-value)?

(A) expanded perlite

(B) expanded polystyrene

(C) fiberglass

(D) polyisocyanurate

3. Heat loss in a building can be minimized by selecting wall materials with high

(A) conductance

(B) enthalpy

(C) permeability

(D) resistance

4. The sketch shown is of a wall in a cold climate. Where should the vapor barrier be located?

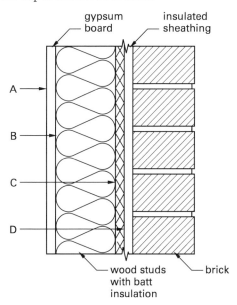

5. The greatest degree of protection from cold winter winds can be achieved with

(A) airlocks

(B) earth sheltering

(C) green roofs

(D) landscaping

Solutions

1. A standard EIFS is designed as a barrier against moisture. The level of moisture prevention depends on the finish and the proper construction of joints and details. An EIFS can experience problems if water leaks behind the finish and insulation and becomes trapped, damaging framing and other building components. Some proprietary systems are available that incorporate the rain screen principle by using a mesh or some other means of allowing pressure to equalize outside and inside of the system. Any water that does leak through is drained to the outside through weep holes.

The other common problem with a standard polymer-based (PB) EIFS is puncturing or denting. This can be addressed by using a polymer-modified system (PM) or by using a high-impact PB system with fiberglass mesh and an extra layer of base coat.

The answer is (A).

2. Polyisocyanurate has the highest R-value. For a 1 in thickness, its R-value ranges from 6.25 ft^2-hr-°F/Btu to 7.20 ft^2-hr-°F/Btu. Polystyrene has the next highest value, at 5.00 ft^2-hr-°F/Btu.

The answer is (D).

3. Resistance is the number of hours needed for 1 Btu to pass through 1 ft^2 of a material of a given thickness when the temperature differential is 1°F. A higher resistance means that heat takes longer to pass through, and thus the material has greater insulation value.

Conductance is the reciprocal of resistance and is the rate of heat loss measured in Btu/hr through 1 ft^2 of a material of a given thickness when the temperature differential is 1°F. Enthalpy is the total heat in a substance, including latent heat and sensible heat. Permeability is the property of a porous material that permits the passage of water vapor through it.

The answer is (D).

4. Vapor barriers always should be located on the warm side of insulation (area B) to prevent moisture from condensing when it cools and reaches the dew point. Moisture penetrating the insulation can reduce the insulation's effectiveness and damage other materials.

The answer is (B).

5. Earth sheltering would offer the greatest degree of protection from cold winter winds. Airlocks only protect door openings. Green roofs are primarily used to protect against solar radiation and to reduce runoff. Landscaping can reduce the negative effects of wind, but not as well as solid earth.

The answer is (B).

28 Doors, Windows, and Glazing

1. In wood door frame construction, the function of the shim is to

(A) provide the required space for hardware

(B) prevent sound from leaking through the opening

(C) hide the gap between the frame and partition

(D) provide for adjustability in setting the frame plumb

2. Which of the following types of glass is the strongest?

(A) laminated

(B) annealed

(C) tempered

(D) heat-strengthened

3. What type of glass would be appropriate for a 10-story building? (Choose the four that apply.)

(A) tempered

(B) heat-strengthened

(C) laminated

(D) annealed

(E) fire-rated

(F) float

4. Which of the windows shown would be best for ventilation during heavy rainstorms?

(A)

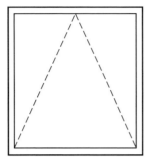

(B)

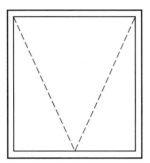

(C)

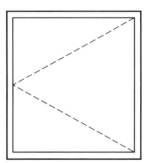

(D)

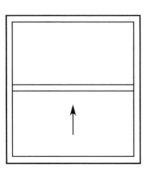

Solutions

1. A shim is a tapered piece of wood that, when used in pairs, allows the position of a door frame to be adjusted along the door's height until the frame is plumb.

The answer is (D).

2. Laminated glass is the strongest of the four types of glass listed. It consists of two or more layers of glass with a layer of plastic bonded in between. If the glazing is broken, the pieces of glass will be held together by the layer of plastic. Laminated glass is used in applications such as bulletproof glazing, car windshields, and skylights.

Annealed glass, or ordinary window glass, is made by floating molten glass on top of molten tin. As the liquid moves through the production process, it is slowly cooled into a perfectly flat sheet of solid glass. Annealed glass may be subjected to processes such as tempering and heat strengthening to change its characteristics.

Tempered and heat-strengthened glass are both formed by heating annealed glass to very high temperatures. Heat-strengthened glass is heated and then cooled slowly. Tempered glass is heated to higher temperatures and then cooled quickly. Tempered glass is about twice as strong as heat-strengthened glass and about four times as strong as

annealed glass. Tempered glass is used in glass doors and windows, as shelving, and for many other uses where a safety glass is required.

The answer is (A).

3. Annealed glass is the standard glass used in most non-critical glazing situations. Float glass is the same as annealed glass and would not be strong enough to be used in high-rise buildings. All of the other types of glass listed have greater strengths and could be used in a tall building with large panels of glass subject to high wind loads and thermal cycling.

The answer is (A), (B), (C), and (E).

4. Option (A) represents an awning window that pivots on the top. As such, the window could be left open during a rainstorm and still keep water out of the building.

Option (B) shows a hopper window. Option (C) illustrates a casement window, and option (D) illustrates a single-hung window. These three options would allow water to enter more easily.

The answer is (A).

29 Finish Materials

1. Which of the following flooring types has the highest resilience?

(A) asphalt

(B) cork

(C) linoleum

(D) vinyl composition

2. Which paint type would serve best as an anti-graffiti coating?

(A) acrylic

(B) alkyd

(C) oil

(D) urethane

3. In order to achieve the most uniform, straight-grain appearance in wood paneling, which of the following should be specified?

(A) plain slicing

(B) rotary slicing

(C) quarter slicing

(D) half-round slicing

4. Which of the following is the most important consideration in detailing a wood-strip floor?

(A) flame-spread rating

(B) expansion space at the perimeter

(C) nailing method

(D) moisture protection from below

5. Ceramic mosaic tile in a public shower room is best installed over a

(A) water-resistant gypsum board

(B) bed of portland cement mortar

(C) concrete block wall coated with a waterproofing membrane

(D) rigid cement composition board made for this purpose

6. A tactile finish should be applied to hardware on a door that leads to a building's

(A) fire stairs

(B) boiler room

(C) restrooms

(D) exterior

Project Planning

7. When specifying a hardwood floor over a concrete slab on grade, which of the following should the architect also specify?

(A) $^3/_4$ in plywood subflooring and 15# building felt

(B) $^3/_4$ in tongue-and-groove plywood placed over a layer of mastic

(C) treated wood sleepers on mastic and a layer of polyethylene vapor barrier

(D) 15# building felt

Solutions

1. Cork is a very resilient material. Its resilience is similar to that of rubber tile.

Asphalt tile, which is seldom used, has the lowest resilience. Linoleum and vinyl composition tile have low to moderate resilience.

The answer is (B).

2. Urethane is a high-performance coating and has superior resistance to abrasion, grease, alcohol, water, and fuels. It resists the adhesion of graffiti to surfaces and allows for relatively easy removal of graffiti.

The answer is (D).

3. Plain slicing produces a figured pattern with a characteristic "cathedral" appearance. Rotary slicing produces the most varied grain pattern, and half-round slicing yields a moderate amount of pattern. Because quarter slicing cuts perpendicular to the growth rings, this gives the straightest pattern of the choices listed. Rift slicing would also give a very uniform grain pattern.

The answer is (C).

4. All of the choices listed are considerations in detailing wood floors, so select the most important. Moisture is one of the biggest problems with wood floors, and keeping moisture out in the first place would minimize other problems such as expansion at the perimeter. Therefore, option (D) is the best choice.

The answer is (D).

5. A full bed of portland cement mortar offers the best durability and water resistance for high-use, wet areas.

The answer is (B).

6. A tactile finish (rough surface) is applied to hardware on doors leading to building areas that would be dangerous for a person with impaired vision, such as a boiler room.

The answer is (B).

7. Wood flooring installed over a slab on grade should be placed on treated wood sleepers that are set in a layer of mastic. Sleepers are generally 2×4s laid flat at 16 in on center. A layer of polyethylene vapor barrier should be placed over the sleepers but under the finish flooring material.

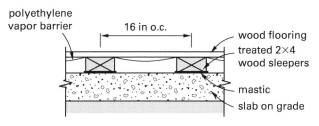

The answer is (C).

30 Building Configuration and Budgeting

1. Which of the following factors accounts for the highest cost of a lighting system over time?

(A) lamps

(B) luminaires

(C) installation

(D) operation

2. A company is considering replacing its existing heating, ventilating, and air conditioning (HVAC) system with a new system at a total cost of $55,000. It is expected that the new, more efficient system will save the company $460 per month in utility costs. The simple payback period of their investment will be _____ years. (Fill in the blank.)

3. Which of the following are true about life-cycle cost analysis? (Choose the four that apply.)

(A) Higher up-front costs often lead to lower operational costs.

(B) Costs presented in the analysis are the only factors that should be considered when making a decision about a material or system.

(C) It is economical to complete a a life-cycle cost analysis (LCCA) if two items have similar installation costs but differing operational costs or projected lifespans.

(D) LCCA evaluates all costs based upon their present value.

(E) An LCCA is similar to a life-cycle assessment (LCA).

(F) Salvage fees may be included in an LCCA.

4. During design development for a small corporate headquarters building, the client informs the architect that, due to poor sales in the previous quarter, the budget for the project must be reduced. Which of the following actions should the architect ignore in order to reduce initial construction costs?

- (A) reducing the number of pieces in the details
- (B) eliminating high maintenance finishes
- (C) suggesting changes that would make custom finishes closer to industry standards
- (D) reducing the number of different details involved in the project

5. Which of the following strategies would be employed in a community adopting the principles of defensible space? (Choose the four that apply.)

- (A) gated streets
- (B) strict enforcement of code regulations
- (C) loan programs for first-time homebuyers
- (D) concentration of all housing in one area
- (E) specification of vandal-resistant materials
- (F) clear distinctions between public and private spaces

6. An architect is considering general planning concepts for a veterinarian hospital and kennel, both owned by the same company. Which is the best design approach for both?

- (A) Combine both functions into one structure to allow sharing of common functions.
- (B) Make the hospital two levels to provide more site space for outdoor runs.
- (C) Design two separate buildings that share the same parking area.
- (D) Develop two wings for different functions but share a common entry suite.

7. A client wants to replace a small office building with an earth-sheltered building. The client wants the new building to have improved energy efficiency and adequate daylighting, while minimizing construction costs. The building site

is in a warm climate and has relatively level topography. The architect prepares the four concept sketches shown.

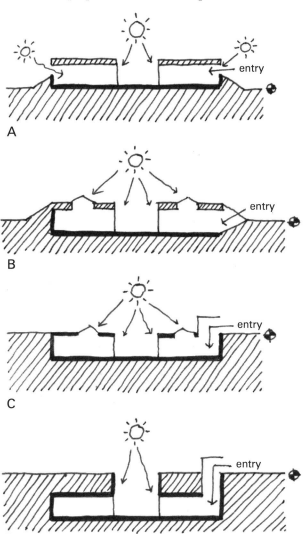

The same amount of foundation work is required for all four concepts. Which concept sketch would best meet the client's goals?

- (A) concept A
- (B) concept B
- (C) concept C
- (D) concept D

Solutions

1. Over the life cycle of a lighting system, the continuing operating cost for electricity is the single largest expense. For nonresidential applications, maintenance (i.e., the replacement of lamps and cleaning of luminaires) is the second greatest expense.

The answer is (D).

2. First calculate the initial (simple) rate of return.

$$\text{initial rate of return} = \frac{\text{annual savings}}{\text{investment}}$$
$$= \frac{\left(\dfrac{\$460}{\text{mo}}\right)\left(12\,\dfrac{\text{mo}}{\text{yr}}\right)}{\$55,000}$$
$$= 0.1003/\text{yr} \quad (10.03\%/\text{yr})$$

The simple payback period is the reciprocal of the initial rate of return.

$$\text{simple payback period} = \frac{1}{\text{initial rate of return}}$$
$$= \frac{1}{\dfrac{0.1003}{\text{yr}}}$$
$$= 10\,\text{yr}$$

Although the simple rate of return and payback period are quickly calculated and can be used as a rough guideline, actual rate of return and discounted payback period calculations are much more valuable when assessing the return on investment and comparing alternative systems.

The answer is 10 years.

3. LCCA allows designers and owners to evaluate the total cost of a product or system over its useful life. This facilitates an objective comparison between two or more options based upon a number of factors, including their initial purchase price, long-term maintenance costs, replacement costs over time, and any portion of the investment that may be recouped through salvage fees. Of course, this analysis is not the only factor that should be considered when making decisions about what to include in a building's design, but it does permit a comprehensive look at the total cost to the owner that decision will incur. An item that looks like a bargain in terms of its present-day purchase price may have steep operational costs or a short lifespan, requiring replacement in just a few years. Life-cycle costing takes all of these factors into consideration and converts all of the costs to present-day values so that they can be compared effectively. An LCA is a

method of evaluating the environmental impact of using a material or product, and it is not the same as an LCCA.

The answer is (A), (C), (D), and (F).

4. Using industry-standard details, reducing the number of components in the construction assembly, and reducing the number of unique details all would help reduce construction costs.

Although life-cycle costs are a consideration in a corporate headquarters (presumably owner-occupied and maintained), the problem refers to initial construction costs.

The answer is (B).

5. Defensible space is a theory that is based on the principles developed by Oscar Newman. The case studies cited in his book describe some of the techniques used to help create a sense of pride of ownership in a neighborhood.

In Dayton, Ohio, mini-neighborhoods were created through the use of gated streets. However, as Newman pointed out, gated streets alone are insufficient; successfully implementing the principles of defensible space requires stricter enforcement of building codes (including attaching criminal charges for noncompliance), help for new homeowners to finance and maintain their properties, and community programs designed to facilitate interaction among neighbors.

At Clason Point in New York City, New York, Newman describes a row house project where the aesthetics of the community contributed to its demise: "temporary" concrete block buildings outfitted with vandal-resistant materials and separated by open spaces that were perceived as dangerous. Newman and the planners introduced barriers such as curbs and fences to define private and semiprivate spaces, limited and widened pedestrian walkways to allow for better visibility and supervision, and refaced existing structures with more "residential" materials that the residents helped to choose. They also allocated a portion of the common grounds to each family and encouraged them to grow grass in order to take ownership of the space outside their homes.

In Yonkers, New York, implementing defensible space principles involved scattering factory-built row houses on a number of sites throughout the city, rather than clustering the low-income residents in a high-rise.

The answer is (A), (B), (C), and (F).

6. Although both types of facilities may share some common functions, such as administrative offices and food storage, the services each provides is unique and the reasons for visiting differ. In addition, a kennel requires adjacent outdoor facilities that a hospital does not. A two-level facility is not efficient for animals or moving supplies because it would require ramps and an elevator. People bring in their animals to each facility for very different reasons, so each should have its own a reception area to avoid potential problems. The best design approach would be to separate the two buildings but to have them on the same site with separate, distinct entrances. However, they could share the same parking area.

The answer is (C).

7. Concept A provides daylighting on sides opposite the central court and requires the least excavation, but it would require extra soil to be imported. Concept C would require extensive excavation and provide no opportunity for side windows. Concept D offers the best earth-sheltering of the four choices, but it has the least amount of daylighting and the highest cost due to excavation, earthwork removal, waterproofing, access stairs and elevators.

Concept B provides the best balance among the three goals of energy efficiency, daylighting, and cost. Much of the building is covered with earth, which would minimize heat gain and loss. Daylighting could be provided by the sunlit central court, skylights, or high windows. The partially buried structure minimizes the cost of excavation and the material excavated could be used to create the berms above grade.

The answer is (B).

Case Studies

Case Study 1

The members of a church plan to add an adjunct structure containing a small chapel and meeting room to the east of the church's present site. This new building will be used for smaller gatherings, meetings, and funeral services. The space requirements are summarized in Resource 4.1.

The required adjacencies are shown in the bubble diagram in Resource 4.2. The heavy lines indicate the closest required proximities. Corridors may be added to the block plan as needed to fulfill site requirements.

The regulatory and developmental constraints are as follows.

Code Requirements

*   There must be 10 standard parking spaces and three accessible parking spaces.

*   No parking is permitted within 10 ft of any property line.

*   A minimum of two exits are required from the new building and from the chapel. One of the exits from the chapel must be a separate exit for funerals. Exits can be no closer together than one-third the diagonal dimensions of the space in which they are located.

*   The maximum length of any dead-end corridor is 20 ft.

Site Requirements

*   Provide seven standard parking spaces and three accessible parking spaces.

*   No parking is permitted within 10 ft of any property line.

*   On the east side of the new building, provide an 80 ft long × 25 ft wide loading area and service drive for funeral procession parking adjacent to a separate entrance of the chapel. The service drive must be one-way, entering and exiting on Hackberry Street (its dimensions are included in the loading area width).

*   There must be one curb cut along Pine Avenue to allow for street parking and one access drive leading to the existing parking area to the west of the new building.

*   Walks and drives must be provided. One walk is to connect the existing church and parking area west of the new building to the new entrance.

Based on the program requirements and bubble diagram, the architect has sketched the rough site plan and block plan shown in Resource 4.2.

Resource 4.1 Summary of Space Requirements

spaces	space required (ft^2)	comments
chapel	1700	separate access for funeral required
activity room	900	directly adjacent to lobby
lobby	500	directly adjacent to chapel
robing room	150	directly adjacent to office
office	300	
storage	200	
toilets	400	
mechanical	400	
corridor(s)		as required

Resource 4.2 Bubble Diagram and Block Plan

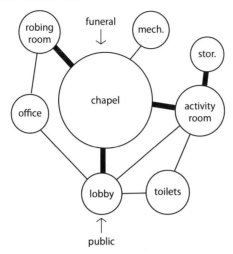

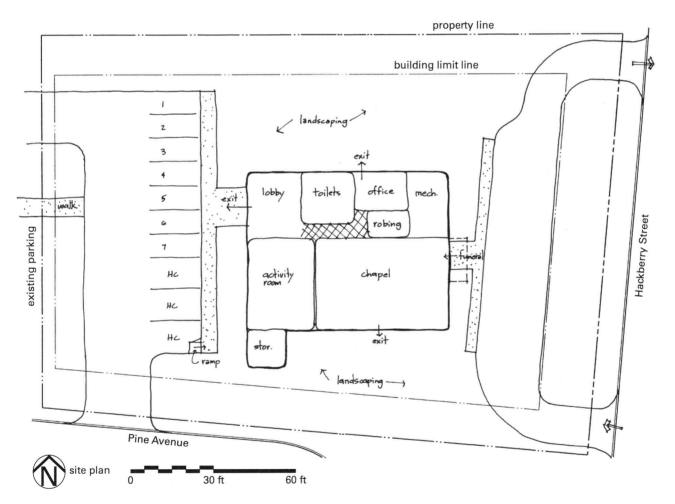

1. In Resource 4.2, what egress problem does the new building present?

(A)   The mechanical room has no exit into the corridor.

(B)   The exit on the south side of the chapel is unnecessary.

(C)   The exits from the chapel are too close together.

(D)   The second corridor exit is through the office.

2. After doing the initial sketch, the architect realizes that the parking area is undersized by three spaces. Why might this be a difficult problem to resolve?

(A)   The accessible ramp intrudes into an accessible parking space.

(B)   The lobby entrance is too far from the accessible parking spaces.

(C)   There is not enough space to expand the parking area.

(D)   The walk from the existing parking area is too narrow.

3. Analyze the preliminary site plan and block diagram shown in Resource 4.2. What improvements could be made to the building and site configuration? (Choose the four that apply.)

(A)   Locate the accessible parking spaces closer to the building entry.

(B)   Improve access between the existing parking area and the west end of the site.

(C)   Switch the positions of the parking spaces and parking access.

(D)   Reverse the direction of the one-way access for funeral processions.

(E)   Switch the positions of the lobby and activity room.

(F)   Incorporate the storage room into the overall block shape of the building.

4. In Resource 4.2, how could the building configuration be improved?

(A)   Add a covered entry next to the lobby.

(B)   Move the robing room closer to the front of the chapel.

(C)   Make the mechanical room accessible from the corridor.

(D)   Move the storage room to the west side to improve building massing.

5. On the illustration shown, place the hot spot marker where the proposed block plan does not satisfy the bubble diagram.

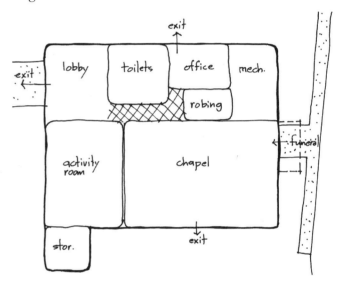

6. The client wants to change the program to increase the size of the activity room by 50% and include a movable wall between the activity room and the chapel, so more people can be accommodated for chapel services when needed. What changes to the site plan would be the best approach for the architect to consider?

(A)   Enlarge the activity room to the west, and move parking slightly to the west as required.

(B)   Enlarge the activity room to the south, and relocate the storage room to the east.

(C)   Move both the west and south walls of the activity room to gain the necessary space increase.

(D)   Rotate the chapel 90°, and move the east wall of the activity room to gain space.

Project Planning

7. Analyze the site plan and program requirements for pedestrian access. What is the greatest deficiency shown in Resource 4.2?

(A) There is no walkway from Pine Avenue to the lobby entry.

(B) The connection between the existing church and new lobby entry is awkward and potentially dangerous.

(C) There is no walkway from the funeral loading area to the lobby entry.

(D) A pedestrian connection between Hackberry Street and the chapel is not provided.

8. The church building committee decides to explore a less expensive alternative to building a separate building for the chapel and other facilities. The committee asks the architect to develop a plan that includes some of the new programmed requirements into an addition directly to the east of the existing church building connected to the existing lobby by a short corridor. The parking and funeral procession access will still be provided on the east side of the new addition. In this proposal, only the chapel, lobby, office, robing room, and a somewhat smaller mechanical room are required. The requirements for the layout are to minimize the distance of expansion to the east, simplify the structure, and minimize cost. A portion of the existing building is shown. (See *Illustration for Prob. 8.*)

Which of the four preliminary alternative block diagrams shown best meets the new requirements?

(A) plan A

(B) plan B

(C) plan C

(D) plan D

Illustration for Prob. 8

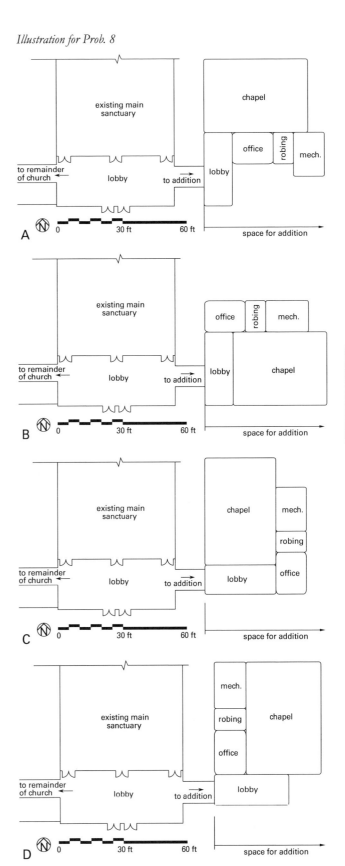

9. The client would like for the chapel to have a high, vaulted ceiling that is expressed from the exterior of the building and that provides opportunities for natural light. The architect's sketches of four simple massing studies are shown.

Which of the options best incorporates these requirements with the low ceiling needs of the other spaces, while maintaining the general spatial relationships shown in Resource 4.2?

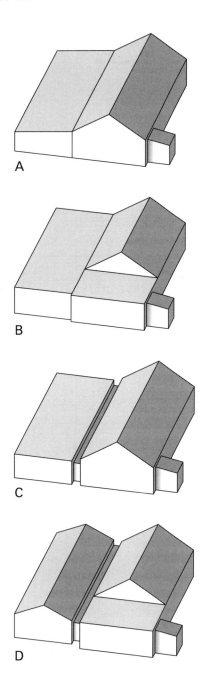

A

B

C

D

10. The architect has developed an alternative shown in the block diagram to meet the program requirements and correct some deficiencies. (See *Illustration for Prob. 10.*)

How can the plan be further improved?

(A) Move the corridor to the west of the office, robing room, and mechanical room.

(B) Relocate the funeral entrance slightly to the south.

(C) Move the ramp from the accessible parking area.

(D) Make the activity room the same width as the chapel.

Illustration for Prob. 10

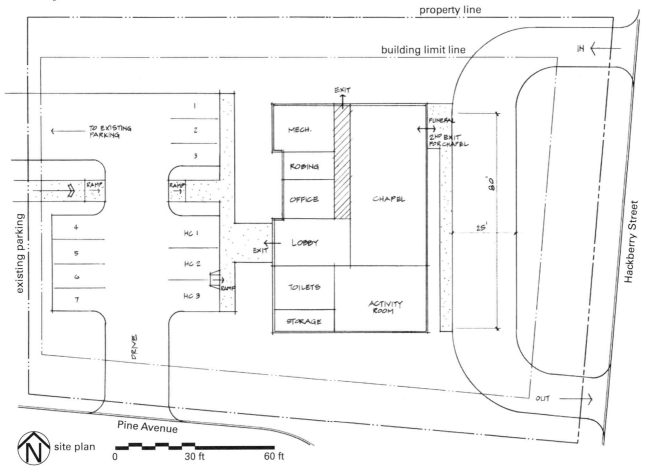

site plan

Case Study 2

As part of the design development phase of a small two-story commercial building, an architect sketches wall section alternatives to meet the exterior design requirements of the building and energy conservation codes. The structure will have a steel frame with a concrete on metal deck second floor and roof. The first floor will be reinforced concrete slab on concrete foundation walls that enclose a usable basement level. The building enclosure will be brick veneer on a metal stud backup wall. One of the architect's sketches is shown in Resource 4.3. The building is a B occupancy located in climate zone 5B (cold, dry) in the midwest United States. The structural frame, floor/ceiling, and roof/ceiling assemblies must have a 1-hour rating.

Resource 4.3 Wall Section Study

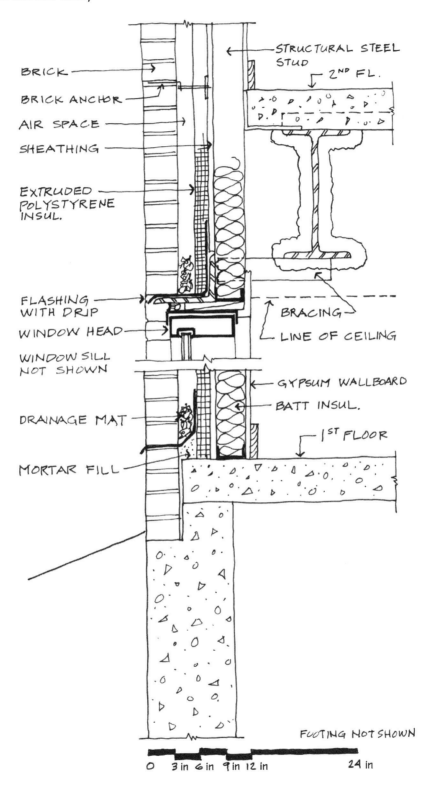

BRICK

BRICK ANCHOR

AIR SPACE

SHEATHING

EXTRUDED POLYSTYRENE INSUL.

FLASHING WITH DRIP

WINDOW HEAD

WINDOW SILL NOT SHOWN

DRAINAGE MAT

MORTAR FILL

STRUCTURAL STEEL STUD

2ND FL.

BRACING

LINE OF CEILING

GYPSUM WALLBOARD

BATT INSUL.

1ST FLOOR

FOOTING NOT SHOWN

0   3 in 6 in 9 in 12 in   24 in

Project Planning

Resource 4.4 Properties for Selected Insulation Types

insulation type	R-value/in (ft^2-hr-°F/Btu)	estimated cost/ft^2 for low end R-19	estimated cost/ft^2 for high end R-19	permeability	air barrier
high density fiberglass batts	3.6–4.5	$4.72	$5.61	class III	no
mineral wool batts	3.5	$1.20	$1.44	class III semi-permeable	no
polyisocyanurate board	5.6–7.7[a]	$2.47	$3.20	class III semi-permeable[b]	yes
mineral wool board	2.4–3.3	$1.50	$2.00	class III	no
expanded polystyrene (EPS)	3.8–4.4[a]	$4.04	$4.32	class II	no
extruded polystyrene (XPS)	5.0[a]	$4.00	$4.37	class II	yes
sprayed closed-cell polyurethane	3.3–5.0	$3.04	$4.06	class II	yes

[a] LTTR: long-term thermal resistance
[b] class I, impermeable if foil faced

Resource 4.5 Code Requirements for Insulation

TABLE C402.1.3
OPAQUE THERMAL ENVELOPE INSULATION COMPONENT MINIMUM REQUIREMENTS, R-VALUE METHOD[a]

CLIMATE ZONE	1		2		3		4 EXCEPT MARINE		5 AND MARINE 4		6		7		8	
	All other	Group R	All other	Group R	All other	Group R	All other	Group R	All other	Group R	All other	Group R	All other	Group R	All other	Group R
Roofs																
Insulation entirely above roof deck	R-20ci	R-25ci	R-25ci	R-25ci	R-25ci	R-25ci	R-30ci	R-30ci	R-30ci	R-30ci	R-30ci	R-30ci	R-35ci	R-35ci	R-35ci	R-35ci
Metal buildings[a, b]	R-19 + R-11 LS	R-19 + R-11 LS	R-19 + R11 LS	R-19 + R-11 LS	R-19 + R-11 LS	R-19 + R-11 LS	R-19 + R-11 LS	R-19 + R-11 LS	R-19 + R-11 LS	R-19 + R-11 LS	R-25 + R-11 LS	R-25 + R-11 LS	R-30 + R-11 LS	R-30 + R-11 LS	R-30 + R-11 LS	R-30 + R-11 LS
Attic and other	R-38	R-38	R-38	R-38	R-38	R-38	R-38	R-38	R-38	R-38	R-49	R-49	R-49	R-49	R-49	R-49
Walls, above grade																
Mass	R-5.7ci[c]	R-5.7ci[c]	R-5.7ci[c]	R-5.7ci[c]	R-7.6ci	R-7.6ci	R-9.5ci	R-9.5ci	R-11.4ci	R-11.4ci	R-13.3ci	R-13.3ci	R-15.2ci	R-15.2ci	R-25ci	R-25ci
Metal building	R-13 + R-6.5ci	R-13 + R-6.5ci	R-13 + R-6.5ci	R-13 + R-6.5ci	R-13 + R-6.5ci	R-13 + R-13ci	R-13 + R-13ci	R-13 + R-13ci	R-13 + R-13ci	R-13 + R-13ci	R-13 + R-13ci	R-13 + R-13ci	R-13 + R-19.5ci	R-13 + R-19.5ci	R-13 + R-19.5ci	R-13 + R-19.5ci
Metal framed	R-13 + R-5ci	R-13 + R-5ci	R-13 + R-5ci	R-13 + R-7.5ci	R-13 + R-7.5ci	R-13 + R-7.5ci	R-13 + R-7.5ci	R-13 + R-7.5ci	R-13 + R-7.5ci	R-13 + R-7.5ci	R-13 + R-7.5ci	R-13 + R-7.5ci	R-13 + R-7.5ci	R-13 + R-15.6ci	R-13 + R-7.5ci	R13 + R17.5ci
Wood framed and other	R-13 + R-3.8ci or R-20	R-13 + R-3.8ci or R-20	R-13 + R-3.8ci or R-20	R-13 + R-3.8ci or R-20	R-13 + R-3.8ci or R-20	R-13 + R-3.8ci or R-20	R-13 + R-3.8ci or R-20	R-13 + R-3.8ci or R-20	R-13 + R-3.8ci or R-20	R-13 + R-7.5ci or R-20	R-13 + R-7.5ci or R-20 + R-3.8ci	R-13 + R-7.5ci or R-20 + R-3.8ci	R-13 + R-7.5ci or R-20 + R-3.8ci	R-13 + R-7.5ci or R-20 + R-3.8ci	R-13 + R-15.6ci or R-20 + R-10ci	R13 + R-15.6ci or R-20 + R-10ci
Walls, below grade																
Below-grade wall[d]	NR	NR	NR	NR	NR	NR	R-7.5ci	R-7.5ci	R-7.5ci	R-7.5ci	R-7.5ci	R-7.5ci	R-10ci	R-10ci	R-12.5ci	R-12.5ci
Floors																
Mass[e]	NR	NR	R-6.3ci	NR	R-10ci	R-8.3ci	R-10ci	R-10.4ci	R-10ci	R-12.5ci	R-12.5ci	R-12.5ci	R-15ci	R-16.7ci	R-16.7ci	R-16.7ci
Joist/framing	R-30	R-30	R-30	R-30	R-30	R-30	R-30	R-30	R-30	R-30	R-30	R-30	R-30[f]	R-30[f]	R-30[f]	R-30[f]
Slab-on-grade floors																
Unheated slabs	NR	NR	NR	NR	NR	NR	R-10 for 24" below	R-10 for 24" below	R-10 for 24" below	R-10 for 24" below	R-10 for 24" below	R-10 for 24" below	R-15 for 24" below	R-15 for 24" below	R-20 for 24" below	R-20 for 24" below
Heated slabs[f]	R-7.5 for 12" below	R-7.5 for 12" below	R-7.5 for 12" below	R-7.5 for 12" below	R-10 for 24" below	R-10 for 24" below	R-15 for 24" below	R-15 for 24" below	R-15 for 24" below	R-15 for 36" below	R-15 for 36" below	R-20 for 48" below	R-20 for 48" below	R-20 for 48" below	R-20 for 48" below	R-20 for 48" below
Opaque doors																
Nonswinging	R-4.75	R-4.75	R-4.75	R-4.75	R-4.75	R-4.75	R-4.75	R-4.75	R-4.75	R-4.75	R-4.75	R-4.75	R-4.75	R-4.75	R-4.75	R-4.75

For SI: 1 inch = 25.4 mm, 1 pound per square foot = 4.88 kg/m^2, 1 pound per cubic foot = 16 kg/m^3.

ci = Continuous insulation, NR = No requirement, LS = Liner system.

a. Assembly descriptions can be found in ANSI/ASHRAE/IESNA Appendix A.
b. Where using R-value compliance method, a thermal spacer block shall be provided, otherwise use the U-factor compliance method in Table C402.1.4.
c. R-5.7ci is allowed to be substituted with concrete block walls complying with ASTM C 90, ungrouted or partially grouted at 32 inches or less on center vertically and 48 inches or less on center horizontally, with ungrouted cores filled with materials having a maximum thermal conductivity of 0.44 Btu-in/h-ft^2-°F.
d. Where heated slabs are below grade, below-grade walls shall comply with the exterior insulation requirements for heated slabs.
e. "Mass floors" shall include floors weighing not less than:
  1. 35 pounds per square foot of floor surface area; or
  2. 25 pounds per square foot of floor surface area where the material weight is not more than 120 pounds per cubic foot.
f. Steel floor joist systems shall be insulated to R-38.

Project Planning

11. In order to meet code requirements, the continuous insulation shown in Resource 4.3 should be _____ in thick. (Fill in the blank.)

12. Place the hot spot marker in the correct location for safing insulation that meets building code requirements.

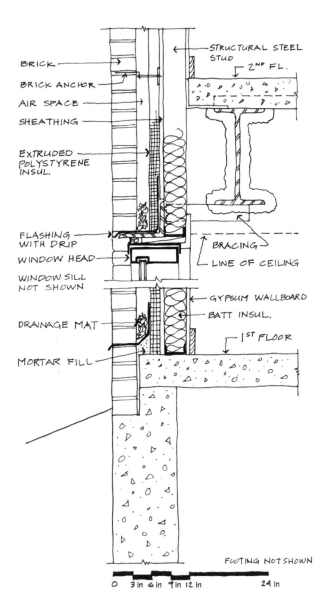

13. In Resource 4.3, consider the tentative construction and the climate. Where should the vapor retarder be placed?

   (A)   on the face of continuous insulation

   (B)   between the continuous insulation and the sheathing

   (C)   between the sheathing and the metal studs

   (D)   between the studs and the gypsum wallboard

14. On the illustration shown, place the building elements in the position on the foundation wall that provides the most complete thermal barrier. Granular backfill will be used. The building elements only represent a partial length of material. Not all elements may be required.

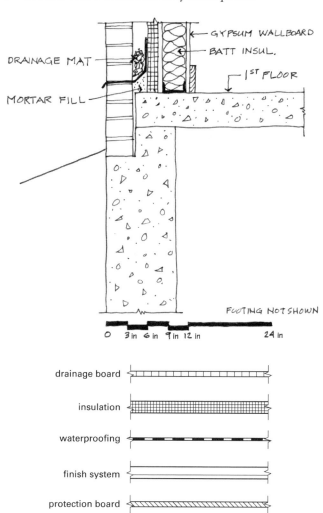

15. Given the tentative construction detailing shown in Resource 4.3, what is the least expensive insulation to use on the exterior of the basement foundation wall?

   (A)   expanded polystyrene

   (B)   extruded polystyrene

   (C)   mineral wool board

   (D)   polyisocyanurate

Project Planning

Solutions

1. The mechanical room does not require an exit into the corridor. The third chapel exit is unnecessary but it does not violate any requirements. The separation of exits in the chapel meets the code requirements. A second exit from the corridor and public spaces would have to go through the office, which could be locked. Therefore, it is prohibited by code.

The answer is (D).

2. The accessible ramp does extend into one accessible space, but this can be resolved by extending the ramp into the walk in front of the parking area and widening the walk as necessary. The accessible parking spaces can be moved north to be closer to the lobby entrance. The requirements do not include any prescribed dimensions for the walk connecting the existing parking area to the new parking area.

The code requirements prohibit parking within 10 ft of a property line, so there is only enough room to expand the parking at the north and south ends of the parking area by one space at each end.

The answer is (C).

3. Option (C) is undesirable because it is safer to exit a car when adjacent to the sidewalk. Option (E) places the activity room away from the chapel, which is contrary to the bubble diagram requirements for the closest required proximity. Although acceptable as shown, moving the accessible parking spaces closer to the building entry would improve access slightly. Because there would be major pedestrian traffic from the existing church and parking area, the walkway should be made more direct and easier to use. The direction of the one-way drive should be reversed to allow for standard drop-off on the passenger side of vehicles. Finally, although not technically incorrect, the position of the storage room looks like an afterthought, shows lack of good planning skills, and might make the design of the exterior awkward.

The answer is (A), (B), (D), and (F).

4. While a covered entry is desirable to keep rain and snow off people entering the building, this could be easily added during design development and is often not part of a simple block diagram. As the bubble diagram indicates, the robing room is directly adjacent to the chapel and is close enough to the front of the chapel to be functional. While the location of the storage room may be problematic, moving it to the west side of the building would not necessarily improve building massing. Even though it is not absolutely necessary, good planning dictates that the mechanical room be accessible from the corridor. If it is

not, then access is necessary through the chapel or from the exterior of the building, both of which are not ideal.

The answer is (C).

5. The entry to the chapel is not in direct proximity to the lobby as indicated by the heavy line in the bubble diagram and by the comments in the list of spaces.

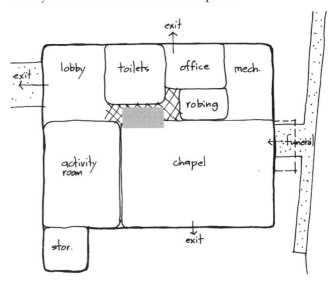

As shown in the block diagram, the closest possible entry to the chapel is in a corridor, which is an intervening space. The shaded area indicates the margin of error for placing the hot spot marker.

6. Option (B) and option (C) are not desirable because they would result in an awkward L-shaped space when the moveable wall is opened. Option (D) would place the entry to the chapel even farther from the lobby, in direct contradiction to the bubble diagram and stated requirement for adjacency. It would also result in a very awkward space when the moveable wall is opened.

The best way to integrate both program changes into the design is simply to extend the activity room to the west. By doing this, the room can be easily enlarged and remain the same width as the chapel. This makes it ideal for using a moveable wall to accommodate more people in the chapel when required. There is enough room on the site to move the parking area to the west as needed to allow for this enlargement.

The answer is (A).

7. Walks from either street to the chapel would be a good addition, but there are no existing sidewalks indicated on the plan, so adding walkways is not a critical requirement, nor is it practical. It is unnecessary to connect the funeral loading area to the lobby entry. The new building is intended as an adjunct to the main church, so the pedestrian access between the two facilities should be as direct, safe, and comfortable as possible. In the present configuration, people would have to squeeze between parked cars to get to the lobby entry. This situation could be improved by creating a walkway extension between parking spaces and providing curb ramps up and down to the drive.

The answer is (B).

8. Option (A) would extend the construction farther to the east than the other options, creating a more expensive configuration. This plan also creates an awkward edge for the funeral procession parking and drive. Option (B) is acceptable for cost and funeral access, but it unnecessarily extends construction further east than it needs to be. Option (C) would make access for funerals very difficult because the chapel is located on the west side of the addition.

Option (D) minimizes the distance of expansion to the east and still provides access on the east side of the building for funeral processions by locating the chapel on the east side, oriented with the long dimension north-south. The office, robing room, and mechanical room are similarly oriented on the west side of the addition. This plan uses a simple block layout, which minimizes foundation and structural costs.

The answer is (D).

9. The low slope roof of option (A) prevents placing windows on the west side and the extension of the south gable prevents any windows being used on the south end of the chapel roof. Option (C) also prevents any fenestration on the south end of the gable portion of the chapel. While option (D) may allow for windows on all four sides of the chapel, the use of a gable roof over the low ceiling spaces visually competes with the vaulted ceiling over the chapel, diminishing its importance and making the building look somewhat industrial. Option (B) best shows the location of the chapel from the exterior and provides opportunities for window locations on the sides as well as at both ends of gable of the chapel. In addition, the peak of the gable is higher, creating greater emphasis and making it more visible from the south over the ceiling of the activity room.

The answer is (B).

10. The corridor is in a good location as shown, allowing access to all adjacent rooms and providing two exits from the lobby to the outside. The funeral entrance at the front of the chapel allows for easy access to hearses. Moving it further south would conflict with the seating in the chapel. The activity room needs to be sized as shown to allow direct access from the lobby. The ramp from the accessible parking cannot encroach into the parking spaces. It should be moved to the east with the sidewalk widened as necessary.

The answer is (C).

11. Find the required insulation value in Resource 4.5. For a metal-framed building in climate zone 5, walls above grade must have an R-13 value for the batt insulation plus an R-7.5ci value for continuous insulation. Resource 4.5 shows that the continuous insulation is extruded polystyrene. According to Resource 4.5, extruded polystyrene has an R-value of 5.0. Therefore, for an R-7.5 value the insulation must be $1\frac{1}{2}$ in thick.

The answer is 1½ in.

12. Safing insulation must be placed between the edge of the second floor slab and the sheathing, within the stud space. This prevents the spread of fire and smoke between the floors. The shaded area indicates the margin of error for placing the hot spot marker.

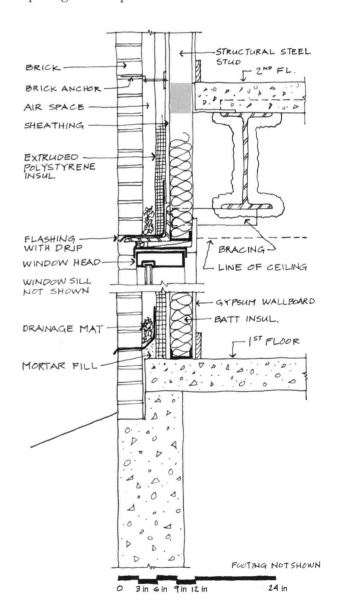

13. For a cold, dry climate such as climate zone 5B, a vapor retarder should be placed on the warm side of the insulation to keep moisture inside the building from migrating to a cold place in the wall where it condenses. Because both batt insulation and continuous insulation are shown in Resource 4.3, the best place would be between the studs and the gypsum wallboard.

The answer is (D).

14. The most complete thermal barrier requires that the insulation to be placed on the inside of the foundation wall where it can be carried up as far as possible to the underside of the concrete floor. Placing insulation on the outside would require it to stop short of grade level, exposing a larger, uninsulated area. The finish system is placed over the insulation. Waterproofing should be placed against the outside of the foundation wall with a protection board over it. A drainage layer is not required if granular fill is being used. Because the elements are only partial lengths they can be placed anywhere along the wall as long as they are in the correct sequence.

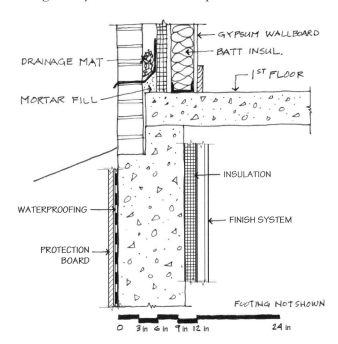

15. In Resource 4.4, the least expensive insulation that is impervious to moisture is mineral wool board, even though it has a lower R-value than polystyrene.

The answer is (C).

DIVISION 5: PROJECT DEVELOPMENT & DOCUMENTATION

31 Integration of Building Systems

1. A designer is planning on using a hydronic distribution system to heat a building and needs to decide which type of system will be best for efficiency and comfort control. To this end, the designer plans on supplying equal flow and fluid temperature to each radiator to yield an efficient return. Which type of piping systems would most likely achieve the best result?

(A) one-pipe system

(B) two-pipe direct return system

(C) two-pipe reverse return system

(D) series perimeter loop system

2. Consider the location for a mechanical system and its vertical distribution tree in a 10-story office building. Which of the following locations should be avoided?

(A) within internal circulation cores

(B) integrated with a building

(C) at the edges of a building

(D) between the internal core and the edge of a building

3. Which type of test is used to determine the required size of a leaching field?

(A) percolation

(B) yield

(C) aquifer

(D) water table

4. Which strategy will most effectively reduce stormwater runoff from a site?

(A) Capture rainwater for irrigation and other nonpotable uses.

(B) Reduce the amount of impervious area.

(C) Construct a garden roof.

(D) Construct an on-site stormwater treatment facility.

5. Which of the following shapes is the most desirable duct shape?

(A)

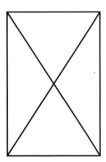

(B)

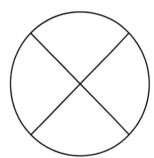

(C)

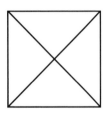

(D)

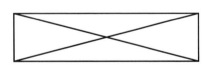

6. An architect is selecting lighting for a computer lab. The candlepower distribution curves for a variety of fixture types are shown. Which candlepower distribution diagram would be most appropriate for this space?

(A)

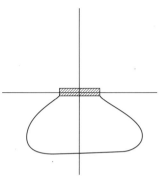

(B)

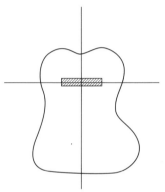

(C)

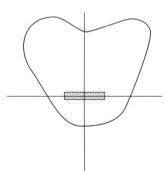

(D)

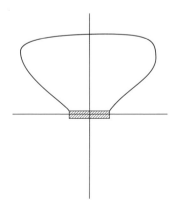

7. Which type of high intensity discharge (HID) lamp must be installed in a specified burning position?

   (A)   mercury vapor

   (B)   metal halide

   (C)   high-pressure sodium

   (D)   low-pressure sodium

8. If not connected to other sections, the section of the soil stack that is located above the highest plumbing fixture in a building is called the

   (A)   vent stack

   (B)   stack vent

   (C)   cleanout

   (D)   vacuum breaker

9. An architect is planning a 100,000 ft^2 university classroom building. The mechanical engineer estimates that the total floor area required for the boiler room and the chilled water plant will be about 3000 ft^2. Which of the following criteria should also be kept in mind when determining the location and design of the mechanical rooms? (Choose the three that apply.)

   (A)   Each mechanical room should have at least one exterior wall.

   (B)   The boiler room should be adjacent to the chilled water plant.

   (C)   Rooms should be as square as possible.

   (D)   Ceilings in both rooms should be at least 12 ft high.

   (E)   Mechanical rooms must be placed on the ground floor.

   (F)   The mechanical rooms should be equal in size.

10. An architect is designing an art school at a major university. Which combination of daylighting and electric lighting would be the most appropriate choice for the painting studios?

   (A)   south-facing windows and incandescent recessed lights

   (B)   north-facing windows and skylights and fixtures with high color rendering index (CRI) fluorescent lamps

   (C)   windows to the east and west and fluorescent fixtures in coves at the perimeter of the studio

   (D)   north-facing skylights and metal halide lamps at each workstation

11. Weatherstripping affects

   (A)   effective temperature

   (B)   thermodynamics

   (C)   ventilation

   (D)   infiltration

12. A main trunk duct is to be placed in the interstitial space above a suspended ceiling and below the structural framing. The space is not constricted. When capacities are equal, which of the following shapes of ducts would be best to use?

   (A)   rectangular, with the long dimension horizontal

   (B)   rectangular, with the long dimension vertical

   (C)   square

   (D)   round

13. Which of the following strategies would effectively reduce the noise caused by a duct system without reducing airflow?

   (A)   Specify duct liners for all supply and return ducts.

   (B)   Specify 90° bends in short duct runs.

   (C)   Provide an active noise-canceling system emitting out-of-phase noise.

   (D)   Specify fiberglass baffles.

Project Development

Solutions

1. In a one-pipe system (i.e., a traditional steam radiator system), it is often difficult to maintain or control temperature, especially to the more remote locations. The return of the condensed water relies heavily on gravity. A two-pipe direct return system does improve on the temperature and pressure issue of the one-pipe system for the remote radiators, but the return loop still relies on gravity. A two-pipe reverse return system distributes the fluid to each of the radiators through a continuous system with individual returns from each unit. This results in a longer overall system but with better control than other types of systems.

The series perimeter loop system has a continuous loop that is pressurized, and temperature is maintained so that individual radiators can tap into it and be controlled individually. The series perimeter loop system typically does not use steam, so chilled water for cooling can be used in the warmer seasons. The loop feeds back to the heat (or cooling) source so that individual returns are not needed.

The answer is (D).

2. The most desirable and preferred areas for leasable office space must be considered. Exterior walls provide the best opportunity to take advantage of natural light, outside views, and natural ventilation. When mechanical systems and their distribution are placed near the center of the building, the exterior wall is made available for other uses.

The preferred areas are reduced when mechanical systems are placed along the outside walls at the edges of a building.

The answer is (C).

3. The required size of a leaching field is determined by the quantity of effluent that must be accommodated and the ability of the soil to let the effluent soak in. This permeability of the soil is measured by the percolation test. None of the other options test either quantity or permeability.

The answer is (A).

4. Reducing the impervious area on a site is the most effective way to reduce stormwater runoff. Impervious area is any area of building or paving that does not allow stormwater to seep into the ground.

Though less effective, installing a garden roof is also a way to reduce stormwater runoff. Reusing captured rainwater for other approved uses, such as flushing toilets and irrigating landscaping, is a good way to manage stormwater and keep it on site. An on-site treatment facility would

help remove contaminants from stormwater before it is released into nearby rivers or streams, but would not reduce stormwater runoff.

The answer is (B).

5. Duct sizes are determined by calculating the cross-sectional area required to accommodate a certain amount of air at a given velocity and then choosing a shape that provides that cross-sectional area and fits within the space allotted for mechanical pathways through the building. The formula for calculating cross-sectional area is

$$A_{in}{}^2 = \left(\frac{\text{volume of air in cfm}}{\text{velocity in fpm}} \right)(\text{friction allowance})$$
$$\times \left(144 \ \frac{in^2}{ft^2} \right)$$

In this problem, the most important variable is friction allowance. Friction allowances vary depending on the shape of the duct; larger, roomier ducts have lower friction allowances than more constricted shapes. A round shape has the least surface area for the same cross-sectional area. Ducts with smooth rounded shapes offer less resistance than ducts with tight spaces or sharp corners. A round duct has a friction allowance of 1.0, making it the least resistive choice; therefore, it is the most desirable.

If round ducts are not feasible, the next best choice is a square or nearly square cross section. Small square ducts (less than 1000 cfm) have a friction allowance of 1.10, while larger ones have a friction allowance of 1.05. Thin rectangular ducts are the most restrictive and have a friction allowance of 1.25.

The answer is (B).

6. The candlepower distribution curve shown in option (D) represents an indirect fixture, which would be a good choice for the computer lab. Indirect lighting would illuminate the ceiling and provide even, diffuse light throughout the space without causing glare or reflections on the computer screens.

The candlepower distribution curve shown in option (A) represents a direct fixture, option (B) represents a semidirect fixture, and option (C) represents a semi-indirect fixture.

The answer is (D).

7. Metal halide lamps are particularly sensitive to orientation, and they lose efficiency and lumen power if not installed correctly. All metal halide lamps are designated with a proper burning position: base-up, base-down, horizontal, or universal.

The other types of HID lamps do not have this characteristic and can be installed in any orientation.

The answer is (B).

8. The stack vent is the portion of the soil stack above the highest plumbing fixture. It serves as a vent for the stack and is open to the outside at the top. A vent stack is a collection of vents from a number of fixtures that share one exterior outlet. A cleanout is an area of the plumbing that can be accessed to clear obstructions from the system. A vacuum breaker is a flap that opens to admit air if there is suction in a water pipe, which prevents siphoning of wastewater back into the clean water supply system.

The answer is (B).

9. Boiler rooms and chilled water plants should be located adjacent to one another when possible; in some buildings, the two functions are placed in the same room. It is imperative that the rooms each have at least one exterior wall to permit access to fuel tanks that may be located outside and to allow for adequate ventilation. Recommended ceiling heights vary depending on the type of equipment chosen, but generally 12 ft is the minimum. The rooms should be long and narrow rather than square and sized to best accommodate the equipment.

Both boilers and chillers are heavy and require additional structural support. It is often most economical to locate them on the ground floor, but this is not required. They tend to be noisy, so the mechanical rooms should be placed in locations within the building where the noise will not disrupt critical tasks. Soundproofing techniques should also be integrated to acoustically separate the mechanical rooms from the occupied spaces.

The answer is (A), (B), and (D).

10. Art studios require optimal color rendering and even daylight. The best combination of natural and artificial lighting techniques would be north-facing windows and skylights along with the best quality high-color rendering index lamps that the budget will allow. Task lighting should also be provided for the students' work areas.

The answer is (B).

11. Weatherstripping helps seal joints and cracks around doors and windows, reducing air infiltration. Air infiltration is a primary factor in heat loss, so sealing these voids improves the performance of mechanical systems and conserves energy.

The answer is (D).

12. A round duct is the most efficient choice and offers the smallest possible perimeter for the same cross-sectional area, thus minimizing friction and pressure loss. A square shape would use the available space most efficiently, but a duct of this shape is not as efficient overall as a round duct. As ducts become more rectangular, they become less efficient and have increased friction loss. A rectangular duct with the long dimension horizontal would only be used if space was a problem.

The answer is (D).

13. An active noise-canceling system would help to reduce the noise in a duct system without reducing airflow. This type of system analyzes the noise from the blowers and other system components and synthesizes a noise that is exactly out of phase with the mechanical noise. The two sounds cancel each other and the result is perceived silence.

The answer is (C).

Project Development

32 Integration of Specialty Systems

1. Which of the following devices would best control entry to a secure laboratory?

- (A) card reader
- (B) central station alarm
- (C) photoelectric cell
- (D) ultrasonic detector

2. Which of the following would be appropriate for fire protection in an elementary school? (Choose the three that apply.)

- (A) ionization detector
- (B) photoelectric detector
- (C) temperature rise detector
- (D) gas-sensing detector
- (E) flame detector
- (F) laser beam detector

3. The pyramidal forms of Manhattan skyscrapers built in the early to mid-1900s were the result of

- (A) the influence of European tastes and style on American architecture
- (B) a response to zoning laws governing setbacks and height restrictions
- (C) an attempt to make buildings safer in case of fire by housing fewer people on the uppermost floors
- (D) the structural limitations of iron as a building material

4. Rehabilitation of a building constructed in the 1860s requires cleaning and repairing the existing brick exterior walls. The brick is in good condition but is very dirty. Portions of the mortar have fallen out, and much of what remains is so soft that it can be scraped away with a fingernail. Which restoration technique should the architect recommend?

- (A) pressure washing with a 10% muratic acid solution
- (B) pressure washing with plain water and repointing the mortar
- (C) hand washing the brick with water and a stiff brush and repointing the mortar
- (D) sandblasting

5. Dock levelers are used to

(A) provide final adjustment for steel angle trim

(B) keep boating piers stable in the water

(C) provide adjustability for various sized trucks

(D) accommodate tolerances in pouring concrete pits

6. Which of the following is required for an access floor system? (Choose the three that apply.)

(A) lifting devices

(B) modular panels

(C) pedestals

(D) stringers

(E) acoustical batts

(F) handrails

7. Which type of lamp typically has the longest life span?

(A) incandescent

(B) fluorescent

(C) metal halide

(D) high-pressure sodium

8. Where would a sound intensity level of 120 dB be found?

(A) in a sewing factory

(B) at a rock concert

(C) in an architect's open plan office

(D) during naptime at a nursery school

9. A lobby is shown.

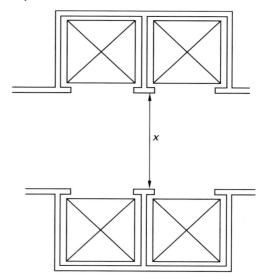

What should be the minimum width (x) of the lobby?

(A) 8 ft

(B) 10 ft

(C) 12 ft

(D) 14 ft

Solutions

1. A card reader is one type of security device that is used to control access.

Security systems are generally comprised of access controls, notification devices, and intrusion detectors. A central station alarm is a method of notification. Photoelectric cells and ultrasonic detectors are devices used for intrusion detection.

The answer is (A).

2. A temperature rise detector would not give early warning to the occupants. A gas-sensing detector by itself would not be appropriate for this application. A flame detector responds to infrared radiation given off by flames and may respond too late to give adequate warning.

If properly located, either an ionization or photoelectric detector would work. Ionization detectors sound an alarm when they sense the products of combustion. Photoelectric detectors monitor smoke. Either would sound an alarm before a temperature rise detector. A laser beam detector is a type of photoelectric detector and would also be appropriate.

The answer is (A), (B), and (F).

3. In 1916, New York City passed a zoning law designed to protect access to light and ventilation for all buildings. Skyscrapers were being built as quickly as possible, and New Yorkers feared that these walls of masonry and steel reaching into the sky would make the street level cold, dark, and cavernous. As buildings rose higher and higher, they were required to comply with more stringent setbacks. In order to build the maximum rentable area on their extremely valuable sites, developers adopted the stepped, wedding cake-like shape.

The answer is (B).

4. The least destructive technique should always be recommended when dealing with historic buildings and fragile old building materials. Hand washing with water and a stiff brush is the gentlest cleaning method and will probably remove most of the dirt from the surface of the brick. Missing or deteriorating mortar should be removed and replaced with compatible mortar, and the mortar should be restruck to shed water from the joints. This process is called repointing or tuck pointing.

Pressure washing (sometimes called power washing) can leave water marks on soft brick and can dislodge crumbling mortar, creating openings and allowing water to be forced inside the wall cavity. Adding an acidic ingredient to the washing solution may cause additional damage to the brick. Sandblasting will likely destroy soft brick and mortar.

The answer is (C).

5. Dock levelers are pieces of equipment used to allow trucks with various bed heights to be serviced from the same dock. The equipment is placed in a pit at the edge of the dock, and a steel panel is adjusted up or down to provide a ramp from the dock to the level of the truck.

The answer is (C).

6. Access floor systems may use stringers, which are rigid connections between pedestals, but they can also be the stringerless type, which rely only on pedestals and panels to keep the system in place.

All access floors use modular panels set on pedestals of some type. Removal of the panels requires a lifting device.

The answer is (A), (B), and (C).

7. Of the four types of lamps listed, the high-pressure sodium lamp generally has the longest life span. A high-pressure sodium bulb can be expected to last around 24,000 hr. A mercury vapor lamp would have a similar life expectancy.

The lamp with the shortest life span is the incandescent bulb. It can be expected to last only about 2000 hr.

The life span of a fluorescent lamp depends on the way the lamp is operated. The life span is affected not only by how many hours the lamp is on but by how many times the lamp is turned on and off. With typical usage patterns, a life span of about 10,000 hr to 20,000 hr can be expected, depending on the type of lamp and ballast used. Depending on the wattage, a metal halide lamp could also be expected to last from 10,000 hr to 20,000 hr.

The answer is (D).

8. A sound intensity level of 120 dB is almost deafening and can be felt throughout a listener's body. It can cause ringing in the ears and a temporary loss of hearing. Hearing protection should be worn during prolonged exposure to sound intensity levels this high.

Common sound intensity levels range from 0 dB, the threshold of hearing, through 130 dB, the threshold of pain.

The answer is (B).

9. The minimum width of the lobby should be 10 ft. A 10 ft wide lobby will allow sufficient space for a group of passengers to gather, but is small enough that a person in the lobby can see all of the elevators while waiting for an available car.

The answer is (B).

33 Loads on Buildings

1. In calculating solar heat gain, what value must be known in addition to the area of the glass?

    (A)   mean radiant temperature

    (B)   design cooling factor

    (C)   equivalent temperature difference

    (D)   coefficient of heat transfer

2. A two-way concrete slab is normally reinforced for

    (A)   bending moment in both directions

    (B)   bending moment in the short direction only

    (C)   bending moment in the long direction only

    (D)   temperature/shrinkage stresses in both directions only

Solutions

1. The design cooling factor and the area of the glass must both be known to calculate solar heat gain.

Equivalent temperature difference is used to calculate heat gain through the building envelope, such as walls and roofs.

2. A two-way concrete system is somewhat square in shape and reinforced for bending moment in both the short and long directions. In the one-way slab, the reinforcement is placed for bending moment in the short direction, while the long direction is reinforced at a minimum ratio for temperature/shrinkage stresses.

The answer is (A).

34 Structural Fundamentals

1. During the final stages of contract document development, the electrical engineer discovers that mechanical ductwork is shown on the mechanical engineering drawings in a position that interferes with electrical conduit. The person responsible for resolving this conflict is the

(A) electrical engineer

(B) mechanical engineer

(C) contractor

(D) architect

2. Adding a shear key to the base of a cantilever retaining wall helps to prevent

(A) sliding of the wall

(B) overturning of the wall

(C) breaking and cracking of the wall base

(D) simultaneous breaking and overturning of the wall

3. Which of the following types of diaphragms has the largest allowable shear value?

(A) blocked plywood diaphragm with a $^3/_8$ in panel of structural I-grade

(B) unblocked plywood diaphragm with a $^3/_8$ in panel of structural I-grade

(C) diaphragm made of steel deck with a 2 in concrete topping

(D) diaphragm that consists of a 6 in concrete slab

Solutions

1. The architect is responsible for the overall coordination of all consultants' drawings and for resolving disputes and conflicts. The electrical engineer should bring the conflict to the architect's attention. The architect can then coordinate with both consultants to resolve the conflict.

The answer is (D).

2. Adding a shear key to the base of a cantilever retaining wall helps prevent sliding of the wall by increasing the contact surface, and therefore the frictional forces, between the base of the wall and the soil.

The answer is (A).

3. Of the listed diaphragm types, the diaphragm that consists of a 6 in concrete slab has the largest allowable shear value. Such a slab would have an allowable shear of about 10,000 lbf/ft. A diaphragm made of steel deck has an allowable shear between 100 lbf/ft and 2600 lbf/ft. Plywood diaphragms generally have an allowable shear value between 100 lbf/ft and 800 lbf/ft.

The answer is (D).

35 Beams and Columns

1. A positive bending moment at a section of a beam implies

(A) compression stress in the top fibers of the beam and tension stress in the bottom fibers

(B) tension stress in the top fibers of the beam and compression stress in the bottom fibers

(C) compression stress in all fibers of the section

(D) that the bending moment is not related to tension and compression stresses

2. When designing a beam, why is it necessary to control deflection? (Choose the four that apply.)

(A) Excessive deflection is visually disturbing.

(B) Excessive deflection can break adjacent windows.

(C) Excessive deflection is a sign that the beam is unsafe in bending.

(D) Excessive deflection is a sign that the beam is unsafe in shear.

(E) Excessive deflection can crack adjacent partitions.

(F) Excessive deflection can crack adjacent plaster ceilings.

3. Neglecting the beam weight, what is the general shape of the bending moment diagram for the cantilever beam loaded as shown?

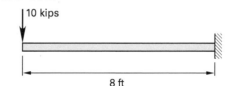

(A)

(B)

(C)

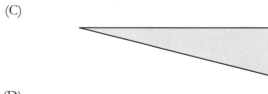

(D)

Project
Development

4. A flat reinforced concrete slab is supported on columns only. The column grid is 24 ft by 24 ft. The tributary area of a typical interior column is approximately

- (A) 140 ft^2
- (B) 290 ft^2
- (C) 390 ft^2
- (D) 580 ft^2

Solutions

1. Sign conventions identify both the bending moment that creates compression stresses in the top fibers of a beam and tension stresses in the bottom fibers of a beam as a positive bending moment. The tension and compression stresses are reversed in option (B), so option (B) is incorrect.

The answer is (A).

2. Excessive beam deflection is visually disturbing and might give the impression that the beam is not safe when it is. An excessive deflection could also damage adjacent building materials, breaking windows or cracking partitions and suspended plaster ceilings.

A beam can have a large deflection and still be safe in bending and shear.

The deflection limits recommended by building codes and standards are often calculated as a percentage of the span. For instance, a limitation of $1/240$ or $1/300$ of the span length, calculated under the total load applied on the beam including all dead and live loads, is often recommended for steel beams so that their appearance is not disturbing. For beams and girders supporting plastered ceilings, a limitation of $1/360$ of the span length, calculated under live load only, is often recommended. This last limitation is explicit in the American Institute of Steel Construction (AISC)

Specification for Structural Steel Buildings, and is frequently used as a guide to whether plaster ceilings are used or not.

The answer is (A), (B), (E), and (F).

3. The bending moment diagram should have the shape of a sloped line for a concentrated load type. This means that diagrams in options (A) and (D) are incorrect. The diagram in option (A) is a horizontal line and corresponds to the general shape of the shear diagram for this beam. Option (D) shows a curved line, which corresponds to the bending moment diagram of a uniformly distributed load. The diagrams in option (B) and option (C) show a sloped line; however, the bending moment at the free left end of the cantilever beam should be equal to zero because the point load is applied there and has no moment at this point. This is shown in option (C).

The answer is (C).

4. The tributary area of a typical interior column in this grid is 24 ft by 24 ft which is about 580 ft^2.

290 ft^2 is the approximate tributary area of a typical exterior column in this grid. This area would be 12 ft by 24 ft.

The answer is (D).

36 Trusses

1. An open-web joist supported floor system is shown.

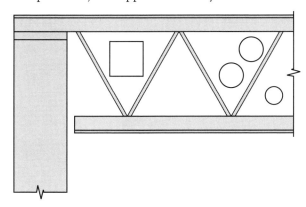

Consider the efficiency of the system and the building floor-to-floor height, and place the appropriate heating, ventilating, and air conditioning (HVAC) duct symbol in the most suitable location.

Solutions

1. A circle symbol is more appropriate for an HVAC duct, and it is integrated within the open-web joist system as shown.

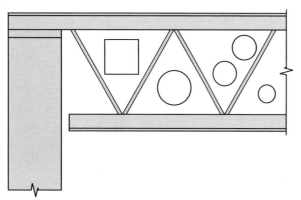

To reduce floor-to-floor height, coordinate duct sizes and open-web joist sizes so that the ducts can be placed between the webs of the joists. Otherwise, ducts must run under the joists, which would increase both the amount of space that must be heated and cooled and the associated energy costs. In the diagram, three of the four options would fit within the empty web space that is shown.

Surface area of metal along the wall of the duct will create a resistance to the movement of air passing through the duct. Of the symbols given, the round duct has the least amount of exposed surface area per cross-section, thus making it the most efficient.

37 Foundations

1. Steel column footing detail is shown. Place the appropriate anchor bolt symbol(s) in the correct location(s) on the illustration.

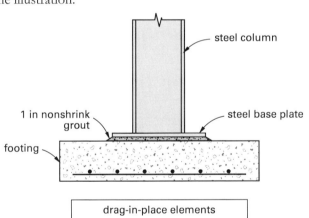

steel column

1 in nonshrink grout

steel base plate

footing

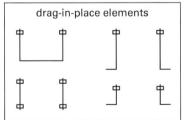

drag-in-place elements

2. In the illustration shown, what is the purpose of the gravel?

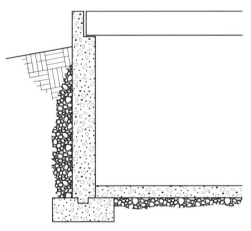

(A) to reduce hydrostatic pressure

(B) to keep the soil from direct contact with the concrete

(C) to provide a firm base for concrete bearing

(D) to hold the membrane in place and protect it

Solutions

1. The L-shaped anchor bolts help connect the steel base plate to the concrete footing. The recommended minimum embedment is 8 in. The steel base plate is normally welded to the steel column and is then placed on 1 in of nonshrink grout to allow for leveling. An anchor bolt must be shown on each side of the steel column.

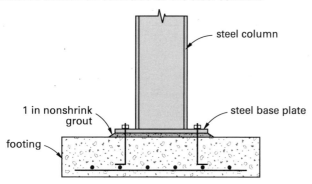

Of the anchor bolt symbols provided, the longer L-shaped anchors are the correct symbols to use and place. The shorter L-shaped anchors do not provide enough embedment depth. The anchors that utilize bolt heads at the bottom do not provide as much surface area for embedment as L-shaped anchors. The U-shaped anchor is not typical in the industry, and it would be difficult to coordinate with multiple base plate anchor holes simultaneously.

2. The gravel provides open spaces for any water under hydrostatic pressure to lose its pressure and drip to drains near the footing. Although it does this by preventing direct contact of the soil with the wall, preventing contact is not the sole purpose.

The answer is (A).

38 Connections

1. Blocking that eases the transition between a roof deck and the parapet wall in a membrane roof installation is known as a

- (A) chamfer
- (B) cant
- (C) transition strip
- (D) scupper

Solutions

1. A cant strip is an angled piece of blocking that eases the transition between the roof deck and the parapet wall when installing a roofing system so that the membranes or roofing felts do not crack or split when they are applied. Rather than bending them at a 90° angle, the cant strip allows the transition to be made with two 45° angles and minimizes the likelihood of damage from cracking or splitting. In addition, the slope helps the water to drain away from the joint and allows the flashing and membranes to be lapped in a way that keeps water from entering.

The answer is (B).

Project Development

39 Building Code Requirements on Structural Design

1. An illustration of stair dimensions is shown.

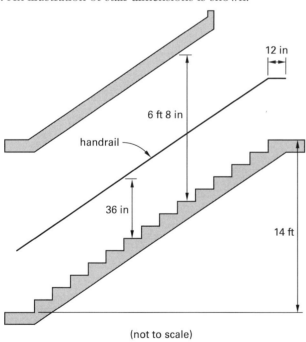

(not to scale)

According to model codes, which of the indicated stair dimensions is a code violation?

- (A) handrail height of 36 in
- (B) headroom height of 6 ft 8 in
- (C) total rise height of 14 ft
- (D) handrail extension of 12 in

2. According to the American Concrete Institute's *Building Code Requirements for Structural Concrete* (ACI 318), what is the maximum permissible spacing of lateral ties in a reinforced concrete column?

- (A) 16 times the diameter of the reinforcing bars
- (B) 48 times the diameter of the lateral ties
- (C) the least dimension of the column
- (D) the least of 16 times the diameter of the reinforcing bars, 48 times the diameter of the lateral ties, or the least dimension of the column

3. According to the *International Building Code* (IBC), a soft story is a story in which the

(A) lateral stiffness is less than 70% of that in the story above or less than 80% of the average stiffness of the stories above

(B) lateral stiffness is less than 60% of that in the story above or less than 70% of the average stiffness of the stories above

(C) lateral stiffness is less than 50% of that in the story above or less than 60% of the average stiffness of the stories above

(D) story lateral strength is less than 80% of that of the story above

4. According to the American Concrete Institute's *Building Code Requirements for Structural Concrete* (ACI 318), a cantilevered reinforced concrete slab spanning 10 ft needs to have a minimum thickness of

(A) 6 in

(B) 12 in

(C) 20 in

(D) 24 in

Project Development

Solutions

1. The maximum allowable height between landings or floors (rise height) is 12 ft. All of the other dimensions are correct. The height from the nosing to the top of a handrail must be between 34 in and 38 in.

The answer is (C).

2. According to ACI 318, the maximum spacing between lateral ties of a reinforced concrete column should be the least of the following three dimensions: 16 times the reinforcing bar diameter, 48 times the tie diameter, or the least dimension of the column.

The answer is (D).

3. According to the IBC, a soft story is a story in which the lateral stiffness is less than 70% of that in the story above or less than 80% of the average stiffness of the stories above.

Option (B) describes an extremely soft story. Option (D) describes a weak story. Option (C) does not correspond to any story type as defined in the IBC.

The answer is (A).

4. According to ACI 318 Table 9.5(a), a cantilevered reinforced concrete slab of a span L must have a minimum thickness of $L/10$.

$$h = \frac{L}{10} = \frac{(10 \text{ ft})\left(12\ \frac{\text{in}}{\text{ft}}\right)}{10}$$
$$= 12 \text{ in}$$

The answer is (B).

40 Wood Construction

1. An illustration of molding is shown.

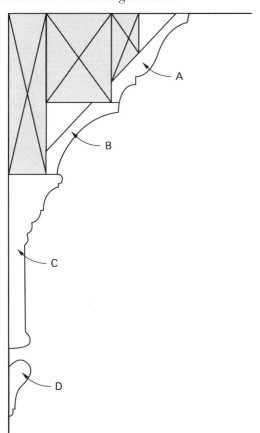

In the illustration, the architrave is located at

(A) A

(B) B

(C) C

(D) D

2. Which is the correct location for a vapor retarder in a cold climate?

(A)
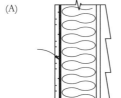

(B)
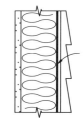

(C)
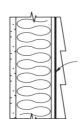

(D)
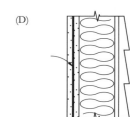

Solutions

1. Heavy crown molds are often made up of a number of different millwork profiles. Millwork is decorative trim produced in a shop, or mill, and delivered to the job site. (Finish carpentry is detailed carpentry completed on site, including installation of the millwork.) An advantage to this type of construction is that it visually minimizes any irregularities between the wall and ceiling surfaces, and any gaps can be sealed with caulk and painted. It also offers the architect the opportunity to design a unique profile using standard components and to control the size and proportions of the trim.

Crown molding, option (A), forms a link between that wall and the ceiling when installed on an angle and often is made up of a combination of straight cuts and curves. A cove molding, option (B), features a smooth concave curve. An architrave, option (C), is a flat piece that is applied directly to the wall.

Picture mold, option (D), is mounted a short distance below the built-up crown molding. Its curved top and the space between the picture mold and the bottom of the rest of the crown allows small hooks to be placed over it so that artwork can be suspended from the wall without putting holes into the wall's surface. The entire assembly,

picture mold included, is often painted the same color to look like one entity.

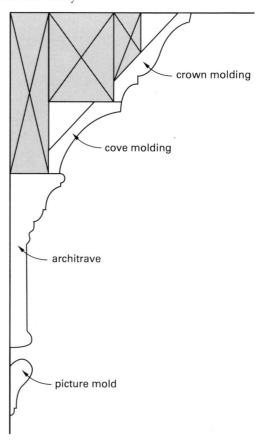

The answer is (C).

2. Vapor retarders (which are sometimes called vapor barriers) are always installed on the "warm" side of a wall, usually between the stud and the interior finish material. The vapor retarder can be made of foil, plastic, or paper and should be applied with no breaks. All seams should be lapped for maximum effectiveness. For this reason, in cold climates it can be preferable to specify unfaced batt insulation and a separate vapor retarder.

If vapor retarders are incorrectly placed on the "cool" side (the exterior of the stud), condensation will develop within the wall cavity, which may lead to decay or mold problems.

The answer is (A).

41 Steel Construction

1. Which of the following factors affect the allowable shear value in a diaphragm system made of steel deck? (Choose the four that apply.)

(A) thickness of the steel deck

(B) size of welds and other connections between deck and framing

(C) spacing of welds and other connections between deck and framing

(D) presence of concrete topping

(E) the location of steel stud partitions above and below the steel deck

(F) whether it is used in a steel frame or concrete frame building structure

2. Which of the following types of metal contains the most copper?

(A) austenitic stainless steel

(B) Monel metal

(C) Muntz metal

(D) nickel silver

Solutions

1. The location of steel stud partitions above and below the steel deck, as well as whether the system is used in a steel frame or a concrete frame building structure do not affect the allowable shear value. The thickness of the steel deck, the size of welds and other connections between the deck and framing, the spacing of welds and other connections between deck and framing, and the presence of concrete topping have an effect on the allowable shear value of a diaphragm made of steel deck.

The answer is (A), (B), (C), and (D).

2. Stainless steel is an alloy of iron, carbon, and chromium. Austenitic stainless steel, the most common type, also contains some nickel and/or manganese. This kind of steel is nonmagnetic and not heat treatable.

Monel is a trade name for a metal alloy of copper and nickel. Muntz metal is a common alloy of 60% copper and 40% tin. Nickel silver is a name given to an alloy of 65% copper, 25% zinc, and 10% nickel.

The answer is (D).

42 Concrete Construction

1. The application of epoxy-coated reinforcing bars would be specified in which type of location? (Choose the four that apply.)

(A) parking garage

(B) fishing pier on the ocean

(C) interior column in an office building

(D) exterior concrete staircase

(E) cold climate highway paving floor slab

(F) floor slab

2. To achieve a slip-resistant finish on a concrete floor slab, the architect should specify a

(A) float finish

(B) broom finish

(C) hard steel-troweled finish

(D) light steel-troweled finish

3. What type of mortar should be specified for a concrete masonry unit (CMU) foundation wall?

(A) M

(B) N

(C) O

(D) S

4. Which of the concrete joints shown connects two successive pours of concrete?

(A)

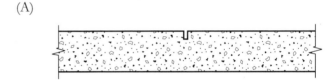

(B)

(C)

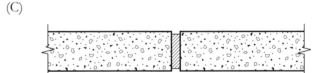

(D)

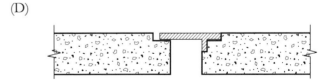

Solutions

1. Epoxy-coated reinforcing bars are used when the concrete will be exposed to chlorides (salts) such as deicing salts and those in seawater. The epoxy coating helps keep the salts from corroding the steel by chemical reaction. An interior column or floor slab is unlikely to be in contact with chlorides, so it is not necessary to specify epoxy-coated rebar in this application.

The answer is (A), (B), (D), and (E).

2. For slip resistance, a broom finish (achieved by passing an industrial broom in parallel strokes across the surface of the uncured concrete) is the best choice.

A float finish is a rough finish intended for outdoor surfaces and interior slabs that will become the substrate for a finish material that does not require a perfectly smooth underlayment, such as carpet or tile. The troweled finishes (hard steel-troweled and light steel-troweled) are very smooth and can be sealed or painted to become the final floor finish, or they can become the substrate for a finish material that requires a perfectly smooth surface, such as vinyl composition tile.

The answer is (B).

3. Type M mortar should be specified for exterior applications at or below grade.

Type N or S is best for exterior applications above grade and for interior load-bearing walls. Type O is well suited for interior and protected exterior non-load-bearing partitions.

The answer is (A).

4. Option (B) shows a construction joint, which would be used to physically connect a new pour of concrete to a previously poured section. In most cases the two sections are connected with a keyed joint. Reinforcing bars across the joint are also commonly used.

The drawing in option (A) shows a control joint. Option (C) shows an isolation joint, which can be used for successive pours of concrete but does not connect the two pairs. Option (D) shows an expansion joint used to allow two sections of a building to move independently.

The answer is (B).

43 Wall Construction

1. Restrictions on surface finishes in all model codes are primarily based on

(A) occupancy and construction type

(B) occupant load and location in the building

(C) location in the building and occupancy group

(D) occupancy group and sprinklering

2. Identify the brick bond shown.

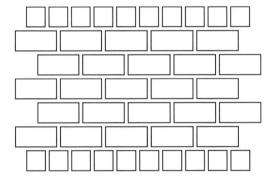

(A) common bond

(B) running bond

(C) English bond

(D) Flemish bond

3. An existing partition separating two rooms is determined to be insufficient for reducing sound transmission. The partition consists of 4 in metal studs spaced 24 in on center with a single layer of $5/8$ in gypsum board on each side. There are no penetrations in the partition. To improve the transmission loss of the partition in the most economical way, which of the following modifications should the architect recommend?

(A) Add resilient channels to one side of the wall and attach a single layer of gypsum board to the channels. Glue an additional layer of gypsum board to the other side.

(B) Add sound-absorbing panels to the noisy side of the partition, and add an additional layer of gypsum board to the opposite side.

(C) Remove one layer of gypsum board, install sound-attenuating insulation, and replace the wall finish with a sound-deadening board and a finish layer of gypsum board.

(D) Cover one side of the partition with an additional layer of gypsum board, and add two additional layers of gypsum board to the other side.

Project Development

4. Calculate the thermal conductivity (*U*-value) for the wall assembly shown at the section indicated on the plan.

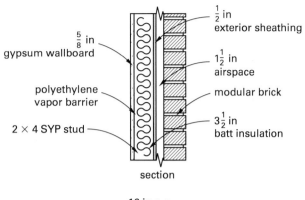

section

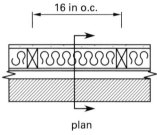

plan

material	R-value (ft^2-hr-°F/Btu)
$5/8$ in gypsum wallboard	0.56
fiberglass batt insulation	3.3/in
brick	0.30/in
$1/2$ in exterior sheathing	0.60
southern yellow pine stud	1.00/in
plastic film vapor barrier	negligible
airspace, still air, no reflective surfaces	0.61
inside air layer, still	0.68
outside air layer, moving winter air	0.17

(A)   0.066 Btu/ft^2-hr-°F

(B)   0.15 Btu/ft^2-hr-°F

(C)   0.20 Btu/ft^2-hr-°F

(D)   15 Btu/ft^2-hr-°F

Solutions

1. The primary restrictions on surface finishes given in model codes (such as in *International Building Code* (IBC) Table 803.5) are the occupancy group and the location in the building according to exiting requirements. Having a building with a sprinkler system only modifies the basic requirements and allows the required flame-spread rating to be dropped one class in some instances.

The answer is (C).

2. The brick bond shown is a common bond. It consists of a header course, five (or more) courses of running bond, and another header course. The pattern then repeats for the height of the wall. Traditionally, in a double-wythe brick wall, the header course "locked" the two wythes together.

The answer is (A).

3. The best way to improve the transmission loss is to add mass and resiliency to the partition. This can be accomplished economically by adding extra gypsum board and mounting one layer on resilient channels.

Sound-absorbing panels would not affect the transmission loss; they would only affect the noise reduction in the room on the side where the panels were installed. Removing the wall finish would not be the most economical method for the results obtained by adding insulation and then replacing new wallboard over sound-deadening board. Adding the extra mass of three layers of gypsum board would not be as effective as using resilient channels with two additional layers of gypsum board as in option (A).

The answer is (A).

4. The U-value, or thermal transmittance, is equivalent to the reciprocal of the sum of the R-values of the materials and airspaces that make up the assembly. To solve this problem, list the materials and determine the R-values for the thicknesses given. Note that some of the R-values are given for the total thickness of the materials, and others are given as R-value per inch. It is easiest to ensure that they are all included by listing them in order from interior to exterior or vice versa. In this case, the stud is excluded because the R-value is calculated at a point between the studs as indicated on the plan. (Do not forget the interior and exterior air layers.)

material	R-value $(\text{ft}^2\text{-hr-}^\circ\text{F/Btu})$
inside air layer	0.68
$\frac{5}{8}$ in gypsum wallboard	0.56
plastic film vapor barrier	–
$3\frac{1}{2}$ in batt insulation (3.5×3.3)	11.55
$\frac{1}{2}$ in exterior sheathing	0.60
$1\frac{1}{2}$ in airspace	0.61
$3\frac{5}{8}$ in brick (3.625×0.30)	1.09
outside air layer	0.17

The sum of the R-values is 15.26 $\text{ft}^2\text{-hr-}^\circ\text{F/Btu}$. The U-value is the reciprocal of that, or

$$U = \frac{1}{R} = \frac{1}{15.26 \dfrac{\text{ft}^2\text{-hr-}^\circ\text{F}}{\text{Btu}}}$$
$$= 0.066 \text{ Btu/ft}^2\text{-hr-}^\circ\text{F}$$

The answer is (A).

44 Lateral Forces—Wind

1. How are the diagonal members of the X-bracing of a tall structure normally designed to minimize costs?

    (A) One diagonal brace is designed to be stressed in tension while the other is not stressed.

    (B) One diagonal brace is designed to be stressed in compression while the other is not stressed.

    (C) Both diagonal braces are designed to be stressed in tension at the same time.

    (D) Both diagonal braces are designed to be stressed in compression at the same time.

2. In wind design, what is the permissible drift of one story relative to an adjacent story in a building where the story height is 12 ft?

    (A) 0.036 in

    (B) 0.36 in

    (C) 0.72 in

    (D) 1.1 in

Project Development

Solutions

1. One diagonal brace is normally designed to be stressed in tension, while the other is not stressed. This is done to minimize costs. Diagonal braces are not designed to work in compression. By designing diagonal members as tension members instead of compression members, their size and therefore their cost is minimized. X-bracing is a common type of lateral bracing for tall structures. Bracing is often placed at the center of the structural framing, such as around the building's central core. When a wind load hits a building from one side, one of the braces acts in tension and the other one is not stressed. When the wind direction is reversed, the brace that works in tension is reversed accordingly while the other is not stressed.

The answer is (A).

2. In wind design, the maximum permissible drift of one story relative to an adjacent story is 0.0025 times the story height.

The story height is 12 ft, and the maximum permissible drift is

$$
\begin{aligned}
d &= 0.0025h \\
&= (0.0025)(12 \text{ ft})\left(12 \frac{\text{in}}{\text{ft}}\right) \\
&= 0.36 \text{ in}
\end{aligned}
$$

The answer is (B).

45 Lateral Forces—Earthquakes

1. The *International Building Code* (IBC) requires that a certain amount of accidental torsion be considered even when a building is symmetrical. Why? (Choose the four that apply.)

(A)   to allow for nonuniform vertical loading

(B)   to allow for asymmetrical floor openings

(C)   to reduce the effect of overturning moments

(D)   to reduce drift

(E)   to allow for eccentricity in rigidity due to non-structural elements and seismic ground motion

(F)   to allow for the fact that positions of loads in an occupied building cannot be exactly determined

2. The intermediate moment-resisting frames in the *International Building Code* (IBC) generally can be used in which of the following seismic design categories?

(A)   categories A, B, and D

(B)   category D only

(C)   category E

(D)   category F

Solutions

1. The IBC requires that a certain arbitrary amount of accidental torsion be considered in a design, even if the building is symmetrical, for all of the listed reasons except option (C) and option (D).

The accidental torsion is not related to either the overturning moment or drift. The code requires that the mass at each level of the building be assumed to be displaced in each direction a distance equal to 5% of the building dimension at that level in the direction perpendicular to the direction of the force.

The answer is (A), (B), (E), and (F).

2. Intermediate moment-resisting frames are generally not permitted in seismic design categories D, E, or F. However, steel intermediate moment-resisting frames with heights up to 35 ft can be used in category D. The design requirements of the intermediate moment-resisting frames are less stringent compared to the special moment-resisting frames. The latter type must be ductile and must satisfy certain provisions of the IBC.

The answer is (A).

Project Development

46 Construction Documentation

1. Software utilizing building information modeling (BIM) provides a digital, spatial, and measurable design tool that may be utilized by the entire design and construction team. This is intended to provide which benefits over a non-BIM design method? (Choose the three that apply.)

(A) collaboration with design team earlier in the design development phase

(B) license sharing with consultants so additional software need not be acquired

(C) utilization of intelligence within models to generate schedules and cost estimates

(D) use of models to facilitate ongoing building maintenance and operations

(E) reduction of time needed to design buildings

(F) elimination of consultants because of the software's ability to analyze BIM data

2. What is used to keep water from penetrating an expansion joint at the intersection of a roof and wall?

(A) base flashing

(B) counterflashing

(C) sealant

(D) coping

3. Which of the following statements about tempered glass is true?

(A) Tempered glass is required in entry doors.

(B) Tempered glass is not a requirement for sidelights with sills below 18 in.

(C) Tempered glass is not a requirement for glazing within 1 ft of doors.

(D) Tempered glass is required in glass within 36 in of doors.

4. A window elevation is shown.

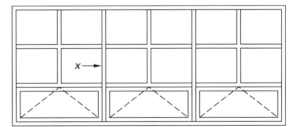

What is indicated by label *x*?

(A) mullion

(B) muntin

(C) stile

(D) rail

Project Development

5. On floors subject to deflection, granite installations should include a

(A) membrane

(B) latex additive in the mortar

(C) type of thinset mortar

(D) sand cushion

6. Which of the following is a requirement of the National Fire Protection Association's *Standard for Portable Fire Extinguishers* (NFPA 10)? (Choose the three that apply.)

(A) Fire extinguisher cabinets must have a vision panel or be clearly marked with a sign.

(B) Fire extinguishers must be tested regularly and have an approved label.

(C) Fire extinguisher cabinets may not protrude into the hallway more than 4 in.

(D) When fire extinguishers are required, no occupant may be more than 75 ft from a fire extinguisher.

(E) Fire extinguishers must be mounted at 48 in above the finish floor.

(F) Cabinets must be locked at all times.

7. An architect is surveying an existing building to determine if the facility complies with *International Building Code* (IBC) requirements for accessibility. Which of the following elements must be modified to satisfy the code requirements?

(A) fire extinguisher cabinet with a "bubble" door that protrudes 5 in from the wall

(B) $^1\!/_4$ in beveled threshold at the main entrance doors

(C) clear floor area 24 in wide on the pull side of the door to the men's restroom from the hallway, which is approached from the front

(D) ramp from the original building to a later addition that rises 6 in over 8 ft

8. Identify the computer data outlet from the electrical symbols shown.

(A)

(B)

(C)

(D)

9. A room 15 ft wide by 20 ft long by $8^1\!/_2$ ft high is finished with the following materials of listed absorptions.

	NRC	125	250	500	1000	2000	4000
floor, wood	0.10	0.15	0.11	0.10	0.07	0.06	0.07
walls, gypsum board	0.05	0.10	0.08	0.05	0.03	0.03	0.03
ceiling, acoustical tile	0.60	0.29	0.29	0.55	0.75	0.73	0.57
window, glass	0.15	0.35	0.25	0.18	0.12	0.07	0.04

On one wall there is a window $3^1\!/_2$ ft high by 8 ft long. What is the total absorption of the room?

(A) 228 sabins (ft^2)

(B) 242 sabins (ft^2)

(C) 266 sabins (ft^2)

(D) 282 sabins (ft^2)

10. What does the electrical symbol shown represent?

(A) triple-position switch

(B) junction box holding three switches

(C) switch for a light controlled from two locations

(D) switch for a light controlled from three locations

11. A spotlight shining perpendicularly to a wall 15 ft away has a candlepower output of 3500 cd. The wall finish is paint with a reflectance of 75%. What is the luminance of

Project Development

the wall at the point where the wall is perpendicular to the direction of light?

(A) 4.90 fL

(B) 11.7 fL

(C) 15.6 fc

(D) 55.7 fc

12. A design for a rest station at an amusement park includes a group of six family restrooms, each containing a toilet, lavatory, and changing table. At least ＿＿＿ of these restrooms must be accessible. (Fill in the blank.)

13. What type of drawings would contain finish floor elevations, information about materials and types of construction assemblies, and window head heights?

(A) floor plans

(B) finish schedules

(C) interior elevations

(D) wall sections

14. What does the material symbol shown represent?

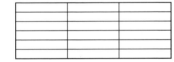

(A) terrazzo

(B) ceramic tile

(C) concrete block

(D) rigid insulation

15. In a full set of construction drawings, the mechanical engineering drawings are typically placed

(A) after the civil engineering drawings and before the architectural drawings

(B) immediately after the architectural drawings

(C) after the structural engineering drawings and before the electrical drawings

(D) after the electrical drawings

16. The symbols shown may appear on a consultant's drawings. Which symbol represents a diffusor?

(A)

(B)

(C)

(D)

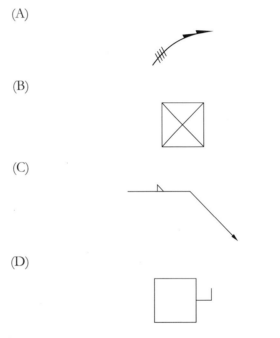

17. In the MasterFormat system, the requirements for testing a plumbing system would be located in

(A) a section of Division 1 of the specifications

(B) Part 1 of Section 22 40 00, Plumbing

(C) Part 2 of Section 22 40 00, Plumbing

(D) Part 3 of Section 22 40 00, Plumbing

Solutions

1. BIM provides an intelligent simulation of architecture that is supposed to achieve an integrated delivery.

Early development of the model is shared with the design team with the intent of identifying issues and locating potential clashes between disciplines. The model intelligence can provide data that is easily incorporated by the software into schedules and cost estimates. The BIM model also may contain data such as installation time, cost, manufacturers' details, sustainability, and maintenance information. Utilizing this information will provide an opportunity for building operations to use the BIM model in maintaining and operating the building long term.

License sharing is not a part of the design process and may be illegal in some cases. The time needed to design a building is not necessarily altered by the design method or efficiency of collaboration. Consultants may utilize the BIM software, but the software itself will not replace the role of the consultant.

The answers are (A), (C), and (D).

2. Base flashing extends from the roof over the cant strip and up the wall. Counter flashing covers the base flashing to extend from the wall over the base flashing and to cover any expansion joint that may occur at this point. Coping protects the top of the parapet. Sealants by themselves are not adequate to cover a major expansion joint as would occur at the roof and wall intersection.

The answer is (B).

3. Safety glazing is required in all areas subject to human impact. This includes glass doors and any glass within 24 in of doors. Glass farther than 24 in from doors and with a sill over 18 in above the floor does not have to be safety glazed.

The answer is (A).

4. Mullions are members that separate large sections of glass, whereas muntins are the framing that separates individual panes of glass. Stiles are vertical members of doors, and rails are horizontal members of doors.

The answer is (A).

5. A membrane is part of a total assembly that also includes reinforcing and a thick bed of mortar on which the granite is laid. The membrane allows the structural slab to move independently of the finish flooring so that any deflection does not crack the floor.

The answer is (A).

6. The National Fire Protection Association's *Standard for Portable Fire Extinguishers* (NFPA 10) is referenced in many codes to provide additional requirements for this type of fire-suppression system. When required, extinguishers must be clearly marked and visible; located no more than 75 ft from each building occupant; properly maintained, tested, and labeled; and readily accessible in case of an emergency.

A fire extinguisher cabinet must not protrude more than 4 in into the hallway and mount no higher than 48 in, but this is a requirement of the *ADA/Accessibility Guidelines*, not NFPA.

The answer is (A), (B), and (D).

7. A change in floor level of $\frac{1}{4}$ in or less is acceptable; the beveled threshold helps to ease the transition and is beneficial at this location. The minimum width of the required clear floor area on the pull side of a door is 18 in when the door is approached from the front, so the provided space is greater than that required. A ramp that rises 6 in over 8 ft (96 in) has a slope of 1:16, which is less than the required 1:12 slope for ramps, and it complies with the accessibility requirements.

A wall-mounted object placed more than 27 in above the floor cannot protrude more than 4 in from the wall. It is reasonable to assume that the cabinet is mounted at a typical height and that the fixture or portions of the fixture are more than 27 in above the floor. Therefore, the fire extinguisher cabinet does not comply with the accessibility requirements and must be removed or replaced with a recessed model.

The answer is (A).

8. Symbol (A) is a computer data outlet. A variation of this symbol is to include a plus sign at the left side and draw the symbol with a point of the triangle at the outlet's location on the wall. If the triangle were not shaded, the symbol would represent a telephone outlet.

Symbol (B) is a duplex floor receptacle. Most types of receptacles can be placed in the floor as long as a protective covering is provided to prevent loose objects, dirt, water, or cleaning products from entering the receptacle. The square around the duplex receptacle symbol indicates that it is located in the floor.

Symbol (C) is a home run to a panel board. The number of arrows should correspond to the number of circuits. If arrows are not shown, it is assumed to be a two-wire circuit.

Symbol (D) is an exit sign. The shaded areas of the symbol represent the faces of the sign. This particular symbol

Project Development

indicates an exit sign that is ceiling-mounted and both sides of the sign are visible. If it were a wall-mounted sign, it would have one face and only one quarter of the symbol would be shaded.

A key to common electrical symbols can be found in *Architectural Graphic Standards* and in the Construction Specification Institute's (CSI's) *Uniform Drawing System*. The symbols depicted in this question are those used by CSI.

The answer is (A).

9. To find the total absorption when calculation at specific frequencies is not required, the noise reduction coefficient (NRC) is used. The total absorption is the summation of all the individual absorptions according to the formula $A = \Sigma Sa$.

floor:	(15 ft)(20 ft)(0.10 sabins/ft^2)	= 30 sabins
walls:	((15 ft + 15 ft + 20 ft + 20 ft) × (8.5 ft) − (3.5 ft)(8 ft)) × (0.05 sabins/ft^2)	= 28 sabins
window:	(3.5 ft)(8 ft)(0.15 sabins/ft^2)	= 4 sabins
ceiling:	(15 ft)(20 ft)(0.60 sabins/ft^2)	=180 sabins
total		242 sabins

The answer is (B).

10. This is the symbol for a three-way switch. This type of switch controls a light from two different switches in different locations.

The "3" in the symbol indicates the number of conductors (not including the ground wire) that make the switch work. A "4" subscript would indicate a four-way switch, or one that can control the same light from three or more different locations.

The answer is (C).

11. In this problem, the footcandle (lux) level of the light shining on the wall must be determined first. Because the direction of light is perpendicular to the wall, the inverse square law is used.

$$E = \frac{I}{d^2}$$
$$= \frac{3500 \text{ cd}}{15 \text{ ft}^2}$$
$$= 15.56 \text{ fc}$$

Once the footcandle (lx) level is determined, it is multiplied by the reflectance to find the brightness. Reflectance is the ratio of reflected light to incident light. The former is measured in footlamberts, the latter in footcandles.

$$(15.56 \text{ fc})(0.75) = 11.7 \text{ fL}$$

The answer is (B).

12. Unisex toilet rooms are required by the *International Building Code* (IBC) where there are more than six separate-sex water closets required, and half of those provided (at least one) must be accessible. The fixtures provided in these rooms may count toward the total fixture requirement. Single-user toilet rooms are preferred by many for privacy and convenience. They are particularly useful in areas where there are lots of children because they make it possible for a parent to accompany a child of the opposite sex to the restroom.

The answer is 3.

13. Wall sections are vertical "slices" of the exterior wall of a building that graphically depict how the building is to be built. They show vertical dimensions, materials, and relationships and how the pieces are intended to fit together.

The answer is (D).

14. Hatches are often used on architectural drawings to indicate materials used, rather than designating the materials with labels or notes. This graphic shorthand allows the drawings to be simpler and less cluttered with text. The material hatch shown represents rigid insulation and is recommended by *Architectural Graphic Standards*.

The answer is (D).

15. The normal sequence of drawings in a full set of drawings is as follows: site drawings, then civil engineering drawings, followed by architectural, structural, plumbing (if not included in mechanical), mechanical, and electrical drawings.

The answer is (C).

16. The symbol shown in option (B) represents a diffusor.

The answer is (B).

17. Requirements for testing of installed systems are in Part 3 of each technical section (if appropriate to the specification). Note that testing requirements for individual products and materials are in Part 2.

The answer is (D).

47 The Project Manual and Specifications

1. In the hearth shown, the height of the fireplace opening is 24 in.

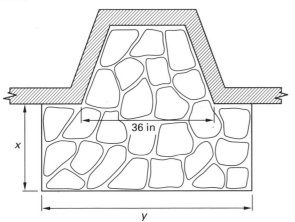

What are the minimum dimensions permitted for the hearth?

(A) $x = 16$ in, $y = 48$ in

(B) $x = 16$ in, $y = 52$ in

(C) $x = 20$ in, $y = 48$ in

(D) $x = 20$ in, $y = 52$ in

2. An architect is designing an addition to a high school to house a new gym and locker rooms. The architect plans to construct the exterior walls with concrete masonry units and apply an exterior insulation and finish system (EIFS) over the block. The new gym will be located adjacent to the school's baseball field. To take advantage of the material's insulative properties and provide the best impact resistance to avoid dents from fly balls, which type of EIFS should be specified?

(A) polymer based (PB)

(B) poly modified (PM)

(C) mineral based (MB)

(D) expanded polystyrene (EPS)

3. Typical 4 in by 4 in ceramic tiles used as wallcovering in an office building's restrooms should be specified as

(A) vitreous

(B) semivitreous

(C) nonvitreous

(D) impervious

4. Which statement concerning fire-rated door assemblies is correct?

(A) Hinges must always be the ball-bearing type.

(B) Under some circumstances a closer is not needed.

(C) Labeling is required for the door only.

(D) The maximum width is 3 ft 0 in.

5. The standardized levels of finish in the gypsum wallboard industry refer, among other things, to the

(A) quality of workmanship of the final finish

(B) number of coats of joint compound used

(C) thickness of joint compound used

(D) type of texturing used

6. Which of the following materials would be used as a firestop?

(A) wood stud

(B) plywood

(C) silicone foam

(D) treated wood blocking

7. Which of the following is the best sealant to use between exterior precast concrete wall panels?

(A) acrylic

(B) butyl

(C) latex

(D) polyurethane

8. Which of the following statements are true about electronic ballasts installed on fluorescent lamps? (Choose the two that apply.)

(A) Flicker is less than with conventional ballasts.

(B) Lamps cannot start in temperatures below 40°F.

(C) Noise is greater than with conventional ballasts.

(D) Lamps cannot be dimmed.

(E) Existing fixtures with conventional ballasts can be retrofitted with electronic ballasts.

(F) Electronic ballasts are less energy efficient.

9. Calculate the number of heating degree days during the following two-week period in March in Williamsburg, Virginia. The base temperature is 65°F.

date	high	low	average
3/1	51°F	31°F	41°F
3/2	79°F	39°F	59°F
3/3	51°F	35°F	43°F
3/4	53°F	31°F	42°F
3/5	54°F	34°F	44°F
3/6	46°F	36°F	41°F
3/7	51°F	27°F	39°F
3/8	58°F	23°F	40°F
3/9	72°F	49°F	60°F
3/10	78°F	63°F	70°F
3/11	70°F	52°F	61°F
3/12	69°F	55°F	62°F
3/13	75°F	55°F	65°F
3/14	70°F	54°F	62°F

(A) 179 heating degree days (°F)

(B) 186 heating degree days (°F)

(C) 230 heating degree days (°F)

(D) 316 heating degree days (°F)

10. An architect is researching folding partitions to be specified to divide a hotel ballroom into two smaller meeting rooms. Meetings will frequently be held in each of the rooms simultaneously, and the presenters often use a lavaliere microphone with an amplification system. The hotel's facilities coordinator specifies that normal speech should not be heard from the other side of the partition, but it is acceptable for loud or amplified speech to be faintly heard. Into which range should the partition's STC rating fall?

(A) 25 to 30

(B) 30 to 35

(C) 35 to 40

(D) 40 to 45

11. Which of the following formulas is a factor in determining cooling load? (Choose the three that apply.)

(A) $q_r = (SG)(SC)A$

(B) $q_m = 1500(BHP)$

(C) $q_{CLTD} = UA(CLTD)$

(D) $q_c = UA\Delta T$

(E) $\mu = \Delta P + T$

(F) $a = A\pi r$

12. A three-phase motor draws a 9 A current at 208 V. The power factor is 75%. The power generated is

(A) 1.4 kW

(B) 2.4 kW

(C) 3.6 kW

(D) 4.2 kW

13. The best measure to use when evaluating how well a window assembly prevents heat gain is the

(A) daylight factor

(B) shading coefficient

(C) solar heat gain coefficient

(D) window-to-wall ratio

14. The pressure in a city water main is 57 psi. The pressure loss through piping, fittings, and the water meter has been calculated as 23 psi, and the highest fixture requires 12 psi to operate. What is the maximum height the fixture can be above the water main?

(A) 9 ft

(B) 24 ft

(C) 50 ft

(D) 78 ft

15. Codes limit the number of conductors permitted in a conduit for which of the following reasons? (Choose the two that apply.)

(A) to maintain maximum ampacity

(B) to control heat buildup in the conduit

(C) to minimize problems with harmonic currents

(D) to prevent damage to the conductors when they are pulled through the conduit

(E) to keep conductors on the same circuit

(F) to allow room in the conduit for data wiring

16. Which of the following statements is true about Division 1 specification sections? The specification sections

(A) establish duties of the owner and contractor

(B) define legal rights of the parties

(C) establish duties of the architect

(D) establish administrative procedures for the project

17. Which of the following materials has the smallest dimensional tolerances?

(A) precast concrete tees

(B) 2 × 4 wood framing at a window opening

(C) steel beams

(D) wood paneling

18. An architect consults with an engineering firm that provides mechanical, electrical, and plumbing services, as well as lighting design. Who is responsible for verifying that recessed downlights do not interfere with the ductwork shown on the plans?

(A) architect

(B) electrical engineer

(C) lighting designer

(D) mechanical engineer

19. A specification section written following the recommendations of the Construction Specifications Institute would include which sections?

(A) general, administration, and execution

(B) administration, products, and execution

(C) general, products, and execution

(D) general, installation, and products

20. In the following specification, which item is described with a performance specification?

Part 2—Products

2.01 Metal Support Material

General: To the extent not otherwise indicated, comply with ASTM C754 for metal system supporting gypsum wallboard.

Ceiling suspension main runners: $1\frac{1}{2}$ in steel channels, cold rolled.

Hanger wire: ASTM A641, soft, Class 1 galvanized, prestretched; sized in accordance with ASTM C754.

Hanger anchorage devices: size for 3 × calculated loads, except size direct-pull concrete inserts for 5 × calculated loads.

Studs: ASTM C645; 25 gage, $2\frac{1}{2}$ in deep, except as otherwise indicated.

ASTM C645; 25 gage, $3\frac{5}{8}$ in deep.

ASTM C645; 20 gage, 6 in deep.

Runners: Match studs; type recommended by stud manufacturer for floor and ceiling support of studs, and for vertical abutment of drywall work at other work.

Furring members: ASTM C65; 25 gage, hat-shaped.

Fasteners: Type and size recommended by furring manufacturer for the substrate and application indicated.

(A) fasteners

(B) hanger wire

(C) hanger anchorage devices

(D) ceiling suspension main runners

21. Which of the following are likely to occur if the drawings and specifications are not thoroughly coordinated? (Choose the four that apply.)

(A) a decrease of the actual cost from the estimated cost because the contractor bid on a less expensive material shown on the drawings, although the same material was called out as a more expensive type in the specifications

(B) the immediate filing of a lawsuit

(C) the need for a change order during construction to account for modifications required to correct discrepancies in the two documents

(D) a delay in construction

(E) an increase in cost because the contractor bid the least expensive choice between two conflicting requirements when the client wanted the more expensive option

(F) the architect may be held financially responsible for the omission

22. Which MasterFormat division would include the specification requirements for metal studs for interior partition walls?

(A) 05

(B) 09

(C) 10

(D) 13

Solutions

1. According to the *International Building Code* (IBC), the minimum depth (x) required for a hearth is 16 in from the face of the fireplace. However, if the fireplace opening is 6 ft^2 or greater, the requirement is increased to 20 in. The opening of the fireplace shown is 3 ft × 2 ft or 6 ft^2.

The hearth must extend at least 8 in on either side of the fireplace opening, so the width of the hearth must be

$$36 \text{ in} + 8 \text{ in} + 8 \text{ in} = 52 \text{ in}$$

The answer is (D).

2. Polymer-modified (PM) mineral-based systems have high impact resistance and provide good insulation. They consist of a base and finish coat of synthetic stucco applied over extruded polystyrene (XPS) insulation board.

Polymer based (PB) systems are made up of a very thin base coat of portland cement and polymer over fiberglass mesh with a thin finish coat of polymer-based synthetic stucco over expanded polystyrene (EPS) insulation board. They are lighter in weight than PM systems, but because their plaster coats are so thin, they do not resist impact well.

Mineral based (MB) systems are basically conventional three-coat portland cement stucco systems. They are very impact resistant, but since the stucco is not applied over an insulation board, the system does not offer the insulation of PB and PM systems.

The answer is (B).

3. For a commercial toilet room, it is best to use impervious tile to withstand moisture and harsh chemical cleaners. Vitrification is a process of applying heat to a tile to fuse the material and make it denser. Denser tile permits less water to be absorbed. Specifying the level of vitrification is a way of classifying tile based upon its moisture absorption rate.

nonvitreous	7% to 15% absorption
semivitreous	3% to 7% absorption
vitreous	0.05% to 3% absorption
impervious	almost no absorption (less than 0.05%)

The answer is (D).

4. Ball-bearing hinges are always required for fire-rated doors. The other statements are incorrect.

The answer is (A).

5. The Gypsum Association publishes *Recommended Levels of Gypsum Board Finish*, which gives six levels of finish. One requirement for these levels is the number of coats of joint compound used. The levels are 0, 1, 2, 3, 4, and 5. Level 0 requires no taping, finish, or accessories, while Level 5 requires three coats of joint compound over joints and fastener heads, as well as a final skim coat over the entire surface of the wall.

The answer is (B).

6. Firestops are materials or systems of materials that are used to seal penetrations through fire walls or smoke barriers. They are always noncombustible and may be factory built or constructed in the field. Depending on the wall type and application, mortar, mineral wool, or silicone foam would be acceptable for use as a firestop.

Draftstops also prevent the passage of fire and smoke but can be made of combustible materials such as treated wood blocking. They are placed between floors and at concealed spaces.

The answer is (C).

7. Polyurethane sealant, either one-part or two-part, provides excellent resistance to weather and is capable of 25% to 50% movement. It can span the wide joints typical of precast concrete, is available in colors, and can be painted.

Acrylics are unsuitable for this situation because of their limited potential for joint movement and their inability to fill the large-width joints that are typical of precast concrete. Butyls are unsuitable because of their limited joint movement and because they are only available in darker colors. They are generally used for areas under water. Latex sealants also have limited joint movement capability and are typically used for joints with no expected movement, such as those around door and window frames.

The answer is (D).

8. Electronic ballasts have many advantages over conventional ballasts. Many annoyances associated with fluorescent lamps, such as humming and flickering, are greatly reduced or eliminated with electronic ballasts. Electronic ballasts permit lamps to be operated at a wider range of temperatures—down to about 0°F—and let lamps be dimmed more easily and economically. In addition, the ballast itself is smaller and lighter in weight and more energy efficient. Existing fixtures with conventional ballasts can be retrofitted with electronic ballasts to realize the advantages of newer technology.

The answer is (A) and (E).

9. Degree days are calculated by comparing the base temperature—in this case, 65°F—to the average temperature on a specific date in a specific location. If the day's average temperature is less than 65°F, subtract the average temperature from the base temperature to determine the number

Project Development

of heating degree days; each degree of difference is equivalent to one degree day. If the temperature is above 65°F, the quantity of heating degree days is 0; however, temperatures above 65°F are recorded as cooling degree days. If the temperature is 65°F, no degree days are recorded for that date. To determine the number of degree days in a specified period of time, simply add the number of degree days recorded for each date.

This problem asks specifically for heating degree days, which are calculated as follows.

date	heating degree days (°F)
3/1	$65 - 41 = 24$
3/2	$65 - 59 = 6$
3/3	$65 - 43 = 22$
3/4	$65 - 42 = 23$
3/5	$65 - 44 = 21$
3/6	$65 - 41 = 24$
3/7	$65 - 39 = 26$
3/8	$65 - 40 = 25$
3/9	$65 - 60 = 5$
3/10	$65 - 70 = 0$
3/11	$65 - 61 = 4$
3/12	$65 - 62 = 3$
3/13	$65 - 65 = 0$
3/14	$65 - 62 = 3$
total	186

The answer is (B).

10. An STC rating of 40 to 45 would provide the desired sound level on the opposite side of the partition.

The answer is (D).

11. $q_c = UA\Delta T$ is the formula for conduction and is a factor in determining total heating load.

The equation used to calculate total cooling load is

$$q_{\text{total}} = q_p + q_m + q_l + q_{\text{CLTD}} + q_r$$

Each of the other equations is a factor in calculating cooling load because they each represent internal heat gains.

$q_r = (SG)(SC)A$ is the formula for calculating insolation, or total radiant heat gain, through windows (r identifies radiant).

$q_m = 1500(BHP)$ allows the designer to calculate heat gain from equipment (m identifies mechanical).

$q_{\text{CLTD}} = UA(\text{CLTD})$ represents the cooling load temperature differential, which allows calculation of heat gain through walls.

Other factors in determining cooling load are q_p, which quantifies heat gain from building occupants (p identifies people), and q_l, which is a calculation of heat gain from lighting fixtures (l identifies lighting).

The answer is (A), (B), and (C).

12. Power, P, is a function of voltage, V, current, I, and the power factor, PF.

$$\begin{aligned} P &= VI(\text{PF}) \\ &= (208 \text{ V})(9 \text{ A})(0.75) \\ &= 1404 \text{ W} \quad (1.4 \text{ kW}) \end{aligned}$$

The answer is (A).

13. The solar heat gain coefficient is the ratio of solar heat gain through a window to the amount of solar radiation striking the window. Because it includes the frame and the glass spacer, the solar heat gain coefficient is a better indicator of heat gain than the shading coefficient, which is a similar measure but does not include the effects of the frame. The daylight factor and the window-to-wall ratio are not measures of heat gain.

The answer is (C).

14. In order to find the maximum height, first take the pressure in the water main and subtract other known pressure losses and the pressure required for the fixture to operate properly.

$$57 \, \frac{\text{lbf}}{\text{in}^2} - 23 \, \frac{\text{lbf}}{\text{in}^2} - 12 \, \frac{\text{lbf}}{\text{in}^2} = 22 \text{ psi}$$

Because 1 psi is needed to lift water 2.3 ft, the maximum height is

$$\left(22 \, \frac{\text{lbf}}{\text{in}^2}\right)\left(2.3 \, \frac{\text{ft}}{\frac{\text{lbf}}{\text{in}^2}}\right) = 50.6 \text{ ft}$$

The answer is (C).

15. Too many conductors carrying too much current in an enclosed area can generate excessive heat. In addition, conductors can be damaged if too many are pulled through a small conduit. For these reasons, the *National Electrical Code* (NEC) limits the number of conductors permitted in a conduit.

The NEC only requires that the ampacity (the current-carrying capacity) of conductors be derated if the number of conductors in a raceway or conduit exceeds three (not counting the neutral conductor). Harmonic currents are only a problem with unconventional electrical loads such as computers, electronic lighting ballasts, and other

Project Development

electronic equipment. When these types of loads are supplied by conductors, the neutral conductor must be counted as one of the three allowable conductors in a conduit before ampacity must be derated.

Data wiring is not allowed to be placed in the same conduit as electrical conductors.

The answer is (B) and (D).

16. The general, supplementary, and special conditions, in addition to American Institute of Architects (AIA) Document A101, *Standard Form of Agreement Between Owner and Contractor*, establish the legal relationship between the two parties and define their rights and duties. The architect's duties in administering the construction contract are also defined by these documents. The administrative procedures for a project are established in Division 1 of the specifications, General Requirements. These sections explain exactly how the contractor is to perform the tasks assigned in the general, supplementary, and special conditions.

The answer is (D).

17. Tolerance is the amount that an element of a building is permitted to be "off" from the specified dimension. Acceptable tolerances for building materials are dependent on their level of quality, their physical properties, the stage in the construction process during which they are to be installed, and the way the materials will be used. Two adjacent, different materials can both be within their acceptable tolerances and not align exactly. For these reasons, it is important the architect's drawings allow for some "play," or dimensional adjustment, and that tolerances specified by the architect agree with cited industry standards for that specific material. Architects should be aware that requiring exceptionally high levels of precision and low tolerances can cause construction costs to escalate; however, if such accuracy is critical to the project, these requirements must be specified.

Wood paneling has the most restrictive tolerances, as even small deviations from the prescribed dimensions are noticeable.

The answer is (D).

18. The architect is responsible for the overall coordination of all the contract documents prepared by his or her consultants.

If the owner chooses to hire engineers outside of the architect's contract, or elects to have some of this work performed by a contractor on a design-build basis, the owner then becomes responsible for coordination of the documents.

The answer is (A).

19. The three-part specification format developed by the Construction Specifications Institute (CSI) and Construction Specifications Canada (CSC) includes sections entitled General, Products, and Execution. The General section includes administrative and procedural requirements specific to the specification. The Products section includes information about materials, systems, manufactured units, shop fabrication, and factory finishing prior to installation. The Execution section gives instructions for on-site incorporation of the products into the project. A detailed description of the various articles and paragraphs included in each part is given in CSI's SectionFormat.

The answer is (C).

20. The specification simply states how the hanger anchorage devices must perform; that is, they must support a certain amount of weight. As long as they do this, they can be any type, size, or style that the contractor selects. The requirements for the fasteners are those selected as appropriate by the manufacturer. The hanger wire specification is a reference type specification because it refers to a particular industry-standard specification. The ceiling suspension main runner is specified with a descriptive specification, which describes various qualities (size, material, and method of fabrication) of the ceiling runner.

The answer is (C).

21. It is commonly believed that the specifications take precedence over the drawings, but AIA Document A201, Sec. 1.2.1, states that these two types of documents are considered "complementary, and what is required by one shall be as binding as if required by all." In cases where there is a discrepancy, the conflict should be brought to the architect's attention. Any time there are conflicts in the project documents, the best that can happen is a quick resolution with no change to the cost, but usually an increase in cost results and the project may be delayed as the parties deal with administrative work. Conflicts in the documents can be corrected with an addendum prior to bidding or negotiation or by change order or construction change directive after the construction contract is signed.

Litigation would be a last resort and other remedies would be sought and implemented before a lawsuit occurred.

The answer is (C), (D), (E), and (F).

22. Light-gage metal framing for interior partitions is specified in Division 09, Finishes. Metal studs are typically specified as a part of gypsum board assemblies.

The answer is (B).

48 Detailed Regulatory and Cost Reviews

1. Installing a sprinkler system in new construction increases the total construction cost by approximately

- (A) 1.5%
- (B) 5%
- (C) 9%
- (D) 15%

2. A new 80,000 ft^2 office building is projected to cost $10,000,000. Approximately what percentages of the construction budget should be allocated to the building's mechanical and electrical systems costs?

- (A) mechanical (5%); electrical (5%)
- (B) mechanical (15%); electrical (5%)
- (C) mechanical (15%); electrical (15%)
- (D) mechanical (25%); electrical (15%)

Project Development

Solutions

1. According to the National Fire Protection Association (NFPA), installing a sprinkler system in a new building adds about 1% to 1.5% to the total construction cost. Retrofitting an existing structure costs considerably more. Sprinkler systems can reduce the risk of death and property loss by one-half to two-thirds, and they are encouraged, if not required, in all types of buildings, including single-family residences, where more than 80% of fire deaths occur.

The answer is (A).

2. For an office building of this size, the total mechanical and electrical costs are in the range of 30% of the total construction budget, about equally divided between the two (15% allocated to each). For smaller office buildings, the total costs are in the range of 20%, also about equally divided.

The answer is (C).

Project Development

Case Studies

Case Study 1

An architect is designing an addition to a two-story wood home in Montclair, New Jersey. The addition is located at the rear of the home, extending into the backyard with a footprint of 24 ft by 24 ft. The front of the existing home faces north. The existing structure has a basement with a footing depth of 7 ft below grade. The addition is to be built on a crawl space without a basement. The frost depth in this locality is at 3.5 ft below the surface of the soil. The architect is preparing a foundation and footing detail for the rear south wall of the addition, as shown in Resource 5.1. The architect is also responsible for detailing the new foundation system to be built on the east and west sides of this addition.

A 4 ft retaining wall is to be built on site in an unrelated location to the addition. This wall will be constructed using standard interconnected stone units from a well-known, local company. A detail of the retaining wall system is shown in Resource 5.2.

Resource 5.1 Foundation Detail at South Addition Wall (N.T.S.)

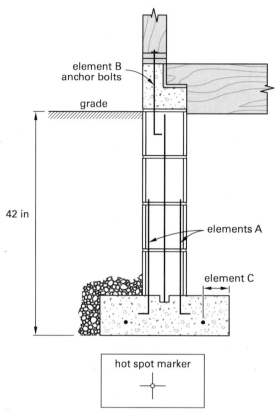

Resource 5.2 Retaining Wall Detail

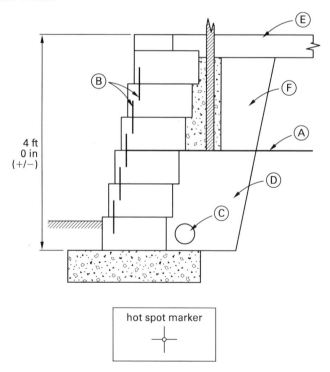

1. The footing detail along the new south addition wall is shown in Resource 5.1. To what depth should the footings along the east and west sides of the addition be constructed?

(A) at 7 ft, the same depth of the existing building foundation footing

(B) at 3.5 ft below grade, the same depth as the new south footing

(C) at 7 ft to start, as a stepped footing, and moving gradually upward to 3.5 ft below grade

(D) at an average depth of about 5 ft below grade

2. On the detail shown in Resource 5.1, why is the depth of the footing shown at 42 in?

(A) The *International Residential Code* (IRC) requires a minimum depth of 3 ft below grade. Making the depth 6 in deeper allows for variations in final grade.

(B) The frost depth in this area is 3.5 ft. Footings need to be at least this deep to avoid heaving in the cold months due to frost in the soil.

(C) The IRC requires that an addition to an existing building has a minimum footing depth of half of the existing building's footing depth. The existing footings are 7 ft deep.

(D) This footing depth is incorrect. It should be 7 ft to align with the existing footing depth.

3. What is the correct location for the transverse reinforcement of the footing? On Resource 5.1, indicate where the hot spot marker should be placed.

4. On the detail given in Resource 5.1, L-shaped rebars that connect the concrete masonry unit (CMU) foundation wall to the footings are shown as elements labeled "A." Which term is commonly used to refer to these elements?

(A) dowels

(B) pegs

(C) pins

(D) bolts

5. In Resource 5.2, a geogrid has been added to the system labeled "A." What is the purpose of this material?

(A) It provides a waterproof membrane to direct water in the soil to weeps in the retaining wall. This reduces the hydraulic pressure behind the wall.

(B) It levels the soil as the wall is being built. This keeps the courses of blocks in the wall plumb and level during construction.

(C) It is a natural material that reintroduces nitrogen and other biological elements back into the soil after backfill. This helps stabilize the soil and promotes biodiversity at the microbial level.

(D) It is a reinforcing mesh that is placed between courses of retaining wall block and extended into the backfill. The geogrid supports the soil and helps resist the tendency for the wall to bulge or blowout.

6. In Resource 5.2, what are the elements labeled "B"?

(A) metal plates connecting concrete units

(B) fiberglass pins

(C) no. 5 rebars

(D) plastic sheets

7. In Resource 5.2, what purposes does the 4 in perforated polyvinyl chloride (PVC) pipe (labeled "C") serve in this retaining wall system? (Choose the two that apply.)

(A) reduces hydrostatic pressure

(B) helps aerate and stabilize the soil after installation of the wall

(C) provides a means for inspection via remote camera that can be inserted into the pipe

(D) reduces moisture in the soil, thus reducing possible freeze or thaw issues

(E) allows any buildup of naturally occurring radon to vent out and not concentrate.

(F) provides a measure of making sure the footing is level during installation

8. In Resource 5.2, the soil layer in which the perforated pipe is buried (labeled "D") should consist of what material?

(A)   sand

(B)   clay

(C)   silt

(D)   crushed stones

9. In Resource 5.1, 0.5 in anchor bolts connect the base plate to the foundation below. According to the *International Residential Code* (IRC), these anchor bolts as must be spaced no more than what distance apart?

(A)   4 ft

(B)   6 ft

(C)   1 ft away from each end and at the midpoint of the wall

(D)   every other stud space

10. Refer to foundation wall detail in Resource 5.1. Element C indicates the coverage of concrete around steel rebar reinforcing in the footing. What is the minimum required concrete cover for the rebars at this location?

(A)   1.5 in

(B)   2 in

(C)   3 in

(D)   5 times the diameter of the rebar

11. On Resource 5.2, place the hot spot marker in the correct location for the low-permeability soil layer in the retaining wall detail.

Case Study 2

An architect is designing a single-story, wood-framed home. The foundation and basement plan are shown in Resource 5.3. The home's dimensions are 40 ft by 45 ft. The foundation is a 12 in concrete masonry unit (CMU) wall. The first floor's main structural system consists of two lines of beams that support the first floor joists. Each line of beams consists of three simply-supported beams spanning 12 ft, 16 ft, and 12 ft. The 12 ft beams are bearing at one end on the foundation wall and on a column on the other end. The 16 ft beams are bearing on columns at each end.

The basement slab is a concrete slab-on-grade. The geotechnical engineer has determined that the site soil bearing capacity is 3500 lbf/ft^2. Per the *International Building Code* (IBC), the floor dead load is 15 lbf/ft^2, and the floor live load is 40 lbf/ft^2.

Resource 5.3 Foundation and Basement Plan

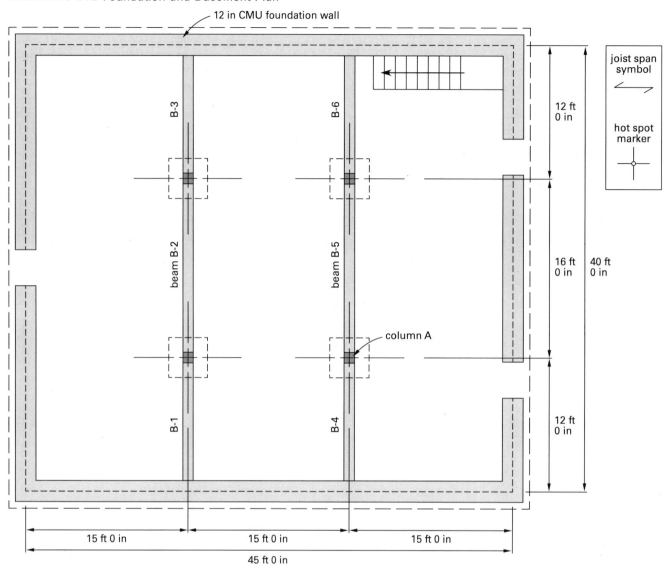

12. Review the foundation and basement plan in Resource 5.3. All materials are readily available and not affected by any market cost influences. Which type of material is likely the most cost-effective option for floor joists?

(A) dimensional lumber

(B) I-joists

(C) laminated veneer lumber (LVL)

(D) glulam

13. The beams shown in Resource 5.3 support only the floor joists for the floor above. What is the total load per linear foot that each beam must support?

(A) 225 lbf/ft

(B) 600 lbf/ft

(C) 825 lbf/ft

(D) 1650 lbf/ft

14. Four columns shown in Resource 5.3 support only the beams and floor joists for the floor above. Approximately, what is the total load supported by each column?

(A) 5.0 kips

(B) 6.6 kips

(C) 8.4 kips

(D) 12 kips

15. On the building's first floor, the architect has been asked to design a load-bearing wall to support future second-story expansion. The total load on column A with the new load-bearing wall above is now 22 kips. The footing is square in shape. The weight of the footing itself is 1 kip. Ignore the load from the slab-on-grade. Based on the soil bearing capacity provided by the geotechnical engineer, what is the size of the footing needed for column A?

(A) 1 ft 9 in by 1 ft 9 in

(B) 2 ft 0 in ft by 2 ft 0 in

(C) 2 ft 7 in by 2 ft 7 in

(D) 3 ft 2 in by 3 ft 2 in

16. On Resource 5.3, place the appropriate floor joist span symbol in the appropriate space(s) and orientation(s) in the plan.

17. On the foundation plan in Resource 5.3, place the hot spot marker in the correct locations for lintels.

18. The American Concrete Institute's *Building Code Requirements for Structural Concrete* (ACI 318) requires a minimum cover over steel reinforcement for all concrete in direct contact with the earth. Foundation footing falls under this rule. What is the required minimum concrete thickness above footing rebars in this example?

(A) 3 in

(B) 6 in

(C) 8 in

(D) 10 in

Solutions

1. The footings cannot be at the same depth as the existing foundation footing. For the east and west foundation walls of the addition, the details must show a stepped footing starting at the same depth as the existing footing and gradually moving upward. This is because the soil immediately next to the existing basement wall is typically backfilled material and cannot be considered stable without confirmation from a geotechnical engineer. Stepping the new footing up from the existing foundation footing will place it on undisturbed soil. The footing can rise by 1 ft for every 2 ft of horizontal distance until it reaches 3.5 ft below grade.

The answer is (C).

2. The IRC does not have a minimum depth, nor does it require that the new footing depth be half the depth of the existing footing. Footing depth is determined by design requirements, soil capacity, and frost depth.

The detail shown in Resource 5.1 refers to the foundation wall on the south side. This wall is separated from the existing footings so that it does not affect them. The factor that should be considered is the depth of the frost line, which is 3.5 ft.

The answer is (B).

3. Continuous rebar runs parallel with the footing and appears in the illustration as small dots in the footer.

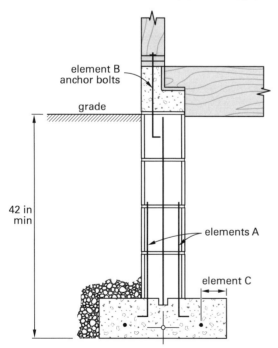

Transverse reinforcement ties these continuous reinforcement bars together. The transverse reineforcement is typically located directly under the continuous rebars in footings. The correct location for the hot spot marker is below the two continuous rebars.

4. L-shaped rebars are commonly called dowels. The dowels are no. 4 bars at least 16 in long, and they connect the CMU foundation wall to its footing.

The answer is (A).

5. A geogrid is a synthetic membrane made of a polymer such as polyester. It is used to reinforce soils behind retaining walls as well as in subbases of roads. Soils tend to fall apart in tension. The soil behind the retaining wall creates a horizontal pressure on the wall itself which is amplified by the height of the wall. The geogrid is strong in tension and takes the "pulling" load of the wall and transfers these forces to a larger area of soil, which is holds the grid due to gravity.

The answer is (D).

6. The typical elements labeled B on the detail consist of straight fiberglass pins that help connect the concrete formed units together. These pins are fiberglass because metal tends to corrode or rust, which can lead to failure in the system or discolorations that leach out to the visible surface of the blocks. The pins connect the block together not only to provide added strength to the system but also to help keep the system aligned and keep the proper angle of the wall during installation.

The answer is (B).

7. The perforated pipe shown in Resource 5.2 is used for drainage. Water is detrimental to wall construction due to the freeze-thaw cycle. In cold weather, water in the soil tends to freeze and expand in volume. This exerts pressure on foundations, retaining walls, and similar structural members, causing these members to crack and fall apart.

Hydrostatic pressures might build up as the soil becomes more saturated with water over time. This drainage will help reduce this pressure.

The answer is (A) and (D).

8. The soil surrounding the perforated drainage pipe must provide a means for any water that enters the area to pass through and drain out through the pipe at the bottom. Of the four choices, crushed stones would be the best solution to accomplish this. The use of sand or silt may allow water to pass, but in an event where large amounts of water are introduced, sand or silt may not allow the water to drain quickly enough. Sand and silt may also clog up the drain pipe over time. Clay would form a

Project Development

dense, possibly impenetrable barrier for the water, not allowing it to drain at all.

The answer is (D).

9. IRC Sec. R403.1.6 addresses foundation anchorage. According to IRC Sec. R403.1.6, these anchors can be no more than 6 ft on center. It is true that anchor bolts must be spaced no more than 12 in from the wall's end, but the spacing between them is still 6 ft at maximum.

The answer is (B).

10. American Concrete Institute (ACI) 318, Sec. 7.7.1, requires a minimum of 3 in of concrete cover to protect the bars if the concrete is permanently exposed to earth. This applies to footings. The cover is the distance from the edge of the concrete to the edge of the rebars. ACI 318 also requires a minimum of 6 in of concrete cover above the rebars in a footing. In this example, 3 in are required at element C.

The answer is (C).

11. The low-permeability soil layer should be behind the wall at the top layer. Having a low-permeability soil layer at this location minimizes the amount of water that could infiltrate the soil and get behind the wall.

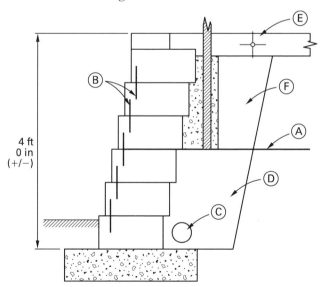

12. I-joists are typically used for spans from 16–20 ft. The size of dimensional lumber is limited by tree sizes, so dimensional lumber length is usually no more than 15–20 ft. For spans longer than 20 ft, engineered wood products such as LVL and glulam can be used. These products are often readily available in lengths up to 28–30 ft and longer if custom-ordered from the manufacturer. However, engineered wood products are more expensive and should be used only if sawn lumber cannot be used. In this case, because the span lengths are about

15 ft, dimensional lumber is the most appropriate and the least expensive material to use.

The answer is (A).

13. The total load per square foot, L, is the sum of the dead load, D, and the live load, L_O.

$$L = D + L_O$$
$$= 15 \ \frac{\text{lbf}}{\text{ft}^2} + 40 \ \frac{\text{lbf}}{\text{ft}^2}$$
$$= 55 \ \text{lbf/ft}^2$$

To calculate the load per linear foot on each beam, multiply the total load by the tributary width, S.

$$w = LS$$
$$= \left(55 \ \frac{\text{lbf}}{\text{ft}^2}\right)(15 \ \text{ft})$$
$$= 825 \ \text{lbf/ft}^2$$

The answer is (C).

14. Each column on the plan needs to support the loads transferred to it by the two beams connected to it. Each beam is simply supported, and the support reactions are equal. Each column supports a 12 ft beam and a 16 ft beam.

The total load on the beam is a product of the total load and the tributary area of the beam, A. The total load per square foot, L, is the sum of the dead load, D, and the live load, L_O.

$$L = D + L_O$$
$$= 15 \ \frac{\text{lbf}}{\text{ft}^2} + 40 \ \frac{\text{lbf}}{\text{ft}^2}$$
$$= 55 \ \text{lbf/ft}^2$$

$$L_{\text{beam 1}} = LA$$
$$= \left(55 \ \frac{\text{lbf}}{\text{ft}^2}\right)\big((15 \ \text{ft})(12 \ \text{ft})\big)$$
$$= 9900 \ \text{lbf}$$

Calculate the support reactions, R_1, of the 12 ft beam by dividing the total beam load by 2.

$$R_1 = \frac{L_{\text{beam 1}}}{2}$$
$$= \left(\frac{9900 \ \text{lbf}}{2}\right)\left(1000 \ \frac{\text{lbf}}{\text{kip}}\right)$$
$$= 4.95 \ \text{kips}$$

Project Development

Similarly, calculate the total load, L, on the 16 ft beam.

$$L_{\text{beam 2}} = LA$$
$$= \left(55 \ \frac{\text{lbf}}{\text{ft}^2}\right)\big((15 \ \text{ft})(16 \ \text{ft})\big)$$
$$= 13{,}200 \ \text{lbf}$$

The support reactions, R_2, of the 16 ft beam are

$$R_2 = \frac{L_{\text{beam 2}}}{2}$$
$$= \left(\frac{13{,}200 \ \text{lbf}}{2}\right)\left(1000 \ \frac{\text{lbf}}{\text{kip}}\right)$$
$$= 6.6 \ \text{kips}$$

The total load to be supported by one column is the sum of the support reactions.

$$L_{\text{column}} = R_1 + R_2$$
$$= 4.95 \ \text{kips} + 6.6 \ \text{kips}$$
$$= 11.55 \ \text{kips} \quad (12 \ \text{kips})$$

The answer is (D).

15. The total load on the footing including the footing weight is

$$L_{\text{footing}} = L_{\text{column A}} + L_{\text{footing weight}}$$
$$= (22 \ \text{kips} + 1 \ \text{kip})\left(1000 \ \frac{\text{lbf}}{\text{kip}}\right)$$
$$= 23{,}000 \ \text{lbf}$$

Calculate the overall footing surface area, A, by dividing the total load on the footing by the value of the soil bearing capacity, q_a. According to the case study description, the geotechnical engineer determined that $q_a = 3500 \ \text{lbf/ft}^2$. The footing surface area is

$$A = \frac{L_{\text{footing}}}{q_a}$$
$$= \frac{23{,}000 \ \text{lbf}}{3500 \ \dfrac{\text{lbf}}{\text{ft}^2}}$$
$$= 6.57 \ \text{ft}^2$$

To determine the side length, d_{side}, of the footing, calculate the square root of the footing area.

$$d_{\text{side}} = \sqrt{A}$$
$$= \sqrt{6.57 \ \text{ft}^2}$$
$$= 2.56 \ \text{ft} \quad (2 \ \text{ft} \ 7 \ \text{in})$$

The answer is (C).

16. The floor joists span the 15 ft length between beams and between the foundation wall and beams. Therefore, the joist span symbol must be drawn parallel to the 15 ft spans in all three bays, as shown. (See *Illustration for Sol. 16*.)

17. Lintels are used above openings to support the loads shown. (See *Illustration for Sol. 17*.)

The correct locations for lintels are above the openings in the foundation walls for door and windows. One lintel is located in the left foundation wall, and two lintels are located in the right wall.

18. ACI 318 requires a minimum of 3 in of concrete coverage around steel reinforcement bars within footings that are in direct contact with the earth and 6 in of concrete above these rebars.

The answer is (B).

Illustration for Sol. 16

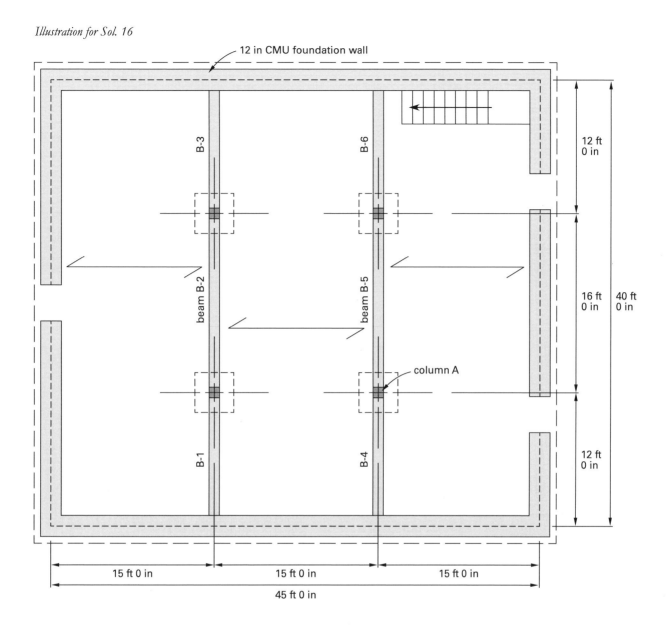

Illustration for Sol. 17

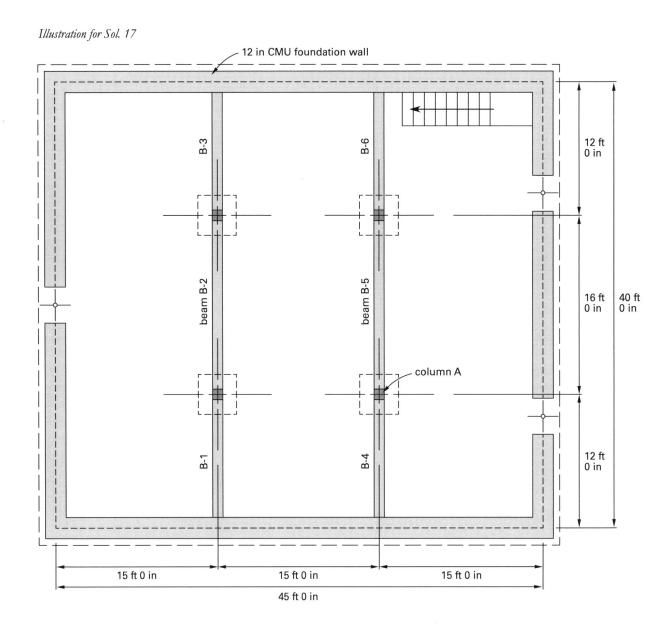

DIVISION 6: CONSTRUCTION & EVALUATION

49 Preconstruction Activities

1. A client has asked the architect to help review information submitted by contractors on American Institute of Architects (AIA) Document A305, *Contractor's Qualification Statement*. Which of the following characteristics is the least indicative of the contractor's ability to complete the project successfully?

(A) number of people on the contractor's in-house staff

(B) financial qualifications and bonding capacity

(C) experience with similar project types

(D) history of finishing projects on time and budget

2. Which of the following are included in the bidding documents? (Choose the four that apply.)

(A) specifications

(B) invitation to bid

(C) owner-architect agreement

(D) owner-contractor agreement

(E) performance bond requirements

(F) change orders

3. An architect has been hired by a design-build firm under the provisions of American Institute of Architects (AIA) Document B143, *Standard Form of Agreement between Design-Builder and Architect*. In AIA Document B143, Article 3, which defines the architect's services, only two tasks have been selected: to complete the design documents and to complete the construction documents. The design-build firm has contracted with the owner to complete the work based on the cost of the work plus a fee, with a guaranteed maximum price. According to the terms of this agreement, what is the architect's obligation to estimate and adjust overall project costs?

(A) Provide an estimate for the architect's portion of the work, which includes the building design only.

(B) Adjust the project size, quality, or budget if the preliminary cost estimate exceeds the budget.

(C) Develop the design and construction documents with cost input from the design-builder.

(D) Make reasonable adjustments in the scope of the project to adjust the cost of the work.

4. An architect completes the drawings for a window replacement project at a private elementary school. The scope of the work includes replacement of all of the operable windows in the classrooms. After the project is awarded and a contractor is signed to do the job, the school's facilities department determines that additional money is available to replace the aluminum storefront at the main entrance to the school. The existing entrance does not comply with current accessibility requirements or security guidelines and cannot be replaced in kind. The school board requests that this work be included in the construction contract. Which of the following statements is true?

(A) The additional work for the aluminum storefront will be incorporated into the contractor's contract through an addendum.

(B) The architect must provide, at no additional cost to the owner, the information necessary for the contractor to prepare a proposal.

(C) The additional work for the aluminum storefront will be incorporated into the construction contract through a change order.

(D) The architectural fees for additional design and coordination will be incorporated into the construction change order and paid by the contractor.

5. A small private college is planning to renovate the locker rooms in the campus fitness center. The work must take place during a three-week semester break. The bids have been received and a construction contract has been awarded. A month before the end of the fall semester, the existing water heater fails and leaves the showers without hot water. The contractor who is onboard for the renovation project is finishing another project with a tight deadline and does not have staff available to address the problem at the fitness center. The college must repair the water heater immediately, so they hire an independent mechanical contractor to replace the unit with the water heater that was specified for the new project. How should this change to the scope of work of the renovation project be addressed?

(A) Prepare an addendum deleting the water heater replacement from the scope of the renovation contractor's work.

(B) Charge the renovation contractor for the water heater replacement materials and labor because they were unavailable to perform the repair.

(C) Adjust the renovation contractor's contract scope and amount by change order.

(D) Revise the documents and rebid the project.

6. Addenda are issued

(A) prior to receipt of bids

(B) after receipt of bids but before work commences

(C) after the award of the contract

(D) during construction

7. Bid documents for an elementary school indicate an area of exterior concrete paving with an indeterminate limit because the owner has not made a final decision concerning the amount of paved area required. In order to compare bid prices fairly for the paving, the architect may request on the bid form that the contractors include

(A) individual quotes

(B) unit prices

(C) fixed costs

(D) contingencies

8. Which of the following statements about bidding is correct?

(A) Bidding procedures vary widely from project to project.

(B) Bidding is not required for federally funded projects.

(C) Open bidding may allow an inexperienced contractor to be awarded a job if the firm submits the lowest price.

(D) Competitive bidding takes less time than negotiation and can result in a lower construction cost.

9. Which of the following variables has the greatest impact on a bid?

(A) contractor's profit margin

(B) influences of the construction marketplace

(C) number of prices received from subcontractors

(D) subcontract bids

10. The final responsibility for awarding a construction contract rests with the

(A) architect

(B) construction manager

(C) owner

(D) owner's legal counsel

Construction & Evaluation

11. The architect is reviewing a critical path method (CPM) schedule from the contractor. The critical path is 200 calendar days, the total float is 30 days, and the contractor is planning for a 5-day work week. Based on this information, the architect could conclude that the construction time

(A)   will be about 40 weeks

(B)   may be as long as 46 weeks

(C)   could be shortened to 32 weeks

(D)   cannot be delayed more than 6 weeks

12. Contractor's overhead and profit typically account for what percentage of the construction cost?

(A)   5–15%

(B)   10–20%

(C)   15–30%

(D)   15–40%

13. Which of the following affects a subcontractor's proposed price? (Choose the four that apply.)

(A)   number of times that equipment must be mobilized

(B)   types of tools needed to build a project

(C)   number of workers needed to complete the work

(D)   stage of the project at which the subcontractor will be on site

(E)   scope of work and quantity of materials required

(F)   insurance and bonding requirements

Construction & Evaluation

Solutions

1. The information requested on AIA Document A305 gives an owner an overall picture of a prospective contractor's capabilities and illustrates the organization of the contractor's firm. This document includes a summary of recent projects and their sizes and budgets, which when combined with additional information about the company's financial qualifications and project performance history, help determine whether the contractor would be a good fit for the proposed work.

The size of the contractor's in-house staff is not necessarily indicative of the firm's capabilities because the contractor may subcontract portions of the work.

The answer is (A).

2. The owner-architect agreement and any change orders are not included in the bidding documents. The project specifications, the invitation to bid, a sample copy of the owner-contractor agreement, and performance bond requirements would be provided to bidders.

The answer is (A), (B), (D), and (E).

3. In AIA Document B143, Sec. 3.2, the architect and design-builder can agree to have the architect provide as few or as many services as are indicated. If evaluation and estimating services are not selected, the architect is only obligated to base the design on the design-build documents, other criteria provided by the design-builder, the proposed project schedule, and the budget for the architect's portion of the project.

In this case, the architect has only been assigned responsibility for providing design and construction documents. The architect is not responsible for estimating the cost of the work. The architect's design will be based on the information provided in the design-build documents, which include, among other things, the project criteria established by the owner, changes to the project criteria proposed by the design-builder and accepted by the owner, and budget established by the design-builder. Because the architect is working as a consultant to the design-builder throughout the design process, the architect must respond to input from the design-builder regarding the cost consequences of a design decision.

If the design-builder's estimate exceeds the budget for the architect's portion of the work, the architect may request additional compensation for revisions to the documents required to bring the project within the budget.

Per AIA Document B143, adjusting the project size, quality, or budget is the design-builder's obligation. The architect may adjust only the scope of the project to accommodate the cost of work if the architect performs budget evaluations according to AIA Document B143, Exhibit B.

The answer is (C).

4. An addendum is used to modify contract requirements during the bidding process only. It would not be used after the construction contract is awarded.

The owner has opted to change the scope of the project, so the architect is entitled to additional compensation for preparing the new entrance design.

A construction change order would not include the architect's fees since the change order modifies only the contract between the owner and the contractor and the architect is not a party to this agreement. To update the architect's contract to include the storefront design, an amendment to the owner-architect agreement is needed. The additional fees due to the architect for design work relative to this change would be agreed upon by the owner and architect and incorporated into the contract amendment. The owner compensates the architect for these design efforts.

A change order would be issued to alter the scope of the contractor's work and modify the terms of the owner-contractor agreement.

The answer is (C).

5. An addendum is used to make changes to the project scope during the bidding process; after the contract is awarded, the contract is modified through either a construction change directive or a change order. The renovation contractor is not responsible for performing work that is outside of the contract requirements and would not be penalized for not being available to perform this emergency work. This repair affects a small portion of the project scope and would not require rebidding.

The most efficient way to proceed is to hire an independent mechanical contractor to address the repair, and then adjust the renovation contractor's contract scope and sum by change order.

The answer is (C).

6. An addendum is a written or graphic document issued by the architect prior to submission of contractors' bids that modifies or interprets the bidding documents. Addenda may be issued in response to errors discovered in the bidding documents, changes the client wants to make, questions from bidders, or additions or deletions needed. Addenda must be sent to all bidders at least four days prior to the bid date. Most bid forms ask bidders to acknowledge receipt of any addenda to help ensure that all bids are based on the same information.

The answer is (A).

7. Unit prices are requested on bid forms when the full extent of the work is unknown, but the type, materials, and quality of work can be defined. A unit price is a set price quote, established by a contractor during bidding, for a specified amount of the work. The unit price is based on cost per unit of measurement, such as square foot, or linear foot, or on individual units, such as a light fixture.

The answer is (B).

8. Bidding procedures are fairly well established in the construction industry, but each project has unique legal, insurance, and administrative requirements that should be shared with all bidders.

Government-funded projects at the federal, state, or local level are generally required to bid.

The bid process can lengthen total project time due to the time allotted for review of the construction documents and contract negotiation, but the competitive nature of bidding allows the owner to compare prices before hiring a contractor. Open bidding means that nearly anyone can bid, regardless of experience. This encourages a variety of contractors to participate, but when bidding is open, it can be difficult to evaluate qualified bidders. In addition, the cost and complexity of advertising and administering the bidding process may increase.

The answer is (A).

9. Labor and materials, by far, have the biggest influence on the cost of a job because they represent about 80% of the cost. Labor and materials costs influence the amount of subcontractors' bids. Profit tends to be based on a percentage of the total project construction cost, and market influences do not have as great an effect on overall costs as the raw costs of the labor and materials required to construct the project.

The answer is (C).

10. The owner is ultimately responsible for deciding which contractor will be hired for a project. The architect is generally involved in the decision-making process, but only assists and gives advice to the owner.

The answer is (C).

11. The critical path is the sequence of events that must happen as scheduled in order for a project to be completed on time. Dividing 5 work days per calendar week into 200 total days gives a 40-week construction time.

Float represents the range of time during which noncritical activities may start or end without affecting the overall schedule. Total float is the individual float times added together, and it does not influence the critical path time interval.

The answer is (A).

12. Contractor's overhead and profit typically constitute 15–40% of the construction cost.

The answer is (D).

13. The stage of the project at which the subcontractor will perform the work would not determine the price of the work. The types of tools needed to complete the job may, under some circumstances, have some bearing on cost if they must be purchased or rented, but normally a subcontractor would have access to the tools required for the trade, and they do not represent a significant portion of the total cost when considered relative to the costs of labor and materials. A subcontractor would be most interested in the number of times equipment must be brought to a job site, the size of the workforce and the skills that will be required, and the owner's requirements for insurance and bonding because all of these have cost implications.

The answer is (A), (C), (E), and (F).

Construction & Evaluation

50 Construction Administration

1. Which of the following statements are true? (Choose the three that apply.)

(A) Shop drawings are usually more detailed than other project drawings.

(B) Shop drawings are usually less detailed than other project drawings.

(C) Shop drawings may be prepared by the general contractor only.

(D) Shop drawings may be prepared by suppliers and subcontractors.

(E) Shop drawings are reviewed by the architect and the general contractor.

(F) Shop drawings are prepared by the structural engineer.

2. How should communications between the contractor and design consultants be conducted the during construction phase?

(A) through the architect

(B) through the owner

(C) through the owner and the architect

(D) directly between the contractor and the design consultants

3. After construction documents have been provided to the general contractor for pricing, an architect decides to change the location of a window by less than 8 in to align it with the center of the room in which it is located. Who is responsible for approving the proposed change?

(A) the owner

(B) the contractor

(C) both the owner and the contractor

(D) neither the owner nor the contractor

4. During the construction of a multi-tenant retail project, one potential tenant requests the addition of 500 ft² of space. Not wanting to lose the potential tenant, the owner agrees and directs the architect to make the changes. The owner and contractor are unable to agree on the cost and timeframe for the change. What should the architect do?

(A) Issue a construction change directive.

(B) Prepare a change order for the contractor to approve.

(C) Revise the contract.

(D) Change the shop drawings.

5. At the beginning of the construction phase, the owner requests a change to the building layout that will require relocating a structural column and modifying the framing in the surrounding area. The column footing has not been constructed. The structural steel shop drawings have been submitted to the architect by the general contractor, but they have not yet been reviewed or approved by the architect or structural engineer. How should the architect initiate this change?

(A) Revise the shop drawings to indicate the new column location and associated framing changes and return the submittal to the general contractor marked "Approved as Noted."

(B) Issue a proposal to the owner for additional design services, and notify the contractor of the pending change.

(C) Consult with the general contractor to establish the cost increase.

(D) Consult with the steel fabricator and supplier to determine the schedule delay.

6. Just before construction is to begin on an office building, an architect receives a request from the owner to add a loading dock to the building. The additional work will extend the construction time by three months and will cost an additional $500,000. Who must approve the change order(s)?

(A) The owner must approve a change order issued by the architect.

√ (B) The owner must approve a change order issued by the architect and signed by the contractor.

(C) The owner and contractor must approve a change order issued by the architect.

(D) The contractor must approve change orders issued by the architect and owner.

7. According to American Institute of Architects (AIA) Document A101, *Standard Form of Agreement between Owner and Architect*, which of the following statements regarding construction observations is correct?

(A) The architect visits the job site only at the beginning and end of construction.

(B) The architect issues an observation report to the owner after each visit.

(C) The architect is responsible for confirming that safety equipment is used.

(D) The architect creates a list of items that have been found incomplete.

8. Which statement describes the architect's responsibility relative to the project schedule?

(A) The architect approves the schedule prepared by the general contractor.

(B) The architect monitors the progress of the work against the project schedule prepared by the contractor.

(C) The architect enforces the schedule.

(D) The architect develops the schedule for the project.

9. An architect is working on a small retail project in a city that has adopted the *International Building Code* (IBC). The owner's agreement with the contractor includes American Institute of Architects (AIA) Document A201, *General Conditions of the Contract for Construction*. During a site visit, the architect discovers that an exterior exit door has been installed backwards, so that the door swings in. The door is shown swinging out on the drawings. Which of the following is an appropriate response from the architect?

(A) Reject the work and instruct the contractor to comply with the requirements of the construction documents.

(B) Revise the drawing and send it to the code official with an addendum to the approved documents stating that the door is no longer an exit door.

(C) Advise the owners that they may choose to accept the nonconforming work and leave the door in place in exchange for a credit from the contractor.

(D) Instruct the contractor to remove the existing door and frame, and order a new door and frame.

10. A contractor installs drywall before the owner's audiovisual system installer has an opportunity to visit the site to review the framing. After inspection on site, the installer contacts the architect and expresses concern that the blocking has not been installed at the correct locations to support the television mounts in a conference room. The required blocking locations and sizes are shown on the contract documents. The architect requests that the drywall be removed in these areas to confirm the concealed construction before the televisions are installed. When the drywall is removed, the architect finds that the blocking has been installed in the correct locations, but it is not the size shown on the drawings and it is inadequate to support the weight of the audiovisual equipment. Who is

Construction & Evaluation

responsible for the cost of uncovering this concealed work and repairing the wall?

(A)   the contractor

(B)   the owner

(C)   the audiovisual system installer

(D)   the architect

11. A project is being completed under the provisions of American Institute of Architects (AIA) Document B101-SP, *Standard Form of Agreement between Owner and Architect, for Use on a Sustainable Project*. When this agreement is used, which aspect of determining construction progress differs from the terms of AIA Document B101, *Standard Form of Agreement between Owner and Architect*?

(A)   The architect must notify the owner of any deviation from the contract documents that could affect the project's sustainability.

(B)   The contractor is required to include specific steps that will be taken to achieve sustainability goals in the overall project schedule.

(C)   The architect must make additional site visits to verify the contractor's compliance with the project schedule.

(D)   The owner must list individual sustainability issues for the architect to verify during site visits.

12. Based on the work observed during a site visit, the architect believes that construction progress is falling behind schedule. The owner-contractor agreement includes American Institute of Architects (AIA) Document A201, *General Conditions of the Contract for Construction*. Which of the following should the architect do first?

(A)   Immediately notify the owner of the problem in writing.

(B)   Detail which portions of the project are lagging in the next field report.

(C)   Determine with the contractor if there is a problem, and suggest ways to correct it.

(D)   Compare the current status of construction with the contractor's schedule.

13. Which party is responsible for the costs associated with special inspections required by the *International Building Code* (IBC)?

(A)   contractor

(B)   architect or design professional

(C)   code official

(D)   owner

14. A specification calls for a window assembly with glazing that meets the following performance criteria.

transmittance	
total solar energy (%)	33%
ultraviolet (%)	10%
visible light (%)	70%
reflectance	
visible light (% exterior)	11%
visible light (% interior)	12%
total solar (energy %)	31%
NFRC U-factor	
winter (nighttime)	$(0.25 \text{ Btu/hr})(\text{ft}^2)(°\text{F})$
summer (daytime)	$(0.21 \text{ Btu/hr})(\text{ft}^2)(°\text{F})$
shading coefficient (SC)	0.43
relative heat gain	$(89 \text{ Btu/hr})(\text{ft}^2)$
solar heat gain coefficient (SHGC)	0.37
light to solar gain (LSG)	1.89

Which performance criteria should be evaluated to determine whether or not the submitted glazing product meets *International Energy Conservation Code* (IECC) requirements for fenestration? (Choose the two that apply.)

(A)   total solar energy transmittance

(B)   NRFC U-factor

(C)   relative heat gain

(D)   solar heat gain coefficient (SHGC)

(E)   visible light transmittance

(F)   shading coefficient (SC)

15. One nondestructive test used to measure the strength of concrete after it has hardened in its final form is the

(A)   core cylinder test

(B)   cylinder test

(C)   impact hammer test

(D)   Kelly ball test

16. If too much water is included in a concrete mix, which of the following problems might develop?

(A) laitance

(B) efflorescence

(C) hydration

(D) segregation

17. Which of the following would be specified in the construction documents?

(A) height of a bottom-dump bucket above the forms as the concrete is being placed

(B) type of vibrator being used to consolidate the concrete after it has been poured

(C) location of the rebar in relation to the forms

(D) method of support of the forms

18. At what temperature do workers need to take steps to protect concrete when cold weather is predicted?

(A) 0°F

(B) 32°F

(C) 40°F

(D) 45°F

19. The contractor is solely responsible for which of the following? (Choose the two that apply.)

(A) field reports to the owner

(B) field tests

(C) scaffolding

(D) reviewing claims of subcontractors

(E) reviewing shop drawings

(F) code review of contract documents

20. When a contractor proposes a substitution of a material or method of construction that is specified in the contract documents, the architect's responsibility in reviewing the substitution is

(A) proving that the proposed substitution is equivalent to the original

(B) finding documentation that relates to the substitution

(C) forwarding the request to the owner

(D) approving or disapproving the request

21. During a site visit, the architect observes the installation of unapproved materials that were not originally specified. Before work can be stopped under the provisions of American Institute of Architects (AIA) Document A201, *General Conditions of the Contract for Construction*, what must occur?

(A) The contractor must provide documentation that the materials installed are equal to those specified.

(B) The owner must issue a written order to the contractor to stop the work.

(C) The architect must give written notice of intent to stop the work and wait seven days before shutting down the job.

(D) The architect must issue a stop work order.

22. During construction, the architect is obligated to visit the site to keep the client informed about the progress and quality of the work. According to the basic provisions of American Institute of Architects (AIA) Document B101, *Standard Form of Agreement between Owner and Architect*, these visits must occur

(A) every week

(B) every two weeks

(C) as appropriate to the stage of the contractor's operations

(D) only if they have been written into the agreement as additional services

23. A change order can be requested by the

(A) architect

(B) owner

(C) architect or owner

(D) architect, owner, or contractor

24. The specifications for a project require moisture tests to be performed on all concrete slabs on which resilient flooring will be installed. According to the requirements of American Institute of Architects (AIA) Document A201, *General Conditions of the Contract for Construction*, which party is responsible for the cost of performing these tests?

(A) architect

(B) owner

(C) contractor

(D) flooring subcontractor

25. Which of the following parties are required to agree to a construction change directive?

(A) architect and owner

(B) architect and contractor

(C) owner and contractor

(D) architect, owner, and contractor

26. During construction, the contractor asks the architect to allow the installation of a different floor tile than originally specified because the proposed new tile can be delivered faster. According to American Institute of Architects (AIA) Document A201, *General Conditions of the Contract for Construction*, which of the following statements are true about this request? (Choose the four that apply.)

(A) The owner's consent is required to allow this change to be made.

(B) The tile, if approved, will not be covered by warranty.

(C) The substitution must be made with a change order.

(D) The architect must evaluate the request and determine that the material is equal to that originally specified.

(E) A change order would be issued if the cost of the new tile is greater than the cost of the specified tile.

(F) The contractor is responsible for any additional cost associated with the change.

27. According to American Institute of Architects (AIA) Document A201, *General Conditions of the Contract for Construction*, the architect's duties when processing the

contractor's application for payment include which of the following? (Choose the four that apply.)

(A) comparing work done and materials stored to the contractor's schedule of values

(B) making an exhaustive on-site inspection to verify that work has been completed properly

(C) approving a certificate for payment if the architect feels the contractor is due payment in the amount stated

(D) using information gathered during previous site visits to determine that the work is in accordance with the contract documents

(E) verifying that subcontractors have been paid from funds dispersed via previous pay applications

(F) determining that the amount of retainage is appropriate to the stage of construction

28. According to the AIA agreements between the owner and the contractor, the amount of retainage withheld from each application for payment is

(A) 5% of the amount due

(B) 10% of the amount due

(C) 10% of the total contract price

(D) as stated in the owner-contractor agreement

29. During a site visit, the architect notices what appears to be an undersized variable air volume box being installed. What should the architect do?

(A) Tell the mechanical engineer to look at the situation during the next site visit by the engineer. Note the observation on a field report.

(B) Find the contractor and stop work on the installation until the size of the unit can be verified by the mechanical engineer and compared to the contract documents.

(C) Notify the owner in writing that the work is not proceeding according to the contract documents, and advise him to stop the work until the architect can arrange a meeting with the mechanical engineer to resolve the situation.

(D) Notify the contractor that the equipment may be undersized, and have the contractor check on it. Concurrently, ask the mechanical engineer to verify the size of the unit against the specifications and report to the architect.

30. When the project is 90% complete, the code inspector requires installation of six exit signs in addition to those shown on the approved plans. Which of the following instruments should the architect use to make this change?

(A) order for minor change

(B) addendum

(C) change order

(D) construction change directive

31. Which of the following statements about submittals are correct? (Choose the three that apply.)

(A) The architect must review submittals before the contractor approves them.

(B) The contractor is ultimately responsible for the accuracy of dimensions and quantities.

(C) Submittals are not considered part of the contract documents.

(D) The contractor can reject submittals and request resubmittal by his or her subcontractors.

(E) The architect can make a change to the scope of work through the review notes on the submittal.

(F) Substitutions may be presented to the architect for consideration at any time during the construction phase.

32. A contractor makes a claim for additional money for extra work caused by unforeseen circumstances. According to American Institute of Architects (AIA) Document A201, *General Conditions of the Contract for Construction*, the initial decision maker (IDM) must respond to this claim within _____ days. (Fill in the blank.)

33. The architect's submittal review includes which of the following? (Choose the four that apply.)

(A) verification or correction of dimensions

(B) notation of action taken

(C) date of receipt of the submittal

(D) determination if the submittal should be reviewed by consultants

(E) verification that the contractor has reviewed the submittal prior to forwarding it to the architect

(F) notes that require the contractor to provide something other than that described in the specifications

34. If a general contractor fails to pay a subcontractor, the subcontractor can protect its financial interests by using a(n)

(A) performance bond

(B) contractor's affidavit of payment

(C) builder's risk insurance

(D) mechanic's lien

35. Which of the following statements is correct?

(A) The architect becomes responsible for a defect in the work if he or she sees the defect during a site visit but fails to report it to the contractor.

(B) The architect has the sole right to make changes in the work.

(C) The architect is responsible for verifying soil test reports provided by the owner.

(D) The architect must update the preliminary estimate of the cost of the work when the construction documents are almost complete.

Construction & Evaluation

Solutions

1. Shop drawings are documents prepared to illustrate the details of a construction assembly or system that the construction team proposes to provide. In many cases, general contractors rely on their subcontractors or suppliers to prepare shop drawings because they will perform the fabrication and installation and they have the most detailed knowledge about the proposed system.

The shop drawings, along with product data and material samples, are sent to the general contractor for review and approval, and then they are forwarded to the architect. The architect (with the assistance of consultants) reviews the shop drawings to confirm that the intent of the project design is being followed.

Shop drawings are typically more detailed than other project drawings because they include information specific to the manufacturer's proposed system. The shop drawings show how a particular product or system will be integrated into the overall project. The architect would not show this level of detail on the construction documents because the supplier of the element may not be known at the time of design. The architect's drawings are intended to convey design intent, and the shop drawings are used to verify that the proposed system complies with the established requirements.

The answer is (A), (D), and (E).

2. During construction observation, definite lines of communication among the parties are established by American Institute of Architects (AIA) Document A201, *General Conditions of the Contract for Construction*. During this time, communications between the contractor and the architect's design consultants proceed through the architect.

The answer is (A).

3. Because construction has not begun, adjusting the location of a window by less than 8 in would be considered a minor change. There would be no change to the quantity of materials utilized and no change to the installation cost or time. The information regarding the change would be issued to the contractor and owner within an addendum, if the contract has not yet been signed, or a bulletin.

The answer is (D).

4. A change order allows a change that affects the project time or cost to be made. In this case, the owner does not want to revise the contract. The architect has no authority to revise the contract between the owner and the contractor. The architect may not make changes to shop drawings, especially if they were reviewed and approved before the change to the construction documents occurs.

The architect may issue a construction change directive to order a change in construction before the owner and contractor agree on cost or timeframe adjustments. As such, the owner can order the change without revising the contract, and the work can continue. The directive must be signed by the owner and architect. The costs and schedule are determined after the directive is issued.

The answer is (A).

5. The architect's first step should be to prepare an amendment to the owner-architect agreement. This design change has been initiated by the owner, and the architect is entitled to additional compensation for the revisions that will be required to move the column. When the amendment is approved by the owner, the architect may proceed with the design work.

The architect should notify the contractor that this change will be made so that construction work that may be affected by the change can be postponed.

Upon receipt of the revised scope of work and request for proposal from the architect, the contractor can prepare a proposal summarizing the cost of the work and the schedule modifications that will be necessary to make the change. The contractor must coordinate with subcontractors and suppliers to determine how the change will affect their schedules.

When the contractor's proposal is approved by the owner, the architect may prepare a change order to modify the construction contract.

The answer is (B).

6. A change order addresses modifications to the project that affect price, time or both. In this case, the change is requested by the owner. A proposal for the work would be solicited from the contractor, and when the owner and the contractor agree on a price, the architect would issue a change order. The change order must also be signed by the owner, contractor, and architect in order for the changes to be incorporated into the contract.

The answer is (B).

7. Construction evaluation services are not required by AIA Document A101. The architect is not restricted from visiting the job site. The architect determines the frequency and time of visits to the job site depending on the complexity of the job. The observation allows the architect to determine work progress and monitor construction quality. It is not typical to visit at only the beginning and end of construction.

The architect does not need to visit the job site with design consultants unless there is a known issue that a specific consultant needs to address.

Creating an observation report for the owner alerts the owner to deficiencies or quality issues that may be of concern. The owner reviews these concerns with the contractors.

Safety on the job site is the responsibility of the contractor.

A list of incomplete items is part of the punch list performed at the end of construction.

The answer is (B).

8. The architect is not responsible for developing, approving, or enforcing the project schedule. The owner and contractor agree upon the project duration in their contract, which establishes the number of days between commencement and substantial completion. The contractor then prepares and submits the schedule for the work based on the parameters established in the agreement. Throughout the course of the project, the contractor is responsible for updating the schedule and sharing the updates with the owner and the architect. The contractor's schedule is presented for information only; the contractor is solely responsible for sequencing the work, so neither the owner nor the architect approve the contractor's schedule.

The architect's responsibility regarding the schedule is to periodically evaluate the progress of the work in comparison to the contractor's stated schedule, and to inform the owner if any deviations from the schedule are identified.

The answer is (B).

9. The architect is obligated to abide by applicable building codes and laws, and this incorrect installation violates the IBC requirements. Because the existing door does not comply with the code requirements, the owner does not have the option to accept it as nonconforming work in exchange for a credit. The contractor controls construction means and methods and may decide to replace the existing door and frame if it cannot be reused and reinstalled. However, this is not the architect's decision.

The IBC requires all exit doors to swing in the direction of egress. Because an out-swinging exit door is a code requirement, it cannot remain as it is; it must comply with the approved construction documents. According to AIA Document A201, Sec. 4.2.6, the architect may reject work that does not comply with the contract documents. It is appropriate, in this case, for the architect to reject the improperly installed door and require the contractor to correct the work.

The answer is (A).

10. If the architect requested that work be removed and the concealed work is correct, the owner is responsible for the cost of this additional work. However, the contractor is responsible for the cost of uncovering and correcting any work that does not comply with the construction documents.

The answer is (A).

11. Under AIA Document B101, the architect is only required to consider environmentally responsible design alternatives, such as material choices and building orientation. These strategies may be adopted as the project budget and the owner's directives allow.

Under AIA Document B101-SP, the contractor is not required to include specific sustainability steps in the schedule. The architect is not required to make additional visits to verify compliance with the project schedule, and the owner is not required to list verifiable sustainability issues for the architect.

AIA Document B101-SP may be used when achieving a stated sustainability goal (such as Leadership in Energy and Environmental Design (LEED) certification, or a certain measurable level of energy efficiency) is a part of the project requirements. The agreement complements the sustainability plan that is developed by the owner and architect early in the design process, which describes the sustainable measures to be employed, implementation strategies, details about design reviews, and documentation required for certification submissions, among other requirements. It also sets forth more specific roles and responsibilities of the architect related to sustainable design, including the responsibility to notify the owner of any known deviations from the contract documents that might affect the achievement of sustainable measures. These changes may be noted during a regular site visit or through other project communications.

The answer is (A).

12. According to AIA Document A201, the contractor must provide a project schedule to the owner and architect prior to the start of construction. This schedule is for information only and neither the owner nor the architect approve the contractor's schedule. The contractor is obligated to perform the work in general accordance with this schedule, but retains all responsibility for sequencing the work. If minor changes to the schedule need to be made to allow the work to proceed, the contractor has the ability to make these modifications.

A conversation with the contractor can allow the architect to determine whether or not there is a serious problem. Some items may be behind schedule, while others may be ahead of schedule. The contractor should be given the opportunity to note where adjustments to the schedule

Construction & Evaluation

may have been made due to delivery timetables, weather conditions, personnel availability, or other factors that fall under the contractor's responsibility to sequence the work, which may help the architect to better understand the project's status. However, the architect should not make suggestions about construction sequencing or procedures, as these decisions are solely the responsibility of the contractor.

The architect should note the field observations and any discussion about the schedule with the contractor in a field report, which will be distributed to both the contractor and owner and serve as documentation of the conditions at the site. AIA Document A201, Sec. 4.2.3, requires the architect to notify the owner of "known deviations... from the most recent construction schedule submitted by the Contractor."

However, before doing any of these things, the architect should first compare the current status of the project with the contractor's original schedule to determine whether or not the work is, in fact, behind schedule.

The answer is (D).

13. The design professional is required to develop a statement of special inspections listing the systems that must be tested and the types and extent of tests that must be performed, and the design professional must submit this to the code official for review and approval. Inspections may be required for seismic resistance, wind requirements, or steel, masonry, or foundation construction, as described in IBC Chap. 17.

The owner (or the architect, acting as the owner's agent) engages a qualified special inspection firm which has the ability to perform the required tests and provide supervision of the work as it progresses. This firm must be independent of the contractor. The owner is responsible for the costs of these services and tests.

The results of the tests and inspections must be submitted to the code official so that the official may evaluate whether the requirements outlined in the contract documents have been fulfilled.

The answer is (D).

14. The IECC establishes performance and area requirements for window and door assemblies. The allowable properties are dependent upon the geographic location of the building (climate zones 1–7 in the United States), the orientation of the assembly (vertical windows and doors or horizontal skylights), and whether the element is fixed or operable. The two criteria cited in the IECC prescriptive fenestration requirements are U-factor and SHGC.

U-factor is the coefficient of heat transmittance. The lower the U-value is, the better the insulating performance

of the glazing. SHGC is a measurement of how much radiation is admitted through a window. A window assembly with a high SHGC transmits more solar heat than an assembly with a low SHGC.

The National Fenestration Rating Council is a third-party testing organization that verifies manufacturers' claims and provides a label stating the window assembly's U-factor and SHGC. The label may also include information on the assembly's performance in visible transmittance and air leakage tests.

The answer is (B) and (D).

15. The impact hammer test involves snapping a spring-loaded plunger against a concrete surface and measuring the amount of rebound. The amount of rebound gives an approximate reading of concrete strength.

A cylinder test requires that a sample be taken at the time the concrete is poured, before it has hardened. A core cylinder test can give the strength of hardened concrete, but the test is destructive to the concrete, and the sample needs to be tested in a laboratory. Both the core cylinder test and the Kelly ball test require the use of fresh concrete.

In addition to these various types of concrete tests, there are also tests that measure the moisture in concrete. These tests are meant for slabs that are to receive moisture-sensitive finishes. They include the following.

- *polyethylene sheet test:* This test uses a plastic sheet taped tightly to a concrete floor. After 16 hours the underside of the plastic is inspected for moisture.

- *electrical resistance test:* This test determines moisture by measuring the electrical conductivity of the concrete between the meter probes.

- *quantitative calcium chloride test:* This test uses a quantity of calcium chloride sealed under a plastic dome placed on the concrete for 60–72 hours. The amount of moisture the chloride absorbs is mathematically converted to a moisture emission expressed in pounds per 1000 ft^2 per 24 hour period.

- *hygrometer test (relative humidity test):* This test determines moisture emission by measuring the relative humidity of the atmosphere confined adjacent to the concrete floor.

The answer is (C).

16. Efflorescence is a white, crystalline deposit of water-soluble salts on the surface of masonry and sometimes concrete. It is caused when water seeps into the masonry and dissolves soluble salts, which are brought to the surface. When the water evaporates, the salts are left on the surface. Hydration is simply the chemical process of the hardening of concrete when water mixes with cement. Segregation is the separation of the constituent parts of the concrete when the concrete is either dropped too far or moved excessively in the horizontal direction while it is being placed.

Laitance is a surface deposit of low-strength material containing cement and fine aggregates (sand) brought to the surface of concrete. It is caused by having too much water in the concrete mix, which results in water bleeding to the top.

The answer is (A).

17. The contractor is responsible for construction means and methods, which would include construction and support of the formwork, the type of equipment used during construction, and the practices employed during placement of the concrete. The size, configuration, and location of the reinforcing bars would be detailed in the construction documents.

The answer is (C).

18. Construction operations are generally discontinued or switch from regular activity to cold-weather mode at 40°F. A concrete pour can proceed at temperatures below 40°F. However, the water and sand must be heated to ensure that none of the constituents have frozen, and the concrete must be heated for at least seven days after placement, during the early curing stage.

Other temperature-sensitive materials, such as sealants, should not be applied when the mercury dips below 40°F.

The answer is (C).

19. American Institute of Architects (AIA) Document A201, *General Conditions of the Contract for Construction*, Article 3.2, discusses the contractor's responsibilities relative to review of the contract documents, which include bringing any noted discrepancies to the architect's attention. The contractor is not responsible for verifying that the design documents comply with code requirements. AIA Document A201, Sec. 3.12.10, states that the contractor is not responsible for providing professional services.

Preparation of field reports to the owner is the responsibility of the architect. If a subcontractor makes a claim to the contractor and the contractor determines it to be valid, the contractor may, in turn, make a claim to the owner. This claim would then be reviewed by the architect. Both the contractor and the architect are responsible for reviewing shop drawings, although only the contractor is responsible for the accuracy of the shop drawings. The architect reviews them for general compliance with the requirements of the contract documents. Scaffolding is

part of the means of construction, which is the contractor's responsibility. AIA Document A201 makes the contractor responsible for arranging and coordinating field tests.

The answer is (B) and (C).

20. Any request for substitution by the contractor must be made in writing and must be accompanied by a complete description of the proposed substitution, including drawings, test data, and other information necessary for an evaluation. The burden of proof of the merit of the substitution falls upon the contractor. The architect is required to review the submission and either approve or disapprove it.

The answer is (D).

21. AIA Document A201, Article 3.4, states that the contractor may make substitutions only with the consent of the owner, after evaluation by the architect and with a change order. Only the owner has the right to stop the work, according to the provisions of AIA Document A201, Sec. 2.3. The owner may stop the work if the contractor fails to correct work that is not in accordance with the requirements of the contract documents or if the contractor repeatedly fails to carry out work in accordance with the contract documents.

The answer is (B).

22. Site visits are part of the basic services of contract administration, but no specific time interval for them is given in the contract. AIA Document B101 states that the architect shall visit the site at intervals appropriate to the stage of the contractor's operations or as agreed by the owner and architect.

The answer is (C).

23. The architect, owner, or contractor may request a change order. A request for proposal is made by the architect, which outlines the anticipated scope of work. A cost proposal is prepared by the contractor, and if accepted by the owner, the architect may prepare the change order to amend the contract. The change order is finalized when all three parties have signed the agreement.

The answer is (D).

24. AIA Document A201, Sec. 13.5, states that tests, inspections, and approvals of portions of the work required by the contract documents or by laws, ordinances, rules, regulations, or orders of public authorities shall be paid for by the contractor. The contractor must also make arrangements for the tests and notify the architect of when they will be conducted.

If testing becomes required after receipt of bids or after contract negotiations and is not part of the original contract documents, then the owner becomes responsible for paying for the testing. This provision applies to testing required by the architect, owner, or public authorities having jurisdiction. This situation might happen if the building field inspector requires a test that was not anticipated. In some situations, the owner may not be legally permitted to pass responsibility for the costs of tests to the contractor; in this case, the owner is responsible for the fees.

The answer is (C).

25. American Institute of Architects (AIA) Document A201, *General Conditions of the Contract for Construction*, Sec. 7.1.2, states that a construction change directive requires agreement by the owner and architect and may or may not be agreed to by the contractor. The construction change directive requires the contractor to proceed with the work. The contract is later modified by change order to reflect the compensation due to the contractor.

The answer is (A).

26. AIA Document A201, Sec. 3.4.2, states that the contractor may make substitutions only with the owner's consent, after evaluation by the architect and in accordance with a change order or construction change directive. The substitution will be covered by warranty. In this case, the substitution is being made for the contractor's convenience. If an adjustment to the cost is necessary, it will be made by change order.

The answer is (A), (C), (D), and (F).

27. AIA Document A201, Sec. 9.4.2, specifically states that the issuance of a certificate for payment is not a representation that the architect has 1) made exhaustive or continuous on-site inspections, 2) reviewed construction means, methods, techniques, sequences, or procedures, 3) reviewed copies of requisitions received from subcontractors and other data, or 4) made examination to ascertain how or for what purpose the contractor has used money previously paid.

The answer is (A), (C), (D), and (F).

28. The amount of retainage withheld from each application for payment is determined by the owner with advice from legal counsel and defined in American Institute of Architects (AIA) Document A101, *Standard Form of Agreement between Owner and Contractor where the basis of payment is a Stipulated Sum*. The exact percentage is whatever is agreed to by the parties to the contract. The contract may specify that the percentage of retainage be reduced as the project nears completion, or it may establish different percentages of retainage for work done and for stored materials.

The answer is (D).

29. The architect has a duty to cooperate with the contractor and should mention the potential problem during the site visit. The contractor then has the opportunity to check on the equipment while the architect is following up with the mechanical engineer. The observation should be noted on the architect's field report to keep the client informed of the progress of the work. If, in fact, the equipment being installed is incorrect, corrective action may be taken. When the contractor is notified immediately, he or she can decide whether or not to suspend work on the installation of the equipment until the situation is resolved.

By the time the mechanical engineer is notified and visits the site, the installation of the equipment may have proceeded to a point where it is difficult to remedy. It is best to act quickly to keep the project moving while the issue is resolved. The architect does not have the authority to stop the work. It is not necessary to advise the owner to stop work which would only delay the project and add expense at this point.

The answer is (D).

30. Because the additional exit signs would necessitate an increase in construction cost and possibly an adjustment to the contract time, an order for minor change would not be appropriate. An addendum can only be used before the contract is signed. It is possible that the contractor and owner might disagree with the cost of the additional exit signs and a construction change directive would be used initially, but it is more likely that everyone would realize the need for the extra signs and agree on a price. Ultimately, a change order would be issued to adjust the contract sum.

The answer is (C).

31. The submittals process allows the architect to verify that the materials the contractor will provide comply with the requirements outlined in the contract documents. The contractor must review submittals prior to giving them to the architect. If the contractor wishes to make a substitution, the contractor must follow the guidelines given in Division 1 of the Specifications. Substitutions are often not accepted after the bid period, or the specifications may require substitutions to be submitted and approved before a specified date. When a substitution is requested, the architect should first verify that the specifications allow this at the current stage of the project. The architect may not add to the scope of work by noting the additional tasks on the submittal. If additional work is necessary, this change should be made through a change order or a construction change directive.

The contractor is responsible for dimensions and quantities of materials. The contractor may require subcontractors to prepare submittal information relative to their work; in this case, if the contractor determines that the submittal data is insufficient or incorrect, the contractor may reject it and require the subcontractor to correct it before it is passed on to the architect. The submittals received from the contractor are not considered a part of the contract documents.

The answer is (B), (C), and (D).

32. The IDM is a person designated to be the first interpreter of the contract documents when disputes arise during construction. The purpose of allowing a third party to make initial judgments on claims is to facilitate conflict resolution and minimize the number of claims that proceed to arbitration or mediation. Traditionally, the architect served in this capacity, and if an alternate IDM is not identified, these responsibilities become the architect's.

The responsibilities of the IDM and an explanation of the claims process are given in AIA Document A201, Sec. 15.2.

This section specifically states that the IDM must respond within 10 days of notification of the claim by the contractor. The IDM may request supporting data to further document the claim.

The answer is 10 days.

33. The architect's submittal review may not change the scope of the work as defined in the contract documents, and it does not include verification or correction of dimensions. If changes to the scope are necessary, they should be made through change order or construction change directive. The contractor is responsible for accuracy and verification of all dimensions.

The architect's submittal review would include notation of action taken, tracking of the date of receipt and distribution of the submittal, determination if the submittal should be reviewed by a consultant, and if so, coordination of this review, and verification that the contractor reviewed the submittal before submitting it to the architect.

The answer is (B), (C), (D), and (E).

34. A mechanic's lien is a claim by one party against the property of another party for the satisfaction of a debt. It can be used by a material supplier, subcontractor, or contractor who has a financial interest in the project to gain payment. (In some states, the architect can file a mechanic's lien to obtain payment for professional services rendered.) In extreme cases, a mechanic's lien can force the sale of the owner's property to satisfy the debt. A lien encumbers the owner's property, making it impossible to sell or transfer the property until the lien is satisfied. This is usually enough pressure to force the owner to resolve the situation. As an alternative to liens, a labor and material payment bond can protect the owner against claims by subcontractors and suppliers who are not paid by the general contractor. The bond gives these parties the right to collect payment from the surety (the company that issued the bond).

The answer is (D).

35. The architect has a responsibility to keep the contractor informed of any nonconforming work and to cooperate in getting the job done, but the architect may not be held legally responsible if the work is not completed or is not in accordance with the construction documents. American Institute of Architects (AIA) Document A201, *General Conditions of the Contract for Construction*, states that the contractor will not be relieved of obligations to perform the work in accordance with the contract documents by activities or duties of the architect. It also states that if the contractor performs any construction activity knowing it involves an error, the contractor will assume responsibility. Changes to the work may be suggested by the architect, owner, or contractor, but the owner must authorize any proposed changes. The architect may rely upon the accuracy of the information provided by the owner.

The architect is responsible for updating the cost of the work at the completion of each stage of the design phase. AIA Document B101, *Standard Form of Agreement between Owner and Architect*, Article 6, discusses architect's obligations to the owner regarding cost. The architect makes periodic updates to the cost evaluation to verify that the proposed design work remains within the owner's budget.

The answer is (D).

51 Project Closeout

1. During the punch list inspection, the architect notices several items that are not completed and that will make it impossible for the client to occupy the space. According to American Institute of Architects (AIA) Document A201, *General Conditions of the Contract for Construction*, which of the following actions must the architect take?

(A)   Notify the owner of the incomplete items.

(B)   Notify the contractor that there are unfinished items that must be finished before the project will be determined substantially complete.

(C)   Prepare a certificate of substantial completion with a list of incomplete items attached.

(D)   Revise the punch list and resubmit it to the contractor.

2. Which of the following may be used to encourage the contractor to finish the job or to satisfy mechanic's lien claims by subcontractors?

(A)   surety bond

(B)   liquidated damages

(C)   retainage

(D)   arbitration

3. Which of the following members of the building team participate in the building commissioning process? (Choose the four that apply.)

(A)   civil engineer

(B)   electrical engineer

(C)   elevator contractor

(D)   interior designer

(E)   owner

(F)   mechanical engineer

4. A project is determined to be "substantially complete" when the

(A)   work is finished except for items on the punch list

(B)   architect has determined that the building is nearly finished

(C)   contractor has notified the architect that the work is complete

(D)   owner can utilize the building for its intended use

Construction & Evaluation

5. Upon completion of the work, which of the following items must the contractor submit? (Choose the three that apply.)

- (A) extra stock of materials as listed in the specifications
- (B) certificate of occupancy issued by the building official
- (C) copies of all change orders completed during the course of the work
- (D) warranties and operating instructions as required in notes on the mechanical and electrical drawings or in the specifications
- (E) certificates of inspection
- (F) certificates of testing

6. According to American Institute of Architects (AIA) Document B101, *Standard Form of Agreement between Owner and Architect*, which of the following services is included in the architect's basic services for project closeout? (Choose the four that apply.)

- (A) forwarding written warranties to the owner
- (B) sending a consent of surety to the owner
- (C) commissioning
- (D) meeting with the owner to determine the need for facility operation services
- (E) post-occupancy walk through within one year
- (F) transfer project insurance from the contractor to the owner

Solutions

1. AIA Document A201, Sec. 9.8.3, requires the architect to complete an inspection of the project upon receipt of the contractor's punch list. The architect must notify the contractor of unfinished items and work that is not in accordance with the contract documents. The contractor must then correct the items on the list so that the owner can occupy the work or a designated portion thereof for its intended use. This must happen before the architect can issue a certificate of substantial completion.

The answer is (B).

2. A surety bond involves a third party (the surety) who ensures completion of the project if the contractor fails to meet his or her obligations. Liquidated damages are an amount specified in advance that the contractor must pay to the owner if the project is not completed on time. Arbitration is a method of resolving disputes between parties to a contract.

Retainage, or an amount of money withheld from each pay application, gives the owner leverage to require the contractor finish the job and provides a reserve in case liens must be satisfied.

The answer is (C).

3. The civil engineer and the interior designer typically would not participate in the building commissioning process because they do not have direct involvement in the design or operation of the building systems.

The answer is (B), (C), (E), and (F).

4. Substantial completion means that the work or a designated portion of the work is sufficiently complete in accordance with the contract documents so that the owner can occupy or utilize the work for its intended use. A building can be substantially complete while still having minor items that the contractor must finish. Substantial completion is addressed in American Institute of Architects (AIA) Document A201, *General Conditions of the Contract for Construction*, Sec. 9.8.

The answer is (D).

5. Copies of change orders are not required at this time, as this paperwork would be issued throughout the course of the project. Certificates of testing are required to be submitted to the architect promptly after each test, not at the completion of the work. Items required by the contract documents must be submitted to the owner before the work is considered complete. This includes extra stock of building materials and warranties and instruction manuals required by the specifications. The contractor must also submit to the architect all documents required with the application for final payment, maintenance contracts, and a set of record drawings if required by the contract documents. Although a certificate of occupancy is issued by the building official, it is normally submitted by the contractor to the owner.

The answer is (A), (B), and (D).

6. AIA Document B101, Article 4, addresses additional services that the architect will provide only if specifically designated or approved in advance by the owner. Commissioning is one of these services, among others, such as programming, geotechnical services, existing facilities surveys, site analysis, landscape design, interior design, detailed cost estimating, on-site project representation, record drawings, and post-contract evaluation beyond one meeting with the owner to review the facility's performance, within one year of substantial completion.

The answer is (A), (B), (D), and (E).

Construction & Evaluation

Case Studies

Case Study 1

A midsize college is constructing a Center for Ethnic Studies, which will offer courses in languages, history, and classical traditions of cultures around the world. Construction of the project is about 60% complete. The building is located on a site on the west side of the college quadrangle. The first floor is approximately 6000 ft^2 and the second floor is approximately 3000 ft^2. A glass storefront system with double doors allows views to the college quad from the building entrance. Parking is provided in a nearby parking garage. Floor plans of the building are shown in Resource 6.1 and some of the applicable building code requirements are given in Resource 6.2.

The two-story structure is being constructed with reinforced-masonry bearing walls, intermediate steel columns and beams, and open-web steel joists. The building's exterior cladding is a terracotta rain screen. Sprinklers are installed throughout the building.

The work is being performed under a standard design-bid-build contract in accordance with American Institute of Architects (AIA) agreements in place between the architect and owner and the owner and contractor. These include AIA Document B101, *Standard Form of Agreement between Owner and Architect*; AIA Document A101, *Standard Form of Agreement between Owner and Contractor where the Basis of Payment is a Stipulated Sum*; and AIA Document A201, *General Conditions of the Contract for Construction*.

The owner has opted to hire the architectural woodwork contractor under a separate contract. This firm will be responsible for the fabrication and installation of all millwork and cabinetry, including the shelving in the library on the second floor.

No other special conditions have been agreed upon between the owner and contractor.

Construction
& Evaluation

Resource 6.1 Floor Plans

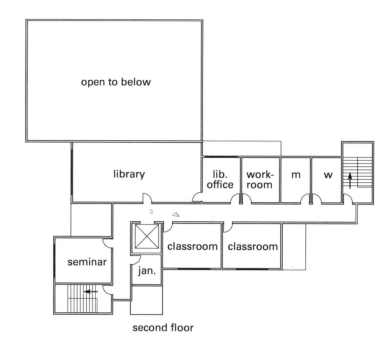

second floor

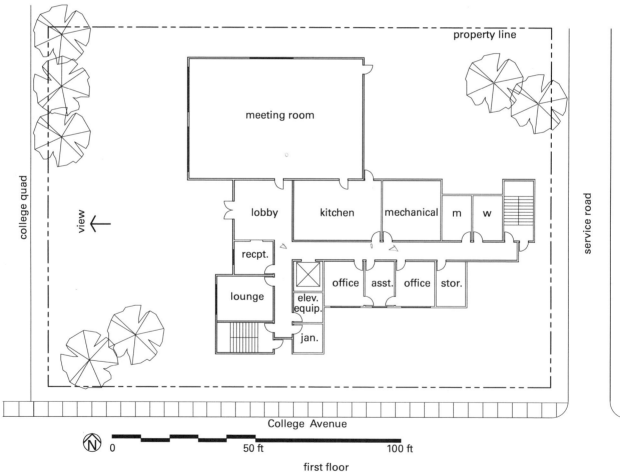

first floor

Resource 6.2 Building Code Excerpt

Building Code Excerpt

Fire-Resistance Rated Construction

1. Partitions along a public corridor must be 1-hour fire rated.
2. Partitions that demise an assembly occupancy of 750 ft^2 or greater must be 1-hour fire rated.
3. Partitions around mechanical rooms must have a minimum fire-resistance rating of 2 hours.

Means of Egress

General Means of Egress

1. The capacity, in inches, of a means of egress for stairways shall be calculated by multiplying the occupant load served by a factor of 0.2 in per occupant for sprinklered buildings and by a factor of 0.3 in per occupant for non-sprinklered buildings. The capacity, in inches, for other egress components shall be calculated by multiplying the occupant load served by a factor of 0.15 in per occupant for sprinklered buildings and by a factor of 0.2 in for non-sprinklered buildings. However, the minimum width of any component shall not be less that that required elsewhere in this code.
2. A minimum of one refuge area for a wheelchair is required in each exit stairway on floors above the first floor. The refuge area must be a minimum of 30 in × 48 in and must not reduce the means of egress minimum width.

Corridors

1. The minimum interior corridor width must be 44 in when the occupant load served is 50 or more, or not less than 36 in when the occupant load served is less than 50. In Group E occupancies with an occupant load greater than 100, the minimum width shall be 72 in.
2. Dead end corridors must not exceed 20 ft 0 in in length.

Stairways

1. The width of exit stairways, in inches, shall be determined as given under the General Means of Egress heading, but in no case may stairways be less than 36 in wide when serving an occupant load of less than 50, or less than 44 in wide, when serving an occupant load of 50 or more.
2. Stairways shall have a maximum riser height of 7 in and a minimum tread depth of 11 in.
3. The width of landings in the direction of travel shall be no less than the required width of the stairway but need be no wider than 48 in.
4. Doors opening onto a landing shall not reduce the landing width to less than one-half the required width. When fully open, the door may not project more than 7 in into the required width.

Fire Protection Systems

1. There must be an audio-visual fire signal device located in each restroom, hallway, lobby, and general assembly area.
2. An audio-visual fire signal device must be visible from any location in the room or space and must be mounted between 6 ft 8 in and 7 ft 6 in above the finish floor.
3. The minimum number of fire extinguishers must be calculated based on one (1) fire extinguisher per 3000 ft^2 of floor area per story.
4. A fire extinguisher must be located no more than 75 ft from the furthest occupant.
5. Fire extinguishers shall be located in conspicuous locations, be readily accessible, and be immediately available for use. The locations shall be along normal paths of travel unless the fire code official determines that the hazard posed requires placement away from normal paths of travel.

Exit Signs

1. Exit signs with an illuminated directional indicator showing the direction of travel to an exit shall be placed in every location where the direction of travel to reach the nearest exit is not apparent.
2. Exit signs shall be placed such that no point in an exit access corridor is more than 100 ft from the nearest visible exit sign.
3. Exit signs are not required for main exterior exit doors that are obviously and clearly identifiable as exits.

Construction & Evaluation

1. During a site visit, the architect notices that one or more electrical rough-ins for exit signs may be missing. While standing at the point where someone would enter the corridor from the lobby on the first floor, where should the exit signs be located? (Choose the three that apply.)

- (A) over the double doors leading to the exterior
- (B) where the east-west and north-south corridors intersect
- (C) outside the door leading to the stairway in the southwest corner of the building
- (D) midway between the lobby and the stairway on the east side of the building
- (E) outside the door leading to the stairway on the east side of the building
- (F) over the door leading to the meeting room

2. The architect did not indicate the required quantity or locations of portable fire extinguishers on the plans for the building, but the general notes and specifications require the contractor to provide and install extinguishers in accordance with the building code requirements. The contractor has issued a request for information asking the architect to describe how many extinguishers are required and where they are to be placed. Which of the following descriptions should be included in the architect's response?

- (A) Provide and install two portable fire extinguishers: one outside the office on the first floor, and one outside the meeting room.
- (B) Provide and install three portable fire extinguishers: one outside the mechanical room, one outside the lobby, and one outside the classrooms.
- (C) Provide and install three portable fire extinguishers: one in the meeting room, one outside the kitchen, and one outside the library office.
- (D) Provide and install four portable fire extinguishers: two on each floor, equally spaced in the corridors.

3. The architectural woodwork contractor arrives at the site to install above-ceiling bracing required to stabilize the book stacks in the library. The contractor determines that the heating, ventilating, and air conditioning (HVAC) ductwork and sprinkler piping have been installed at locations that will conflict with the bracing installation. The existing above-ceiling elements make the installation more difficult, and additional materials and time will be necessary to install the bracing.

The general contractor counters that the architectural woodwork contractor did not inform him that bracing would be needed above the ceiling. The general contractor understood that all millwork installation would take place below the finished ceiling. The general contractor notifies the architect that installation of the finished ceiling in this area will be delayed because of the additional time requested by the architectural woodwork contractor to complete the bracing.

What should the architect do upon hearing about this issue?

- (A) Inform the architectural woodwork contractor that the woodwork contractor is responsible for any additional costs, including the costs of delay, incurred to resolve the problem.
- (B) Inform the owner of the situation and notify the owner that the general contractor may make a formal claim against the architectural woodwork contractor.
- (C) Remind the general contractor that the general contractor is responsible for coordination with the architectural woodwork contractor and is required to absorb the additional costs.
- (D) Notify the owner that it is the owner's responsibility to coordinate between the general contractor and the architectural woodwork contractor and to pay for the extra costs to resolve the issue.

4. During a site visit, the architect notices that the number of floor tiles on the stair landings differ from what is shown in the architect's drawings, possibly indicating that the landing in the east stairway has been constructed smaller than indicated in the drawings. To verify compliance with code requirements, which of the following dimensions should the architect document? (Choose the four that apply.)

- (A) available egress width on the landing when the door is opening
- (B) available egress width on the landing when the door is fully open
- (C) depth and width of the refuge area
- (D) distance between handrails
- (E) length of the handrail extension
- (F) width of the landing

5. While observing the installation of gypsum wallboard, the architect notes that the partitions around the mechanical room have not been constructed in accordance with the specified wall-type design and, as built, will not have the required fire-resistance ratings shown on the drawings. How should the architect respond?

- (A) Reject the work, notify the owner, and instruct the contractor to correct the problem.

- (B) Tell the wallboard subcontractor's employees in the field to construct the partition according to the drawings.

- (C) Inform the owner of the problem, and ask the owner to stop work.

- (D) Issue a change order directing the contractor to make the correction.

6. The structural engineer contacts the architect from the construction site and explains that some of the masonry reinforcement in the exterior walls around the meeting room does not appear to have been installed properly. The engineer emails the architect a few photographs of the locations in question, which were taken during the site visit today, and also attaches photos taken during the last site visit one week ago when the contractor had just started building the wall. The photos show that the reinforcement installed near the top of the wall does not look the same as the reinforcement installed last week in the lower part of the wall. The contractor has confirmed that the walls around the meeting room are complete. The roof framing has not yet been started. What action should the architect take?

- (A) Require the engineer to instruct the contractor to remove the upper part of the masonry walls course by course so that each reinforcement section can be inspected.

- (B) Notify the owner, and require the contractor to remove enough of the masonry to allow the structural engineer to inspect the work.

- (C) Notify the owner in writing of the need to stop all work until the issue can be resolved.

- (D) Require the contractor to retain a third-party inspection and testing service to review the work.

7. During a construction phase walk-through with the architect, the owner decides to replace the single door from the lobby into the meeting room with a double door and instructs the architect to proceed with the change. The single door opening has already been framed and the wall has been finished. The specified door assembly is on

site but has not yet been installed. How should the architect proceed?

- (A) Issue a construction change directive until the owner and architect can decide on the desired type of double door.

- (B) Verbally instruct the contractor to make the change and provide a sketch showing the new set of doors.

- (C) Prepare specifications and drawings for the new door opening, request an estimate from the contractor, obtain approval from the owner, and then issue a change order with the owner's signature.

- (D) Issue American Institute of Architects (AIA) Document G710, *Architect's Supplemental Instructions*, to the contractor with a drawing and specification for the new doors.

8. At the beginning of the project, the contractor provided the requested submittal package for the acoustical ceiling systems to the architect. The submittal was reviewed, approved, and returned to the contractor. When the contractor attempted to arrange delivery of the material to the site, however, the distributor notified the contractor that the manufacturer of the specialty acoustical ceiling system specified for the meeting room had gone bankrupt a few months earlier and that the approved system is no longer available. The contractor notified the architect immediately, and, with the owner's approval, the architect specified an alternate system.

Today the architect received shop drawings and product information for the new ceiling materials from the contractor, and the cut sheets showed a different product from the replacement system the architect specified. The contractor's schedule shows that this ceiling is to be installed at the end of the month. Because of the time crunch, the general contractor passed the shop drawings on to the architect without review. The time available to order any system is running short, and this issue has the potential to cause a construction delay.

What is the architect's best course of action?

- (A) If the submitted system is an acceptable substitute for the one specified, approve the submittal.

- (B) Require that the manufacturer submit documentation that the new system is equal to the one specified.

- (C) Ask the owner to allow the architect to review a nonspecified product.

- (D) Return the submittal to the contractor without review.

9. When reviewing an application for payment from the contractor, the architect notices a line item for finish materials that the architect has not seen at the job site. When contacted by the architect, the contractor says that the items were purchased and delivered early to avoid a price increase and have been stored off site at the contractor's warehouse. The contractor has receipts for the items. How should the architect process the application for payment?

    (A)   Refuse to approve the amount the contractor claims for the stored materials.

    (B)   Request to view the stored materials before processing the application.

    (C)   Ask the owner if there is any objection to approving the application as submitted.

    (D)   Approve the application in its entirety after talking with the contractor.

Construction & Evaluation

Case Study 2

Unison Medical Group is opening a convenient care center inside Melody Marketplace, a large grocery store. The staff of nurse practitioners and physician's assistants will provide care for minor injuries and illnesses and administer immunizations at this location.

The total area of the building is 45,000 ft^2 and all areas are fully sprinklered. Two-thirds of the building houses retail space (i.e., the grocery store and the leased tenant spaces); the other one-third houses the loading dock, storage area, and other back-of-house activities. There are six 1200 ft^2 leasable spaces near the entrance. Four of these spaces are occupied by a coffee shop with seating for 30 patrons, a tax preparation service, a hair salon, and a dry cleaning drop-off and pick-up point. Unison Medical Group was the last tenant to sign a lease, and the clinic will occupy the remaining two spaces.

Dorian Associates, an architecture firm specializing in medical facilities design, has developed construction documents for fitting out the Unison Medical Group space. The clinic will include a reception and waiting area, two patient exam rooms, restrooms, a nurses' station, an office for the clinicians, a supply storage area, and a small break room.

The bid package for this project includes an invitation to bid; American Institute of Architects (AIA) Document A701, *Instructions to Bidders*; the bid form and other required paperwork such as bond forms; and the contract documents, including drawings and specifications. The contract will be based on AIA Document A101, *Standard Form of Agreement between Owner and Contractor where the basis of payment is a Stipulated Sum*, and AIA Document A201, *General Conditions of the Contract for Construction*.

The project was advertised in several local newspapers, and the architecture firm oversaw distribution of the bid documents to those who responded to the notice. Unison Medical Group also reached out to some of the firms who had worked on the construction of their other facilities in the area to notify them that this project was out for bid.

Although Unison owns and operates numerous primary care and specialty medical offices, this will be the first time that they open a convenient-care clinic. This design is intended to serve as the prototype for similar facilities that will be constructed at other retail locations in the future, including many of Melody Marketplace's other store locations. Unison is hoping that it can build a good relationship with a contractor who will become familiar with the work and to whom they can award future projects, all of which will be built using the same layout and finishes. However, the contractors were only asked to bid on this single project.

The architects received 15 requests for the bid documents and seven of those contractors submitted bids. After reviewing the proposals, the project was awarded to Chord Construction Services, the lowest bidder on the project.

Resource 6.3 Floor Plan

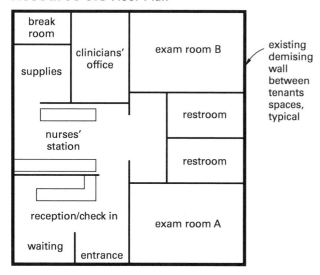

Resource 6.4 Code Excerpt

Code Excerpt

Classification. Structures or portions of structures shall be classified with respect to occupancy in one or more of the groups listed below.

Assembly: Group A-1 (fixed seating); Group A-2 (food or drink consumption); Group A-3 (worship, recreation, or amusement); Group A-4 (indoor sporting events); Group A-5 (outdoor activities).

Exceptions: A building or tenant space used for assembly purposes with an occupant load of less than 50 persons shall be classified as a Group B occupancy.

Business: Group B (office, professional, or service-type transactions)—Business occupancies shall include, but are not limited to, the following: ambulatory health care facilities, banks, barber and beauty shops, civic administration, outpatient clinic, dry cleaning and laundry pick-up and delivery stations, professional services.

Mercantile: Group M (Display or Sale of Merchandise)—Mercantile occupancies shall include, but are not limited to, the following: department stores, drug stores, markets, retail or wholesale stores, sales rooms.

Storage: Group S-1 (moderate-hazard), Group S-2 (low-hazard/noncombustible).

Mixed Use and Occupancy. Each portion of a building shall be individually classified as noted. Where a building contains more than one occupancy group, the occupancies shall be separated with fire-resistance-rated construction or shall comply with the provisions noted.

Accessory Occupancies: Accessory occupancies are those occupancies which are ancillary to the main occupancy of the building or portion thereof. Aggregate accessory occupancies shall not occupy more than 10% of the total building area of the story in which they are located. No separation is required between accessory occupancies and the main occupancy unless required by another provision of this code.

Nonseparated Occupancies: No separation is required between nonseparated occupancies.

Separated Occupancies: Individual occupancies shall be separated from adjacent occupancies in accordance with the provided table. Required separations shall be fire barriers or horizontal assemblies constructed in accordance with the requirements of this code so as to completely separate adjacent occupancies.

Resource 6.5 Required Separation of Occupancies (hours)

occupancy	A-1, A-2, A-3, A-4, A-5		B, M, S-1		S-2	
	S	NS	S	NS	S	NS
A-1, A-2, A-3, A-4, A-5	N	N	1	2	N	1
B, M, S-1	1	2	N	N	1	2
S-2	N	1	1	2	N	N

S: buildings equipped throughout with an approved automatic sprinkler system
NS: buildings without an approved automatic sprinkler system
N: no separation requirement
NP: not permitted
1: 1-hour
2: 2-hour

Resource 6.6 Application and Certificate for Payment

APPLICATION AND CERTIFICATE FOR PAYMENT   Page 1 of 2 Pages

To Owner: Unison Medical Group	Project: Unison Clinic	Application#: 2 Period To: Project NOS:	Distribution To: ☐ Owner ☐ Const Mgr
From Contractor: Chord Construction Services	Via Architect: Dorian Associates	Contract Date: May 31	☐ Architect ☐ Contractor

Contract for: General Construction

CONTRACTOR'S APPLICATION FOR PAYMENT

Application is made for payment as shown below, in connection with the Contract. Continuation Sheet is attached.

1. Original contract sum................................. $ 285,625
2. Net change by Change Orders .... $ 0
3. Contract sum to date (line 1 +/– 2) .... $ 285,625
4. Total completed & stored to date............ $ 42,300
   (Column G on Continuation Sheet)
5. Retainage:
   a. __5%__ of Completed Work .... $
      (Columns D+E on Continuan Sheet)
   b. __10%__ of Stored Material .... $
      (Column F on Continuation Sheet)
      Total Retainage Line 5a+5b or
      Total in Column 1 of Continuation Sheet.. $
6. Total Earned Less retainage..................... $
   (Line 4 less Line 5 Total)
7. Less Previous Certificates for Payment
   (Line 4 less Line 5 Total)........................... $ 22,625
8. Current Payment Due.............................. $
9. Ballance to Finish, Including Retainage
   (Line 4 less Line 5 Total) $

Change Order Summary	Additions	Deductions
Total changes approved in previous month by Owner.		
Total approved this Month		
Totals		
Net Changes by Change Order		

The undersigned Contractor certifies that to the best of the Contractor's knowledge, information, and belief the Work covered by this Application for Payment has been completed in accordance with the Contract Documents, that the amounts have been paid by the Contractor for Work for which previous Certificates for Payment were issued and payments received from the Owner, and that current payments there in is now due.

Contractor:

By: James Chord   Date: June 1

State of: _____
County of: _____
Subscribed and sworn to before
me this _____ day of _____

Notary Public: _____
My Commission expires: _____

CERTIFICATE FOR PAYMENT

In accordance with Contract Documents, based on on-site observations and the data comprising application, the Architect certifies to the Owner the to the best of the Architect's knowledge, information, and belief the Work has progressed as indicated, the quality of the Work is in accordance with the Contract Documents, and the Contractor is entitled to payment of the AMOUNT CERTIFIED.

Amount Certified ....$_____

(Attached explanation if amount certified differs from the amount applied for. Initial figures on this application and on the Continuation Sheet that are changed to conform to the amount certified.)

Architect:

By: _____   Date: _____

This Certificate is not negotiable. The AMOUNT CERTIFIED is payable only to the Contractor named herein. Issuance, payment, and acceptance of payment are without prejudice to any rights of the Owner of Contractor under this Contract.

Construction & Evaluation

10. The invitation to bid for this project states that the contract will be awarded to the "lowest responsive and responsible bidder." Which of the following statements are true? (Choose the three that apply.)

- (A) A responsive bidder is capable of performing the work as described in the bidding documents.
- √ (B) A responsive bid is one which satisfies all of the requirements of the bidding documents.
- √ (C) A responsible bidder is a firm with the financial backing and workforce required to satisfy the requirements of the contract.
- √ (D) A contractor must submit a performance and payment bond to be considered a responsible bidder.
- (E) The apparent low bidder will be announced at a public bid opening.
- (F) If there is an error in the paperwork submitted by the low bidder, that bidder will be deemed not responsible.

11. Unison Medical Group plans to construct multiple clinics using the same basic plans and specifications that have been developed for this project. The architecture firm suggested to the owner that they undertake a value engineering exercise to identify elements of the design that could be refined or modified to be more economical. Which of the following statements about value engineering are true? (Choose the three that apply.)

- √ (A) Value engineering is most effective when it is performed in the construction documents phase.
- (B) The value engineering study should be performed by the architect and the results reported to the owner.
- √ (C) The value engineering exercise always results in a project with a lower cost.
- (D) Value engineering is a collaborative process involving the designer, owner, and a third-party facilitator.
- (E) Value engineering analysis can be beneficial at any stage of the project.
- (F) It is the owner's responsibility to define what characteristics of the project add "value."

12. Refer to the information given in the case study narrative. To solve this problem, it may be helpful to complete a table to keep track of the data. (See *Table for Prob. 12 and Prob. 13*.)

What is the retail area of the Melody Marketplace grocery store?

- (A) 22,800 ft^2
- (B) 30,000 ft^2
- (C) 40,200 ft^2
- (D) 45,000 ft^2

13. To solve this problem, it may be helpful to complete a table to keep track of the data. (See *Table for Prob. 12 and Prob. 13*.)

The Cadence Coffeehouse should be classified as a(n)

- (A) assembly occupancy
- (B) business occupancy
- (C) accessory occupancy
- (D) mercantile occupancy

14. What is the required fire rating of the nonbearing partition wall between the grocery store's retail space and the stockroom?

- (A) No separation is required.
- (B) 1-hour
- (C) 2-hour
- (D) nonbearing partition is not permitted between retail space and the stockroom

15. Which one of the following documents can be used to modify a project's scope of the work during the bid phase?

- (A) change order
- (B) addendum
- (C) request for information
- (D) substitution

Table for Prob. 12 and Prob. 13

	Melody Marketplace (retail area)	Melody Marketplace (stockroom)	Unison Convenient Care Clinic	Cadence Coffeehouse	Tempo Tax Services	Sharps Salon
area						
occupancy classification						

16. The architect receives a submittal from Chord Construction for the interior framing and drywall systems that will be provided for the project. The submittal package consists of the contractor's generic cover sheet showing the date of submission and the general specification section number, plus a brochure from a gypsum-board manufacturer showing the manufacturer's full line of products. The contractor has not indicated which products will be provided. How should the architect respond?

(A) Review the brochure, and conduct Internet research to determine which of the manufacturer's products most closely match those specified.

(B) Inform the contractor that the information submitted is incomplete, and hold the original submittal until the subcontractor provides additional information.

(C) Mark up the submittal, and indicate which products are approved for use on the project.

(D) Reject the submittal, and require the contractor to resubmit with the proposed products clearly identified.

17. Chord Construction Services submitted the application for payment included in Resource 6.6. An excerpt from this form is shown. (See *Illustration for Prob. 17.*)

To date, the value of the completed work is $30,300, and the value of the stored materials is $12,000. The contractor has previously been paid $22,625. Using the information on the application, the amount of the payment due is _____. (Fill in the blank.)

Illustration for Prob. 17

CONTRACTOR'S APPLICATION FOR PAYMENT

Application is made for payment as shown below, in connection with the Contract.
Continuation Sheet is attached.

1. Original contract sum............................... $ | 285,625
2. Net change by Change Orders .... $ | 0
3. Contract sum to date (line 1 +/− 2) .... $ | 285,625
4. Total completed & stored to date............. $ | 42,300
   (Column G on Continuation Sheet)
5. Retainage:
   a. __5%__ of Completed Work $ | _____
      (Columns D+E on Continuan Sheet)
   b. __10%__ of Stored Material $ | _____
      (Column F on Continuation Sheet)
      Total Retainage Line 5a+5b or
      Total in Column 1 of Continuation Sheet.. $ | _____
6. Total Earned Less retainage...................... $ | _____
   (Line 4 less Line 5 Total)
7. Less Previous Certificates for Payment
   (Line 4 less Line 5 Total)........................... $ | _____
8. Current Payment Due............................... $ | _____
9. Balance to Finish, Including Retainage
   (Line 4 less Line 5 Total) $ | _____

Change Order Summary	Additions	Deductions
Total changes approved in previous month by Owner.		
Total approved this Month		
Totals		
Net Changes by Change Order		

Solutions

1. Refer to the exit signs section of the building code excerpt given in Resource 6.2. An exit sign is not required for a main exit door that is obviously identifiable as an exit. The corridor is less than 100 ft in length, so an intermediate exit sign is not required. The door leading to the meeting room is not an exit and a sign should not be installed at this location.

A directional exit sign is required just outside the lobby so that the direction to an alternate exit is visible from both the north-south corridor and the east-west corridor. Exit signs are also required outside the doors to both stairways because these lead to exterior exits.

The answer is (B), (C), and (E).

2. The fire protection systems section of the building code excerpt in Resource 6.2 states that a minimum of one extinguisher is required for each 3000 ft^2 of floor area.

From the floor plans in Resource 6.1, the area of the first floor is approximately 6000 ft^2, and the area of the second floor is approximately 3000 ft^2. Based on the area requirements, at least two extinguishers are required on the first floor, and at least one extinguisher is required on the second floor.

Use the scale accompanying the floor plans to estimate the length of the corridors. The north-south corridor is about 30 ft long, and the east-west corridor is about 70 ft long. If one extinguisher is placed in the first floor corridor outside the kitchen, it would be within 75 ft of almost all of the first floor occupants except those in the most distant part of the meeting room. The meeting room is the largest space in the building and has the greatest number of potential occupants. Therefore, a second extinguisher should be placed in the meeting room in a visible location.

On the upper level, one extinguisher mounted outside the library office would place it within 75 ft of any occupant on the second floor.

Option (A) describes an insufficient number of extinguishers for the area. The locations described in option (B) satisfy the maximum distance requirements, but an extinguisher mounted outside of the meeting room would be inaccessible to meeting room occupants. The number of extinguishers described in option (D) fulfills the area requirements, but describing the mounting locations as being "equally spaced" is vague and could result in the same situation as option (B): there may be no extinguisher in the meeting room, and one of the extinguishers may be more than 75 ft from the meeting room's most distant occupant.

The answer is (C).

3. The owner is responsible for coordinating the activities of the owner's own forces and those of each separate contractor hired directly by the owner with the work of the general contractor. If the architectural woodwork contractor needed to install bracing at a particular point in the contractor's schedule, the owner (or the millwork contractor acting on behalf of the owner) should have notified the general contractor before the project began. The coordination issue is the owner's responsibility and, therefore, any additional costs or schedule delays caused by failure to coordinate the work would be charged to the owner.

American Institute of Architects (AIA) Document A201, *General Conditions of the Contract for Construction*, requires the general contractor to report promptly to the architect any problems in a separate contractor's work that would interfere with the general contractor's work. Failure of the contractor to notify the architect of any condition or work performed by separate contractors constitutes an acknowledgment that the separate contractor's work is acceptable. In this case, the general contractor promptly notified the architect of the issue, and it would be within the general contractor's rights to make a claim for additional time or money or both according to the provisions of AIA Document A201, Article 4.3. The general contractor, however, does not have a contract with the architectural woodwork contractor, so the claim would not be against the architectural woodwork contractor's company; it would be against the owner.

According to AIA Document A201, Article 6, the owner is responsible for the coordination between the general contractor and the architectural woodwork contractor, as well as for any additional expenses or delay to the general contractor caused by the owner's failure to coordinate the work.

When notified of the problem, the architect should inform the owner of the situation, point out this part of the agreement, and explain that the general contractor has the right to make a claim. The architect is not under any further obligation regarding this issue until a formal claim is made by the general contractor. At that time, the architect would need to make a determination about the claim, in his or her role as the initial decision maker (IDM), according to AIA Document A201, Article 4.4.

The answer is (D).

4. While the distance between handrails and the length of the handrail extension must comply with the code requirements, these measurements are not critical in determining whether the stair construction complies with the landing width requirements.

If the second floor stair landing has been constructed smaller than shown on the architectural drawings, the final construction may not satisfy accessibility and egress requirements and the work must be rejected. The architect should verify the dimensions in the field and check the approved shop drawings; if it is determined that the designed dimensions and actual dimensions do not match or that the built conditions do not comply with the code requirements, this work will need to be replaced.

From the stairways section of the building code excerpt in Resource 6.2, the top landing must be at least as wide in the direction of travel as the required width of the stairway. The architect should begin by verifying this measurement.

Any door that opens into the required landing width cannot reduce the required egress width by more than one-half. When fully open, the door cannot reduce the required egress width by more than 7 in.

There must be a minimum refuge area of 30 in × 48 in provided on the landing, and the refuge area cannot reduce the required egress minimum width.

The answer is (A), (B), (C), and (F).

5. Under American Institute of Architects (AIA) Document A201, *General Conditions of the Contract for Construction*, Article 12, all communications with subcontractors must go through the general contractor.

A change order is neither necessary nor appropriate because it is clear that the work does not conform to the requirements of the contract documents.

The architect is required to keep the owner informed of defects and deficiencies observed in the work. It is unnecessary to stop all work on the project while the issue is resolved.

If work is rejected by the architect or fails to conform to the requirements of the contract documents, the contractor must promptly correct it at the contractor's expense. This requirement applies to work discovered before or after substantial completion, and it applies regardless of whether or not the work is fabricated, installed, or completed.

The answer is (A).

6. Although the structural engineer is responsible for structural observations, only the architect has the contractual right to require that work be uncovered and corrected. Stopping all work would be an excessive action; work on other parts of the building can continue while the reinforcement issue is being resolved. An outside inspection and testing service is not required in this case, because the architect and engineer can determine whether or not the reinforcement is in compliance with the contract documents.

American Institute of Architects (AIA) Document A201, *General Conditions of the Contract for Construction*, allows the architect to request that work be uncovered—even if the architect has not specifically requested the opportunity to examine it prior to its being covered—when the architect believes that some aspect of construction is not in compliance with the contract documents. In this case, the problem was first noticed by the structural engineer, who has photographic documentation that some portions of the reinforcement have not been installed correctly. The architect should ask the engineer to identify which part(s) of the masonry walls need to be removed to verify compliance. With this information and the owner's consent, the architect should request that the contractor remove those portions.

If, after inspection, it is determined that the reinforcement is in compliance with the contract documents, the cost of uncovering the work will be paid by the owner through a change order. However, if the reinforcement is incorrect, the cost will be borne by the contractor. In this case, the structural engineer's photographs show that the reinforcement was installed differently at different times, so it is likely that the cost of uncovering the work will be the contractor's responsibility.

The answer is (B).

7. A construction change directive is used only when something needs to be completed immediately but the owner and contractor cannot agree on a price or time extension. It is unlikely that making this change to the door is something that requires immediate attention at this stage of construction.

Option (B) is incorrect because this change will affect the project cost, time, or both, and should be documented in a more formal manner than through sketches and verbal instructions.

AIA Document G710 is used when there are minor changes to the work (i.e., changes that can be made without adjustment to project cost or time). The timing of the request for this particular change will necessitate an increase in the contract sum and possibly an extension of the contract time. Therefore, a change order must be used. The architect must give the contractor specifications and drawings as necessary to describe the change, sign and process the change order, and then issue it to the contractor. The owner will be responsible for all additional costs associated with this change.

The answer is (C).

Construction & Evaluation

8. This issue does have the potential to cause a construction delay, but the architect should still follow the standard process for reviewing submittals. A substitution such as this can be made only after evaluation by the architect and with the consent of the owner, according to American Institute of Architects (AIA) Document A201, *General Conditions of the Contract for Construction*. To perform that evaluation, the supplier or subcontractor must submit the necessary documentation to show that the proposed manufacturer provides a system equal to that specified. A change order must also be issued. The contractor failed to assemble the review the required documentation properly. The architect cannot determine if the product is an acceptable substitute with the data given.

Allowing the contractor to skip the review step may actually prolong the review. Without the contractor's initial check that all documentation is complete and accurate, the paperwork may have to go back and forth between the contractor and architect multiple times.

The architect is obligated to evaluate the submittal before making a recommendation to the owner and would not need to ask the owner for permission to do the evaluation.

All submittals must be reviewed and stamped by the contractor before they are forwarded to the architect for review. The contractor must verify field measurements, check materials, and coordinate other criteria before submitting the product data to the architect. If the architect receives submittals that do not have the general contractor's review stamp, the architect should return them to the contractor without review. The best practice is to adhere to the submittal review procedures and return the documents to the contractor with a request that they do the same.

The answer is (D).

9. Under American Institute of Architects (AIA) Document A201, *General Conditions of the Contract for Construction*, an application for payment only covers completed work and materials and equipment delivered and suitably stored at the site. If the contractor wants to store materials off site, the arrangements for, and location of, this storage must be agreed upon with the owner in advance.

The owner and contractor used a standard design-bid-build contract with no special conditions, so the contractor may not request payment for these materials until they are physically located at the construction site. The architect should refuse to approve the amount claimed for the stored materials.

The answer is (A).

10. A responsible bidder is one capable of performing the work. The criteria for evaluating whether or not a contractor is a responsible bidder may vary from project to project and may depend on the owner's objectives. For example, the owner may decide to require a minimum number of years of experience on similar projects, or that a contractor must have a minimum bonding capacity. When such requirements are imposed, the owner may choose to prequalify contractors, so that any bids received are from firms that have already been vetted. In such cases, the contractor may be asked to submit American Institute of Architects (AIA) Document A305, *Contractor's Qualification Statement*, to provide additional information. Additionally, the owner could request that the bids and the qualification documents be submitted in separate, sealed envelopes; the qualifications documents are reviewed first, and only the bids from contractors determined to be responsible will be opened. State procurement laws vary; architects and owners should confirm their state's definition and interpretation of the term "responsible bidder" to ensure compliance with bidding regulations.

Usually, assessment of the contractor's ability to perform the work is based on an evaluation of the business's qualifications (such as holding a contractor's license enabling them to perform work in the project's jurisdiction, or having a permanent place of business), as well as their financial standing, which may include their ability to secure appropriate insurance coverage and required bonds. Assessment may also include consideration of the contractor's performance on previous projects for this owner, references, and reputation.

The architect and owner generally refer to the bidder submitting the lowest price as the apparent low bidder until they have had the opportunity to verify that the contractor's bid has been properly submitted and is valid. A determination of whether or not a bid is responsive depends on assessment of the documentation submitted and its compliance with the instructions in the bidding documents. Evaluating whether a bidder is responsible requires more information than that provided on the bid forms. A contractor has the right to protest or appeal an owner's decision that the firm is not responsible. Therefore, the evaluation criteria should be stated in the bidding documents, and legal counsel should be consulted before eliminating bidders from consideration.

Bidding documents often state that the project will be awarded to the lowest responsive and responsible bidder. A responsive bid is a bid that satisfies all of the requirements and follows all of the instructions outlined in the bidding documents. A contractor must ensure that the bid is submitted on time and to the correct location, the paperwork is completed correctly and all required signatures are in place, the bid itself is accompanied by any required supplemental information or required bonds, all requested unit prices have been provided, and receipt of all addenda has been acknowledged.

The answer is (B), (C), and (E).

11. Value engineering is the process of analyzing aspects of the project's program, proposed solution, and budget to determine whether refinement or modifications to the design may result in increased value. The objective is to realize as many of the owner's goals as possible at the lowest cost. The earlier in the project that value engineering analysis is conducted, the greater the potential savings. However, value engineering can be beneficial at all stages of design and construction.

Value engineering usually requires the participation of the designer, the owner, and a third-party consultant who facilitates the discussion. The consultant's role is to understand the project's objectives and constraints, to help the project participants look at aspects of the project in different ways, and to offer alternative design solutions. The efforts may not necessarily result in a lower project cost. However, value engineering should result in the owner getting more for the money, or increased return on their investment, through greater efficiency, increased functionality, lower operating or life cycle costs, or quicker construction.

The answer is (D), (E), and (F).

12. Complete a table to keep track of the data required to solve the problem. (See *Table for Sol. 12 and Sol. 13.*)

The total area of the building is 45,000 ft². Two-thirds of the building is retail space. The other third is warehouse and storage space.

$$A_{\text{retail}} = \frac{2}{3} A_{\text{total}} = \left(\frac{2}{3}\right)(45{,}000 \text{ ft}^2) = 30{,}000 \text{ ft}^2$$

$$A_{\text{stockroom}} = \frac{1}{3} A_{\text{total}} = \left(\frac{2}{3}\right)(45{,}000 \text{ ft}^2) = 15{,}000 \text{ ft}^2$$

The retail area for the Melody Marketplace also includes six tenant spaces; each one is 1200 ft². Two will be occupied by the convenient care clinic, for a total area of 2400 ft². The other tenants—Cadence Coffeehouse, Tempo Tax Services, Sharps Salon, and the dry cleaner—each occupy 1200 ft².

tenant space	area (ft²)
Cadence Coffeehouse	1200
Tempo Tax Services	1200
Sharps Salon	1200
Dry Cleaner	1200
Unison Convenient Care Clinic	2400
total	7200

To find the retail area of the Melody Marketplace grocery store, subtract the total tenant space area from the total retail area.

$$\begin{aligned} A_{\text{Melody}} &= A_{\text{retail}} - A_{\text{tenant}} \\ &= 30{,}000 \text{ ft}^2 - 7200 \text{ ft}^2 \\ &= 22{,}800 \text{ ft}^2 \end{aligned}$$

The retail area of the Melody Marketplace is classified as a Group M, Mercantile occupancy.

The stockroom is a Group S-2, Storage (low-hazard/non-combustible) occupancy.

The answer is (A).

13. Because the aggregate area of the tenant spaces is more than 10% of the building area of the story, the tenant spaces cannot be considered accessory occupancies and must be classified depending on their individual use.

$$\begin{aligned} A_{\text{aggregate tenant spaces}} &= (\text{no. of spaces}) A_{\text{retail}} \\ &= (6 \text{ spaces})(1200 \text{ ft}^2) \\ &= 7200 \text{ ft}^2 \\ A_{\text{total,story}} &= 45{,}000 \text{ ft}^2 \\ A_{\text{building,story}} &= \left(\frac{A_{\text{aggregate tenant spaces}}}{A_{\text{total,story}}}\right) = \left(\frac{7200 \text{ ft}^2}{45{,}000 \text{ ft}^2}\right) \times 100\% \\ &= 16\% \end{aligned}$$

Cadence Coffeehouse is a space used for assembly purposes as described by Group A-2 but has an occupant load of less than 50, so according to the code, it is classified as a Group B, Business occupancy.

The Unison Convenient Care Clinic is a Group B, Business occupancy (clinic-outpatient). Tempo Tax Services is a Group B, Business occupancy (professional services).

Sharps Salon is also a Group B, Business occupancy (barber and beauty shops).

The answer is (B).

Table for Sol. 12 and Sol. 13

	Melody Marketplace (retail area)	Melody Marketplace (stockroom)	Unison Convenient Care Clinic	Cadence Coffeehouse	Tempo Tax Services	Sharps Salon
area	22,800 ft^2	15,000 ft^2	2400 ft^2	1200 ft^2	1200 ft^2	1200 ft^2
occupancy classification	Mercantile (M)	Storage (S-2)	Business (B)	Business (B)	Business (B)	Business (B)

14. The Melody Marketplace building is fully sprinklered; therefore, according to the required separation of occupancies table in the code excerpt in Resource 6.4, the separation required between the grocery store's retail space (M, Mercantile) and the stockroom (S-2, Storage) is 1-hour.

The answer is (B).

15. A change order is used to modify the project cost or time after the contract has been awarded.

A request for information is prepared by the contractor to obtain information or clarification of the project requirements from the architect. If the architect determines that clarification is required to address a question submitted in the bid phase, the architect will issue an addendum, which will incorporate the response into the contract requirements. It is the architect's formal response through the addendum, not the contractor's request, that modifies the scope of the work.

The architect may require all requests for substitutions to be submitted during the bid phase. Merely submitting a request for a substitution does not change the project requirements. If a substitution is requested and the architect agrees that the alternative product meets the project requirements and is acceptable for use, the architect will issue an addendum to this effect.

An addendum is a document issued by the architect during the bid phase to make a change to the scope of work defined in the bid documents. The architect can use an addendum to repond to a request for information or a request for a substitution received from a bidder, or to provide additional information about the project, to make corrections, or to clarify items in the drawings or specifications. The addendum becomes a part of the contract documents, and only information provided in this format is binding.

The answer is (B).

16. The contractor's submittals should be organized in a way that corresponds to the specification requirements. When product data is submitted, the document should be clearly marked to identify which product is intended for use for each application. This initial review and coordination is the responsibility of the contractor. Ideally, a submittal that does not include this information would be returned to the subcontractor or supplier by the contractor before it is forwarded to the architect.

If the architect receives a submittal that is unclear or incomplete, the best course of action is to reject it, return it to the contractor, and request that it be resubmitted. If the architect holds onto a portion of the submittal while awaiting supplementary information, it is possible that the new information will not be coordinated with what the architect already has received. The architect is not responsible for performing research that may be necessary to determine if a submitted product is equal to the specified product; this is the contractor's responsibility. The architect's review of the submittal should be limited to evaluating whether the products submitted conform to the requirements of the contract. The work of selecting and coordinating materials, confirming dimensions, and determining installation methods is the responsibility of the contractor.

The answer is (D).

17. Use the information provided to complete the application for payment and determine the amount due to the contractor.

The total project amount is $285,625, which is given on Line 1. This application states that there have been no approved change orders (Line 2), so the total project amount has not been changed (Line 3). The value on Line 4 is the amount that has been completed or stored to date. All of this information is provided on the application for payment in Resource 6.6.

The information given in the problem statement can be used to determine what portion of the total amount is work that has been completed (which is, therefore, subject to a 5% retainage) and what portion is stored but not yet installed, upon which 10% retainage will be held. The value of the completed work is $30,300. The value of the materials stored is $12,000.

The retainage is determined as follows.

$$\text{Line 5a} = (5\%)(\text{completed work})$$
$$= (0.05)(\$30,300)$$
$$= \$1515$$
$$\text{Line 5b} = (10\%)(\text{stored material})$$
$$= (0.1)(12,000)$$
$$= \$1200$$
$$\text{total retainage} = \text{Line 5a} + \text{Line 5b}$$
$$= \$1515 + \$1200$$
$$= \$2715$$

The retainage held is subtracted from the total amount earned to determine the total earned less retainage, Line 6.

$$\text{Line 6} = \text{total amount earned} - \text{total retainage}$$
$$= \$42,300 - \$2715$$
$$= \$39,585$$

The contractor has previously been paid \$22,625. This value is inserted on Line 7.

The current payment due (Line 8) is equal to the total earned less retainage (Line 6) minus the total amount that has previously been paid (Line 7).

$$\text{Line 8} = \text{Line 6} - \text{Line 7}$$
$$= \$39,585 - \$22,625$$
$$= \$16,960$$

The answer is \$16,960.

Illustration for Sol. 17

CONTRACTOR'S APPLICATION FOR PAYMENT

Application is made for payment as shown below, in connection with the Contract. Continuation Sheet is attached.

1. Original contract sum.............................. $ 285,625
2. Net change by Change Orders .... $ 0
3. Contract sum to date (line 1 +/– 2) .... $ 285,625
4. Total completed & stored to date............. $ 42,300
   (Column G on Continuation Sheet)
5. Retainage:
   a. __5%__ of Completed Work $ 1,515   5% of \$30,300 (from problem statement)
      (Columns D+E on Continuan Sheet)
   b. __10%__ of Stored Material $ 1,200   10% of 12,000 (from problem statement)
      (Column F on Continuation Sheet)
      Total Retainage Line 5a+5b or
      Total in Column 1 of Continuation Sheet.. $ 2,715   \$1,515 + \$1,200
6. Total Earned Less retainage...................... $ 39,585   \$42,300 – \$2,715
   (Line 4 less Line 5 Total)
7. Less Previous Certificates for Payment
   (Line 4 less Line 5 Total)........................... $ 22,625   (from problem statement)
8. Current Payment Due................................ $ 16,960   \$39,585 – \$22,625
9. Ballance to Finish, Including Retainage
   (Line 4 less Line 5 Total) $

Change Order Summary	Additions	Deductions
Total changes approved in previous month by Owner.		
Total approved this Month		
Totals		
Net Changes by Change Order		

Construction & Evaluation